THE REVOLUTION OF THE SAINTS

A STUDY IN THE ORIGINS OF RADICAL POLITICS

D1262888

THE
REVOLUTION
OF
THE SAINTS

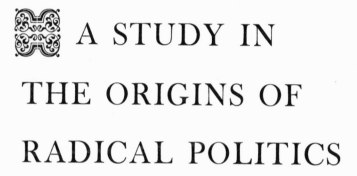 A STUDY IN

THE ORIGINS OF

RADICAL POLITICS

MICHAEL WALZER

HARVARD UNIVERSITY PRESS

CAMBRIDGE, MASSACHUSETTS

LONDON, ENGLAND

Library of Congress Catalog Card Number 65-22048

Printed in the United States of America

Publication of this book has been aided by a grant from the Ford Foundation

Second printing, 1982

TO MY MOTHER AND FATHER

 PREFACE

I began this book hoping to write sympathetically about a human choice which I thought strange and disturbing: the decision to be a Puritan, to repress oneself and others, to act out a conception of holiness at once abstract and urgent. Calvinist saintliness, after all, has scarred us all, leaving its mark if not on our conscious then on our clandestine minds, and it is always worthwhile to go back and puzzle over the wounds. But in the course of my work, I decided that the choice of Puritanism is not really so different from other, later choices which I find neither strange nor disturbing. The Calvinist saint seems to me now the first of those self-disciplined agents of social and political reconstruction who have appeared so frequently in modern history. He is the destroyer of an old order for which there is no need to feel nostalgic. He is the builder of a repressive system which may well have to be endured before it can be escaped or transcended. He is, above all, an extraordinarily bold, inventive, and ruthless politician, as a man should be who has "great works" to perform, as a man, perhaps, must be for "great works have great enemies."

In describing Puritanism as the earliest form of political radicalism, I have not intended to write a complete history either of the English Puritans or of the English Revolution. Nor have I intended my portrait of Puritan thought and action to replace, but only to supplement, other interpretations of seventeenth-century history. The "rise" of the gentry, the "crisis" of the old aristocracy, the "winning of the initiative" by the proud Commoners: all these processes (and the economic transformations which underlay or accompanied them) are presupposed throughout my book. Puritanism is related to such processes, however, in a special way which has never, I think, been made entirely clear: not as their reflex in religious thought, but as a creative response to the difficulties they (and other social changes as well) posed for individual men and women.

Though my treatment is roughly chronological, I have jumped over the years rather freely when it suited my purposes and, particularly in writing about Puritan ideas, have collected material from the Tudor, Stuart, and revolutionary periods, sometimes assuming, sometimes arguing the existence of a common world view. The revolutionary crisis, of course, had its slow development, a steady accumulation of mistakes by those in authority and defiances by those in opposition, a history of lost opportunities for compromise and peace. This I have not made any attempt to trace. But the revolution also had its foundation, a firm basis in radical aspiration and organization which goes back to Calvin himself and to the work of the Marian exiles. It is this foundation which I have tried to describe and explain.

In doing so I have by and large ignored those tiny sects on the left-wing, so to speak, of English Protestantism, whose members have so often been treated if not as the counterparts then at least as the ancestors of modern democrats, socialists, and communists. That treatment does not seem to me very useful. However important they are to latter-day genealogists, the sects (even, the Levellers) are of very minor importance in seventeenth-century history. The case for Puritan radicalism, if it is to be made at all, must be made with the Disciplinarians of Elizabethan times and the Presbyterians and Congregationalists of the Stuart period, that is, with the Puritan mainstream, the true English Calvinists. That these groups differed among themselves and changed over the years is certainly true; nevertheless, I have tried to argue that all of them all the time shared certain key ideas incompatible with the traditional system in church and state, ideas which tended continually to produce radical and innovative political activity.

I hope at some later time to continue my study of radicalism and to describe more fully, perhaps with reference to other countries and histories, those peculiar circumstances which make political zeal and discipline possible and even necessary. And that will be the time to suggest what is obviously true, that radical politics can take different forms, and to develop a critique of the increasingly total forms it has taken in our own time. Such a critique is by no means implicit in anything I have said here, for I have no wish to repeat or carry backwards in time that easy and false equation of radicalism and totalitarianism which has been so common among historians, sociologists and political scientists in the last fifteen or twenty years. My only object is to make Puritan radicalism, so unattractive to my contemporaries, humanly comprehensible.

Throughout the book I have expanded all abbreviations and modernized all spelling both in quotations and book titles. This seemed advisable not only for technical but also for editorial reasons. The retention of the old spelling and abbreviations makes Puritan writing seem hopelessly distant and even quaint, at least to readers not experienced in the study of sixteenth- and seventeenth-century texts. Yet the literature of the English saints, at its best, is marked by a marvelous colloquial eloquence and a simple and moving urgency. I have chosen a minor sacrifice in accuracy for what I hope will be a gain in immediacy and understanding. Only when quoting poetry (or some old word or phrase no longer in use) have I retained the original spelling.

This book was first written as a doctoral dissertation and both in writing it and in preparing to write it I have incurred obligations to more people than I can possibly name here. Many of my teachers, at Brandeis, Cambridge and Harvard Universities, will recognize in these pages a phrase, a snatch of conversation, an odd notion — and these may have been as important to me as the more systematic knowledge they taught. I am grateful to all of them. I owe them a debt which can only be repaid by passing on in my own fashion something of what I learned from them.

My wife, Judith Walzer, has been my constant companion and critic during the years that I struggled to understand the Puritan saints and to write this book. Its various metamorphoses, and my own as well, are in large part her work. Professors Carl J. Friedrich, Louis Hartz, and Barrington Moore all read early versions of several chapters and their encouragement and their advice were equally helpful to me. My Princeton colleague Paul Sigmund read the section on the ancient science of angelology and corrected many foolish errors.

For five years at Harvard I worked closely with Professor Samuel Beer. His ideas about the proper study of politics have been the major inspiration of my own thought on that same subject. His course, Social Science 2, provided me with the first forum from which I could elaborate a view of Puritanism. A meeting of Social Science 2 teachers, now historians, sociologists, and political scientists at various universities, provided me with my first set of academic critics. I am grateful to all the participants: Samuel Beer, Norman Birnbaum, William Chambers, Harry Eckstein, Klaus Epstein, George Nadel, Melvin Richter, Charles Tilly.

A Fulbright grant from the United States Government in 1956-57 and a fellowship from the Social Science Research Council in 1959-60 made possible the research for this book. A grant from Princeton University provided for the typing of the final manuscript. I wish to acknowledge the kindness of the editors of *History and Theory* and *The American Political Science Review* in permitting me to reprint sections of articles which originally appeared in their pages. And finally, I am grateful to the editors of Harvard University Press, and especially to Miss Ann Orlov, for having so greatly eased the trauma of publication.

MICHAEL WALZER

Princeton, N.J.
June 8, 1965

CONTENTS

THE REVOLUTION OF THE SAINTS

A STUDY IN THE ORIGINS OF RADICAL POLITICS

. . . you have great works to do, the planting of a new heaven and a new earth among us, and great works have great enemies . . .

Stephen Marshall
1641

CHAPTER ONE · THE EMERGENCE OF RADICAL POLITICS

A politics of conflict and competition for power, of faction, intrigue, and open war is probably universal in human history. Not so a politics of party organization and methodical activity, opposition and reform, radical ideology and revolution. The history of reform and revolution is relatively short compared, for example, with that of the political order itself or of the power struggle. The detached appraisal of a going system, the programmatic expression of discontent and aspiration, the organization of zealous men for sustained political activity: it is surely fair to say that these three together are aspects only of the modern, that is, the postmedieval political world.

The study of modern politics might begin at many points in the sixteenth century: with Machiavelli and the new political realism, with Luther and the German princes and their attack upon Roman internationalism, with Bodin and the sovereignty of the new monarchs. The concern of this essay, however, is not with reason of state, the national church, or the idea of sovereignty. It lies instead with another of those startling innovations of sixteenth-century political history: the appearance of revolutionary organization and radical ideology.[1] Revolution as a political phenomenon and ideology as a kind of mental and moral discipline are both, of course, closely related to the rise of the modern state. Yet the idea that specially designated and organized bands of men might play a creative part in the political world, destroying the established order and reconstructing society according to the Word of God or the plans of their fellows—this idea did not enter at all into the thought of Machiavelli, Luther, or Bodin. In establishing the state, these three writers relied ex-

[1] H. G. Koenigsberger, "The Organization of Revolutionary Parties in France and the Netherlands during the Sixteenth Century," *The Journal of Modern History* 27:335-351 (1955).

clusively upon the prince, whether they imagined him as an adventurer, a Christian magistrate, or a hereditary bureaucrat. All other men remained subjects, condemned to political passivity. But this was an incomplete vision, for in fact the revolutionary activity of saints and citizens played as important a part in the formation of the modern state as did the sovereign power of princes. In Switzerland, the Dutch Netherlands, Scotland, and most importantly in England and later in France, the old order was finally overthrown not by absolutist kings or in the name of reason of state but by groups of political radicals, themselves moved by new and revolutionary ideologies.

It will be argued below that it was the Calvinists who first switched the emphasis of political thought from the prince to the saint (or the band of saints) and then constructed a theoretical justification for independent political action. What Calvinists said of the saint, other men would later say of the citizen: the same sense of civic virtue, of discipline and duty, lies behind the two names. Saint and citizen together suggest a new integration of private men (or rather, of *chosen* groups of private men, of proven holiness and virtue) into the political order, an integration based upon a novel view of politics as a kind of conscientious and continuous labor. This is surely the most significant outcome of the Calvinist theory of worldly activity, preceding in time any infusion of religious worldliness into the economic order.[2] The diligent activism of the saints—Genevan, Huguenot, Dutch, Scottish, and Puritan—marked the transformation of politics into work and revealed for the first time the extraordinary conscience that directed the work.

Conscience and work entered the political world together; they formed the basis for the new politics of revolution and shaped the character of the revolutionary. They also provided, it should be said, an internal rationale for the diligent efficiency of the modern official and the pious political concern of the modern bourgeois. But both these eminent men were revolutionaries in their time; they had first of all to construct a world in which their efficiency and concern would be respectable—and to attack an older world that had made them both objects of mockery or

2 This is suggested in C. J. Friedrich, *Constitutional Reason of State: The Survival of Constitutional Order* (Providence, R. I., 1957), p. 59.

disdain.[3] In politics as in religion the saints were oppositional men and their primary task was the destruction of traditional order. But they were committed after that to the literal reforming of human society, to the creation of a Holy Commonwealth in which conscientious activity would be encouraged and even required. The saints saw themselves as divine *instruments* and theirs was the politics of wreckers, architects, and builders—hard at work upon the political world. They refused to recognize any inherent or natural resistance to their labors. They treated every obstacle as another example of the devil's resourcefulness and they summoned all their energy, imagination, and craft to overcome it. Because their work required cooperation, they organized to carry it through successfully and they joined forces with any man who might help them without regard to the older bonds of family and neighborhood. They sought "brethren" and turned away if necessary from their relatives; they sought zeal and not affection. Thus there arose the leagues and covenants, the conferences and congregations which are the prototypes of revolutionary discipline. In these the good work was carried forward; at the same time, new saints were trained and hardened for their unremitting labor. The results of that labor can best be seen in the English Revolution of 1640.

In Elizabethan and Jacobean drama the Calvinist saints who later played such a crucial part in that revolution were described as men of hypocritical zeal, meddlesome, continually on the move, nervously and ostentatiously searching for godly things to do—thus Ben Jonson's Puritan, Zeal-of-the-Land Busy.[4] Zeal-of-the-Land was a comic figure, but he was also a new man, especially susceptible to caricature. The saint's personality was his own most radical innovation. It was marked above all by an uncompromising and sustained commitment to a political ideal (which other men called hypocrisy), and by a pattern of rigorous and systematic labor in pursuit of that ideal (which other men called

[3] Crane Brinton argues that the Jacobin clubs, all unknowingly, played an important part in training the bureaucrats and petty officials of the Napoleonic era; see *The Jacobins: An Essay in the New History* (New York, 1930), pp. 230-231. A similar argument, connecting Puritanism with the rise of parliamentary power and the training of parliamentarians, will be made below.

[4] Jonson, *Bartholomew Fair*. See W. P. Holden, *Anti-Puritan Satire, 1572-1642* (New Haven, 1954).

meddlesomeness). The origins and consequences of this godly commitment and this godly business will be examined below. It is necessary first to suggest how new both were in the sixteenth century, with what incomprehension the contemporaries of Calvin and then of Cromwell approached the savage struggles into which godly zeal and business plunged them, how frequently they doubted the "sincerity" of the saint—long after he had, one would have thought, sufficiently demonstrated it. In discussing rebellion and sedition, for example, both Bodin and Francis Bacon still thought in terms of the ragged plebians of the classical cities and the "overmighty subjects" of bastard feudalism. Bacon, perhaps, had some foreboding of what was to come in England when he wrote a warning against unemployed scholars; such men would indeed become, though not merely because they were unemployed, the alienated intellectuals who fed the minds of the lay saints.[5] But King James' Lord Chancellor had no sense of what this intellectual food would be like or of its consequences in human behavior. Even the great Clarendon, writing after the event, still saw the English Revolution as a conspiracy of discontented noblemen. He barely noticed the Puritans and examined their faith only as a species of hypocrisy and an excuse for "turbulence."[6] Clarendon was very wrong; yet his opinions surely reflected the wisdom of the ages. The active, ideologically committed political radical had never before been known in Europe. Medieval society was, to use the word of a modern theorist, a society largely composed of *nonparticipants,* inactive men.[7] A brief glance at the history of that society will suggest the novelty of Calvinist politics.

II

Writing in the second century A.D., the Stoic philosopher Epictetus listed politics among those things which are "not in our power." "Be ready," he advised his fellow Romans, "to say that it does not concern you." His was a warning against ambition and the pursuit of office, but it also represented a turning away

---

5 Bacon, *Essays,* "Of Sedition and Troubles." Jean Bodin, *Six Books of the Commonwealth,* trans. M. J. Tooley (Oxford, n.d.), p. 113.

6 Edward Earl of Clarendon, *The History of the Rebellion and Civil Wars in England* (Oxford, 1827), especially bk. III.

7 See Daniel Lerner, *The Passing of Traditional Society* (Glencoe, Ill., 1958).

from political interests and activity, a radical severance of private needs and aspirations from the public world of cities and empires. The philosopher cultivates internal things; he must be prepared "in every [external] thing to have the inferior part, in honor, in office, in the courts of justice, in every little matter."[8] He is ready to do his duty, to perform any public tasks for which he may be made responsible by birth or by appointment. But since he has no public vision, no idea of the state reformed, no particular political purpose, he will aim in his office at nothing more than an honorable performance. His narrow sense of duty narrows in turn his political imagination and discovers no ideal to be patiently and systematically pursued. The philosopher forms no party. Himself a slave, Epictetus wrote in an age when citizenship had lost its meaning and all men had become, in one way or another, subjects, whose political existence had but one essential characteristic: that they obeyed impersonal, more or less legal commands.

The collapse of the universal sovereignty of the empire shattered even this politics, subjecting men to a frightening variety of extralegal commands and forcing them to make private and personal arrangements. The feudal system that eventually emerged from these arrangements virtually precluded political relations.[9] For the formal, impersonal, legal and functional-rational ties established by a conventional political system, it substituted the extended family and the private treaty, relations intensely personal and in substance at least putatively natural, patriarchal, and affective. For the interests and ideals that bound men together in the pursuit of political goals, it substituted the bonds of personal loyalty, kinship, and neighborhood. For the rational consideration of political methods, it substituted a blind adherence to customary ways. Men came to inherit not merely their lands and possessions, but also their social place and their moral and personal commitments. Reverence for tradition paralleled the reverence for fathers and lords and similarly precluded impersonal devotion to ideas, parties, or states. Familial or dynastic

8 Epictetus, *The Enchiridion,* trans. George Long (Chicago, 1954), I, XXIX.
9 The following several paragraphs are based largely on Marc Bloch, *Feudal Society,* trans. L. A. Manyon (Chicago, 1961), and Walter Ullmann, *Principles of Government and Politics in the Middle Ages* (New York, 1961).

aggression or retreat replaced political activity. Distant and largely powerless kings retained some vestiges of authority and some claim to dominate the world of feudal arrangements only by invoking divine right and acting out the magical rites of religious kingship. But if this increased somewhat the respect with which monarchy was regarded, it also intensified the apathy of subjects —leaving the kings no dependable supporters except God and their relatives. As much under the aegis of Christianity as through the subversive survival of pagan cults, politics became a distant realm of magic and mystery. Ordinary men lived in a narrower world, tied to family, village, and feudal lord, and forgot the very ideas of citizenship and the common good. Religion reinforced the philosopher's advice: politics ought never to be the concern of private men.

When in the eleventh and twelfth centuries, the feudal system was given theoretical form, it was described, of course, as a political community—but not as a community dependent upon the will or activity of its members and not as a community of equal citizens. In the work of a writer like John of Salisbury, for example, political society was seen as a great organism, a body politic not open to man-made transformations, as natural as was the family.[10] Men were not properly speaking citizens of this body, but literally *members*, related to the bodily whole in a functional-organic way. These members obviously shared an interest in the well-being of the body, but they were never called upon to decide together the precise nature of that interest. If the idea of the body politic suggested a higher degree of social integration than was in fact achieved by the feudal system, it also suggested that the sole agent of that integration was the ruler. It served the interests, then, of the new monarchs of the high Middle Ages. And it left politics a mystery still, open to the understanding of the rational head, but impenetrable to the mindless members. How could the foot challenge the authority or wisdom of the head?

Organic imagery also served to justify the hierarchy of persons which had gradually supplanted the chaos of feudal arrangements. Barons and lords might well yield theoretical supremacy to the king; they gained an assured place within a hierarchical system,

---

[10] John of Salisbury, *Policraticus*, partially reprinted by John Dickinson, *Statesman's Book* (New York, 1927), pp. 64ff. See also Dickinson's Introduction.

a natural and inevitable ranking of excellence and honor which was rarely challenged in the premodern period, even though precedence in its upper reaches was always in dispute. This social hierarchy was thought to be reflected not only in the human organism, but also in the cosmos, in God's universe: as the head rules the body, medieval writers argued, so God the world and the king the polity; as the angels stand below God in nine ranks and orders, so the nobler parts of the body politic below the king and the priests of the body of Christ below the pope. The inequality thus defended established patterns of obedience and deference which made independent political activity as difficult in practice as it was inconceivable in theory.

Efforts to restructure or reform the feudal system could only be made from above, as in any unchallenged hierarchy, by popes and new monarchs, or from outside, by monkish enthusiasts of one sort or another. Neither popes, kings, nor monks, however, dared suggest to lesser men, certainly not to laymen, that politics involved sustained, methodical endeavor or free and rational association—though indeed the papal bureaucracy came to incorporate elements of both. The Hildebrandine reform, fostered over the years by Roman officialdom, was surely part of a rationalizing process, involving as it did a determined attack upon those mysteries (such as the cult of the thaumaturgic king and the sacramental character of coronation) that had invaded the political world.[11] The reformers sought to restrict mystery to the religious sphere (and to organize its administration there) and at least partly on the basis of this restriction to limit the authority of secular kings and establish a papal overlordship and a new moral order. But the new overlord could hardly suggest a new *civisme* to his subjects—it seems fair to argue that Gregorian Christianity was "civic" only to its priests—nor could he urge upon them any new forms of political activity. Himself a defender of hierarchy in the secular as in the ecclesiastical order, the pope chose among feudal factions but created no new political associations.[12] Methodical, systematic endeavor remained a monkish characteristic,

[11] Fritz Kern, *Kingship and Law in the Middle Ages*, trans. with intro. by S. B. Chrimes (Oxford, 1948), pp. 54ff.

[12] Perhaps the best discussion of the Gregorian reforms is to be found in Gerd Tellenbach, *Church and Society at the Time of the Investiture Contest*, trans. R. F. Bennet (Oxford, 1940).

imitated perhaps in the papal bureaucracy and again in the religious orders of crusading knights but without significance in the politics of laymen. Calvinists would one day look back to the crusades as a fine example of religious activism, but they could find few other examples in the Middle Ages. Feudal wars were largely the chaotic struggles of aggressive noble families, "overmighty subjects" of weak kings. Rebellions were most often the desperate, furious risings of nonpolitical peasants or proletarians, unorganized, helpless, with only the crudest of programs.

The traditional world view of medieval man, with its conception of an unchanging political order, hierarchical and organic, and its emphasis upon personal and particularistic relations, probably precluded any sort of independent political aspiration or initiative.[13] Something of both, however, was surely present in the great cities of the late medieval and Renaissance periods—as the long struggles for democracy in the guilds and for the leadership of the guilds in the government demonstrate. But even in fourteenth- and fifteenth-century Italy where urbanization was most advanced, it would be difficult to discover a politics characterized by zealous, systematic, and sustained activity. There did emerge, among Florentine humanists for example, a new and striking sense of the virtues of political life and the civic duty of citizens. But in practice the intense antagonisms of classes and families among the Italians culminated in conspiracy, assassination, riot, and internal *coup,* rather than in systematic organization, sustained activity, or revolution. Civic virtue never triumphed over familial loyalty; the idea of shared citizenship never overcame an extraordinary concern with hierarchical status; the class struggle with its usual accompaniment of shared interests and enthusiasms never entirely replaced the feudal vendetta.[14]

13 The term traditional is used here in Max Weber's sense to indicate a society and mentality founded on custom and personalistic relations. Thus the feudal hierarchy was a *chain of being* and not a hierarchy of office; it was not open to planned reconstruction; Weber, The *Theory of Social and Economic Organization,* trans. A. M. Henderson and Talcott Parsons (Oxford, 1947), pp. 324ff.

14 "A popular radicalism in the form in which it is opposed to the monarchies of later times, is not to be found in the despotic States of the Renaissance. Each individual protested inwardly against despotism but was disposed to make tolerable or profitable terms with it rather than combine with others for its destruction." Jacob Burckhardt, The *Civilization of the Renaissance in Italy: An Essay* (London, 1955), p. 39. See also G. A. Brucker, *Florentine Politics and Society: 1343-1378*

In the early sixteenth century, Machiavelli's *Discourses* offer an imaginative and realistic discussion of political life and are filled with a genuine yearning for civic virtue and citizenship. His *Prince,* however, is not a program for activist citizens, but a handbook for adventurers. The new consciousness of politics as a matter of individual skill and calculation, which Machiavelli best embodies, was as yet unaccompanied by a new ideology that might give form to the creative work, limiting and shaping the ambition of princes and making available to them the willing cooperation of other men. The new consciousness thus produced only an intensely personal, faction-ridden politics. Artistry freed from form gave rise to the political *condottiere,* the virtuoso of power. Whatever the reality of Weber's description of Italy's economic life, the importance of the adventurer in her politics can hardly be denied.[15]

Savonarola may well be an exception, if the martyr is not in fact a kind of religious adventurer. It was his endeavor, he wrote, to "make [Florence] virtuous, create for her a state that will preserve her virtue."[16] This might have provided an ideal around which to shape political activity and organize a party of zealots. But the single motor force of the Savonarolan reform was a charisma so purely personal, so incapable of organizational expression, that there remained after the death of the man himself nothing more than an exotic memory and a rather uninteresting collection of sermons. The Florentines were entirely correct to recognize in Savonarola a man but not a movement, a passion but not an ideology. Half a century later the people of Geneva would discover that precisely the opposite was true of John Calvin.

III

Machiavelli's adventurer-prince is one of the first of the "masterless men" of the sixteenth and seventeenth centuries. These were the heroes and villains of the age, cut loose from organic,

(Princeton, 1962), pp. 28, 35, 125-126; and Lauro Martines, *The Social World of the Florentine Humanists: 1390-1460* (Princeton, 1963), pp. 50ff.

15 See Max Weber, *The Protestant Ethic and the Spirit of Capitalism,* trans. Talcott Parsons (New York, 1958), pp. 58ff.

16 Quoted in Roberto Ridolfi, *The Life of Girolamo Savonarola,* trans. Cecil Grayson (New York, 1959), p. 105.

hierarchical, and particularistic ties—ambitious, calculating, ir-reverent—insensitive to the ancient mysteries but not yet inte-grated into a modern social system. Some of these men eventually found a new master in Calvin's God and then they set to work creating a new society in which he could be glorified and they could be active. Calvin pursued power in Geneva with all the artfulness of a Machiavellian adventurer; the same might be said of his followers in England. Yet the elements of seventeenth-century revolutionary politics need only be listed to suggest the distance the English Calvinists had come not only from the pas-sivity of medieval members, but also from the pure self-aggrandize-ment of Renaissance princes.

First, the judicial murder—and not the assassination—of King Charles I; the trial of the king in 1649 was a bold exploration into the very nature of monarchy rather than a personal attack upon Charles himself. Secondly, the appearance of a well-disci-plined citizens' army in which representative councils arose and "agitators" lectured or preached to the troops, teaching even privates (cobblers and tinkers in the satiric literature) to reflect upon political issues. Thirdly, the first effort to write and then to rewrite the constitution of a nation, thus quite literally con-structing a new political order. Fourthly, the public presenta-tion of whole sets of clamorous demands, many of them from previously passive and nonpolitical men, for the reorganization of the church, the state, the government of London, the educa-tional system, and the administration of the poor laws. Fifthly, the formation of groups specifically and deliberately designed to implement these demands, groups based on the principle of voluntary association and requiring proof of ideological commit-ment but not of blood ties, aristocratic patronage, or local resi-dence. Sixthly, the appearance of a political journalism in re-sponse to the sudden expansion of the active and interested public. Finally and above all, the sharp, insistent awareness of the need for and the possibility of *reform*. Surely one of the decisive characteristics of the new politics, this passion to remake society was clearly manifest in a sermon preached before the House of Commons in 1641:

Reformation must be universal [exhorted the Puritan minister Thomas Case] . . . reform all places, all persons and callings; reform the benches of judgement, the inferior magistrates . . . Reform the universities, reform the cities, reform the countries, reform inferior schools of learning, reform the Sabbath, reform the ordinances, the worship of God . . . you have more work to do than I can speak . . . Every plant which my heavenly father hath not planted shall be rooted up.[17]

The same spirit was present sixty years earlier in a group of Puritan ministers who drafted a parliamentary bill which with its first clause would have thrown down all existing "laws, customs, statutes, ordinances and constitutions" of the English church.[18] It is hard even to conceive of a politics of such destructive sweep in the Middle Ages. It is at least equally hard to imagine the magistrates, scholars, or soldiers who would happily have set about providing new laws, customs, statutes, ordinances, and so on. In his own fashion, however, Cromwell was such a man; John Milton, who served him, was surely another. Not only the church, but the state, the household, the school, even the theater and the sports arena—religion, culture, family, and politics—all these the great Puritan poet would have made anew.[19]

The very word *reform* took on a new meaning in the course of the sixteenth and seventeenth centuries: it had once suggested renewal, restoration to some original form or state.[20] This was the connotation it probably carried for early Protestants with their vision of the primitive church and for many French and English lawyers who conceived and glorified an "ancient constitution." But the changes proposed in the name of these two myths were often so radical and represented, despite the appeal to custom and precedent, such a sharp departure from current practice, that reform came eventually to mean simply improvement, change for the better, indeed, radical change for the better. By the 1640's the word implied transformations of the sort associated today with revolution. That was the sense it already had for the conservative Hooker who saw reform as an endless process: "There hath arisen a sect in England which . . . seeketh to reform

17 Thomas Case, *Two Sermons Lately Preached* (London, 1642), II, 13, 16. (The spelling has been modernized here and in all subsequent quotations and titles.)

18 Quoted in J. E. Neale, *Elizabeth I and Her Parliaments: 1584-1601* (London, 1957), p. 149.

19 See especially Milton, *Works*, ed. F. A. Patterson, et al. (New York, 1932), III, part I, 237ff. and IV, 275ff.

20 *Oxford English Dictionary, s.v.* reform, reformation.

even the French [that is, the Huguenot] reformation." It had a
similar meaning in Milton's work: "God is decreeing some new
and great period in his church, even to the reforming of reformation itself."[21] Preachers and lawyers continued, of course, to appeal to primitive and ancient practices, but the shift in meaning
is clearly visible in the gradual replacement of the cyclical view of
history that underlay the idea of renewal with a progressive view
that provided a theoretical foundation for the idea of improvement.[22]

The development of a theory of progress is only another sign
of the new political spirit, the new sense of activity and its
possibilities, the more radical imagination that mark the sixteenth
and seventeenth centuries. The origins and nature of this new
spirit are suggested by the fact that progress was first imagined
in terms of a Christian history and an imminent millenium, or
again, by the fact that it was a minister who preached so ener-
getically of reform to the gentlemen, lawyers, and merchants of
the English Commons. The Puritan cleric insisted that political
activity was a creative endeavor in which the saints were privileged
as well as obliged to participate. The saints were responsible for
their world—as medieval men were not—and responsible above
all for its continual reformation. Their enthusiastic and purposive
activity was part of their religious life, not something distinct and
separate: they acted out their saintliness in debates, elections, administration, and warfare. Only some sensitivity to religious zeal
can make the behavior of the English in the sixteen-forties and
fifties explicable. Politics for the moment was the pursuit of a
religious goal; its end was joy—if only spiritual joy—as Milton
surely knew and even the most somber and dutiful of the saints
must dimly have sensed.

But Puritan zeal was not a private passion; it was instead a
highly collective emotion and it imposed upon the saints a new
and impersonal discipline. Conscience freed the saints from medieval passivity and feudal loyalty, but it did not encourage the
individualist, Italianate politics of faction and intrigue. Puritan

21 *Of the Laws of Ecclesiastical Polity*, Everyman's Ed. (London, 1954), bk. IV,
VIII, 4. Milton, *Works*, IV, 340.
22 See E. L. Tuveson, *Millenium and Utopia: A Study in the Background of the
Idea of Progress* (Berkeley, 1949).

ministers campaigned against the personal extravagance of the
great Renaissance courtiers and deplored the role of "private
interest" in politics. The conscientious activity that they favored
is perhaps best revealed in Cromwell's New Model Army, with
its rigid camp discipline, its elaborate rules against every imaginable sin from looting and rapine to blasphemy and card-playing
and finally its workmanlike and efficient military tactics. Such a
discipline, emphasizing self-control (or mutual surveillance), sustained commitment and systematic activity might well have its
parallel in politics. Indeed, the new spirit of the Puritans can be
defined as a kind of military and political work-ethic, directly
analogous to the "worldly asceticism" which Max Weber has
described in economic life, but oriented not toward acquisition
so much as toward contention, struggle, destruction, and rebuilding.[23] Calvinist conscience gave to war and to politics (and if
Weber is right to business as well) a new sense of method and
purpose. It is this above all that distinguishes the activity of the
saints from that of medieval men, caught up in the unchanging
world of tradition, fixed in their social place and loyal to their
relatives; and also from that of Renaissance men, pursuing a
purely personal ambition.

IV

The purposive and systematic activity of the saints is at least
logically dependent on four other developments in social and
political history—aspects of the gradual transformation of a traditional into a modern society. These are not quite accurately described as the preconditions of Calvinist radicalism, for they were
themselves the products of human willfulness and even of the
willfulness of the saints. They are developments parallel and related to the emergence of radical politics; they helped make
ideological commitment and political reconstruction possible.
Three of these developments can be described by simply para-
phrasing Max Weber's outline of the social basis of the new eco-
nomics.[24]

(1) *The separation of politics from the household.* Already in
the Middle Ages, the reordering activity of papalists and new

[23] Weber, *Protestant Ethic,* pp. 95ff.
[24] *Ibid.,* pp. 21-22.

monarchs had required a long and only partially successful war against the proprietary rights and legal privileges of the feudal families. It has been pointed out by many observers, however, that popes and kings waged this war not by abolishing but by seeking to appropriate and monopolize these rights and privileges for themselves, for the pope as bridegroom of the church and for the monarch as father of the country. Thus the familial aggression of an earlier period was replaced by dynastic aggrandizement and the petty patriarchies of feudal lords by the grand patriarchies of powerful kings. Such changes obviously did not rule out the continuation of familial politics, in the form of aristocratic faction and bureaucratic nepotism. But they did tend to reduce somewhat the importance of kinship in political life, if only by suggesting that all the king's subjects were equally his children. The activity of the Calvinist saints, however, required a recognition that all subjects were knowledgeable and active citizens rather than naïve political children, that government was not a household, the state not an extended family, and the king not a loving father. Radical politics was dependent upon the breaking up of the traditional family and all its magnified and distorted images. That it also had a part in the reconstruction of the family in a more modern form will be argued below.

(2) *The appearance of formally free men.* In the sixteenth century it is first possible to glimpse that illegal man who has become so common in modern times, the political exile. He has an importance in the history of politics something like that of the runaway serf in a broader social history. He is the runaway subject, a very different figure from the defeated feudal lord, the banished baron who traveled in countries not precisely foreign and graced the courts of his relatives. The exile first appears in Italy, among the faction leaders of the Renaissance city-states who so often found themselves condemned to wander abroad or to live in embittered isolation on their country estates. But the new, sixteenth-century radical was more likely than the Renaissance politician to be self-exiled for ideological reasons, the victim not of a feud but of a persecution. The religious Reformation, destroying or significantly undermining the corporate church, had set loose a new group of men, freelance preachers and vagabond scholars. Often driven from their native land, these new

intellectuals nourished their fervor as well as their resentment and organized an opposition that reached considerably beyond the factious intrigues of the Italians. The mere presence of the exile, however, whether in Italy or in the north, is sufficient indication of the existence of many more persons detached from feudal bonds and obligations. These are the "masterless men" of Hobbes' description; their lives are reflected also in the new literature of the *picaresque*. In Hobbes' work and in the novels they most often appear as rogues—dangerous or delightful depending on one's point of view. But they were also pilgrims and so they are described in the sermon literature of the Puritans.[25] Only such men would be capable of organizing themselves voluntarily upon the basis of ideological commitment. Only with them might the politics of dynastic aggrandizement be replaced by the politics of individual, party, class, and national aggrandizement.

(3) *The rational, amoral, pragmatic consideration of political methods.* A truly realistic sense of the methodology of power, its acquisition, preservation, and use, probably appears first in the Italian cities. The relative weights of skill, energy, and luck in political affairs were there calculated with great care and dedicated interest. On the basis of an accumulating record of actual political experience the appropriateness of various means to various ends was lengthily debated. The long-term effect of such debates was to end the usefulness of mystery as a political limit: nothing was exempt from the vigorous, pragmatic concern of a man like Machiavelli. Though with obviously different purposes, something of this same concern survived and was even extended and made more profound in the political casuistry of Calvinist and Jesuit writers.[26] The exhaustive and often tedious deliberations of priests and saints as to whether this or that political means might legitimately be employed by Christians had a dramatic effect: the passionate pursuit of personal power was transformed into a collective and conscientious endeavor and the devilish study of the art of politics into a godly science. Every act of every king was opened to the second guessing of alert, calculating, and

[25] The best discussion of the theme of pilgrimage in Puritan literature is to be found in William Haller, *The Rise of Puritanism* (New York, 1957), especially pp. 147ff. On the picaresque, see F. W. Chandler, *The Literature of Roguery* (New York, 1907).

[26] G. L. Mosse, *The Holy Pretence* (Oxford, 1957).

religious subjects—and this pious second-guessing was even more dangerous to kings than was the cool pragmatism of a Machiavellian adventurer. Conscientious men required the careful casuists, but once they had been told that power was legitimately their goal they were extraordinarily effective in pursuing it and probably even more ruthless than the adventurer in adopting the necessary means.

(4) *The rise of large-scale political units.* Only in the modern state are the various centers of traditional political life—family, corporation, town, and so on—overwhelmed and then transformed into minor units through which children are socialized and taught obedience and economic or local interests represented. And only when this, or something like this, is, so to speak, in the works, is the stage set for the full development of radical politics. A recent student of revolution is surely correct to argue that a full-scale party organization of political rebels is the historical parallel of the complicated, powerful apparatus of the modern state; the two appear together in the sixteenth century.[27] But this is not merely a matter of the challenge of absolutist kings and the response of radicals and heretics. In a sense, the two groups of men, kings and rebels, work together—whatever the tension, even the wars between them. The suppression of smaller political units in which energy and zeal had been dissipated (for example, by Hussite heretics in a semifeudal Bohemia), the destruction of feudal, familial, and local loyalties, the reappearance (out of the medieval organism) first of the subject and then of the citizen: these may well provide the social basis for that obedience which new monarchs required; they also provide the basis for ideological commitment and voluntary association.

V

The breakdown of feudal patriarchy; the emergence of free men, whether exiles or vagabonds, pilgrims or rogues; the rational calculation of political means; the rise of the modern state —these developments suggest the historical situation in which the saint appeared. He was the man who possessed that "unusu-

---

[27] Koenigsberger, "Revolutionary Parties," p. 335. On the development of the institutions of the modern state in England, see G. R. Elton, *The Tudor Revolution in Government* (Cambridge, Eng., 1953).

ally strong character" (to use Weber's phrase) which was necessary to overcome political traditionalism and to survive in the dangerous world of masterless men.[28] In a rough way, he corresponds to Weber's economic entrepreneur, who differed from the cautious medieval burgher and the Italian adventurer-capitalist much as the new saint differed from the medieval subject and the Renaissance *condottiere*. Radical politics was the saint's creation, developed through a difficult process of invention and experimentation. Its systematic and sustained character was the saint's own character, acted out in worldly endeavor. Its particular methods were produced in much the same way as modern military tactics were evolved out of feudal disorder and personal combat, that is, in the course of the political conflict itself, by men systematically active, imaginatively responsive to opportunity, seeking victory.

> Good brother, we must bend unto all means
> That may give furtherance to the holy cause.[29]

Thus spoke Ben Jonson's Tribulation Wholesome as he led one of the Puritan brethren into the shop of the ungodly alchemist. He suggested the conscientious recklessness of the political entrepreneur. Tribulation, like his brother Zeal-of-the-Land, was a caricature; yet the audience that watched Jonson's play undoubtedly had some acquaintance with him. The saint to be described below is in some ways a "type"—the sociological version, perhaps, of caricature. Yet particular historical men fashioned themselves as best they could in his image, and some of them certainly sought every available means to further the holy cause. It is with these political entrepreneurs that the following pages are concerned. In every country, their features were roughly the same; hence the usefulness both of the "type" and the caricature.

It must always be remembered, of course, that these were men of diverse interests and capacities, of different social backgrounds, participating in various ways in the going system and committed with varying intensity to the new order. Individuals were drawn into the formal life of the reformed churches whose deepest loyalties covertly lingered behind; others, genuinely committed, nevertheless maintained anachronistic or disjointed patterns of

---

[28] Weber, *Protestant Ethic*, p. 69.
[29] Jonson, *The Alchemist*, III, i.

thought, expression, or conduct. Despite all this, however, the saint is visible, open to caricature and idealization, the new politics inexplicable without him. His presence in this world of confusion, caution, and perennial half-heartedness suggests a series of questions. Genevan Calvinists, French Huguenots, Scottish Covenanters, English Marian exiles, Disciplinarian ministers, Puritan saints: what was it that moved particular men to join these associations of godly strangers? What were the concrete needs that sainthood served, with its rigid self-discipline and its nervous, incessant activism? What was the basis in routine reflection and day-to-day activity of that "unusually strong character" that enabled the saints to experiment politically and ignore, whenever necessary, the age-old customs, the trained passivity, and the traditional loyalties of their fellows?

The purpose of this book is to answer these questions through an historical and sociological study of Calvinist politics during the hundred years that preceded the English Revolution. At the end of the book it will be possible to state in theoretical terms the argument already suggested in this introduction: that Calvinist politics, indeed, radicalism in general, is an aspect of that broad historical process which contemporary writers call "modernization." Calvinism taught previously passive men the styles and methods of political activity and enabled them successfully to claim the right of participation in that ongoing system of political action that is the modern state. Not that modernity is in any sense the intentional creation of political radicals: few of the elements of the modern ("rational-legal") order detailed by Weber, for example, have much to do with radical aspiration.[30] Calvinism is related, as the final chapter of this study will argue, not with modernity but with modernization, that is, with the process far more significantly than with its outcome. The saint appeared at a certain moment in that process and is remembered afterwards for the dramatic part that he played and for the effects that he had rather than for his own motives and purposes. But he cannot be understood unless the historical sources of his sainthood are carefully examined and his purposes distinguished from the results of his activity.

[30] Weber, *Theory of Economic and Social Organization*, pp. 329ff.

In the history of Western Europe, and especially of England, the sixteenth and seventeenth centuries mark a crucial phase of the modernizing process, a "crisis" manifest finally in the mid-seventeenth-century English Revolution in which the Puritan saint is the central protagonist. In a sense, the saint is the cause rather than the product of that crisis; it occurs, in different countries at different times, whenever a group of men, hardened and disciplined by an ideology, decisively challenge the old order, offering their own vision as an alternative to traditionalism and their own persons as alternatives to the traditional rulers. But in another, equally important, sense, the saint is a product of his times: for men are open to ideological discipline only at certain moments in history. Most often, they are immune, safe from whatever it is that inspires self-discipline and activism, disdainful of all enthusiasm. The crisis of modernization might be defined as the moment when old immunities are suddenly cancelled, old patterns of passivity and acquiescence overthrown. It is only then that groups of men seek (and indeed, require) some such strengthening of character as Weber describes. Different ideologies, of course, can serve their purposes; clearly Calvinism is not the unique form of political radicalism. Parallels with Jacobinism and Bolshevism will be suggested below. But it is probable both that radicalism was first expressed through the medium of religious aspiration and that Calvinism was the ideological system through which men were first organized for the new sorts of wordly endeavor which have been described above.

For this reason, the study begins, in Chapter Two, with an examination of Calvinism as an ideology, marked by its critical view of the patriarchal and feudal world, its political realism, its bold suggestion for social reconstruction and its extraordinary capacity for organizing men and sending them into battle against Satan and his allies—even when those allies turned out to be kings and noblemen. The immediate effects of these views are examined in Chapter Three through two case studies: the French Huguenots and the English Marian exiles. Here the appeal of Calvinism to particular social groups can be analyzed and the various approaches of individual men to sainthood—awkward, anxious, and enthusiastic—systematically described. Only some understanding of the human needs that Calvinism met, both for

Calvin himself and for the later saints, will make it possible to understand the appearance of such a totally new world-view at this particular moment in history. For needs are causes, in a way, though this is not to suggest that men always or ever get what they need.

The two social groups in England whose members were most likely to adopt the Calvinist ideology, to become saints, and to shape sainthood to their own needs, were the clergy and the new class of educated laymen. Professional intellectuals play a vital part in the modernization process everywhere and they are usually seconded by those amateurs of knowledge who arise out of the economic and social transformations of the traditional order, usually as leaders of the new middle classes. The role of the minister in sixteenth- and seventeenth-century England provides the occasion for an analysis of the radical intellectual as the man who first freed himself from the controls of a corporate church and who proved (perhaps because of this freedom) most sensitive to the strains of social change, most open to conversion, and most ready to experiment with underground organization and radical ideology. The sociology and politics of the Puritan clergy are examined in Chapter Four; their new ideas, the day-to-day artic- ulation of their discontent and new-found godliness in sermons, diaries, and theological tracts, are studied in Chapters Five and Six. The highly regulated life of the ministers, the modes of their organization, the very tone of their literature, all suggest, it will be argued, a new world of discipline and work in which me- dieval hierarchy and patriarchy, organismic feeling, and corporate association are left far behind.

The lay saints, most often or most importantly pious gentle- men like Oliver Cromwell or university-educated merchants and lawyers who aspire to gentility, are described in Chapter Seven. Puritanism proved admirably adapted to the needs of these men —just as radicalism in different forms has often since proven it- self functional to the "rise" of new social classes, or at any rate of the educated members of such classes. The annoying word "rise" which seems to denote some collective and impersonal ascent actually conceals a vast amount of painful human endeavor requiring willfulness, calculation, nerve, and perhaps above all an anxious, introspective discipline and self-control—requiring, that is, a conscience such as Calvinism supplied to its saints. At the same time, the acceptance of the new ideology by gentlemen and merchants made radical politics possible. Without the power and prerogatives of gentility, Calvinist zeal would have remained a private matter, giving rise at best to a helter-skelter rebellious-ness like that of the medieval and Reformation sects or to a fur-tive and futile conspiracy of heretical prophets. (The English sec-tarians, it should be said, will not be discussed in the pages that follow; interesting as they are, they are not the crucial innovators in English political history.)

The reception of Calvinist ideas in the social milieu that pro-duced Hampden, Pym, and Cromwell made practically possible the two forms of the new politics which followed historically upon the secret organizations of the intellectuals: godly magistracy and religious soldiery. The culmination of the two was revolution—manifest in the usurpations of Puritan parliamentarians and the "providential" victories of the New Model army. Underlying both was not only the ambition of a class but also the Calvinist con-science, with its extraordinary view of politics as work and of work as a permanent effort and an endless struggle with the devil. In the course of this struggle the discipline of an army at war and the nerves of a soldier on guard became elementary necessities of political men: the new conception of politics as a kind of war, which underlies the view the saints themselves took of the revolution, is described in Chapter Eight. Perhaps the char-acter of these political soldiers was best revealed in the reiterated theme of a sermon preached by John Arrowsmith to the House of Commons in January of 1643, when the war was already begun. "I am confident," Arrowsmith declared, "you never dreamt of reforming a church and state with ease."[31] If indeed men did not dream of a peaceful change, if they had been brought somehow to view violence and systematic warfare as the necessary price of reformation, this was because of the training that Calvinism provided. The traditional mentality, for which such a struggle might well have been inconceivable, was slowly worn away and finally altogether replaced by the collective and modernist con-science of the saints.

[31] *The Covenant-Avenging Sword Brandished* (London, 1643), p. 14.

CHAPTER TWO   CALVINISM

Richard Hooker, it has been said, is the title of a book rather than the name of a man: we know so little about him.[1] Calvin, though we know far more, might best be called the name of a doctrine: an organized system of ideas that seems to exist quite independently of its creator. From the appearance of the *Institutes* in 1536, it is possible to speak only of Calvinism, and in fact the man himself would have considered this self-effacement as a most godly achievement, as well as a clear argument for the objective truth of his ideas. For Lutherans, the private feelings and the mystical experiences of the German reformer must be of great importance; they seek to regain his religious condition, to relive something of his ordeal in order to achieve something like his faith. But the private Calvin is of no historical significance. He is immediately a public figure; he has only public opinions; his religious experience is not especially interesting. That internal activity of the spirit which, as Calvin believed, creates certainty in God's prophets seems in his own case to have involved the gradual enlightenment of a stubborn and finely logical mind, rather than any dramatic inspiration or personal crisis.[2] Though he affirmed over and over again the inscrutability of God, Calvin had little taste for the private mysteries. From inscrutability a rational man turns away, but mystery is compelling and exciting. Calvinism was the product of an extraordinarily successful effort to resist the religious compulsions of the personal and the emotional.

It was partly for this reason that Calvin's ideas were carried so

1 Christopher Morris, Introduction to Richard Hooker, *Of the Laws of the Ecclesiastical Polity*, Everyman's ed. (London, 1954).

2 For a discussion of Calvinist conversion, see R. E. Davies, *The Problem of Authority in the Continental Reformers* (London, 1946), p. 99. Beza's conversion, at the end of a long physical illness, was apparently more dramatic; Paul Geisendorf, *Theodore De Bèze* (Geneva, 1949), pp. 27f.

much farther than Luther's and adapted to so much wider a range of social and economic circumstances. They possessed the authority of objective and impersonal doctrine and the scope and appeal of an opinion meant to be public. Luther in his old age was a provincial figure and a political conservative—and this was a posture, unlike that more energetic conservatism of the nineteenth century, of resignation and quietude. Calvin in his last years was an international figure and, some would have said, the inexhaustible source of sedition and rebellion. The attraction of a set of ideas, then, its appeal to ordinary men of all classes, is by no means determined by its emotional intensity or depth. For Luther was surely closer to the human root of the problems that agitated men in the sixteenth century; he alone had the temerity to live out the great dilemmas of authority and masterlessness, anxiety and justification.[3] Driven by the extraordinary difficulties of his private life he produced a theology that dramatized the most extreme religious experiences. Never unwilling to contradict himself, possessed of a vulgar eloquence that knew no compromise, he suggested an intensely personal transcendence of contradiction and polarity. Calvin, on the other hand, who wrote a brilliantly logical prose, was a master of equivocation. His work possessed the great political virtue of ambiguity. It was subject not so much to a private process of internalization and emotional recapitulation, as to a public process of development, accretion, distortion, and use.

These differences in personality and style suggest a more fundamental distinction. Luther was a theologian whose compelling concern was always with the private knowledge of God. He stands in a medieval tradition that includes such very different figures as Francis and Bernard—in this tradition rather than that, for example, of the Conciliarists whose primary interest was in church government. Luther never really devoted his best energies to the theoretical problems of ecclesiastical organization, perhaps because he had not originally intended to face them at all; he had not planned a new church. Calvin, however, who belonged to the next generation of Protestants, was from the beginning of his career a man committed to systematic innovation, and his innova-

[3] See Erik Erikson, *Young Man Luther: A Study in Psychoanalysis and History* (New York, 1958).

tions were far less important in theology than in moral conduct and social organization. He was concerned primarily with the church which would replace Rome and with the method of that replacement. On the most important theological questions—the mystery of God's being and the grace he extended to men—Calvin by and large refused to speculate, arguing that speculation on such matters was sinful self-indulgence. The relevant passages in the *Institutes* are strangely short and cryptic. And after the *Institutes,* the Genevan legislator wrote only biblical commentaries, sermons, letters, polemics, and exhortations: all these in an intellectual but unspeculative style, always ready to fall back upon common sense, sharply practical though not above elaborate confusion.

The theological thrust toward God and grace was deliberately inhibited in Calvin's writing. He wrote what might be called a theology anti-theological: "not to indulge curiosity"; "not to speak, or think, or even desire to know, concerning obscure subjects, anything beyond the information given in the Divine Word"; to forsake "unprofitable speculations," which have neither "certainty" nor "daily use"; "to leave to God the knowledge of himself."[4] Nor was Calvin sympathetic to men tortured by the problem of salvation; the clear probability, he believed, was that they were not saved. It was a terrible sin "when miserable man endeavors to force his way into the secret recesses of Divine wisdom . . . that he may discover what is determined concerning him at the tribunal of God."[5] To do so was to plunge into an abyss of anxiety. While there were theological helps for this anxiety within the body of Calvinist thought, it must be said that these were less spiritually conclusive than merely edifying. Calvinism was far more importantly a doctrine of discipline and obedience than of justification. "By bringing men into the obedience of the Gospel, to offer them as it were in sacrifice unto God": that, Calvin wrote, was the duty of a Christian pastor. "And not as the papists have hitherto proudly bragged, by the offering up

---

4 John Calvin, *The Institutes of the Christian Religion,* I, xiii, 3, 21; I, xiv, 4. All quotations from the *Institutes* are taken from the translation by John Allen (Philadelphia, 1921), from the Latin collated with the last French edition.

5 *Institutes,* III, xxiv, 4.

of Christ to reconcile men unto God."[6] Obedience and not reconciliation—and this meant that Calvinism was more a social and moral system than a personal and religious one. The overcoming of anxiety became for Calvinists a specifically worldly, rather than an otherworldly, activity.

The distinction was by no means so clear, of course; Catholics had always striven to combine Christian morality and salvation, with the ancient theology of the overlapping visible and invisible churches as one of their methods. And no Christian could easily give up the attempt. Yet it is true that Protestantism tended to push visibility and invisibility, morality and salvation, further and further apart. In Lutheranism, the invisible church became a sharp reality to the individual believer who had experienced justification: the religion tended, therefore, to multiply pietistic sects in which this experience was cultivated. In Calvinism, on the other hand, the religious energies of the believer were publically disciplined, directed into and through the forms of the visible church. As these differences became more and more apparent, Protestant Christianity came to suggest either a privately cultivated communion with God or a social religion.

II

Calvin's relations to his political predecessors are similar to his relations to the theologians and reformers of the Middle Ages. He did not produce anything that resembled a major political philosophy, and this was once again because he was only barely interested in the internal ordering of the mind, in the construction in depth of a philosophical position. Yet any minor summation of his "contribution" to political history would be inadequate. It is hardly enough to say that Calvinism included a group of interesting—if rather unoriginal—political ideas, which take their place in the intricate history of theory, nor that it provided a new (and newly necessary) justification for political order, nor that it suggested a utopian scheme of edification and moral discipline. Its most characteristic productions were, in fact, quite different; they tended to be practical and social, programmatic

[6] Calvin, *A Commentary upon the Epistle of St. Paul to the Romans,* trans. Christopher Roadell (London, 1583), p. 192.

and organizational. Manifestoes, exhortations, polemics—these were the forms of its literary expression; covenants, assemblies, congregations, and holy commonwealths—these were the results of its organizational initiative. Lutheranism was not similarly expressed, nor did it have similar results. The Lutheran saint, in his pursuit of the invisible kingdom of heaven, turned away from politics and left the kingdom of earth, as Luther himself wrote, "to anyone who wants to take it."[7] Calvin was driven by his worldly and organizational commitments to "take" the earthly kingdom, and to transform it.

Calvin's politics was based upon a recognition and a demand: first, a surprisingly realistic and unmoralizing recognition of political reality; secondly, a demand that politics be bent to serve a religious purpose. Neither of these involved him in a discussion of the forms of authority or the content of law. Once again he inhibited his theorizing at these crucial points and consequently his recognition of political facts could never constitute their rationalization. It was a detached and pessimistic acknowledgment of the ways of the world, but never an internal, imaginative analysis of the forms of order and legality. In secular dress, Calvinism might look much like the nominalism of Hobbes. It was saved from this nominalism, of course, by its theory of the objective Word. In politics Calvin recognized authority in its most brutal forms only in order to invest it with the Word and thus make the Word brutally and firmly authoritative in the world.[8]

Calvin's thought moved between wordly fact and divine command, and the bareness and rigidity with which he conceived of each effectively undercut the broad theorizing of the medieval schools. There was no room in Calvinism for the moralized nature and the condescending, one might almost say, socializing God of Aquinas. This unifying view, like that of the overlapping visible and invisible churches, was shattered by Protestantism, and politics for the moment appeared to offer only two possibilities: a cruel and immoral tyranny—appropriate indeed for a world

---

7 Martin Luther, *Works*, ed. C. M. Jacobs (Philadelphia, 1915-1932), III, 248.

8 The best studies of Calvinist politics, relied on frequently in this chapter, are Georges Lagarde, *Recherches sur l'esprit politique de la Réforme* (Paris, 1926) and André Biéler, *La Pensée économique et sociale de Calvin* (Geneva, 1959); see also Marc-Edward Chenevière, *La Pensée politique de Calvin* (Paris, 1937).

from which the saints have fled—or a religious discipline. Luther's doctrine of the bloody sword amounted to an acceptance of the first possibility; Calvin, though he never believed the sword dispensable, opted finally for the second.

Detached from the traditional forms of theological and philosophical speculation, Calvin might be described most simply as a practical man of ideas: a French refugee intellectual caught up in Genevan politics. He was uninvolved in either the elaborate theoretical processes of religious justification or political rationalization. And it was precisely this freedom which enabled him to establish a new connection to the world of activity, a connection which is best explained by calling him not primarily a theologian or a philosopher but an ideologist. The power of a theology lies in its capacity to offer believers a knowledge of God and so to make possible an escape from the corrupted earth and a transcendental communion. The power of a philosophy (at least in the traditional sense of that word) lies in its capacity to explain to its students the world and human society as they are and must be and so to win for them that freedom which consists in an acknowledgment of necessity. The power of an ideology, on the other hand, lies in its capacity to activate its adherents and to change the world.[9] Its content is necessarily a description of contemporary experience as unacceptable and unnecessary and a rejection of any merely personal transcendence or salvation. Its practical effect is to generate organization and cooperative activity. Calvinist ideology can be briefly summarized in these terms.

The permanent, inescapable estrangement of man from God is the starting point of Calvin's politics. Unlike Luther once again, he did not believe reconciliation to be possible and sought rather to cope with the secondary effects of Adam's Fall. He explored the social implications of human alienation and searched for a social remedy. Fearfulness and anxiety, distrust and war, he thought, were the key experiences of fallen men (they were the key experiences more particularly of sixteenth-century Europeans), cut off not only from God, but also from all stable and meaning-

---

[9] Ideology is not used here in the Marxist sense to suggest the role of ideas in veiling and justifying concrete group interests. See Marx and Engels, *The German Ideology* (New York, 1947), pp. 14f, 30ff, 39.

ful association with their fellows.[10] Calvin used the old doctrine of the Fall to explain to his contemporaries the world around them. And because he firmly believed that the terrors of contemporary life could be politically controlled, he became an activist and an ecclesiastical politician. Privately, he responded to those terrors with a self-control so rigid and apparently so successful as to leave no record of the troubles he must have known. Publicly, he advocated a systematic discipline designed to make possible a similar response on the part of society as a whole. In his political as in his religious thought, Calvin sought a cure for anxiety not in reconciliation but in obedience.

The reintegration of the old Adam into a disciplinary association—church and state combined—would be the beginning at least of salvation. Calvin's views took their final form while he was still a young man, and he promptly engaged in a sharp polemic against the Anabaptists, whose goal was not so much the reconstruction as the dissolution of the political world. Anticipating this goal, many of the Anabaptist saints refused to go to court or serve in the army or associate themselves in any way with the political order. They sought an immediate blessedness and reunion with God. In his attack upon this sort of Christian radicalism, the future reformer of Geneva insisted that the mitigation of anxiety and alienation could only be achieved in a Christian commonwealth.[11] He seemed to forego any suggestion of otherworldliness. Calvinism was thus anchored in thisworldly endeavor; it appropriated worldly means and usages: magistracy, legislation, warfare. The struggle for a new human community, replacing the lost Eden, was made a matter of concrete political activity.

Finally, Calvin demanded of his followers wholehearted participation in this activity. They presumably shared the anxiety and alienation; they must join in the work of reconstruction. It was this demand which established ideology as a new factor in the historical process. Although initially made only upon the king, it was subject to gradual extension until finally every man (or at

10 For an especially vivid description, see *Institutes*, I, xvii, 10; the theme of alienation is discussed in Biéler, *Pensée économique et sociale*, pp. 186ff.

11 Calvin, *A Short Instruction For to Arm All Good Christian People against the Pestiferous Errors of the Common Sect of Anabaptists* (London, 1549). See also Lagarde, *Recherches*, pp. 217-218.

least every saint) was called upon to do his share for the holy
cause. This "devolution" (as Richard Hooker called it)[12] was
possible because Calvin was not searching, in the manner of medieval writers, for a moral king, but rather for a man, *any man*,
ready to be God's instrument. It was not reverence, but cold
practicality which led him to start with the French Monarch.
Eventually, he could hardly help but light upon himself, and
upon others like himself. At the same time, however, he was never
willing to rely on individual instruments, however high their
social status or great their inspiration. He relied above all on
organizations, and imparted to his followers an extraordinary
organizational initiative and stamina. There have been few men
in history who loved meetings more. Hence the plethora of new
associations in which the discipline of the holy commonwealth
was previewed. The enlisted members of these groups were drawn
into all sorts of new activities—debating, voting, fighting for a
cause—and were slowly taught the new forms of order and control that were intended to free them from Adam's sin and its
worldly consequences.

Medieval Catholics had also organized the faithful, but they
had done so without removing them in any way from the existing political and feudal worlds, or from the complex bonds of
local and patriarchal connection. Only in the clergy and in monas-
tic orders were men exposed to a radically new organizational
life. Calvinists sought to make this exposure universal. To be
sure, their early congregations sometimes looked very much like
the *eigenkirche* of some powerful nobleman. The saints, whatever the extent of their alienation, were forced into all sorts of
compromises with the world. In theory, however, and to a considerable extent in practice as well, Calvinism was not compatible
with feudal organization. Its forms of association and connection
already existed, so to speak, at a considerable distance from the
old order and appealed to men who had in some way been set
loose from that order.

The impact upon individuals of such a new and disciplined
organizational life was obviously various. Upon many the effects
were minor: an order and control gratefully accepted, quietly

[12] Richard Hooker, *Ecclesiastical Polity, Book VIII*, ed. R. A. Houk (New York,
1931), p. 249.

circumvented, or fearfully and covertly resisted. For some, the
Calvinist organizational system provided a new method of social
advance. For some, its offices brought an enhancement of uneasy
prestige—the mitigation of a different sort of anxiety than that
with which Calvin was primarily concerned. But there were others
who reacted more intensely; they became the saints. Of them it
seems fair to say that they were the creations of an ideology, that
they were somehow reshaped, their energy channeled and controlled by the new discipline. The pious and rigorous routine of
their lives brought them a sense of self-assurance, which was the
end of alienation and which in politics often looked very much
like fanaticism.

THE STATE AS AN ORDER OF REPRESSION

Calvin's thought thus begins with alienation and ends with a
new religious discipline. But there is an intermediate stage between these two. Sure that the saints will not always and everywhere impose their discipline upon the fallen world, Calvin describes and justifies a purely secular repression. And he argues
that this repression, brutal and bloody as it must be, nevertheless
represents a considerable gain for a humanity alienated from
God. This is, as it were, the minimum program of Calvinist ideology. But even the maximum program, the godly discipline, must
be seen against the background of secular repression if it is to be
fully understood. Calvin's realism is the basis of his radicalism.
His followers never forgot the lessons that realism taught. The
wickedness of men and the eternal need for control and restraint
are ever-present axioms of Calvinist politics. They justify, under
certain conditions, the secular state; they condition and qualify
the holiness of the holy commonwealth.

Had the Fall never happened, had Adam not lost his original
divine nature, there would be no politics to discuss. Calvin re-
affirmed the traditional Christian view, made much of by Luther,
that man in his innocence carried the law in his heart and required no external authority, no coercive political structure.[13]
In this innocence, however, the French theologian had little
interest. He could hardly imagine any other man than the fallen

13 Calvin, *Sermons upon the Book of Job* (London, 1574), sermon 152, p. 780.
Also *Sermons upon the Fifth Book of Moses* (London, 1583), sermon 101, p. 620.

Adam. As he had only a formal faith in the reality of an earlier condition, so he was disinclined to believe in some future state of earthly redemption.

The Fall had created a second nature and an asocial man, a creature hating submission and continually striving to dominate others. "I say that the nature of man is such that every man would be a lord and master over his neighbors and no man by his good will would be a subject."[14] Calvin also referred frequently to some lingering remnant of Adam's original innocence, but he showed little concern with this primary nature and little interest in fixing its precise form. A remnant it surely was, and painfully obscure amidst human corruption. In contrast to Catholic theologians, Calvin apparently did not believe that it survived as a kind of powerless rationality. He more frequently identified the remnants of goodness as instinctive: a "natural instinct," "some sense," "a sentiment of the conscience," "an instinctive propensity."[15] He invoked this natural sense in justifying the sex taboos, and occasionally implied its connection to a larger "natural order." More than this, he apparently believed that some propensity toward society lingered ineffectively in the human heart, some uneasy and rudimentary conscience of right and wrong.[16] These too presumably reflected something of a larger world order, though what the method of this reflection was or what the nature of this order, Calvin was quite unwilling to say.

The difficulty, and at the same time the final emphasis of his view, can best be gathered from his reaction to one of the medieval arguments in defense of natural law theory. This was an argument rooted in the considerable but uneasy respect which medieval scholars had felt for the men of the classical world. Clearly, society and law—perhaps in their finest forms—had existed among these heathen, and this seemed to demonstrate that the Fall had not left them in any very desperate condition, at least as far as secular affairs might go. The Fall, in other words, had been a religious but not a political disaster; man retained even in pagan times a rational capacity for law-making. This ar-

14 Calvin, *Job*, sermon 136, p. 718.

15 *Institutes*, I, xvi, 3, 5; II, ii, 22. See Lagarde, *Recherches*, pp. 138-139 and E. Doumergue, *Jean Calvin*, vol. V: *La Pensée ecclésiastique et la pensée politique de Calvin* (Lausanne, 1917), pp. 466ff.

16 *Institutes*, II, ii, 13, 22, 24. See Chenevière, *Pensée politique*, pp. 61-67, 71-73.

gument from pagan society to natural law was common among
medieval writers; it served not only the purposes of Christian
classicists, but yielded law as much to Moslem as to Athenian and
Roman determination. It amounted, then, to a denial of radical
demands for "Christian dominion." In the *Sermons on Timothy,*
Calvin came very near to restating this position: "Did not the
heathen know what justice meant and what it was to be a magistrate?"[17] But in the *Institutes,* he presented a very different point
of view. The political laws of the heathen, he suggested, need not
be ascribed to human nature at all; they were rather "the most
excellent gifts of the Divine Spirit."[18] That an inscrutable God
may thus have granted blessings to the Greeks far above any he
had yet presented to Christian nations did not bother Calvin. The
essential point was that these blessings were not the rewards of
merit or the achievements of natural man. And this must be
taken as his final verdict: the first nature was so nearly dead that
its existence had virtually no political significance. Human asociability was the political equivalent of man's moral corruption;
this last was so terrible that even Calvin's considerable rhetorical
powers had to be extended to make it clear.[19]

In political thought the asocial second nature of man had two
immediate negative results. It meant first that society and the
state were not natural associations—as they had been described
by medieval Aristotelians. They were entirely distinct, for example, from the family; while obedience to parents was natural,
political subjection was not. That was why God, at once cunning
and gentle, called rulers fathers: "to draw us to [subjection] by
a more loving manner." Affectionate submission to the father

17 Calvin, *Sermons on the Epistles of St. Paul to Timothy and Titus* (London,
1579), sermon 39, on Timothy, p. 452.
18 *Institutes,* II, ii, 16; Lagarde, *Recherches,* p. 176. Man understands the
necessity for law, Calvin writes; it is even true "that some seeds of political order
are sown in the minds of all" (II, ii, 13). But the reformer apparently does not feel
that these "seeds" are sufficient to account for the splendid growth of Greek political
life. See the discussion of this point in François Wendel, *Calvin: The Origins and
Development of his Religious Thought,* trans. Philip Mairet (London, 1963), pp. 164,
192-194.
19 For a view of Calvin on natural law very different from that presented here,
see J. T. McNeill, "Natural Law in the Teaching of the Reformers," *Journal of
Religion* 26:179ff (1946). McNeill argues for the importance of natural law in the
work of the reformers, but does not deal sufficiently with the radical theory of the
Fall.

was in some general way a preparation for political life, a conditioning of human depravity; it "mollifies and inclines our minds
to a habit of submission."[20] But in fact magistrates were not
fathers and men were under no obligation to love them. Love for
those in authority was the frequent prescription of Luther; in
Calvin's writing it was almost always replaced by "esteem,"
"honor," "pray for," "obey."[21] There was then no historical or
moral progress from the family to more complex societies, and the
state, once it was established, could not profitably be described
with familial imagery. Calvin set himself apart from the vast
majority of sixteenth-century theorists who, if not actually insisting that the state was only a family writ large, still found paternity
the most useful metaphor for political authority. Indeed, Calvin
was quite likely to turn the metaphor about and suggest that
fatherhood was really an office very much like magistracy.[22]

   If political society did not develop organically from the family,
neither was it founded by a process of consultation and contract;
this was the second negative outcome of human asociability. Rational savages were not led to social order in any such manner as
Hobbes and Locke were later to describe, by reflecting upon the
inconveniences of their natural condition and covenanting with
others who had similarly reflected. Calvin admitted the awfulness
of nature and frequently enjoined men in society to be wonder-
fully grateful. "We know that men are of so perverse and crooked
a nature, that everyone would scratch out his neighbor's eyes if
there were no bridle to hold them in." Government was "equally
as necessary to mankind as bread and water, light and air, and
far more excellent."[23] Yet while men ate and drank quite by themselves, government was apparently not within their power.

   In his *Commentary on Genesis*, Calvin suggested that lordship
and servitude did have a naturalistic origin; they arose from
human second nature through which the original natural order
had been "violently corrupted." Lordship had its beginning, apparently, in the fierceness of a few savage chiefs who had forced
others to submit. Servitude was at first unlawful, but "the use . . .

20 Calvin, *Fifth Book of Moses*, sermon 36, p. 213; *Institutes*, II, viii, 35.
21 See list of quotations in Lagarde, *Recherches*, p. 247.
22 See, for example, *Institutes*, IV, xiii, 14.
23 Calvin, *Fifth Book of Moses*, sermon 142, p. 872; *Institutes*, IV, xx, 3.

was afterwards received, which necessity excuseth."[24] This description was obviously inadequate, and for reasons that even Hobbes recognized when he required that conquest be seconded (though only theoretically) by a contract. Otherwise it established no legitimacy, no conscientious reason for obedience. For Calvin neither of these could possibly be the creation of men. "They have such a lustiness in them as provoketh them continually to be desirous to exalt themselves too much. By means whereof there will never be any willing subjection until God hath wrought it."[25] Actually, Calvin went further: there would not even be unwilling subjection, not even fearful obedience to overwhelming power, unless God acted to transform lusty sinners.

Man in nature was thus solitary and powerless. Fallen from divine grace, he was incapable even of the consolations of human association. His alienation was double in character—from God and from society. The fallen Adam lived like a terrified animal, and all the other, more ferocious animals were "armed for [his] destruction." It was a life which might well be described, had the adjectives occurred to Calvin, as nasty, brutish, and short. Men have no fixed dwelling and no clear line of work, he wrote, they "wander about in uncertainty all their days."[26] Human life was an anxious business at best; Calvin, like Hobbes, seems somewhat inordinately aware of its dangers; underlying his concern for discipline and subjection was an extraordinary fearfulness. In long, self-indulgent ruminations, he dwelt on the uncertainties of existence; disaster, he insisted, is always imminent.[27] Finally, of course, only divine grace could deliver man from this "extreme anxiety and dread." But for all men, and not only for the elect, God had established social and political order; if these did not provide deliverance they would at any rate bring "tranquillity" and "safety."[28]

24 Calvin, *A Commentary Upon the First Book of Moses, Called Genesis,* trans. Thomas Tymme (London, 1578), p. 270.

25 Calvin, *Fifth Book of Moses,* sermon 36, p. 217. Calvin continues with a perfectly Hobbesian description of human nature; "we have naturally in us the cursed root of desirousness to climb . . ."

26 *Institutes,* I, xvii, 10; III, x, 6. See discussion in Biéler, *Pensée économique et Sociale,* pp. 236-245.

27 Calvin, *Of the Life or Conversation of a Christian Man,* trans. Thomas Broke (n.p., 1549), sig. G_8 verso–H_1; *Institutes,* I, xvii, 10.

28 *Institutes,* IV, xx, 2.

II

The order of nature, Calvin wrote, is obedience to God. If he had previously denied the naturalness of the state, this statement may be said to call into question the naturalness of nature. In Calvinist thought nature ceased altogether to be a realm of secondary causation, a world whose laws were anciently established and subject to God's will only in the extraordinary case of a miracle. Providence no longer consisted in law or in foresight: "providence consists in action." The eternal order of nature became an order of circumstantial and particular events, the cause of each being the immediate, active (but inscrutable) will of God. Any other view would leave "no room for God to display or exercise his paternal favor or his judgements . . . as though the fecundity of one year were not the singular benediction of God, and as though penury and famine were not his malediction and vengeance." Again, even more clearly: "no wind ever rises or blows, but by the special command of God."[29] God's commands did, of course, create something of a pattern, and it was this pattern that Calvin sometimes called natural. Yet he always insisted that it arose from no "perpetual concatenation and intricate series of causes, contained in nature," but from "God the Arbiter and Governor of all things . . ."[30] This same omnipotent and ever-active God could at will violate the patterns of nature and at his command his saints might do the same. Their violations were no more arbitrary than was the pattern itself.

In this order of divinely ordained facts, lordship and servitude had their place. Not the products of natural propensity or rational calculation, authority and submission were both creations of God, who could teach the fear of magistrates to brute beasts if he wished.[31] It was God who instituted princes and it was God who implanted fear in the hearts of their subjects. This is proved, Calvin wrote, whenever we see thousands of men, ambition fired in them all, living in quiet obedience to a prince. For "what is the cause hereof, but that God doth arm with sword and power whom he will have to be excellent in the world." More than this,

[29] *Institutes*, I, xvi, 4, 5, 7.
[30] *Institutes*, I, xvi, 8; see also xvi, 9: "What God decrees must necessarily come to pass; *yet it is not by absolute or natural necessity*" (emphasis added).
[31] Calvin, *Fifth Book of Moses*, sermon 36, p. 214.

he also "inspires in men that fear without which it is certain they would never submit."[32] God was the cause of all political facts—and especially of such incredible facts as order and subjection.

At the same time as he thus established obedience, God began the even more difficult task of making it conscientious. He published a new edition, as it were, of the forgotten laws of nature and innocence. This is the Decalogue, which may be taken for all practical purposes as a full and complete restatement of the old natural law. In contrast with the Catholic view, repeated by Hooker at the very end of the sixteenth century, which found room in its theory of natural law for the imaginative investigations and crafty adaptations of human reason, Calvinists reconstructed the theory as a tight and authoritative system of "Thou shalt" and "Thou shalt not." By their persistent identification of natural law with the Ten Commandments, they transformed the flexible generalities of the Catholic theorists into a series of positive decrees.[33] The same process was at work in their treatment of law as in their treatment of authority: both were placed beyond the limits of human nature and human reason; both represented a bridle entirely external, though the one coerced the conscience and the other only the body.

Restraint was necessary as a remedy for the Fall.[34] But the Fall was not the cause of political organization; this would suggest that men had themselves sought and found a remedy for their misery. In fact, social order, command, and obedience were created by God for his own inscrutable reasons and were only incidentally useful to humanity: "the authority possessed by kings and governors over all things upon earth is not a consequence of the perverseness of men, but of the providence and holy ordinance of God, who has been pleased to regulate human affairs in this manner."[35] God's socializing law as well as his saving grace were

---

32 Calvin, *Commentaries upon the Prophet Daniel*, trans. by Arthur Golding (London, 1570), p. 85; *Homilies on I Samuel*, quoted by Doumergue in *Jean Calvin*, V, 493.

33 Calvin, *Institutes*, IV, xx, 16; Lagarde, *Recherches*, p. 177; Cheneviere, *Pensée politique*, pp. 73-77.

34 Not as a punishment: Doumergue, *Jean Calvin*, V, 400 and 400n.

35 *Institutes*, IV, xx, 4; Chenevière, *Pensée politique*, pp. 125-128. For a different interpretation of the passage, see Sheldon Wolin, "Calvin and the Reformation: The Political Education of Protestantism," *American Political Science Review* 51:441-442 (June 1957).

always and entirely in his own power. His law (which required the faithful to love their neighbors) would be "incumbent on [a man's] conscience, though there were not another man existing in the world."[36]

Calvin often argues from the utility of political order to the need for obedience: ". . . princes do never so abuse their power in vexing the good and the innocent, but in their tyranny they retain some show of a just dominion: there can be no tyranny which in some respect is not a defense to conserve the society of men."[37] Asociability, however, was so terrifying that it could never be an alternative to enforced socialization, and so utility never became a critical standard. Even if the conservation of human society had actually been God's purpose in establishing government, it still did not provide any criteria by which mere subjects could frame political judgments. Since there had been no secondary causes in the creation of states, so there were no human purposes against which to measure their forms and activities. The fallen Adam was politically helpless; he would often have to make do with a king like the one Calvin described in his *Sermons on Timothy*—who came to office by violence, who was a condemner of God, a hypocrite, a man of no religion, a dolt, a rapist, a beast, an effeminate person, and a murderer. In this case Calvin did not bother with a utilitarian justification; he fell back upon the only power that might make such a monster ruler of his fellows: "yet would God honor him, he knoweth why: therefore must I be content to be subject."[38]

This was the Christian reason for submission; it revealed the full meaning of the command to obey for conscience's sake. A pagan, of course, would have no such reason, nor indeed would an unregenerate Christian. They had not received the divine command, nor could they realize in their fallen condition the utilities of social life. They submitted only to force, to the facts of power. But did the true Christian do anything different? God's command to obey princes was actually only an "improvement" for Christian consciences. While it legitimized authority in general, it granted legitimacy to no particular sovereign—except to

---

[36] *Institutes*, III, xix, 16.
[37] Calvin, *Romans*, p. 173.
[38] Calvin, *Timothy and Titus*, sermon 46, on Tomothy, p. 552.

the one who actually held and exercised power. In fact, obedience was always imposed by force, since it was only by its forcefulness that it could be recognized. "So long as he will have them to reign . . . kings are armed with authority from God, in that they are able . . . to retain under their hand and at their appointment great multitudes of men . . ."[39] Calvin ignored the medieval distinction between legitimate rulers and usurpers; in fact, he condemned any effort to make lawful distinctions: "It belongeth not to us to be inquisitive by what right and title a prince reigneth . . . and whether he have it by good and lawful inheritance . . ." "To us it ought to suffice that they do rule. For they have not ascended unto this estate by their own strength, but they are placed by the hand of God."[40] The Christian had a new reason to obey such kings, but no new way to recognize them; his conscientious obedience changed nothing in the nature of authority.

The argument must be carried one step further, to its inevitable Hobbesian conclusion: a particular sovereign was only to be obeyed so long as he possessed the power to impose obedience; his legitimacy could not survive his defeat, for a defeated sovereign was deposed by God. In the 38th chapter of the Book of Jeremiah Calvin found this doctrine presented. The prophet ordered the people of Jerusalem to surrender to the Chaldean invader, and Calvin wrote:

> Though . . . the people had pledged to the end their faith to the king, yet as God had now delivered the city to the Chaldeans, the obligation of the oath ceased; for when governments are changed, whatever the subjects had promised is no longer binding . . . when a foreign enemy takes possession of the whole land, the obligation of the oath ceases, for it is not in the power of the people to set up princes, because it belongs to God to change governments as he please . . .[41]

III

Calvin's harsh vindication of political reality was in no sense softened by his demand for conscientious obedience. Indeed, even conscience was bound more by power than by goodness or legality,

39 Calvin, *Daniel*, p. 84 verso.

40 Calvin, *Timothy and Titus*, sermon 46, on Timothy, p. 550; Calvin, *Romans*, p. 172.

41 Calvin, *Commentaries on the Book of the Prophet Jeremiah*, trans. John Owen (Edinburgh, 1850), Lecture 147; III, 387-388.

for men were subject to God's authority only because they were creatures of his formation. And as God's own power was not a matter for human investigation, so the powers that he established on earth were not to be studied too closely by mere subjects. Calvin specifically inhibited discussion on two of the most crucial points of political thought: first on the question of governmental form; secondly, on the content of positive law. The first to violate such prohibitions, of course, was Calvin himself; in the *Institutes* and the many *Commentaries* he several times returned to the question of constitutional form and affirmed his preference for some sort of aristocratic and free state.[42] He could hardly avoid an embarrassed manner, however, in thus succumbing to that speculative itch "with which our minds are always tickling us." Nor is it difficult to detect a touch of flattery aimed at the Genevan burghers who were his first audience. More important, though, was the firmness with which he so uncharacteristically discounted his own opinions. "All these remarks, however, will be unnecessary to those who are satisfied with the will of the Lord. For if it be his pleasure to appoint kings over kingdoms and senators or other magistrates over free cities, it is our duty to be obedient to any governors whom God has established over the places in which we reside."[43] Calvin recognized that different circumstances required different governmental forms: it was another example of his respect for political facts. "The principles to guide [discussion] must depend on circumstances." Yet discussion was not really very profitable; particular peoples at particular times received from God's hands the forms they required. Though he had not been so merciful to other nations as he had been to the ancient Jews, all political systems were equally divine in their origin.

What of their content? In a passage in the *Sermons upon the Fifth Book of Moses*, where Calvin's equivocation fell just short of artistry, the problem was presented:

When God ordaineth kings, princes and magistrates, therewithal he giveth them authority to make laws. True it is, that they ought to

---

[42] See especially *Fifth Book of Moses*, sermon 101, p. 621; sermon 105, pp. 645ff. and *Institutes*, IV, xx, 8.

[43] Calvin, *Institutes*, IV, xx, 8. Calvin's disclaimer is by no means taken seriously enough, nor its full import understood, in J. T. McNeill, "The Democratic Element in Calvin's Thought," *Church History* 18:153-171 (1949).

learn them in his school, according as it is said that laws and ordinances which are made in commonweales do take their force of God's
wisdom. But yet, for all that, civil or politic laws are made by men.
Yet notwithstanding God hath not resigned anything, that he should
not still hold the sovereign dominion over men, I mean even in respect of outward policy.[44]

"True it is, that . . . But yet, for all that . . . Yet notwithstanding
. . . I mean even"—this was indeed the rhetoric of confusion.
Calvin's point of view must be drawn forth, almost against his
will, by examining the possibilities his rhetoric concealed. In
doing this, the work of Zwingli is crucially important, for the
earlier Swiss reformer had suggested just that radical position
which Calvin's confusion was meant to deny, if not to obliterate.

Zwingli had sacrificed natural law—even as Calvin was to do—
to the radical Protestant theory of the Fall: "The first thing to
consider is that man is not able to find the law of nature in himself . . ." The second Adam was morally helpless until God inter-
vened and provided the Ten Commandments. Zwingli, along
with most other Protestants, then rediscovered a narrowly con-
strued natural law in the Decalogue. But the Decalogue contained
also the first revelations of true religion and from this the Zurich
reformer drew an all-important conclusion: "The natural law is
nothing else than true religion and only the believer is able to
understand it."[45] Such a view would make it difficult indeed to
cope with the polity of the Greeks—though Zwingli, a greater
admirer of the classical world than was Calvin, came very near
to describing the statesmen of ancient Greece and Rome as members of God's elect.[46] For his contemporaries, however, Zwingli's
position required quite simply that their laws be biblical and
their rulers Christian. Calvin's hesitation at just this point was
crucial for his entire view of politics: in backing cautiously away
from the earlier reformer's radicalism, he found no easy stop-
ping point.

Calvin was quite unwilling to admit that every non-Christian
ruler was illegitimate. He was too preoccupied with the problem

---

44 Calvin, *Fifth Book of Moses*, sermon 4, p. 21. See discussion in Lagarde,
Recherches, pp. 203ff.
45 Quoted in Lagarde, *Recherches*, p. 143.
46 Wendel, *Calvin*, pp. 192-193.

of order to set about overthrowing, even in theory, states and kingdoms that God had established. Indeed, he tended to feel that any authority, by its very existence, proved its legitimacy. On the other hand, he could hardly grant to the natural powers of non-Christian (or unregenerate) men the capacity for morally appropriate laws. Pagan politics, if necessary and even legitimate, was surely not desirable; the laws and customs of the heathen would often be repugnant to true Christians. Nor would the Christian conscience, co-witness with God to the Ten Commandments, feel any moral connection to merely secular law, any internal acknowledgment of its justice. Yet the Christian must obey, bound by the previous and general command of God to submit himself to the powers that be. Calvin concluded that only this commandment was binding upon the Christian conscience; no specifically human laws had any similar binding power.[47] Matters of secular concern were left free and indifferent, at least with regard to conscience; men must obey but could withhold internal consent. At the same time, there was no need to protest publicly even against the most barbarous customs. In his *Commentaries upon the Prophet Daniel,* Calvin demonstrated his pious equanimity. He noted that when Daniel's accusers had been thrown, in their turn, to the lions, their wives and children had been cast into the pit along with them. This might seem to be against equity, Calvin wrote, yet it should not be publicly condemned.

. . . it is better to leave this at liberty. For we know that the kings of the East . . . did exercise cruel and barbarous dominion or rather tyranny toward their subjects. Therefore there is no cause why any man should contend much about this question.[48]

The disapproval of any aspect of political existence was properly an internal matter.

Calvin's view of positive law appears very similar to that radically nominalist position which later emerged clearly in the work of Hobbes. Indeed, the only choices available to the Genevan reformer, once he had expressed his relative disinterest in natural law, would seem to be Zwingli's biblicism or an extreme

---

47 Calvin, *Fifth Book of Moses,* sermon 20, p. 118 and *Institutes,* IV, x, 5. On the effect of this view, see Lagarde, *Recherches,* pp. 193ff.
48 Calvin, *Daniel,* pp. 114-115.

nominalism. It is fair to say that in his argument for the independent legitimacy of a secular, non-Christian politics, Calvin chose the second position.[49] His practical nominalism had, of course, the authority of an inscrutable God, and he protected conscience from its morally corrosive impact by permitting it to withhold consent from evil laws. In all this, however, he really achieved little more than did Hobbes with his doctrine of the private judgment. Hobbes' private judgment, it may be suggested, was a secularized reduction of the Calvinist conscience.[50] In both Hobbes and Calvin this limited inner freedom was preserved only by setting positive law beyond the reach of the individual subject; since conscience was not connected to the law and not bound by it, so it could not make effective judgments.

IV

These inhibitions on political speculation were inherent in Calvin's thought: paradoxically, they were rooted in his acknowledgment of the independent value of the political world. In Aquinas' theory, this same acknowledgment had followed from a pious compromise with nature and had made possible a long discussion of law and of the possible types of government. Calvin made no such compromise; his validation of politics was no offer of secular free play, no recognition of value in the old Adam. Rather it grew out of a stern and often harsh sense of the necessities of human second nature. With the alienation and anxiety of natural man always before his eyes, "to the intent that men should not be as cats and dogs in snatching one at another . . ."[51] Calvin accepted politics in any form it took, so long as it fulfilled its general purpose and established an *order of repression*. This indeed may be taken as his definition of the state.

Although it had no connection whatsoever with divine grace, political discipline represented the first triumph over secular anxiety—the instability and terrors of life without repression. Pro-

49 What may be called the Hobbesian implications of Calvin's thought were presented explicitly in the seventeenth century by the Huguenot minister Élie Merlat, who quoted extensively from Hobbes himself. See the discussion of Merlat's ideas in G. H. Dodge, *The Political Theory of the Huguenots of the Dispersion* (New York, 1947), pp. 7-9.

50 Thomas Hobbes, *Leviathan*, ed. Michael Oakeshott (Oxford, 1960), p. 243.

51 Calvin, *Timothy and Titus*, sermon 14, on Titus, p. 1208.

tection against anxiety was afforded first by the mere existence of the institutions of social life. God had established vocations, Calvin wrote, "lest of all adventures, [man] should be driven about all the course of his life." "It will also be a small alleviation of his cares, labors, troubles and other burdens . . ."[52] In his vocation he might develop a precise and limited sense of responsibility as well as a more or less permanent daily routine. God had also provided for the existence of positive law and for the cruel punishment of those who violated its precepts—for without law and punishment "many men must needs be injured for no private man's right can be stable and sure . . ." He gave the sword to magistrates "to hurt and to destroy" the wicked and to secure peace and "tranquillity."[53] Social tranquillity was in fact the great achievement of political repression. Curiously, Calvin used the same word to describe the effect of divine grace: "A tranquil God tranquillizes all things . . ."[54]

Law and political discipline might also produce a kind of internal tranquillity. Law fixed the range of human activity and of this-wordly endeavor, and if it could not bind conscience, it at least set reasonable limits to sin and so eased the terror of the conscientious. Calvin's treatment of the usurer provides an interesting example of this psychological process. He viewed the usurer as a frightened man, excitedly murmuring to himself:

I must use such a mean, I must practise such a feat, I must look into such a business, or otherwise I shall be behindhand in all things, I shall but pine away, I shall not get half my living, if I proceed not in this manner . . .[55]

Calvin assured this wretched sinner that he would be held accountable to God, but meanwhile he offered a kind of secular comfort: "It would be wished that all usury . . . were first banished from the earth. But as this cannot be accomplished, it should be seen what can be accomplished for the public good."[56] Usury was thus treated as a political problem. Calvin dissolved the medieval

[52] Calvin, *Life or Conversation*, sig. K₂; *Institutes*, II, x, 6.
[53] Calvin, *Daniel*, p. 97 verso; *Romans*, p. 173; and *Institutes*, IV, xx, 2.
[54] *Institutes*, III, xxiv, 4. Calvin is quoting St. Bernard, who does not appear frequently in the pages of the *Institutes*.
[55] Calvin, *Fifth Book of Moses*, sermon 134, p. 821.
[56] Calvin, "Letter on Usury," in *Usury Laws . . . The Opinions of Jeremy Bentham and John Calvin* (New York, 1881), p. 34.

distinction between natural increment represented by rent on land and unnatural increment represented by interest on money: if one did not "stop at words" but rather "investigated the things," it was obvious that rent and interest were similar economic and social facts.[57] In determining the public good with regard to such facts, scriptural passages were also of little use; Calvin was hardly interested in the traditional arguments from either nature or theology. He appealed instead to the "rules of equity"— and what were these but the positive laws? An early Huguenot synod, under Calvin's strict guidance, adopted precisely this position: "All persons shall carefully observe the king's edicts and the rules of charity about interest in money." The true function of the king was made more clear in another case considered by Huguenot casuists: whether goods sold by pirates might be bought. The ministers replied: "If the magistrate consent unto their sale, they may with a *safe conscience*, but if the sale be clandestine, they ought not . . .[58]

Given the laws of Geneva and of France, Calvin was willing to grant "that before men [usury] shall not be condemned for theft . . ."[59] It was only a question of fixing the rate and that was a matter which political authority determined. The obedient citizen might still be a sinner before God, but by regulating his sinfulness, the state modified his anxiety. At the same time it opened him for still further regulation and control. And this must be considered the true meaning of Calvin's occasional comments on usury. While hardly representing any very enthusiastic recommendation of business as a way of life—a seventeenth-century commentator is surely right to say that Calvin treated interest the way an apothecary does poison[60]—Calvin's views continued a pattern of frank recognition of wordly activity. The underlying purpose of this recognition was to fix all activity within politically acceptable limits and to prepare men for Christian discipline.

---

57 Quoted in Henri Hauser, *Les débuts du capitalisme* (Paris, 1927), pp. 54-55; see discussion pp. 66f.

58 *Synodicon in Gallia Reformata: or, the Acts, Decisions, Decrees and Canons of those Famous National Councils of the Reformed Churches in France*, ed. John Quick (London, 1692), pp. 9, 34 (emphasis added).

59 Calvin, *Fifth Book of Moses*, sermon 134, p. 821. A somewhat different interpretation of these and other texts is suggested by Biéler, *Pensée économique et sociale*, pp. 453-473.

60 Quoted in Hauser, *Les débuts*, p. 45.

The mitigation of secular anxiety was achieved first of all through obedience to the commands of established authority. Calvin had nothing to say of the emotional overcoming of terror and loneliness through love. His prince or magistrate was no father who mixed paternal affection with discipline. In keeping with his entirely unemotional attitude toward political reality, Calvin saw the magistrate as an officeholder, without a significant personality, evil as all men were, entirely lacking in charisma. No special virtue adhered to power, the powerful were "no better than other folks," and their subjects obeyed them coldly saying "Very well Lord, these reign in thy name . . ."[61] Calvin's recognition of political authority was also the end of political mystery. The state was a fact, a matter of force and organization. It was useful and necessary because of man's dramatic helplessness; in addition, political order was comforting and consoling. But that was all.

A politics of this sort obviously missed by some distance any transcendence of anxiety. It offered no sense of human freedom or of brotherly union. As in his theology, Calvin was always and insistently concerned with obedience, but not with reconciliation. It is not even unfair to suggest that he sought to maintain a certain fundamental anxiety, because without it political discipline would have no hold upon men. In his theology he viewed the uncertainties and doubts which afflicted the pious as helpful exercises to strengthen their faith. Disorder and tumult played a similar role in strengthening the bonds of authority. In order that men not become too secure God "permits them to be frequently disquieted and infested with wars . . ." He saw to it that "there [was] no firm nor stable state in the earth,"[62] and thus emphasized anew both the precariousness of order and the necessity for repression.

THE STATE AS A CHRISTIAN DISCIPLINE

Secular repression was only the foundation stone of a Christian polity; it provided the very minimum of social control and consolation; it revealed only the most rudimentary achievement of

---

[61] Calvin, *Fifth Book of Moses*, sermon 36, p. 216; *Job*, sermon 131, p. 674.
[62] *Institutes*, III, ix, 1; *Daniel*, p. 63.

God's sovereign power and man's brute force. Nevertheless, Calvin seemed at times to argue that the old Adam could expect nothing better. Listing the political duties of kings and magistrates, he demanded only "justice":

They who rule well can in no other way administer righteousness and judgement than by being careful to render to everyone his own, and that by checking the audacity of the wicked and by defending the good and the innocent; *this is only what can be expected from earthly kings.*

Now in policy *there is nothing more to be looked for,* than that no man attempt anything against his neighbor, that men do one another no harm, that men work no displeasure one to another, neither in goods, nor in person, nor in name, and that whosoever offendeth, be punished.[63]

At other times, however, Calvin insisted upon the religious duties of the magistrates and denied that a purely secular justice was of any value whatsoever:

All laws are preposterous which neglect the claims of God and merely provide for the interests of men.

What then are the states of honor and all the dignities of the world? They are all means to bring to pass that God may reign over us . . . So then, what ought kings, emperors and magistrates to do? They ought to see that God be exalted and magnified . . .[64]

Taken out of context like this, these different formulations appear patently contradictory. In any given sermon or treatise, however, Calvin's artfulness conceals the difficulties of his position. The defense of secular repression and the assertion of "the claims of God" are so closely woven together that it is extremely difficult to disentangle them. And to do so is perhaps not entirely fair to Calvin's intentions. But it is the only way of explaining his achievement at Geneva and of revealing the sources within his thought of that radicalism that continually burst forth among his followers. Calvin's ideology is rooted in the secular pessimism

63 Calvin, *Jeremiah,* lecture 85; III, 142; Calvin, *Fifth Book of Moses,* sermon 116, p. 710 (emphasis added).

64 *Institutes,* IV, xx, 9; Calvin, *Fifth Book of Moses,* sermon 4, p. 22. See also the Dedication to the *Institutes:* "For where the glory of God is not made the end of government, it is not a legitimate sovereignty, but a usurpation . . ."

of the first two quotations, but it is fully developed only in the godly assertiveness of the last two.

Even while defending the most brutal repression, Calvin insisted upon its inadequacy. He sought to establish a greater degree of control over the old Adam and a qualitatively different tranquillity: the two together were to be the products of Christian discipline. Reconciliation and reunion were still not Calvin's goals; he dismissed utopia as "a foolish fantasy the Jews had."[65] His morbid insistence upon human wickedness determined the quality of his new discipline as of the old and familiar repression: fallen man was the object of both. But Christians, Calvin thought, ought to be the subjects as well as the objects of social control, for what God claimed was voluntary obedience. Like the secular state, the Christian commonwealth would be coercive; unlike the secular state, it would be founded upon the consent of conscientious men. Calvinism brought conscience and coercion together—in much the same way as they were later brought together in Rousseau's General Will. Indeed, the two views of political life which appear in Calvin's thought may be imagined as Christian anticipations of the two different authoritarianisms of Hobbes and Rousseau. As with the later French writer, Calvin was acutely aware of the vast increase in social control that would result if human beings could be made to will that control themselves and to consent to it in their hearts. This was precisely what the Christian believer did in Calvin's theory, and this is what the Calvinist saints actually did in their private lives, in their churches and congregations, and in those states and commonwealths where they managed to seize power.

II

Whereas the secular order could only repress nature, religion could transform it. This was most clearly and dramatically demonstrated in Calvin's treatment of the family. The state was an order entirely distinct from the family; in Calvin's writing no connection was described between them. The state was not su-

---

[65] Calvin, *Against the Anabaptists*, sig. E$_3$. Biéler calls Christian discipline "la société provisoire" because it falls short of the ultimate goal of history: Christ's kingdom; see *Pensée économique et sociale*, pp. 256-265.

perior, only different; it required no change in family relationships, neither a reinforcement nor a loosening of domestic bonds.
But Christian fellowship tore those bonds apart. No man, Calvin wrote, could "continue steadfastly in the Gospel but with the
condition of forgetting his father and mother and of forsaking his
wife and giving over his own children." This was, of course,
traditional evangelical doctrine and Calvin quoted with approval
the injunction of Luke: "We cannot be the disciples of . . .
Christ, except we hate both father and mother" (and, Luke continued, wife and children, brothers and sisters).[66] Again, Calvin
cited the passage in Exodus where Moses led the slaughter of
the golden-calf worshippers: "you shall show yourselves rightly
zealous of God's service," Calvin commented, "in that you kill
your own brethren without sparing, so as in this case the order of
nature be put underfoot, to show that God is above all . . ."[67]
Fanaticism of this sort, as will be seen, might have its political
as well as its evangelical purposes. But it also served a more immediate end, reflecting and justifying something of the experience of the early reformers.

Calvin wrote frequently and insistently to French converts urging them to leave parents and homeland and join the "fellowship
of faithful men" in Geneva.[68] Had not Abraham, as Theodore
Beza declared, "Left Parents, countrie, goods with gods and all?"[69]
Beza's trilogy of renunciation (which may be summed up: father,
fatherland, and father's land), became a set piece of Calvinist
rhetoric. It was altered somewhat for women: "How many Christian women are there," Calvin exclaimed, "who are held captive
by their children!"[70] Christian fellowship required the sacrifice
of all familial ties. This indeed had been the experience of Calvin
himself, of Beza, Hotman, and many another sixteenth-century
Protestant.

The family thus torn apart, at the command of God and for
the sake of fellowship, was shortly reconstituted. Whereas the

---

66 Calvin, *Fifth Book of Moses*, sermon 194, pp. 1203-1204; Luke 14:26.

67 *Ibid.*, the reference is to Exodus 32:27.

68 *Letters of John Calvin*, ed. Jules Bonnet, trans. David Constable (Edinburgh,
1855), I, 371-373; II, 78, 165-167.

69 Theodore Beza, *A Tragedy of Abraham's Sacrifice*, trans. Arthur Golding
(London, 1577), ed. with intro. Malcolm Wallace (Toronto, 1906), p. 18.

70 Calvin, *Letters*, II, 78.

evangelical attack had hardened into the institutions of celibacy and monasticism, Calvin brought family and world together as proper arenas for the exercise of Christian piety. But he did not reconstitute the family as a natural association. Indeed, he was fond of reminding fathers that "it is not without the appointment of Divine Providence that they have attained that station . . . The title of father is a mark which God hath set upon men." Marital union, explains one of Calvin's most enthusiastic students, is only the condition of procreation; God is the cause. Paternal authority, then, was not entirely natural: "if men and women have children, they must understand that there is no subjection due unto them, except they themselves be overruled by God."[71] For what had Calvin done when he left France, but obeyed God rather than his father?

"The family of a believer must be as it were a little church . . ." This was Calvin's often repeated description of Christian familial relationships. Among heathen, Calvin continued, the family would be "an image and figure of public government," that is, of secular order. But among Christians the family was to be ordered in strict obedience to God's commands. Fatherhood was transformed into a religious office, with its duties and its obligations prescribed in the Word—and these did not differ from those enjoined upon the Christian magistrate: to govern his subjects (here: wife, children, and servants) so that God would be honored among them.[72] In order that the family might become a constituent element of the Christian discipline, Calvin radically deemphasized the natural and affective aspects of fatherhood, and dramatically stressed its authoritarian features. The father became, as it were, the representative of God and the Christian magistrate in the family.

That extension of paternal care which masked the actual forms of feudal dominion and servitude could logically find no place in Calvinist thought. The reconstructed family formed a *"little church"* and its members were members also of the greater church established in their neighborhood, subject to the discipline

71 Doumergue, *Jean Calvin*, V, 508; *Institutes*, II, viii, 26; *Fifth Book of Moses*, sermon 36, pp. 213-215.
72 Calvin, *Timothy and Titus*, sermon 23, on Timothy, p. 282. See Biéler, *Pensée économique et sociale*, pp. 259f.

of the elders as well as the father. The long-term tendency of
Calvinism was to limit the extent of paternal power by setting
the family within a larger disciplinary system. Even in bourgeois
Geneva this tendency was apparent, but it was more clearly
visible among the French Huguenots. Since Huguenot ministers
deferred on all important matters to Calvin's opinion, it may be
assumed that their struggle with the prerogatives of feudal lordship was his also. The ministers required of the nobility that its
members, like all men, form their families into churches, the male
members into consistories. But they could hardly approve of that
"church" which a nobleman formed by keeping a private pastor
and making his court into a private congregation. Ministers are
"given to the service of the church," decreed a Huguenot synod,
"and not to the persons and palaces of great lords, although their
families may equal in number some churches . . . their Lordships
shall be desired not to carry away with them in their removals . . .
the church's ministers."[73] When noblemen were not following the
king about, the Huguenot Discipline declared, they were to join
themselves to a regular church and submit to its authority. In
effect, they were to think very narrowly of their family and its
private devotion, limiting the extent of the first, conducting the
second themselves. And they were to accept something like equal
membership, along with all their dependents, in the local society
of Christians. In her memoirs, Mme. de Mornay, the wife of
Philip, the Huguenot "pope" and most likely author of the
Vindiciae contra Tyrannos, angrily described what such membership involved. Barred from communion because of the way
she wore her hair, she watched in fury while her servants were
admitted. For months afterward the puritanical ministers and
the noblewoman who insisted on dressing according to her station, debated the Christian uses of hairpins and wires. The deadly
seriousness of both suggests a truly titanic struggle of aristocratic
pride and clerical pretension. Though its outcome was suitably
indecisive, the effect of such contention upon the feudal order
may easily be imagined.[74]

[73] *Synodicon*, p. 66.
[74] *A Huguenot Family in the Sixteenth Century: The Memoirs of Philippe de
Mornay, Sieur de Plessis Marly, Written by his Wife*, trans. with intro. by Lucy
Crump (London, n.d.), pp. 64, 198ff. "M. Bironier and another elder were . . . sent

Not directly involved in such social conflicts, Calvin's final attitude toward feudal lordship was one of compromise. He permitted servitude and only required that the lord remember God's office: "the great ones must understand that they are to show the way to their inferiors and underlings . . ."[75] This was to become the frequent injunction of Calvinist writers; recalling God's command to Abraham that he circumcise his servants, they would urge the nobility to spread the true religion among its dependents. So long as lordship remained a useful instrument available to Christian hands, its Calvinistic reconstitution would be problematic.

III

The use of feudal authority to convert servants and dependents suggests that the church was something more than a collection of pious fugitives from parents and lords. It was also a coercive institution designed to bring men into the "obedience of the Gospel," which is to say: not to open them for grace, but to expose them to command. Religion produced a counterpolity to the state; as a prelude to admitting the state to the world of religious purpose, Calvin admitted politics to religion. He often described the church as a commonwealth and the metaphor is a significant key to his thought. Politics had long played its part, of course, in the Catholic church, but a recent writer is entirely correct to view Calvin as the political educator of Protestantism.[76] Luther's absolute distinction between spiritual and temporal existence had suggested that the state could only be an order of repression and politics only of interest to sinners. Christians already dwelt in another world, to which organization, authority, and coercion did not pertain. Regenerate men, wrote the German reformer, "have no need of any human relations. They communicate internally by the Word . . ."[77] Calvin would have recognized this as a description of the invisible church, and he would not have been much concerned with it. He suspected, perhaps, that piety would be of little value, even to God, unless it could be organized.

---

to her to declare that she could not be admitted wearing a wig, but as for her men-servants, they might . . . be admitted" (p. 211).

[75] Calvin, *Fifth Book of Moses,* sermon 166, p. 1028.

[76] Wolin, "Calvin and the Reformation," especially p. 440.

[77] Quoted in Lagarde, *Recherches,* p. 296.

As a social order, the church required the apparatus of worldly government. Calvin described this government at great length, and over the next hundred years Calvinists of various sorts probably wrote more treatises on ecclesiastical organization than on any other subject. The burden of this enormous literature was that the forms of church polity, unlike those of the secular order, did not depend upon circumstances, upon the facts of power or the patterns of legality, but had been set for all time in the Word of God. The secular state was subject quite simply to change, but the church only to corruption and reform.[78]

The Calvinist church was an inclusive organization of professing Christians, saints and hypocrites alike, governed by a select committee of ministers and laymen. The admission of laymen to the government of the church was the result of that demystification which the clergy had undergone in the course of the Reformation. Clerics undoubtedly continued to exercise a considerable power, but they no longer possessed any personal superiority. All the awe that the presumption of celibacy once inspired was gone forever. This new equality of believers might have produced a new democracy in the church: the lay elders who sat alongside the ministers and who were always in the majority were supposedly chosen by the congregation. In reality, they were coopted by the existing church leadership and, unless active (and godly) opposition developed, the tacit consent of the membership was assumed.[79] The political value of lay participation, however, did not depend upon its formal procedures; the eldership, along with the office of deacon, effected a certain social integration in the church polity, formerly impossible because of the moral gap between laymen and their clerical governors.

Calvin had an acute sense of the church as a political society; he designed the moral discipline to tighten and stabilize the bonds of fellowship. The assembly of ministers and elders was given great powers of investigation and "spiritual" chastisement—"an absolute and irresponsible authority of censure, enforced by the power of

78 See Calvin's description of the ancient church as "an actual exemplification of the Divine institution," *Institutes*, IV, iv, 1.

79 In Geneva, the elders were elected by the town's Council of Two Hundred from a list of names submitted by the Small Council (and recommended, after Calvin's final victory, by the ministers); see James Mackinnon, *Calvin and the Reformation* (London, 1936), pp. 80-81.

excommunication."[80] But such power could only be exercised if
it met with some degree of acquiescence on the part of the people.
As it would be impossible without lay participation, so it would
not be fully effective unless that participation was universal.
The investigations of the church elders depended upon the
"mutual surveillance" of the church members. Calvinist discipline
required a direct and willful obedience to the Word of God as represented in the regulations of the consistory. It thus differed from
the controls established by the secular state, where obedience was
imposed by force and determined by a law which made no claim
upon conscience. Religious discipline intensified the order already
achieved by secular repression.

In practice, all the church's members did not respond willingly
to the new discipline: there were many who had to be watched,
investigated, chastised and, if they remained recalcitrant after
many warnings, finally excommunicated. Because of Calvin's
exalted view of God's sovereignty, he could not claim that the
church's excommunication was an absolute condemnation to an
eternity in hell; on the other hand, he dared not surrender such
a powerful disciplinary instrument. "The church binds him whom
it excommunicates," he wrote, "not that it consigns him to perpetual ruin and dispair, but because it condemns his life and manners, and already warns him of his final condemnation."[81] Ultimately, as will be seen, the condemned sinner would be driven
from the holy commonwealth: excommunication was a worldly
writ. Similarly, those whom the church admitted to communion
were "warned" of their final salvation. But they were thisworldly
saints and reaped immediate rewards for their godly lives and manners. They were the ones who watched, investigated and chastised
the others.

Calvinism tended to set its communicants apart, not only from
the excommunicants, but also from all those whose obedience was
not perfect or who did not participate enthusiastically in the
communal government. The saints were a tightly disciplined
group, the supreme example of the new ideology's organizing

[80] Mark Pattison, "Calvin at Geneva," *Essays of the Late Mark Pattison*, ed.
Henry Nettleship (Oxford, 1889), II, 25. This is an excellent characterization of the
Calvinist discipline. See also *Institutes*, IV, xii, 1ff.
[81] *Institutes*, IV, xi, 1.

power. As they had proven their regeneracy by their rigorous self-control, so they acted it out in the world. They did not withdraw to some private ecstacy. "It is certainly the duty of a Christian man," wrote Calvin, "to ascend higher than merely to seek and secure the salvation of his own soul." Instead, he was to "set before him as a prime motive of his existence zeal to show forth the glory of God . . ."[82] While insisting in conventional fashion that the earth should become "vile in our estimation," Calvin simultaneously reevaluated it as the theater of God's glory. Here the religious man discovered his true function. The saint was the militant Christian activist, and his activity carried him outside the church. He not only participated in congregational government, he also created the holy commonwealth.

<h4 style="text-align:center">IV</h4>

The offices of the church tended fairly regularly to be filled by the most rich and powerful members of the lay community; at the same time, men who rose within the ecclesiastical organization, acquiring new prestige and self-esteem, might well move into some governing position in the state. In either case, lay participation brought the church effectively into the secular order. In Geneva, except at the very height of Calvin's power, the result was actually to hand ecclesiastical supremacy to the city council. But citizens serving on the consistory could hardly avoid some imitation of its moral tone, especially when that tone was dictated by such authoritative figures as Calvin or his first disciple Beza. They carried back to the assembly of burghers an elevated sense of religious responsibility, which was soon manifest in civil laws and decrees. A conscientious reciprocity between political and religious office thus provided the basis for their integration, even when that integration was never legally completed, as Calvin, convinced both of the precarious nature of faith and of the preponderant power of the secular order, was certain it never should be. He was content to appeal to the lay conscience, so long as he could make that appeal from some independent religious position. "*If . . . you see* that our advice is from the holy

---

82 *Reply by John Calvin to the Letter of Cardinal Sadolet to the Senate and People of Geneva* (1539), in *Theological Treatises*, trans. with intro. J. K. S. Reid (Philadelphia, 1954), p. 228.

word of the Gospel," Calvin wrote to the Genevan magistrates, "take good care that these observances be received and obeyed in your city . . ."[83]

This religious responsibility of the Christian magistrate was paralleled by the equally religious duty of ordinary citizens. If the average man did not have much chance of becoming an elder, he might still (with God's aid) become a father—an office with similar duties though they extended over a more narrow society. As the "holy father of a family," he would be constantly engaged in "pious exertions" to govern that little church which was his household. Family devotion reproduced the communal devotion of the larger church, worship and discipline were doubled, and men subject to the power of the consistory exercised that power in their own homes. In doing so they prepared themselves to be conscientious citizens of the Christian state.

It was assumed that the coincidence of believer and citizen would be a permanent feature of the new discipline. Calvin required this much cooperation from secular law: the final punishment of an unrepentant excommunicant was exile.[84] He insisted upon this not so much because "civil death" would prefigure the sinner's spiritual death, but rather in order to maintain the moral purity of the Christian state. That purity would not be perfect, for many citizens of the state would exist in some kind of spiritual limbo while being warned or chastised by their consistorial inquisitors. But the price of final defiance was to be made clear.

The identity of believer and citizen was dramatically manifest in the civic oath which, in effect, turned Geneva into a covenanted community. Calvin led the ministers in demanding, in 1537, that the entire city make public profession of its new faith; he wished, as an historian of Geneva has written, that "civil society be integrally composed of all the Christian members of the religious society, and of them alone."[85] Though the triumph proved only temporary and had later to be confirmed, the ministers had their way: the people of Geneva accepted the confession of faith and swore to obey the Ten Commandments—at the same time as they

[83] *Articles Concerning the Organization of the Church and of Worship at Geneva* (1537), in Calvin, *Theological Treatises*, p. 49 (emphasis added).
[84] Georges Goyau, *Une ville-église: Genève* (Paris, 1919), I, 32-33, 65.
[85] *Ibid.*, p. 51.

swore their loyalty to the city.[86] This was the first of those national or civic oaths and covenants that Calvinists were to undertake; obviously modeled on the biblical covenants between God and the Jews, they provided something of the same sense of choosing and being chosen. The idea of the covenant is an extremely important clue to the nature of that higher repression which Calvin saw as the object of Christian politics.

In his theology, Calvin distinguished between covenants of law and of grace. The covenants of the Old Testament upon which the Geneva oath was modelled were combinations of the two. Since no human being could perfectly obey the Deuteronomic code, God offered his grace—to ancient Jews as well as to sixteenth-century Christians, for Calvin always insisted that the two testaments were essentially similar.[87] At the same time, however, as he granted a grace supposedly "independent of the works of believers," God required that his laws be substantially obeyed. He would not have "his goodness . . . become an object of contempt."[88] The emphasis of Calvinist theology thus alternated: law, then grace, then law again—with the significant difference that law in the third stage was internally accepted by the men who had received grace. In another sense, too, Calvin's emphasis was alternative: the initial covenant made with the Jews was national and social, but God's grace as described in the New Testament was offered only to individuals. And yet once again, the acceptance of grace reformed a community. If at first this was only a free association of believers, it quickly became a political society, responsible not alone for the earthly proclamation of grace, but also for the fulfillment of the legal requirements of the covenant—so that God's glory be suitably acknowledged. The alternation here is social, personal, and social again; the covenant in the third stage rests, as does the law, upon the new willingness of God's saints.

For an understanding of the oath that Calvin required of all Genevans, the last term of each of these alternations is most relevant. The covenant, then, represented a social commitment

---

86 The preceedings are described in J. T. McNeill, *The History and Character of Calvinism* (New York, 1957), p. 142: "groups of people, summoned by the police, gave their adherence."

87 *Institutes*, II, x, 2.

88 *Institutes*, III, xvii, 5-6.

to obey God's law, based upon a presumed internal receptivity and consent. It was a self-imposed submission to divinely imposed law, but this self-imposition was a social act and subject to social enforcement in God's name. With the covenant, Christian discipline was definitely substituted for secular repression; all the citizens of the new commonwealth conscientiously accepted an absolute dominion which they recognized as godly. And this presumably brought with it an end to such anxiety as could have an earthly end, for it vastly increased the effectiveness of the repression of the old Adam. Social discipline took on new meaning when enforced through conscience, instead of being imposed on consciences that were free, or modified by the intervention of nature, blood, or patriarchy with all their affective and emotional connotations.

RESISTANCE, REFORMATION, AND GODLY WARFARE

That God rather than man must always be obeyed is probably the most significant platitude in the history of political thought. Like most platitudes it offers neither clear-cut definitions nor a program for action. Obedience to God may involve submission to any number of well-established earthly authorities which claim to speak in God's name; it may also describe the spontaneous heroism of a conscientious individual who challenges the powers that be. It is certain only that the precept rests upon an appeal to conscience and that conscience, unless bound by an authoritative church, has no rules. Franz Neumann has summed up the difficulty: "There cannot be a universally valid statement telling us when man's conscience may legitimately absolve him from obedience to the laws of the state. Every man has individually to wrestle with the problem."[89] It was a fundamental commitment of Calvinist writers, however, that this difficulty could be resolved, and resolved before men began to wrestle with it as individuals.

The first Protestants relived in spirit the enthusiasm of the first Christians. Obedience to God involved for them only passive resistance and a quick martyrdom or flight from their homeland and a weary exile. Both of these were individual responses to persecu-

---

[89] Franz Neumann, *The Democratic and The Authoritarian State: Essays in Political and Legal Theory*, ed. H. Marcuse (Glencoe, Illinois, 1957), p. 158.

tion. Judging from his letters, Calvin preferred the second of the
two, if only because he needed the exiles in Geneva. But he could
hardly suggest emigration as a long-term policy for the Protestant
nobility of France. Nor would he have wished to do so, for in his
view the nobles had a political part to play in their own land.
What he required of them was not so much religious enthusiasm
as a conscientious performance of their political duties.[90] Here
was what Calvin meant by obeying God. He sought to organize the
noblesse de la religion at home and so to impose a Christian commonwealth upon the French. If the saints held office—and Calvin
had already described even feudal lordship as a vocation—their
day-to-day activity would transform ordinary repression into godly
discipline.[91] It was something like this that Calvin preached to
the young noblemen who asked his advice. He did not demand of
them any spontaneous activity, any purely personal courage; he
probably thought martyrdom naïve. Calvinist conscience was collective and it would be acted out, as long as Calvin himself was
in control, in an orderly, disciplined, and systematic fashion.

But suppose the French king forbade such activity? Given Calvin's vindication of secular authority, it is difficult to see how he
could justify any kind of political opposition, however godly in
intention. If the established powers were indeed divinely ordained and therefore always legitimate, then Calvin's French
followers could do nothing but pray to God for the king's conversion. A tyrannical or even a heretical monarch would appear
to them as God's scourge; they would search natural and political
history for omens of further punishment or merciful relief. Bred
to activism and diligence in the church, the saints would be passive
in the state. But this was not the conclusion that Calvinists drew
from the theory of God's sovereign power. For the view of political reality as the embodiment of divine will had this fundamental
ambiguity: the divine will must be active also in any group of men
actually in revolt, manifest in revolutionary organizations as much
as in the institutions of government. And did not the Calvinist
saints know themselves to be instruments of that will? God had
put his mark upon them and that mark was conscience, a piece

90 See *Institutes,* III, ix, 4, 6, where all men are warned to remain at their posts,
and magistrates and fathers especially.
91 Cheneviere, *Pensée politique,* pp. 150-154.

of divine willfulness implanted in man. Conscience would be the saint's warrant to free himself from political passivity and success would be the divine sign justifying whatever he did.

Calvin himself, however, while not absolutely precluding this sort of activism, sought a greater certainty in politics than mere sainthood could provide.[92] He too wished to escape from political passivity, but at the same time he was terribly afraid of an anarchy of pious endeavor. Since conscience was public among the saints, there needed to be a way to recognize it publicly, to know without any doubt whom God had chosen to be his instruments and what tasks he had assigned. Calvin's theory of an ever-active God led him to search in history for some divine ordination of resistance and reform: the great reformer still looked for precedents and omens, for the divine in the factual. Against the fact of Catholic monarchy in France, for example, Calvin struggled to set a *counter-fact*, an opposing force as real, as worldly, as ordinary as tyranny itself—the power of the Protestant nobility. He exploited what may be called the ambiguity of the factual, but he intended the exploitation to be limited. He taught his followers to appeal from established law to historical precedent and from historical precedent to providential force, but he himself made such appeals only with the greatest hesitation.

His own prejudice was clearly in favor of those social groups which had already left their factual mark—in history, law, and tradition. And so he inserted in the *Institutes* a careful justification of resistance by the "lesser magistrates" of the feudal world. They and they alone might defend true religion against heretical kings. Calvin's views did not differ from those both Luther and Bucer had expressed many years earlier, though his statement probably benefited from his superior powers of equivocation.[93] The significance of his theory, however, did not lie in its cautious reformulation of the privileges of feudal magistracy, but rather in

[92] Though the saints were supposed to enjoy great peace and certainty as to their salvation, Calvin was quite unwilling to make that certainty the basis for political action. This may be one reason for the extraordinary equivocation of the sections on certainty in the *Institutes* (see especially III, ii) and for his warning (III, ii, 11) that "experience shows, that the reprobate are sometimes affected with emotions very similar to those of the elect, so that, in their own opinion, they in no respect differ from the elect."

[93] *Institutes*, IV, xx, 31; see Hans Baron, "Calvinist Republicanism and its Historical Roots," *Church History* 8:30-42 (1939).

its more fundamental and fully developed conception of political
office as a religious vocation.

That nobles might act to bridle the king was an old medieval
idea, but in medieval times they had always acted as representatives of the community or of one of the estates or corporate bodies
which made up the community. They had defended law, custom
or common interest against a tyrant. Although this view played
its part in Huguenot theory, it was not the basic Calvinist conception. Calvin never imagined officers or nobles as representatives;
he found no human community capable of organizing itself and
appointing delegates or spokesmen.[94] Although constitutional
structures varied a great deal, particular officers were created only
by God. Political duties were determined by the divine will.
Resistance was thus not a representative but a conscientious act,
public not in a secular but in a religious sense. Magistrates were
morally (not civilly) guilty if they failed to resist a tyrant, because "they fraudulently betray the liberty of the people, *of
which they have been appointed protectors by the ordination of
God.*"[95]

Conscience, as always among the Calvinists, was supported by
fact. Many magistrates and nobles actually possessed the power to
resist a king. More than this, long traditions of provincial auton-
omy, municipal privilege, and feudal rights had accustomed them
to the use of their power. The development of legal theory and
practice in the course of the sixteenth century, however, undermined the authority of these men and of the corporate bodies
for which they spoke. As all political and legal power was drawn
together into a unified sovereignty, each individual officeholder—
feudal as well as royal—came to be regarded as a "member and
collateral" of the king. Royal lawyers denied his independence
and royal courts, more or less effectively, enforced the denial.[96]
Calvinists tended to oppose this drainage of power out of society,

---

94 Calvin writes that the Jews had the "liberty to choose their own judges," but
he treats this as a special gift of God; *Fifth Book of Moses,* sermon 101, p. 620. On
the other hand, see Calvin's view of the choice of Saul as king: "He is elected not
by the council of men but by the will of God alone." Quoted in Doumergue, *Jean
Calvin,* V, 481.

95 *Institutes,* IV, xx, 31 (emphasis added).

96 See W. F. Church, *Constitutional Thought in Sixteenth Century France: A
Study in the Evolution of Ideas* (Cambridge, Mass., 1941), p. 39 and *passim.*

perhaps because it limited and reduced the opportunities for conscientious activity. Calvin's own refusal to recognize the new sovereignty of kings was based upon a significant interpretation of Scripture. It would be a great abuse, he argued, to deny the plurality of the "powers that be"; the New Testament texts provided "a common reason for recommending the authority of *all* magistrates . . ."[97] Only later, however, would Beza and the Huguenot writers bring forth a developed theory of shared sovereignty. Meanwhile, Calvin might exercise his talent for fine distinctions. A rebellion of the nobles against the Guise would only be justified, he wrote shortly before the Conspiracy of Amboise, if it were led by a prince of the blood; but if only one prince were to take part, then it would have to be the leading one, nearest by birth to the royal house.[98]

In defending the remnants of a feudal politics, neither Calvin nor any of his followers restated the traditional medieval arguments. They did not urge the naturalness of hierarchy (or invoke the usual analogy with the orders of angels), nor did they treat with any especial reverence the familial and patriarchal bonds that had been so important to feudal society. And since they did none of these things, their theory suggested what was perhaps obviously true: that the old authorities could only endure if they were radically reconstituted. Wherever this reconstitution took place, or was vigorously attempted, Calvinism with its realistic politics and its disciplined organizational system might well provide ideological support. The revival of Stoicism among the Catholic nobility at the same time that Protestantism was spreading rapidly through France suggests that the need for some new ideological brace was widely felt.[99] Both Stoicism and Calvinism, it may be argued, were world views admirably suited to educated young aristocrats in the process of becoming local officeholders, lawyers, and administrators.

II

The theory of office provides the key to a new view of political activity, which may be summed up in the single word *reform*.

97 Quoted in Doumergue, *Jean Calvin*, V, 501; the reference is to I Peter 2:13-14.
98 Cheneviere, *Pensée politique*, pp. 341-346.
99 See Léontine Zanta, *La Renaissance du Stoïcisme au XVIe siècle* (Paris, 1914), especially pp. 243ff on the royal officeholder William Du Vair.

A conscientious magistrate was obliged not only to resist a plundering or heretical tyrant; it was also his constant duty, in a world whose normal progress was degenerative, to "attempt to lead men back to the pure worship of God." Because of human corruption, reform was a permanent necessity. Resistance was only one, and by no means the most important, of the activities which office required. Calvin's letters to Protector Somerset of England illustrate another kind of activity, once again fundamentally religious and in no sense representative. Somerset might expect the rage and violence of a large majority of his subjects, Calvin coolly wrote, nevertheless, he should employ his sword to bring them all "to the clear light of the Word." He warned Somerset over and over again of his "responsibility," his "charge," his "duty."[100] The pious magistrate must be as vigilant and active as God himself. In the important *Sermons on the Fifth Book of Moses*, Calvin returned to the attack with a sharp denunciation of passivity and lassitude among officeholders. "Inquire diligently . . ." he urged the magistrates and judges, "be rigorous in making search . . . search out matters to the very bottom."[101] Only thus might Satan and his followers be rooted out of earthly societies.

Calvin insisted upon the same duty in the lord of a manor and the head of a family as he here urged upon the effective ruler of a nation: each man in his office must do all that is legally within his power. Though the emphasis was on orderly and disciplined behavior, the suggestion was clearly revolutionary. Calvin opposed the more spontaneous kinds of reform: he denied the political right of tyrannicide, he denounced religious iconoclasm and condemned the unordained, vagabond prophets of an enthusiastic Protestantism.[102] But he did require activity: "it is meet that everyone (to his power) do apply himself faithfully to [give God his glory] by all the means that he can, considering always the state in which he is . . ."[103] The duties of any given vocation, needless to say, were subject to debate and even to experiment.

100 Calvin, *Letters*, II, 171, 172, 183.

101 Calvin, *Fifth Book of Moses*, sermon 120, pp. 737-738.

102 For Calvin's condemnation of tyrannicide, see *Institutes*, IV, xx, 26 and *Life or Conversation*, sig. K₂ verso. On religious vagabondage, see *Letters*, I, 293.

103 Calvin, *What a Faithful Man Ought to Do*, sig. B₇; see also *Daniel*, sig. B₂ verso (epistle): "Now it is your part . . . as far as every man's office and power shall lead him, to be careful with all his heart, that the true religion may recover its pure and perfect state."

This last requirement of activity and reform took on greater significance when the idea of office was extended beyond the political sphere, where its legal definition was at least a possibility, to the religious and "providential" spheres where its precise nature was far more difficult to determine. Calvin's recourse to an avenging Providence was, of course, less a program for action than a rhetorical warning to tyrants, but the idea had a peculiar suggestiveness about it. God sometimes raised up "providential liberators," "public avengers," Calvin wrote; "let princes hear and fear." Such men, whenever they made their appearance, had a "legitimate commission" from the Lord; "being armed with authority from heaven, they punish an inferior power by a superior one . . ."[104] It was hard to see how their legitimacy could be known, however, except by their success; Calvin had merely readmitted the tyrannicide under the cover of divinity. In so doing he revealed that the legality of resistance was at least in part a *post facto* ascription.

More interesting still was his discussion of the powers of religious office, that is, of the minister and the prophet. Both were presumably excluded from any political activity. But the Calvinist effort to enforce the moral law with secular and religious power altered the nature of their exclusion. Religious office involved the duty of moral censure—and it was surely not difficult to see that the denunciation of kings by prophets and ministers was a political matter.[105]

Why are prophets and teachers sent? That they may reduce the world to order: they are not to spare their hearers, but freely to reprove them whenever there may be need; they are also to use threatenings when they find men perverse . . . prophets and teachers may take courage and thus boldly set themselves against kings and nations, when armed with the power of celestial truth.

Rulers must be obeyed, but certain of the saints have a special office to rebuke their evil-doings. Undoubtedly Calvin was one of these, and this must be the explanation of his own repeated denunciations of kings, especially in the *Commentary on Daniel*, where the references to France were made explicit in the pref-

---

104 *Institutes*, IV, xx, 30-31.
105 Calvin, *Jeremiah*, lecture 2; I, 44.

So similar to Luther

ace.[106] But the French king, who recognized within limits the protests and rebukes of parliamentarians and estates' representatives, might well have asked to know Calvin's office.

The Genevan reformer sought persistently to stabilize the calling of ministers and prophets, and to reduce the risks inherent in his own ideas. Despite this, the risks remained great: stability was not in the nature of Protestant prophets. Even Calvin himself, a firm and exemplary exception, had to admit that the office of prophet was not readily subject to organization and control. Here, as with the "providential liberator," conscience was set free. "If you entertain some doubts about [my calling]," Calvin wrote to a Genevan burgher in 1538, "it is enough for me that it is quite clear to my own satisfaction."[107] At this point he was not far from a reduction of the theory of office to a radical and anarchistic individualism. Actually, of course, he had a stern sense of the public duties of officeholders and of the elaborate organizational training and testing that had to be undergone before personal calling could be publicly recognized. It was indeed the shift in emphasis from religious calling to political office (without any major change in content) that established his position. He linked private conscience to public duty in order to produce political activity. As a direct consequence of this, however, he could hardly avoid the admission that such dramatic forms of activity as tyrannicide and prophetic denunciation might well be conscientious and dutiful. Secular order was thus subject to disruption by conscientious men: it was a difficult, even an untenable, position for a theorist whose fundamental teaching was one of discipline and obedience.

With this difficulty it might be well to end the discussion of Calvin's political ideas. Yet there is one further aspect of his thought as a whole that greatly increased the revolutionary potential of the theory of religious office. Pervasive in his work was a view of the life of the saint as a perpetual, almost military, struggle with the devil. It was because of the devil, and his vast cohorts of earthly followers, that the conscientious, reforming activity of religious men so often resulted in or required violence

106 Calvin, *Daniel,* see especially p. 97.
107 Calvin *Letters,* I, 71.

and warfare. Whenever the Gospel had appeared, Calvin wrote, in the early days of Christianity and again in his own time, "there was not, so to speak, a corner of the earth that was not horribly afflicted. The uproar of war, like a universal fire, was kindled in all lands . . . a chaotic confusion of order and civil polity [followed] . . . [so] that it seemed as if the world was presently about to be overturned."[108] One could almost test the divinity of the Word by the violence of Satan's opposition.[109] Because of his activity, the life of the godly was something like permanent warfare. Calvin's description was perhaps not unreal to men in the sixteenth century. God permitted the devil, he wrote, "to exercise the faithful with fighting, attack them in ambuscades, harass them with incursions . . . throw them into confusion, terrify them . . ."[110] The imagery of warfare was constant in Calvin's writing, and while it was at least partly a rhetorical device, it also suggested the tendency of Calvinist energy to organize itself for worldly struggle.

When the offices became military posts, new possibilities were opened to the saints who held them. Calvin himself drew back from any very radical projection of his military rhetoric and suggested that the right of Christians extended no further than defensive war. But others might not feel themselves so bound, for if warfare were permanent, the careful distinction between defense and offense would eventually lose its meaning. While Calvin sought to limit and define the range of permissible activities, and to establish resistance as a particular and circumscribed legal duty, his dramatic view of Satanic strife suggested something quite different: in time of war, the old Roman maxim went, the laws are silent. Military discipline then replaces legal order; peace and tranquillity wait upon victory.

---

108 Calvin, *Letters*, II, 172. See *Timothy and Titus*, sermon 9, on Timothy, p. 100: "For the devil cannot abide that they should preach the Word of God purely, but he will resist it . . . he will attempt all that he can. Therefore we must be ready to fight." Also, *Daniel*, sig. B₂: "And the devil doth prick forth those that he hath . . . with most excessive fury and outrage, to being all to hurly-burly . . . Hereof come battles and wars."

109 "It is the native property of the Divine Word never to make its appearance without disturbing Satan and rousing his opposition. This is the most certain . . . criterion by which it is distinguished from false doctrines which are . . . received with applause by the world." *Institutes*, Dedication.

110 *Institutes*, I, xiv, 18.

CHAPTER THREE · TWO CASE STUDIES IN CALVINIST POLITICS

Ideologies undergo a process of change and development, which is an aspect of political and social history as much as it is a part of the history of ideas. Men act and explain their actions in ideological terms. They organize and explain their organizations to each other. In doing these things, they continually transform the language, images, and concepts that are their means of expression. This transformation is worked out in different ways. Frightened and uncertain men often bring extraordinarily different, even contradictory expressive modes into uneasy and usually temporary harmony: so the Huguenots, moving cautiously between the old and the new, mixed the metaphors, so to speak, of feudalism and Calvinism. On the other hand, men driven by the pressures of rapid social change or political defeat and persecution may adopt a new ideology with astonishing recklessness, cutting themselves off from a long intellectual tradition. In this manner the Marian exiles expounded Calvin's ideas with a logic and boldness that greatly disturbed the master himself. To a certain extent, an ideology is self-limiting in the ideas it can express; hence it appeals only to certain groups of men and moves them only in certain directions. But the men themselves, selfish, brave, enthusiastic, cynical or absurd, are always capable of confusion and extravagance.

The work of French Huguenot theorists and English Marian exiles affords a clear illustration of the interaction of concrete, interested men and abstract symbols and ideas. The contrast between the two groups of writers is especially interesting because both worked with essentially the same intellectual stockpile—medieval commonplaces along with the newer Protestant notions—and both worked in the shade of Calvin, under the immediate impact of his systematic ideology. John Knox and Philip de Mornay would not have been strangers to one another had they ever met, though de Mornay would undoubtedly have felt more comfortable with his English counterpart (and friend) Sir Philip Sidney. Whatever their probable ideological sympathies, however, there was an immense social distance between de Mornay, a son of the French nobility attached to the court of Henry of Navarre, and Knox, a son of the Scottish peasantry who labored in the French galleys and lived as an embittered exile in England and Geneva.

Knowing the men, it might be possible to anticipate their ideas. Both produced political ideologies that are filled with a Calvinist sense of conscience and duty. Both urged upon their fellow men explicit programs of political action. Both were themselves activists, de Mornay an advisor and ambassador for the Huguenots during the French civil wars, Knox one of the leaders of the Scottish reformation. But the men for whom de Mornay wrote, Protestant though they were, were also noblemen, younger sons of gentry families, wealthy burghers, and lawyers. Frightened by the growth of royal power, uncertain of their own political functions, they sought not only religious reform, but a new constitutional order in which they might play a secure and significant part. Already men of status and prestige, they cultivated a conscience that at once befitted their position and, by enhancing their self-esteem, prepared them to improve it. The intellectuals who gave form to their rough aspirations emphasized and extended Calvin's theory of political office, with its heavy overtones of duty and discipline. They made of Calvinism a doctrine that trained and fortified the French nobility for a new political role. This was by no means an automatic reflection of aristocratic self-interest; it represented instead an ideologically controlled sense of what that interest was—a sense not shared by all the members of the nobility and firmly grasped by very few of them indeed.

John Knox, on the other hand, wrote for a group of angry and alienated intellectuals, exiles from their native land, their old ties broken, ready to be singleminded in the hope of discovering a new legitimacy and a new rectitude. Knox transformed Calvin's conception of the saint into an ideal around which men without established social interests might rally. His description of the saint's political activity reached far beyond the doctrine of official responsibility developed in Huguenot tracts. Himself an outlaw, the exiled minister felt little obligation to legal order. This did not set him outside the world of social control; Calvinism taught the saint a kind of self-discipline, much as it did the Huguenot nobleman. But if the self-discipline of the Huguenot was in the service of constitutional order, that of the Marian exile was shaped to the necessities of revolutionary organization.

THE HUGUENOTS

There is a striking chronological coincidence between the large-scale reception of Calvinism in France and the appearance of the nobility in Protestant ranks. French Lutheranism had appealed almost entirely to men of the lower classes: artisans (especially migrant workers and *chambrelans*), monks, mendicants, rural clerics, schoolmasters. Calvinism, on the other hand, spread through the political elites of sixteenth-century France. If it was quickly uprooted among those social groups that depended most directly upon the crown—the *noblesse de la robe,* the legists, and parliamentary *avocats*—it continued to gain ground among the older political classes that had maintained some sense of independent authority.[1] As late as 1558, Calvin might still complain of the insufficient status and dignity of his French followers, but by then fully a third of the French students at Geneva were of noble birth, while in France itself Genevan Protestantism was the religion of an increasing number of aristocrats and gentlemen and was on the way to becoming the hereditary religion of their families.[2] The library of the provincial nobleman Charles du Vergier, seized by the king's officials in 1556, already contained the psalms of Marot and Beza and a copy of Calvin's Genevan catechism.[3] Du Vergier, even in his obscurity, was typical of the

1 On the early spread of French Protestantism, see Henri Hauser, "The French Reformation and the French People in the Sixteenth Century," *The American Historical Review* 4:218ff. (January 1899). On the changing composition of the Protestant communities, see Impart de la Tour, *Les origines de la Réforme,* vol. IV: *Calvin et l'Institution Chrétienne* (Paris, 1905), pp. 473ff., and Lucien Romier, *Le royaume de Catherine de Médicis: La France à la veille des guerres de religion* (Paris, 1922), II, 257f.

2 Statistics on the French students in Geneva are supplied in R. M. Kingdon, *Geneva and the Coming of the Wars of Religion in France, 1555-1563* (Geneva, 1956), pp. 6ff. On Calvinism as an hereditary religion, see É. G. Léonard, *Le Protestant Français* (Paris, 1953), pp. 8, 62.

3 De la Tour, *Calvin,* p. 489. For another example of Calvinism in the country, see *A Huguenot Family in the Sixteenth Century: The Memoirs of Philippe de*

men who provided leadership and support for the Huguenot movement.

Virtually all the Huguenot publicists were noblemen, writing first of all for their peers. Beza, de Mornay, Languet, La Noue—even that French "congregationalist" Morely—all were of noble birth. Many of them, not choosing to live in exile and seclusion at Geneva, spent their lives in the service of Huguenot lords or German Protestant princes, moving back and forth over the French frontier and serving a cause that often enough seemed international. The Huguenot ministry also included in its ranks a considerable number of the lesser nobility; their large estates were a frequent concern of Protestant casuists. At various of the twenty-eight synods held between 1559 and 1659 (the years of the first and last national Protestant assemblies) the proportion of aristocrats among the clerical representatives approached one-third.[4] The church had obviously remained an honorable calling. Despite a long history of internal struggles between noblemen and commoners, the political and cultural tone of French Protestantism was largely determined by the aristocracy. That process which a recent historian calls the *embourgeoisement* of French Protestantism did not really begin until the eighteenth century.[5] During the years of the religious wars only the letters and occasional proclamations of the Huguenot aldermen of La Rochelle can be said to represent a bourgeois viewpoint, and even in that heroic city military leadership was in the hands of a very model of Protestant chivalry, François de la Noue ("dit Bras de Fer").[6]

Between Calvinism and the still-feudal nobility, there occurred a kind of historical tug-of-war—a struggle typical, perhaps, of periods of cultural transformation. At times, Calvinist organiza-

---

Mornay, Sieur de Plessis Marly, Written by his Wife, trans. with intro. by Lucy Crump (London, n.d.).

4 *Synodicon in Gallia Reformata: or, the Acts, Decisions, Decrees and Canons of those Famous National Councils of the Reformed Churches in France,* ed. John Quick (London, 1692). This book provides lists of participants in all the Huguenot synods. On ministers' estates, see p. xxiv: "Ministers, though they have estates and lands of their own, may yet nevertheless take wages from their flocks."

5 Léonard, *Protestant Français,* pp. 63ff.

6 The Huguenot aristocracy, however, granted a considerable latitude to its burgher supporters and some effort was made, especially in La Rochelle, to create free cities analogous to those of Germany. See Georges Weill, *Les théories sur le pouvoir royal en France pendant les guerres de religion* (Paris, 1892), pp. 127-129.

tion appeared on the verge of total absorption into the old patterns of feudal order; at times, individual noblemen broke their
feudal ties (often enough, by going into exile) and seemed to behave like proper saints; probably more rarely, some unification
of lordship and religion was achieved in the person of a pious
gentleman. It was entirely possible for the two different organizational systems—congregation, classis, and synod on the one hand,
feudal hierarchy and local connection on the other—simply to
coexist, although curious jurisdictional tangles might be the
result. When the minister Pierre Fournelet wished to change
congregations, for example, he required three letters of release
from his duties at the Neuchatel church: one from the agent of
Léonor d'Orléans, Due de Longeuville and sovereign lord of
Neuchatel; a second from the city's council of burghers; and a
third from the local classis.[7] Despite the large amount of synodi-
cal legislation attempting to establish control over the feudal
household and the system of patronage, the balance clearly leaned
toward the older forms. The frequently reiterated demands of
church officials for discipline and religious order are themselves
indications that in countless local instances the consistory could
exercise little power over an unruly nobility. The almost plain-
tive note sounded at the La Rochelle synod of 1581 was typical:
"Princes and great lords shall be advised to observe the articles
of our discipline."[8]

Protestantism in France was gradually, if somewhat chaotically
and unevenly, integrated into a going system of feudal connection
and patronage, which—whatever its economic and political weakness—was still significantly a form of military organization. It
was a system out of use, perhaps, since the Italian wars, but still
eminently usable. "The time had not yet come," writes Imbart
de la Tour, "when the noble would be transformed into a courtier."[9] Nor, it should be said, was he likely—and here he differed

7 Kingdon, *Coming of the Wars*, p. 27. The existence of a double form of
organization—a combination of aristocrats and a confederation of congregations
—is also noted by J. W. Thompson, *The Wars of Religion in France: 1559-1576*
(Chicago, 1909), p. 313, and by J. E. Neale, *The Age of Catherine de Medici*
(London, 1943), p. 31.

8 *Synodicon*, p. 137; see also pp. xxi and lv of the Huguenot Discipline reprinted
in the same book.

9 De la Tour, *Calvin*, p. 487.

greatly from his English counterpart—to have had a university education or to have served as a local official of the crown. The first duty of the nobility, Hubert Languet might still insist, "is to fight the enemies of the nation . . . The recompense of the fatigue and danger to which the nobles are exposed is the honor granted them by the other orders of the state. . ."[10] And it was as a soldier and an old-fashioned feudal lord that the French nobleman first established his connection with the Protestant congregation. In a period of increasing violence, he offered the protection of his sword and his men, and became, as it were, the feudal patron of Calvinist worship. Soon enough he was a religious patron as well, himself a duly elected elder, the minister very likely a member of his household, though perhaps an uncomfortable one.[11] The various truces during the intermittent civil wars usually permitted nobles enjoying the feudal right of high justice to have preaching on their estates. Although Catholics insisted that the privilege of hearing the sermon extended no further than the lord's household and tenants, no further, that is, than the right of justice itself, in practice the privilege was stretched to include the local Huguenot congregation—a very important extension, but one rendered ambiguous by its circumstances. The price that had to be paid in congregational independence may easily be guessed. Disputes between ministers and noblemen were frequent, but it is clear that the lord of the manor possessed superior power. And given his new position as protector and patron of the reformed church, what was more likely than that he justify his feudal lordship by reference to his religious vocation? "God has established me," wrote the Seigneur de la Feste-Fresnel, "with power over many men, and by this means one of the most superstitious countries of the kingdom will be gained for Christ."[12]

De la Feste-Fresnel's boast did not yet, however, constitute a developed ideological position. The Catholic historian, Imbart de la Tour, is probably correct to argue that the French nobility, even at the climactic moments of its struggle with the king, never

10 Quoted in Henri Chevreul, *Hubert Languet* (Paris, 1852), pp. 115-116.
11 Romier, *Royaume de Catherine de Médicis*, II, 263ff.
12 Quoted in Hauser, "French Reformation," p. 226.

developed a new and independent ideology. Its ideas, born of the needs or passions of the moment, were often little more than outbursts of regret or anger. The nobility, de la Tour writes, knew only force and warfare and always believed (incorrectly) "that a revolt was a revolution."[13] Except for those who went into exile, the nobility continued to move within a world where honor, loyalty, and chivalry were the cardinal virtues. The Calvinist shaping of the aristocratic conscience was never a completed process, precisely because the deepest feelings of the vast majority of aristocrats were never sufficiently emancipated from the feudal and patriarchal world: there was too much regret, an emotion on which Calvinism does not thrive. When the warrior La Noue admitted that the medieval romances of Amadis still caused "un esprit de vertige" among the men of his generation—the generation of the Huguenots and of the religious struggles—it was as if he opened up a secret world, unsubmissive surely to Genevan rigor.[14] Another element of this same world was revealed in one of the verses celebrating Poltrot, the Protestant assassin of the Duke of Guise:

> L'example merveilleux
> D'une extresme vaillance
> Le dixiesme de preux
> Liberateurs de France.[15]

Le preux—the gallant knight, the man of valor; here is a figure not easily absorbed into the Calvinist categories of saint and worldling. More properly Protestant poetry celebrated the assassin as an instrument of God and said nothing of his personal *vaillance*.

The work of the Huguenots does represent, however, the nearest approach of the French nobility of early modern times to an independent ideological position. It attempts a highly rationalized and legalized view of the rights and duties of the

13 De la Tour, *Les origines de la Réforme*, vol. I: *La France moderne* (Paris, 1905), p. 374.

14 Quoted in J. Huizinga, *The Waning of the Middle Ages* (New York, 1954), pp. 79-80; see La Noue, *Discours politiques et militaire* (n. p., 1612), pp. 133-147. In Geneva a man was admonished by the consistory for possessing a copy of the medieval romance *Amadis de Gaules;* see Williston Walker, *John Calvin, the Organizer of Reformed Protestantism* (London, 1906), p. 304.

15 Quoted in Charles Labitte, *De la démocratie chez les prédicateurs de la ligue* (Paris, 1841), p. lii.

aristocracy, considering its members not as heads of feudal households, but as officers of the realm. Huguenot theory may be considered an unsuccessful effort to transform feudal status into constitutional position. It was an effort made at the last possible moment, for most noblemen were already detached from practical politics and local administration and were more and more dependent, both for legitimacy and self-esteem, upon the sheer fact of their status and its attendant honors.[16] Protestant writers sought to discover a passageway for the old nobility into the political order of the modern state. Many aristocrats, however, had already decided that their more natural path led from the feudal household into the king's court, where honor, loyalty, and chivalry enjoyed a somewhat artificial but highly elaborate existence. Other men, mostly younger sons, rowdy, ambitious, and usually uneducated, welcomed an opportunity to fight as Protestants, but were hardly willing to accept that combined military and ecclesiastical discipline that Calvinists sought to impose on their soldiers. Such men were adventurers, without complicated motives, without economic or political function, largely devoid of Protestant piety. They were hardly the sternly dutiful officials in whose interests Hotman and de Mornay elaborated a new view of the French constitution.

French Calvinism worked itself out politically, then, as an effort to reorganize the feudal system—not only its constitution but also its "spirit." It was an attempt to turn the "valiant knight" into a conscientious officeholder. For this purpose, Calvin's conception of the duties of the lesser magistrates was stressed and elaborated by Huguenot intellectuals. A massive effort was made to prove that the theory was based upon historical fact; endless legal precedent was mustered. The feudal oath and the system of vassalage were transformed and then incorporated into a far larger and more modern structure of constitutional obligation. Unfortunately, the men who were to animate this structure existed in numbers far too small to be effective. Huguenot constitutionalism had a brief, and largely mental, existence. Philip de Mornay suggests the historical figure who might have given the theory practical significance: he was a country gentle-

---

[16] De la Tour, *France moderne*, pp. 375ff., and Romier, *Royaume de Catherine de Médicis*, I, 170-171.

man of puritanical temperament, intelligent, incorruptible, humorless, yet possessing a considerable political imagination.[17] He lived uneasily at Henry of Navarre's court, could not forgive the future king his mistresses, but suffered them with "mute reproach." Piously, he presented Henry with the gift of a carefully worked-out daily schedule—for a "well-arranged" day has plenty of time for "serious business."[18] Navarre himself was the other side of the Huguenot coin. The unchallenged leader of the Protestant party, he changed it into a feudal faction by his very presence. He is the prototype of that "discontented person" of "greatness and reputation" against whom Bacon warned in his essay "Of Sedition and Troubles." De Mornay and others like him stayed in the background: the prince of the blood took the lead; a Cromwell was not yet imaginable.

II

The tracts of the English Marian exiles often read like sermons; they are above all exhortations to political good works. But the tone of much of Huguenot literature—when it is not hysterical and vituperative—is that of a clerical conference considering difficult problems of conscience and casuistry. That this should be the character of polemical works usually written by laymen suggests the extreme uncertainty with which Huguenot ideas of office, duty, and political activity were received. Sixty or seventy years before, French knights had ridden off to the Italian wars in high spirits and with no moral qualms. Many would fight again in the same mood; they were permanently at arms, with few interests and little proficiency except in war and the chase. But this was not true for some at least of the aristocratic converts to Calvinism, youthful de Mornays who lived in the provinces of southern or western France, or who studied at Bordeaux or Geneva. They were newly pious and diligently so; and if they no longer could follow enthusiastically in the train of some marauding baron, they would need new reasons for activity and warfare, reasons that would speak to their nervously Calvinist con-

---

17 Hubert Languet was apparently a similar type: a man who dreaded light conversation, hated all forms of luxury, and cultivated an "austerity of manner" for which he was praised by Melancthon; see Chevreul, *Languet*, pp. 15, 172-173.

18 *Huguenot Family*, pp. 59-60.

sciences and overcome any vague nostalgia for the old ways. He wrote his treatise, declared Theodore Beza, "that the consciences of many may be satisfied." His new Protestant sense of conscience as a public affair led him to a careful, systematic effort to reach large numbers of men with political argument. A troubled conscience, he argued, permits even private citizens to violate Calvin's earlier prohibition and open a public discussion of law and government:

> If . . . the conscience of some be at a loss, they can and are . . . under an obligation to examine (albeit discreetly and in a peaceful manner) what elements of reason and justice are to be found in the command by which they are bidden or forbidden to do something.[19]

The same motivation is described in the second dialogue of the important pamphlet *Réveille-Matin*. *Politique* is asked to discuss the problem of resistance "in terms both of conscience and of the state" for the sake of the "timid and the scrupulous." Such men must be "confirmed and resolved by arguments, authorities and examples."[20]

Huguenot writing was a kind of political casuistry, specifically designed to convince the scrupulous, to soothe their consciences, and order their conduct. Like any casuist, the Huguenot was bound by his cases; he found these cases in history, the theater of God's judgment, to which Calvinists usually looked for the tokens and prescriptions of an ever-active divine will. The interpretation of history became a religious act, or, as Hotman put it, an "act of piety."[21] The citation of historical example is the single major method of argumentation in Huguenot writing. Nothing served better to settle the minds of sixteenth-century Frenchmen. It is this fact which helps explain the great importance attributed by his contemporaries to Francis Hotman's *Franco-Gallia* and also makes comprehensible the length and detail of the historical illustration in both Beza's tract and the *Vindiciae contra Tyrannos*. Such detail is not supplementary but essential, far more important than any reasoning from abstract principles. Having

---

19 Theodore Beza, *Concerning the Rights of Rulers over their Subjects and the Duty of Subjects towards their Rulers*, trans. Henri-Louis Gonin, intro. A. A. Van Schelven, ed. A. M. Murray (Capetown, 1956), p. 26.

20 Eusebe Philadelphe Cosmopolite [Nicolas Barnaud?], *Le Réveille-Matin des Français et de leurs voisins* (Edinburgh, 1574), dialogue II, p. 75.

21 See Weill, *Théories sur le pouvoir royal*, p. 105.

presented his historical illustration, Beza considered himself virtually finished: "These . . . examples . . . are so reliable and authentic that they alone should be adequate to strengthen the consciences of subordinate magistrates."[22]

The Calvinist view of the factual world led to a new evaluation of history, and especially of a history called objective. This new view of the past was, of course, common to many men during the Renaissance and Reformation, when the pervasive force of established custom was undermined both by historical analysis and by the evocation of primitive purity.[23] The myth of origins has, so far as modern times are concerned, its own origin here. But to this more general trend, Calvinists lent a particular emphasis, and, what is perhaps more important, a new intensity of interest. It was this intensity that drove Hotman to rely for his analysis on nothing but original sources and to answer his critics with the characteristically vigorous (and mistaken) assertion that "the book is historical; it is the history of a fact. The whole discourse is dependent upon fact."[24] And facts, he might have added, are the work of God, the details of a permanent revelation. Indeed, Hotman suggested no abstract principles whatsoever to justify the constitution he had discovered in French history; the only universality he recognized was a pretended universality of fact: he collected examples at random from the histories of Germany, Sparta, England, and Aragon (in that order) and concluded that his idea of liberty had been the "constant and universal law of all nations."[25] Hotman's history provides a dramatic example

22 Beza, *Rights of Rulers*, pp. 42-43; for another example of this sort of argumentation, see the anonymous tract *Le politique, dialogue traitant de la puissance, autorité, et du devoir des princes*, in *Mémoires de l'état de France sous Charles neuviéme* (Meidelsbourg, 1576), III, especially pp. 131-134.

23 For a discussion of French work on political history during the sixteenth century, see W. F. Church, *Constitutional Thought in Sixteenth Century France: A Study in the Evolution of Ideas* (Cambridge, Mass., 1941), pp. 83ff., 157ff., 203ff.

24 Quoted from one of Hotman's letters, in Beatrice Reynolds, *Proponents of Limited Monarchy in Sixteenth Century France; Francis Hotman and Jean Bodin* (New York, 1931), p. 80. For the Huguenot view of historical objectivity, see de Mornay's letter to Hubert Languet in which he criticizes Jean Sleidan's history of the Reformation: "I dare to blame many historians for having given their judgments on affairs . . . I have often thought that the historian, who is like the reporter of a trial, ought to leave judgment free to the judges, without prejudicing them by a first opinion . . ." Quoted in Paul Méaly, *Les publicistes de la Réforme* (Paris, 1903), p. 228.

25 Francis Hotman, *Franco-Gallia or, An Account of the Ancient Free State of France* (originally published 1573; in English, London, 1721), p. 71. See also de

of the method—later used by English common lawyers—which makes *precedent* the very opposite of *custom*. It suggests the rational use of historical example to underpin political innovation.

Calvin could write casually that the usual course of human history was degeneration.[26] Something like this attitude always lay behind the insistence that the only reform necessary was a dramatic return to primitive purity. But the mere description of an original state of political virtue was not sufficient to convince the consciences of men still caught up in traditional modes of thought and behavior. The Huguenot noble had no desire to make so radical a break with the political order as the Reformation had already made with the traditional religion. He was, after all, a man of established (if often decaying) position, possessed of practical military skills and a mind to accompany them—a combination of status, function, and mentality not conducive to extended or radical speculation. In addition to the myth of origins, he required a myth of persistence, of what Beza called "uninterrupted usage." He needed to be told that the original rights and duties were his still, or at least that he had been deprived of them so recently that time had not yet covered the wounds. " 'Tis plain," wrote Hotman, "that it is not yet a hundred years complete, since the liberties of Franco-gallia and the authority of its annual General Council flourished in full vigor . . . our commonwealth, which at first was founded upon the principles of liberty maintained itself in the same free and sacred state . . . for more than eleven hundred years." Similarly and equally incorrectly, the author of the *Réveille-Matin*: "It is not more than sixty years," he insists, "that the liberty of the estates has been oppressed."[27] The French constitution was thus reconstructed as a kind of static force in political life, deriving its legitimacy from uninterrupted usage—and yet challenging existing institutions. It was not something that had grown through the ages, like customary law, incorporating wisdom and experience. It was rather a secular revelation, discovered in the history books and legitimizing political

---

Mornay's letter to Hotman, urging him "to deduce our right from the constitutional law [jure et lege] of the kingdom rather than from natural equity [justa re] . . ." Quoted in Reynolds, *Limited Monarchy*, pp. 93-94.

26 Calvin, *Institutes of the Christian Religion*, IV, ix, 8.

27 Hotman, *Franco-Gallia*, p. 122; *Réveille-Matin*, Dialogue II, p. 89.

activity for men not yet ready to rely on religious revelation alone, nor to take risks—as Cromwell would one day do—in the hope of providential vindication.

Except in Hotman's work, the Huguenot view of history never led to any very extended treatment of persistence, development, or change. In the introduction to the *Franco-Gallia,* Hotman described the state as a body politic with a familiar history: "even as human bodies decay and perish . . . so commonwealths are brought to their period . . ."[28] Organic imagery of this sort rarely reappears in Huguenot writing. History is as unnatured in its usual treatment by Protestant publicists as is nature itself in Calvin's work. Each historical event, like each breath of wind, is particularly and specially willed by God. History is the casuist's case-book; it is not a continuous development, but a collection of discrete facts, examples, and precedents. The only necessary distinction is offered by *Histographique* in the second dialogue of the *Réveille-Matin*: the judgments of God are known in biblical history with "truth and certainty," while in profane history they are known "only by conjecture."[29] Actually, this distinction is rarely made in practice; the typical writer simply proliferates examples, drawing apparently on whatever history he knows best, biblical, classical, or feudal. Any of these might serve, and not only for historical purposes; the new moral image of the French noble was also compounded of three historical types: the biblical saint, the stoical aristocrat, and the "gallant knight." At the price of considerable intellectual confusion, history thus provided the earnest, active Huguenot with a multiple legitimacy.

III

Every example is an argument and Hotman's history the most impressive argument of all. Whatever the historical value of the *Franco-Gallia*—and modern writers have rightly tended to be hard on it[30]—it can best be read as an elaborate treatise designed to convince the subtle but tenacious Calvinist conscience. Resistance to tyrants, Hotman sought to prove, was not opposition to God or even to God's appointed vicar on earth. A close study of

28 Hotman, *Franco-Gallia*, preface, pp. v-vi.
29 *Réveille-Matin*, dialogue II, pp. 39-40.
30 See August Thierry, *Récit des temps mérovingiens* (Paris, 1878), pp. 32-40.

French history revealed that the divine will had established alternative powers, equal with the king in rights and responsibilities. The "public council" of the French kingdom possessed a *"sacred authority"* legally founded upon an ancient, longstanding constitution. The power which its officers possessed was as divine—he had only to say *as real*—as was the power of the king.[31] Its exercise was a matter of practical judgment and constitutional usage; often in the past the council had opposed, had even deposed, the king. Conscience could thus be resolved by legal fact. Itself an assemblage of legal facts, the political order was as sacred for Hotman the lawyer as it had been for Calvin the theologian, but the lawyer had now demonstrated that resistance to tyranny was a part of this order, historically verifiable, legally justified, and hence divinely ordained.

God himself wills the political order; its officers act in his name. Given this axiom, it was at last possible to answer the ancient question, Who can act effectively for God on earth? *La noblesse de la religion* presented itself—however surprisingly—as the appointed divine instrument. And there the Huguenot search ended. The resistance of the Protestant nobles, their insurrection, was nothing more than the performance of that duty which God had prescribed, according to the procedures that he himself had established. Hotman's discovery of these constitutional procedures made the resistance possible; legal and historical argument eased consciences that might otherwise have been disturbed. Even violent political change was legalized and made over, as it were, into something routine and orderly. How was it possible, asked a Huguenot pamphleteer calling himself Nicholas de Montand, that Capetian kings had dispossessed the Carolingians? He answered, in effect, that it was no very difficult matter, having been ordered first "by the will of God, who changes kingdoms and empires as he pleases. By what means? *By the political order which he has established in the world.*"[32] And that meant: by the established political officers.

Despite Calvin's recognition of the "providential liberator," Huguenot writers were extremely wary about justifying tyranni-

---

[31] Hotman, *Franco-Gallia*, pp. 53, 64ff, 77 (emphasis added).
[32] Quoted from Nicholas de Montand, *Le miroir des Français* (1581) in Weill, *Théories sur le pouvoir royal*, p. 154 (emphasis added).

cide. They spurned the luxury, and also avoided the political dangers, of such a chancy miracle. Discussing affairs in England, the author of the *Réveille-Matin* admitted that some miraculous act of God might well end the life of the troublesome Mary Stuart; he would prefer, however, her legal execution.[33] Cast in a similar mold was Beza's insistence that there were ways to oppose tyranny "derived from human institutions." His extreme preoccupation with worldly means gives a curiously nonreligious tone to the political writing of Calvin's successor, until it is understood that this very preoccupation had its theological reasons. Beza recognized, for example, that the judges of Israel, like the Old Testament tyrannicides, had been stirred to their famous deeds by some special motion of God; precisely these cases had been cited by many writers who would have removed the tyrant without bestirring themselves. Beza would have nothing to do with such political lassitude; that God had had to arouse the Israelites "in a special way" only indicated, he wrote, that their spirit had been broken by tyranny. For men (or rather, some men) actually possess "an ordinary right . . . to defend the lawful constitution of their country."[34] Such "ordinary rights" were the routine provisions of divine providence; miracles were unnecessary.

The second contract of the *Vindiciae* also represented an attempt to place political activity and resistance within the ordinary world of fact and law.[35] It is instructive to notice what de Mornay did with the older medieval ideas of which he made such obvious use in his tract. Medieval writers had sometimes defended resistance by arguing that kingship was nothing more than an

---

33 *Réveille-Matin*, dialogue II, p. 16.

34 Beza, *Rights of Rulers*, pp. 29, 34.

35 Junius Brutus [Philip de Mornay], *Vindiciae contra Tyrannos* (orig. published 1576; English ed. 1689; repr. with intro. by H. J. Laski, New York, n.d.), pp. 71ff. De Mornay's authorship has been disputed and it is possible that Hubert Languet wrote the section expounding the second contract (between king and people). See Laski's introduction and Raoul Patry, *Philippe de Plessis-Mornay: un Huguenot homme d'état (1549-1623)* (Paris, 1933), pp. 277-278. Joint authorship has been the favored theory of those commentators who see the religious argument of the first sections as an addition to what was originally a secular and rationalist position. It will be maintained below that a Calvinist spirit pervades the whole book and that its various parts form an argument that is, by and large, consistent, though certainly confused in its details. Hence, for convenience' sake, De Mornay will be cited as the sole author.

office rationally designed to meet certain limited human needs. When the temporary officeholder failed to meet the needs or over-stepped the limits, reasonable men might well remove him from office. "The king is made for the people, not the people for the king."[36] But Huguenots could no more be satisfied with such a secular and theoretical utilitarianism than with an unpredictable divine intervention. Utilitarian argument remained largely ab-stract and formal. With his contract de Mornay sought to trans-form utility into a legal reference, a set point of political order, to which Calvinists might appeal, so to speak, in the strenuous court of their practical conscience. He strove to avoid any merely moral obligation or any obligation binding only upon rational men. At great length de Mornay repeated the medieval discussion of the ends of monarchy, but he was not satisfied until he had fixed the end as a bond and the bond as a legal contract. Having done that he immediately sought historical verification of the contract's actual existence. Through his discussion of the corona-tion oaths of feudal kings, of the rights and powers of parliaments, diets, estates and councils, of ephors, tribunes and senators, he sought to establish the right of resistance in history and constitu-tional reality.[37]

IV

Against a conqueror or a usurper this right might be exercised by any private citizen; he would require only ordinary boldness, not divine inspiration. In the more likely case of a legitimate tyrant, the "ordinary right" of constitutional defense belonged only to those public men who occupied constitutional offices. This had been the view of medieval writers also, but in Huguenot literature it took on a new meaning. Pressing their political spec-ulation considerably beyond the historical casuistry of Hotman, Protestant writers developed two key ideas. First, they sharply insisted upon the conventional nature of all human order (ex-cept in the church) excluding the very possibility of both pater-nalism and charisma and opening the way for a straightforward

---

[36] For a discussion of the medieval view, see Fritz Kern, *Kingship and Law in the Middle Ages*, trans. S. B. Chrimes (Oxford, 1948), pp. 119ff. The utilitarian view of kingship is argued in the *Vindiciae*, pp. 139ff.

[37] *Vindiciae*, especially pp. 127ff, 176ff.

constitutional politics. Secondly, they infused this newly narrowed order with a religious conscience and discipline. If it was history and law that made Huguenot activity legitimate, it was Calvinist conscience that made it obligatory and defined its goals. And conscience worked within the forms of office; it was, in effect, God's call to political action. Hotman's history had braced the Protestant nobleman for his worldly tasks, helped him to overcome his lingering "esprit de vertige." De Mornay's first covenant—a development in feudal imagery of Calvin's conception of political office—revealed the impulse which would send conscientious men into action.

"The nature of a king," wrote de Mornay in the *Vindiciae*, "signifies not an inheritance, not a propriety, nor a usufruct, but a charge [and an] office." The man who holds such an office is still only a man; if king he is nothing more than the "administrator of the commonwealth." He did not emerge from the womb with a crown upon his head and he possesses no such natural supremacy over his subjects as does a father over his children. Touching upon an eternal theme of political radicalism, de Mornay insisted that subjects were the brethren of the king.[38] Political inequality was thus entirely and explicitly detached from natural hierarchy—a separation already implicit in Calvin's work. An even more dramatic denial of patriarchy as an element in political order is found in the *Dialogue between Archon and Polity*: "There is only one Father," exclaims the anonymous Huguenot author, "master and lord common to all men and to nature. Except for him . . . there is no other paternity, mastery or domination; earthy superiors being only his ministers and lieutenants . . ."[39]

As natural hierarchy and paternity were pushed outside the political world, so headship could have no meaning within it; but if the king were not a head, the state could no longer be a body politic. In fact, then, political organization was artificial (the creation of God or of men), defined by its constitutional structure and no longer explicable as a part of the natural, organic world. Huguenot writers, as has been seen, tended to reify this structure and assign it an entirely ahistorical existence—almost as

---

38 *Ibid.*, pp. 156, 170; see also *Le politique*, in *Mémoires*, III, 98.
39 *Le politique*, in *Mémoires*, p. 156; compare Matthew 23:9.

if, newly ordinary and matter-of-fact, it had become an object of secular awe. Since they possessed little idea of historical development, this was easy enough to do. It was, moreover, a happy solution to many of the problems raised for the French aristocracy by the new and obviously growing power of the king. For in their treatment of the constitution, Protestant nobles were seeking above all a basis for their own permanence, an extension, as it were, of the persistence they found in history. They were forced to seek that permanence, however, in the name of their official "vocations" and not of their personal status, for with the feudal hierarchy in decay the magic of the king's person overrode every other claim unless the basis of the claim was impersonal. "A kingdom has within itself," Hotman wrote, "a perpetual and sure principle of safety in the wisdom of its senators and of persons well-skilled in affairs."[40] But if a particular man failed to fulfill the purposes of his office, if a senator was not wise, that purpose remained "official" and wisdom was still to be assumed in senators. Neither human failure nor prescription of time could alter the constitutional structure. Founded upon the fact of magistracy, ordained by God for human benefit, the offices were eternal: "the commonwealth never dies."[41]

Beza's discussion follows the same pattern, similarly switching the emphasis from natural endowment or feudal rank to political office and basing office on the ahistorical fact of sovereignty. Calvin's disciple distinguished carefully between the domestic servants of the king, responsive to his every pleasure (and, according to Hotman, debauched by luxury), and the independent nobility and civic officials. The latter relied on the "supremacy as such" and not on the monarch; in effect they shared the crown. "L'état," the Huguenot officials might have said, "c'est nous." So long as all men were conscientious, neither a unified nor a personal sovereignty could exist: any pious or willful magistrate might act independently of the king, for the good of the kingdom or the glory of God. The only price of his independence was his conscientiousness. Even if the offices of some noblemen have become

[40] Hotman, *Franco-Gallia*, p. 108.
[41] *Vindiciae*, p. 137. The author is arguing that "neither can the lapse of time nor changing of individuals alter in any sort the right of [the] people." He has previously (p. 126), described the magistrates as the eternal guardians of the "rights and privileges of the people."

nothing more than hereditary titles of honor, wrote Beza, "they have in no way lost their original right and authority," nor, it need hardly be said, have the men been relieved of the duties their honor entails.[42]

Huguenot conscience was so closely bound to the forms of office that it seemed at times to be an attribute rather of the position than the individual. Each man is obliged to defend the "good law," declared Beza, "in accordance with the station he has obtained in the constitution of the community." That such duty was neither natural nor universal was evident in Beza's absolute denial of any political power in slaves and in the *Vindiciae*'s refusal of any "public command" to private persons.[43] The Calvinist devaluation of the personal thus led among the French Huguenots to an exaltation of the official. But this was only possible because the officer was God's deputy, or in Huguenot imagery, his vassal. "All the inhabitants of the earth," wrote de Mornay, "hold of [God] that which they have and are but his tenants . . . all men, of what degree soever they be, are his servants, farmers, officers and vassals and owe account and acknowledgment to Him . . ."[44] The first covenant of the *Vindiciae* was an effort to give formal expression to this relation. Through the covenant God worked his will upon the men who held offices; they could not consent rationally but only conscientiously obey, and obedience required earnest, disciplined, sustained activity for the glory of God.

Although some Huguenot ideologists sought to restore the representative quality of political office, which Calvin had denied, obligation and duty for most of them were simply built into the reified constitutional structure, fixed by God and co-witnessed by conscience. It was for this reason that Calvinist writers were so ready to dispense with majorities.[45] They sought indeed to integrate the people into the constitutional structure, but not the people as they had been described in medieval literature, a corporate community held together by love and fellowship, nor

42 Beza, *Rights of Rulers*, pp. 38-40; see the similar argument in *Vindiciae*, pp. 126-127.

43 Beza, *Rights of Rulers*, pp. 74, 77; *Vindiciae*, pp. 109-110.

44 *Vindiciae*, p. 68.

45 See especially the discussion in the *Vindiciae*, pp. 100ff., answering the question, what may be done when the "better part" of a people consents to tyranny?

yet the people as they would later be described by liberal writers, an assembly of selfish, crafty individuals. The Huguenots envisioned instead a Protestant populace, leaders and followers alike possessing a single conscience, tightly united by the recognition of a joint responsibility before God. The "whole body of the people," declared de Mornay in the *Vindiciae,* should be considered as "the office and place of one man." The people collectively were a magistrate; they too had a vocation and a set of political duties—and this was the beginning of their discipline. They were no longer to behave like fallen men and "run in mutinous disorder." As a mere collection of private persons, "they have no power, they have no public command, nor any calling to unsheathe the sword of authority." The covenants were collective; they could "in no way appertain to particulars."[46] Huguenot writers continually insisted that their followers do nothing recklessly, "but in due order and in a disciplined fashion as far as shall be possible."[47] And this meant that the magistracy of the people was to be acted out only by the people's magistrates. Without the godly officials, the people did not constitute an organized or a politically or legally competent body.

The two covenants of the *Vindiciae* established not a representative government, and certainly not a system of popular sovereignty, but a very special sort of trusteeship. The basis of constitutional trust was the identity of godly consciences. For this reason, Huguenot "due order" did not preclude, in fact it required, the people's understanding of what they did, even when all they did was to obey and follow their pious magistrates. These magistrates, wrote de Mornay, were a "substitute" for the collective people, standing in the same place and bound by the same religious obligations. "All men are bound to serve God, but some . . . have received greater authority . . ."[48] Thus conscience made political discipline possible once natural hierarchy had been overthrown. Calvinism suggested to all men a new asceticism of duty; in the somber and devoted person of the magistrate the

---

[46] *Vindiciae,* pp. 90, 97, 109.
[47] *Rights of Rulers,* p. 35.
[48] *Vindiciae,* p. 110. "When we speak of all the people, we understand by that only those who hold their authority from the people, to wit, the magistrates, whom the people have substituted, or established, as it were, consorts to the empire . . . ," p. 97.

old Adam, fallen and corrupt, would hardly be visible; and among the newly disciplined people, the memory of the mutinous mob was exorcised.

Mere private persons have no role in Huguenot theory; by definition they are undisciplined and disorderly. Calvin's letters provide frequent examples of his extreme dislike for the wandering preacher or the free-wheeling prophet.[49] Beza's disdain for that insurgent Protestant philosopher Peter Ramus was precisely similar to his master's attitude. "He always wishes to appear, not as a disciple, but as a doctor," wrote the archdisciple of Geneva. "Ramus, who does not know the first thing about all these questions and who, I know, had never studied deeply either the Bible or any of its sacred interpretations, throws himself into battle armed only with his self-confidence."[50] With the picaresque man as with the picaresque mind, Calvinists were uneasy and unreconciled. They would have sought to organize even Don Quixote— but they would also have set him upon enemies more substantial than those he pursued. They would have drafted him into one of their armies.

The army the Huguenots actually assembled suggests the nature of their discipline far better than the constitutional order they never achieved. In the *Mémoires de l'état de France* there are preserved forty articles adopted by a Huguenot assembly of the *Midi* for the "regulation of affairs of war."[51] These articles are the earliest version of those extraordinarily precise and rigorous disciplines enforced some seventy years later in the Scottish Presbyterian and New Model armies of the English Revolution. In the forty Huguenot articles, military and ecclesiastical discipline were woven together. They were "two excellent nerves," wrote the author of the *Réveille-Matin,* "in order to hold vices in check and soldiers to their duty." Special police were established by the Huguenot assembly to enforce the "law of God and the policy of the army." Religious discipline and military police together ensured the "good and modest conduct"

---

49 See for example, Calvin, *Letters,* ed. Jules Bonnet, trans. David Constable (Edinburgh, 1855), I, 293.

50 Quoted in Paul Geisendorf, *Théodore de Bèze* (Geneva, 1949), p. 304.

51 "Articles pour le règlement des affaires de guerre," *Mémoires,* II, 164ff. The articles were drawn up at a synod held in Bearn in 1572, and adopted at Millau in 1573.

of the Christian soldier.[52] In his *Discours politiques et militaires,*
François de la Noue described the nature and effects of the Huguenot discipline—at least as it prevailed during the first civil
war:

When the war started there were some chiefs and captains who
spoke of military discipline, but much more effective were the sermons
in which we were admonished not to oppress the poor people . . . The
noblesse showed itself in these early days quite worthy of its name . . .
If any soldier was guilty of violence, he was banished or put in cus-
tody . . . Among such a large gathering we heard no-one blaspheme
the word of God . . . You could not find a box of dice or pack of cards
in the camp . . .[53]

Surely there is a great distance between the new soldier and the
gallant knight of feudal story. The knight was still an individual
of sorts, chivalrous, personally pious, riding alone or in a motley
band. The soldier was the disciplined member of an army, whose
piety was ideological and collective, confirmed by public prayer
—itself one of the chief innovations of the Huguenot camps. Perhaps the Protestant *vicomtes* of the second civil war still resembled gallant knights, or more likely, marauding feudal
barons. But the psalm-singing soldiers recruited from the Calvinist congregations were different men. "What manner of
churches are these, which turn out captains?" demanded a Catholic officer; he might equally well have asked "What manner of
captains . . . ?"[54] Like the political people, the religious army was
bound by a "common severity" and a common conscience in the
duties of its office. It was involved in a sustained and disciplined
struggle in defense of what was already called "the Cause."[55]

v

This was the heart of Huguenot theory: political order was a
permanent system of shared sovereignty, a specific and precise
allocation of duties, enforceable on the one hand at law and on
the other in conscience. Resistance was nothing more than a

[52] *Réveille-Matin,* dialogue II, p. 103; "Articles," *Mémoires,* II, 173.
[53] *Discours,* pp. 571-572; quoted in Sir Charles Oman, *A History of the Art of
War in the Sixteenth Century* (London, 1937), pp. 399-401.
[54] Quoted in C. G. Kelly, *French Protestantism: 1559-1562* (Baltimore, 1918),
p. 82.
[55] "Articles," *Mémoires,* II, 169. See also p. 165 describing the collective oath of
the Huguenot army.

disciplined acting out of constitutional and moral obligations. Arguments from natural law, communal will, and secular utility were all supplementary to this fundamental conception.[56] Order, organization, discipline, duty: these were the ideas at the center of Huguenot thought; they reveal more clearly than anything else the deepest hopes and fears—but perhaps especially the fears— of those educated Protestant noblemen, exploring the style and uses of piety, seeking somewhat worriedly a politics in which they could both exercise their new devotion and maintain their ancient authority.

It was in many ways an age of fear. That profound pessimism which Huizinga has described as a characteristic of the late medieval mind lingered still as an element of the aristocratic temperament.[57] It can be seen in Hubert Languet's dour but warm letters to the young Sidney. "From your letters," wrote Sidney, "I fancy I see a picture of the age in which we live: an age that resembles a bow too long bent; it must be unstrung or it will break." In some men, the accumulating tension released new energy; others it broke; all men of any sensitivity were aware of it. Languet's letters were full of the calm assurance that disaster was imminent. Horrifying war among Christians, new conquests by the Turks, the fall of Italy, perhaps all Europe, before the barbarians: all these gloomy anticipations he urged upon Sidney.[58] Himself a Protestant stoic rather than a Calvinist, he held before the young Englishman only a stern image of aristocratic duty, devoid of all enthusiasm. Theodore Beza could not always react with the same stoical calm. News of the Bartholomew's Night massacre released in him a terrible fear: "Here we are certainly exposed to the same danger," he wrote from Geneva to a Zurich friend, "and this will be, perhaps, the last time I write

---

56 Many historians of political theory have seen these elements of Huguenot argumentation as the chief French Protestant "contribution" to the development of political thought. This may or may not be true; it is not relevant to the argument here. See Méaly, *Les publicistes,* and more especially Harold Laski's Introduction to the *Vindiciae.*

57 Huizinga, *Waning of the Middle Ages,* pp. 31ff.

58 *The Correspondence of Philip Sidney and Hubert Languet,* ed. W. A. Bradley (Boston, 1912), pp. 40, 49 and *passim.* See also p. 101: "I consider that in these days men do a great deal, if they do not actually betray their friends; any additional good feeling must be set down as clear gain . . ."

to you. It is impossible to doubt that this is an universal plot . . ."[59]

But Turkish invasions and popish plots were not the real source of the Huguenots' fearfulness. They were more afraid of the logic of their own ideas and of the dangerous activity into which they were driven. "We feel," one of the pamphleteers wrote, "the effects and the bitterness . . . of war."[60] Of course, Calvin had taught his followers to expect war and the French aristocracy had long ago learned to enjoy it. But a sustained war against the king had implications from which even the *noblesse de la religion* drew back. They justified their resistance in the new language of conscience, but their conscientious activity was in fact cautious and moderate. French Calvinism never gave rise to a religious zealotry. The Huguenot nobility had a very limited sense of possibility; they fought what was really a very limited kind of war—and were glad enough, by and large, when it was over.

Huguenot discussions of warfare, as of politics, were casuistic in tone. Their purpose was to justify the activity of Protestant soldiers, but also to limit and control that activity. "Yea, if they be assailed by surprisals," de Mornay wrote in the *Vindiciae*, "they may also make use of ambuscades . . . there being no rule in lawful war that directs them . . . provided always that they carefully distinguish between advantageous strategems and perfidious treason, which is always unlawful."[61] Men might use the means which they possessed, Beza argued; he went on to deny "that the means by which the objects and affairs of this world are defended, such as both courts of law and armed force . . . differ from the means by which things spiritual can be defended."[62] It was the ultimate tribute to the conventional world. But Beza's flexibility was also a recognition of limits. In a burst of almost hysterical venom, the author of the *Réveille-Matin* suggested a different warfare: "If ever there were a time to use profitably Italian ruse and malice, it is now. And if there were ever men against whom it was necessary to employ both beak and claw . . . it is against these furious and maddened beasts."[63] A politics of beak

---

59 Quoted in Geisendorf, *Théodore de Bèze*, p. 306.
60 *Le politique, Mémoires*, III, 83.
61 *Vindiciae*, p. 96.
62 Beza, *Rights of Rulers*, p. 82.
63 *Réveille-Matin*, dialogue II, p. 112.

and claw, however, would probably have been more frightening to the Protestant nobility than to their enemies.

A cautious, essentially defensive war led by the godly magistrates and aiming at a restoration of the "ancient constitution"— this was the intention of the nobility. But the goals of God, after all, reached beyond the limitation of kings and so Huguenot warfare was always in danger of moving (at least in theory) beyond resistance and defense. The Huguenot nobles were, paradoxically, made uneasy by their own rationalizations. They could not be conscientious in the Calvinist sense without seeking continually to reorganize the political and social orders for the greater glory of God. It was their duty not merely to resist heretical kings but to transform the secular state into what de Mornay called "the temple of God."[64] The purpose of well-ordered polities," wrote Beza, "is not simply peace and quiet in this life . . . but the glory of God toward which the whole present life of man should be directed."[65] De Mornay's first covenant, as has been seen, was an effort to fix this religious obligation in legal form. It should be said, however, that he never offered a political description of the "temple of God." Neither he nor any other Huguenot produced a utopian tract, which perhaps suggests that they were not entirely serious about transforming the state. Certainly the men for whom they wrote were not serious; revolution was their greatest terror and what disturbed them most about their own insurrection was precisely its similarity to revolution.

Nevertheless, the support of the *Calvinist* church and the extension of the *reformed* religion became, in Huguenot literature, the duties of political officials. It need hardly be said that these were obligations for which historical justification and constitutional ground would be difficult indeed to discover. "I declare," wrote Beza, assuming a pontifical rather than a casuistical air, "that it is the principal duty of a most excellent and pious ruler that he should apply whatever means, authority, and power has been granted him by God to this end entirely—that God may be recognized among his subjects."[66] The argument was carried

---

64 *Vindiciae*, p. 67: "There are no estates which ought to be esteemed firm and stable, but those in which the temple of God is built, and which are indeed the temple itself . . ."
65 Beza, *Rights of Rulers*, p. 83.
66 *Ibid.*, p. 82.

further in the *Vindiciae*: magistrates, its author insists, are obliged by covenant to maintain the true religion; ever more, they must "extend the confines of the church . . . and in failing hereof, if they have the means to do it, they justly incur the penalty of high treason against the Divine Majesty."[67] De Mornay's only example of such activity was the crusades. It must have been crusading warfare, also, which the author of a Huguenot "sonnet in paradoxes" meant to describe:

> La paix est un grand mal, la guerre est un grand bien
> La paix est nostre mort, la guerre est nostre vie.
> La paix nous a espors, la guerre nous rallie.
> La paix tue les bons, la guerre est leur soustien.
> Paix est propre au meschant, la guerre au vray chretien.[68]

As if dissatisfied with a merely civil war, some Huguenot theorists strove to make it international. Referring to the French as "this poor afflicted people," they called upon some neighboring prince "to be a liberator." It is a title that conquerors have claimed ever since.[69] Themselves members of an international class as well as of an international church, Huguenot intellectuals were doubly driven to a view of war which obviously approaches that of revolutionaries in a later age. "The church of God . . . being extended over all the earth, is not enclosed in any limits. [Its] defense . . . is equally and indifferently recommended to all the princes of the earth . . . any prince who is concerned to do his duty, ought to search out, chastise and combat those of his companions who make war against God."[70]

In reality, however, an international Protestant crusade was not what the Huguenots had in mind. By and large, they sought to restrain their warfare, to make it respectable, to deny its implications. They struggled to maintain a defensive posture even when they were palpably on the offensive. They insisted that arms could only be used in defending the true religion, and in defending it, Beza added, only where it had been "lawfully . . . settled and confirmed by public authority."[71] (But that would exclude

---

67 *Vindiciae*, p. 109; see also pp. 218-220.
68 *Le politique, Mémoires*, III, 142.
69 *Réveille-Matin*, dialogue I, p. 143; see *Vindiciae*, p. 229, and discussion in Méaly, *Les publicistes*, pp. 143f.
70 *Réveille-Matin*, dialogue II, p. 29.
71 Beza, *Rights of Rulers*, p. 85.

France!) Force of arms could not, after all, be employed to advance the cause of religion, but only to defend the true church from the perpetual onslaught of its enemies. In Huguenot literature, resistance was most consistently described with the imagery of defensive war: "when the godly have been assailed by open war . . . *then* they take arms and *wait* their enemies' assaults."[72]

The extraordinary ecclesiastical organization of the Huguenots —in effect a state within a state and surely the most original of their achievements—found no reflection whatsoever in their writing, except perhaps in the incipient federalism of the *Vindiciae*. The political and military organization that paralleled the Calvinist church was assimilated in theory to that band of feudal barons, the fifteenth-century League of the Public Weal.[73] Huguenot publicists persisted in viewing resistance as a newly conscientious and highly rationalized, but essentially medieval activity. Revolution was their greatest fear, not the fulfillment of their conscientious and constitutional activity, but its nemesis. Once they had seen the radicalism of the Catholic League, the Protestant nobility was willing enough to welcome even a *politique* king—who could not possibly make the state a "temple of God." "The nobility alone has not deviated from the correct path," one of them wrote in 1593, when Huguenot political activity was at an end, "it has understood that if there were no longer a king, each village would free itself from its gentleman."[74] Here indeed was the secret terror that must explain much of Huguenot ideology. For a man who still *possessed* a village could hardly be a wholehearted member of a Calvinist congregation, nor would he dare explore the logic of Calvinist thought.

THE MARIAN EXILES

In the years after Catholic Queen Mary came to the throne, some 800 English Protestants went into exile on the continent.[75]

---

72 *Vindiciae,* p. 106 (emphasis added).

73 The "Rule of Millau," adopted in 1573 by the same synod which adopted the articles of military discipline established the Huguenot organization, but still defended it in feudal terms: it demanded that "the statutes, municipal privileges, franchises and liberties of the corporate towns and other places" be respected, but hardly suggested a justification of the discipline and independence of the Protestant congregations. See Weill, *Théories sur le pouvoir royal,* p. 130.

74 Quoted, *ibid.,* p. 258.

75 On the Marian exile, see the excellent study by C H. Garrett, *The Marian*

About a hundred of these were men not very different from the exiles of previous ages, noblemen and their followers who fled upon the victory of one or another feudal faction. Mostly younger sons of gentry families, these most recent exiles traveled little farther than the coast of France; there they stayed to intrigue, spy upon one another, and play the pirate. They had been supporters of Northumberland, adherents of the unfortunate Queen Jane, Kentish companions of the rebel Wyatt. Their Protestantism was a function of their politics, and their politics of their familial and local interests. Intrigue at home and exile abroad led them to no generalized political viewpoint; in their letters they developed an elaborate but highly personal apologetic; of theoretical justification they offered little. A few among these younger sons, tired perhaps of fruitless conspiracy, stayed only briefly in France and then went on to Italy, where they studied the new ways of the Italian courts, absorbing Renaissance manners and, more rarely, Renaissance art. One of them was Sir Thomas Hoby, translator of Castiglione's *Il Cortegiano* and a future Elizabethan official. Hoby provides an interesting and revealing family history: his father was a simple country gentleman of Hereford; his older half-brother held abbey lands, was an Edwardian ambassador and friend to Titian and Aretino; his son would be an uncompromising Puritan.[76] Sir Thomas himself, cultivated in the new manner, a traveler before and during his exile, was a middleman of ideas who carried back to England a rich intellectual booty; his immediate companions, in France and in Italy, were men of adventure, freebooters of another sort.

The majority by far of the exiles were different men, separated by a great gulf from the times and manners of the banished feudal lord. They did not stop in France, a country receptive to English conspirators but not to English Protestants, but moved on instead to the reformed cities of south Germany and Switzerland. There they established self-governing religious communities, replacing the spying and intrigue of the adventurers with political and theological controversy. Perhaps half of these exiles

---

Exiles (Cambridge, Eng., 1938); also M. M. Knappen, *Tudor Puritanism: A Chapter in the History of Idealism* (Chicago, 1930), chs. vi-viii.

76 See *The Diary of Lady Margaret Hoby 1599-1605*, ed. with an intro. by D. M. Meads (London, 1930), introduction; also *DNB s. v.* Hoby.

were clergymen of one sort or another (ex-monks and friars, deacons, priests, freelance preachers) or theological students of
Cambridge and Oxford. Only a very small and insignificant number of the clerics and clerics-to-be were of gentle birth. The students were usually poor; they apparently traveled in groups and
lived together, their expenses paid by "godly merchants." Very
few merchants, however, followed them into exile. The number of gentlemen was far larger, reaching to a third or more of
the Englishmen in the German and Swiss towns—the largest
group after the ministers and students. A few of these carried
their establishments into exile with them; the Duchess of Suffolk, for example, was accompanied by a major-domo, a "gentlewoman" and six servants, including a "Greek rider of horses,"
and a fool. But the Duchess was an exception; few of the gentry
could maintain such formidable households. Exile (and often,
poverty) forced upon them a new equality with their clerical
colleagues. Finally, a small group of artisans, mostly weavers,
also went abroad, gathering at Geneva and Aarau, but playing
hardly any role in congregational politics.[77] Their insignificant
number contrasts sharply with the large artisan majorities among
Protestant refugees from France and Flanders. Because of the
presence of the gentry and the predominance of clerical intellectuals, the Marian exile took on a new political and ideological
importance.

The major role in the politics of exile clearly belonged to the
ministers: this is, perhaps, the primary difference between the
Marian exiles and the later Huguenot movement, whose intellectuals were almost all laymen and aristocrats. The position
and power of the ministers was greatly enhanced by exile, for
while the gentry left their land behind, the clerics carried their
books along. Although the degree of participation in communal affairs was high, intellectual expression remained a
clerical monopoly. Young gentlemen in exile tested their capacity for political intervention and theological controversy, but
the ministers were the leaders of the congregations as of the student bands.[78] And these were the only exilic communities, for
the refugees, refusing allegiance to their adopted towns, were fur-

77 See the statistical breakdown of the exiles in Garrett, *Marian Exiles*, p. 41.
78 [William Whittingham?], *A Brief Discourse of the Troubles at Frankfurt*

ther cut off from their German and Swiss neighbors by an almost total ignorance of foreign languages. Exile for most of them was a distinctly narrow and at the same time intensely collective experience.

For five years, then, the Marian exiles lived "outside the limits of any effective jurisdiction." "They were free men," Miss Garrett goes on, "free to come and go as they chose, to bear arms or not as they chose, and above all free to order the internal affairs of their own little communities as they chose."[79] With time on their hands (except for a few weavers and printers the exiles engaged in no other economic activity than the collection and distribution of charitable funds), the English Protestants turned their self-government into a hectic, time-consuming business. They experimented, it may be suggested, with new kinds of political activity. The major tendency of their politics can be grasped from a comparison of the two "disciplines" (church constitutions) of the Frankfurt community. The "old discipline," imposed early by the more conservative among the exiles, was just 12 articles in length, provided for some 8 church officers, and by its very vagueness maximized the authority of the single minister. The "new discipline," adopted after much controversy and a small-scale revolution, was 73 articles in length, provided for 16 church officers (the congregation at the time of its adoption had 62 male members) and explicitly, with elaborate care, limited the authority of the two equal ministers.[80] The tendency, then, was to shatter and divide authority, to increase the number of offices, to proliferate constitutional detail. In all this, the energetic activity, polemical skillfulness and organizational experience of the ministers played a major part.

The ministers and students themselves fall into two groups, which may briefly, if not quite satisfactorily, be designated as future Anglicans and future Puritans. The latter group, a minority among the refugees, underwent, as it were, a double exile:

(first published in 1574; ed. and repr. by Edward Arber, London, 1908). This book describes and documents the most crucial of the controversies among the exiles.

79 Garrett, *Marian Exiles*, p. 18.

80 The two disciplines are printed in *A Brief Discourse*, pp. 143-149 and 150-205. On the struggle within the congregation, see Garrett, *Marian Exiles*, pp. 22ff., and Knappen, *Tudor Puritanism*, ch. iv.

first leaving their homeland, then separating themselves from the majority of their fellow emigrees. Most of the Englishmen abroad strove to maintain what one of them called the "English face" of their refugee churches, to continue using the English ritual and the last legally proclaimed Edwardian prayer book.[81] Although exiled they refused to consider themselves outlawed. The radicalism of the Puritan minority, on the other hand, was characterized by a refusal to submit religion to either civil law or national allegiance. In their fervent pursuit of Protestant logic the Puritans arrived finally at Calvin's Geneva; they had fled, defeated, from the English community at Frankfurt. In Geneva they established a congregation and a discipline that set the standards of future Puritan ambition and they produced a translation of the Bible whose marginal notes carried Puritanism into countless English households.[82] More than this, they addressed to their countrymen at home a series of extraordinary political tracts, in which they elaborated a far more radical view of political activity than the Huguenots were to attain and developed what was probably the first justification of revolution.

Their political theory stands in a close relation to their political experience. The radicalism of their views was the intellectual outcome of a long process of alienation and detachment, culminating finally in the physical fact of their double exile and setting them altogether free of English convention and law. Crossing the channel, they left behind a world of political habit and routine with which they had become increasingly impatient. Many of their fellow ministers mistook this new freedom for mere irascibility; thus Jewel, a future Anglican bishop, despaired of a similar future for Christopher Goodman: "he is a man of irritable temper, and too pertinacious in anything he has once undertaken."[83] Fuller's judgment of Anthony Gilby was similar: "a fierce, fiery and furious opposer."[84] And surely these were angry

81 *A Brief Discourse*, p. 54.

82 On the ideological tone and influence of the Geneva Bible, see Hardin Craig, Jr., "The Geneva Bible as a Political Document" *Pacific Historical Review* 7:40-49 (1938).

83 J. Jewel to Peter Martyr in 1559, *Zurich Letters*, first series, ed. and trans. H. Robinson (Cambridge, 1842-1845), p. 21.

84 Fuller's comment is quoted in a note by the editor, John Knox, *Works*, ed. D. Laing (Edinburgh, 1846-1848), IV, 546.

men, inexperienced in gentility, narrowly educated, with small talents. Yet exile provided them with an environment as narrow, intense, and restricted as were their own minds. Radically disillusioned with the Henrician reformation, feeling little loyalty even to the progressively more Protestant formulations of Edward's reign, they made foreign Geneva the prototype of a new, tightly disciplined perfection.

For these future Puritans, exile had been a great release; this was symbolized, perhaps, in the torrent of violent rhetoric which they loosed at England from their continental refuge. Freed of the court and its factions, independent of the great noblemen, the ministers discovered themselves for the first time as free intellectuals with commitments of their own and a deeply felt urge to remake the world in their own image. They proceeded to take their full rhetorical revenge upon Henry VIII and his secular reformation—in which they had played so small a part. "Thus was there no reformation but a deformation," wrote Gilby, "in the time of that tyrant and lecherous monster . . . he cared for no manner of religion. This monstrous boar . . . must needs be called the Head of the Church . . . in his best time, nothing was heard but the king's book and the king's proceedings, the king's homilies in the churches where God's Word should only have been preached."[85] Such language must have been a satisfaction to the new and nervous egotism of the ministers. In this sense, at least, they prospered in exile. There is hardly a word in their letters or tracts to suggest nostalgia or sorrow for England.

In England the ministers had been nothing more than church officers, obedient to their bishop, to the convocation and to the Supreme Head. Politically they were private persons, holding no office at all. It was a distinction which even John Knox might observe. "I am not minded," he wrote in 1552, ". . . to move contention . . . because I am but one, having in my contrair magistrates, common order, and the judgements of many learned . . ."[86] In his first admonitory letter to England, in 1554, he insisted upon

85 Anthony Gilby, *An Admonition to England and Scotland to Call Them to Repentance*, originally published together with Knox's *The Appellation* (1558) repr. in Knox, *Works*, IV, 563-64.

86 Knox, *Epistle to the Congregation of Berwick*, in Peter Lorimer, *John Knox and the Church of England* (Edinburgh, 1875), p. 156.

the same point: "Shall we go and slay all idolators?" he inquired.
"That were the office, dear brethren, of every civil magistrate
within his realm . . . the slaying of idolators appertains not to
every particular man . . ."[87]

But the men of Geneva, unlike the other exiles with their
"English face" and law, could no longer pretend even to official
status in a church—except in that tiny religious commonwealth
which was entirely their own creation. They had no legal
or public calling to address Englishmen at all. Facing England
from exile, then, they sought a new office and found it not in
men's constitutions but in divine prophecy. They thus seized
upon an aspect of Calvinist thought that never interested the
Huguenots. In the person of the Old Testament prophet, the men
of Geneva found their new public character. "I, a man sent of
God"—thus did John Knox designate himself—"to call . . . this
people . . . again to the true service of God."[88] They described
prophecy as a Calvinist *office,* in which individual inadequacy
and corruption were overcome by the discipline of duty and divinely ordained status. God's ministers, Knox wrote, "as they
be the sons of men, of nature are they liars, unstable and vain;
but His eternal Word which He putteth in their mouths and
whereof they are made ambassadors is of . . . truth, stability and
assurance."[89] He would not speak, declared Gilby, "from men's
wisdom, vain eloquence, or subtle reasons, but from the infal-
lible truth of God's Word." He was called to deliver "God's curse
and threatenings."[90] Christopher Goodman, in a more gentle
mood, called the ministers "stewards of God's holy mysteries, and
that not at the appointment of men, or for themselves, but by the
ordinance of our saviour . . ."[91] The prophet of doom, however,

87 Knox, *A Godly Letter of Warning or Admonition to the Faithful in London,
Newcastle and Berwick* (1554) in *Works,* III, 194; see also *A Comfortable Epistle to
Christ's Afflicted Church* (1554) in *Works,* III, 244.

88 Knox, *The Appellation from the Sentence Pronounced by the Bishops and
Clergy* (1558) in *Works,* IV, 474.

89 Knox, *The Copy of an Epistle* (1559) in *Works,* V, 486. See also Edwin Muir,
John Knox: Portrait of a Calvinist (London, 1939). This is the most interesting of
the modern biographies of Knox; it attempts, not always successfully, a psychological
examination of the tension between man and "instrument."

90 Gilby, *Admonition,* in Knox, *Works,* IV, 554.

91 Christopher Goodman, *How Superior Powers Ought to be Obeyed* (1558) repr.
Facsimile Text Society (New York, 1931), p. 31.

was a more frequent and more self-enhancing image than was the steward of mystery. Neither, it should be noted, required an English ordination. He was a "trumpet" of God, Knox wrote to his confidant Mrs. Bowes. "Albeit I never lack the presence and plain image of my own wretched infirmity, yet seeing sin so manifestly abound in all estates, I am compelled to thunder out the threatenings of God against obstinate rebels."[92]

In the world of religious office, conscience played a part very similar to its political role: it freed men from old loyalties, enforced a new sense of duty and required obedience to a willful God. The prophet, Knox assured his readers—though they might well have had their doubts—does not relish the doom he foretells. If it were not for his conscience, he would flee his task as Jonah did. "If I should cease, then should I do against my conscience, as also against my knowledge, and so should I be guilty of the blood of them that perisheth for lack of admonition . . ."[93] The initial duty of the prophet did not go beyond such trumpeting; prophecy was not yet a political office. But in its very freedom from legal limitation it already had political implications. The prophet was a special officer of God, an "instrument" directly employed. His status and function were not determined by a constitutional structure, were not regulated and controlled by law or custom; he was, in a sense, beyond such control. Like the exile he was outside any effective political jurisdiction. He could range freely, disregarding legal rules and social boundaries. Calvin had already announced the right of prophets to chastise kings. A courageous preacher might even exercise the right: the Puritan Edward Dering would one day speak bluntly to Elizabeth.[94] But it was a far more significant political fact when the chastisement was not delivered face-to-face in the comparative privacy of the court, but rather in the public forum, in pamphlets, and to the nation. Inevitably then, chastisement became rebellion: "let a thing be here noted," Knox wrote ominously in 1554, "the prophet of God sometimes may teach treason against kings, and yet neither he, nor such as obey the word spoken in the Lord's name by him,

92 Knox, *Works*, III, 338.
93 Knox, *Godly Letter*, *Works*, III, 108.
94 Edward Dering, *A Sermon Preached before the Queen's Majesty* (n.p., n.d.).

offends God."[95] It was a discovery whose boldness was made possible by the new identity of the minister in exile.

II

The most immediate product of these divine "instruments" was a literature of denunciation: a vigorous, at times hysterical, often ugly revelation of what Knox had meant when he promised indulgence to the prophet's "spiritual hatred." Denunciation was restrained only by a single, frequently reiterated prophetic vision:[96]

And albeit that abominable idolators triumph for a moment, yet approaches the hour when God's vengeance shall strike [and] not only their souls but their vile carcasses shall be plagued . . . Their cities shall be burnt, their land shall be laid waste, and their daughters shall be defiled, their children shall fall on the edge of the sword, mercy shall they find none because they have refused the God of all mercy.

But this was only pious hopefulness. Denunciation unrestrained was of more interest; its intellectual outcome was quite extraordinary. The thrust of a harsh, but logical and almost continuous invective was toward the radical devaluation of the conventional world, of the political, legal, and intellectual *status quo*. In the polemic and prophecy of the exiles in Geneva, there appeared a steadily growing emphasis on the utter and total corruption of this world, of "men's wisdom," of tradition and law, of the opinion of the multitude. Every earthly authority was undermined, every merely human or rational justification of authority was called into doubt. Knox and the other prophets described what was almost a Manichean universe in which an earth corrupt "in all its estates" was ruled by a stalwart Satan: ". . . albeit it is contrary to our fantasy, yet we must believe it, for the devil is called prince and god of this world, because he reigneth and is honored by idolatry in it."[97]

Since Mary was a legal queen and the prophet an illegal man, it was inevitable that he sound his trumpet against authority.

95 Knox, *Godly Letter, Works*, III, 184.

96 *Ibid.*, pp. 166-167.

97 Knox, *Faithful Admonition, Works*, III, 285. For Knox's theological difficulties with the problem of the effective power of Satan, see his tract on predestination, *An Answer to a Great Number of Blasphemous Cavillations, Works*, V, 35-36.

Himself in "league with God," he defended a narrowly conceived divine truth against the sinfulness and ignorance of mankind and its governors. In more traditional thought, it was these governors who were called "gods of this world"—a title Knox gave to the devil. The magistrates were only fallen men; neither their reason nor their human nature would be any basis for a godly politics. "The true knowledge of God," wrote Knox, "is not born with man, neither yet cometh it unto him by natural power." Reason, education, study: all these brought men far short of that true knowledge which the prophet had in "the grace of his election."[98] True knowledge was thus identified with religious illumination (or, since the prophets were not mystics, with religious dedication) and the identity was also a restriction. Knox recognized the "daily delectations" that classical literature might bring; he condemned it nevertheless—indeed, all the more enthusiastically—because he saw no value except in the "perpetual repetition" of God's word.[99] In the writings of Knox, Goodman, and Whittingham, the wealth of classical reference so common in the sixteenth century, so common even in the work of other Calvinists, virtually disappeared. Writing his tract against women, Knox dragged it all in again, presumably using the current handbooks, but classical learning was never a key element in his argument. Nor would his politics be based on such conventional knowledge as might also be available to magistrates and lords. His appeal was always to a special truth; tutored by the Holy Ghost, he boasted an understanding of what was "already appointed in the counsel of the eternal."[100]

Custom provided no surer evidence of this counsel than did reason. Knox recited the usual arguments by which men sought to justify their actions: "They are laudable, they are honest and decent, they have good significations, they pleased our fathers and the most part of the world used the same"—and he condemned them all. "And thus into idolatry the corrupt children follow the footsteps of their forefathers."[101] Whittingham's conclusion was

---

98 Knox, *Godly Letter, Works*, III, 204; *An Answer, Works*, V, 28.

99 Knox, *A Letter of Wholesome Counsel* (1556), *Works*, IV, 135.

100 "God shall always raise up some to whom the verity shall be revealed, and unto such ye shall give place . . . ," *First Blast of the Trumpet Against the Monstrous Regiment of Women, Works*, IV, 379.

101 Knox, *Godly Letter, Works*, III, 180.

similar: "so that custom and company . . . draw us to perdi-
tion . . ."[102] The example of the father was of no more value than
was that of the queen—would-be mother of her subjects. Histori-
city was not the equivalent of sanctity—as in some Huguenot writing—it was rather a cause for suspicion; what did it indicate but
prolonged acquiescence by corrupt worldlings? Nor might the
prophet's purposes be served by law, and still less by popular
election. Knox's sweep was grand: ". . . neither the consent of the
people, process of time, nor multitude of men," he wrote to Queen
Elizabeth in 1559, "can establish a law which God shall approve
. . . It appertaineth to you, therefore, to ground the justness of
your authority, not upon that law which from year to year doth
change but upon the eternal providence of [God] . . ."[103]

Given the range of their denunciation, it was hardly necessary,
or possible, for the prophets to elaborate a political theory. The
traditional subject matter of such a theory was of little interest
to them; they had virtually no sense of the history, secular purposes, or constitutional form of the state. Their concern was extraordinarily singular: no one might be chosen king or governor,
Christopher Goodman wrote, "what title or right soever he
seems to have thereunto by civil policy, except he be a promoter
and setter-forth of God's glory."[104] Whatever his title, here was the
magistrate's function, and beyond this the prophets were unwilling to go. It is obvious that only a Christian could fulfill this
function; only a Christian, therefore, could legitimately be king.
In the interests of political order and "civil policy," Calvin had
accepted the possibility of a heathen ruler although he yearned
for someone better. Goodman rejected this possibility not because
he was uninterested in order, but because he no longer recognized
even the possibility of heathen (or heretical) civility. The only alternative to the world of wickedness was the Christian commonwealth.

It is useful to compare Goodman's statement with a description
of royal duty from the pen of another minister. The concern
of John Ponet, an Edwardian bishop who lived in Strasbourg with
the future Anglicans, was obviously more profane than holy: "The

102 See Whittingham's Introduction to Goodman, *Superior Powers*, sig. A$_2$.
103 Knox, *Works*, IV, 49.
104 Goodman, *Superior Powers*, p. 51.

prince's watch," he wrote, "ought to defend the poor man's house, his labor the subject's ease, his diligence the subject's pleasure, his trouble the subject's quietness." Home, ease, pleasure, and quietness: these were hardly the paramount Calvinist virtues. Ponet suggested an identification of tyranny with theft; good government he saw as a protection for property.[105] The prophets at Geneva, on the other hand, singlemindedly described the tyrant as an idolator; they were as little interested in the new defense of private property as in the older defense of common land. Their attack upon Satan's world left them with virtually no social connections or sympathies, and with but one political passion: to drive fallen man "up the Lord's hill." God's prophet fastened his narrowly religious purpose upon the secular and political world. He proposed to call all rights of succession, all established law and custom, all dynastic, national, or even class loyalties—valueless. The effect of prophetic denunciation was thus to deepen the practical alienation of the exiles and to give it an intellectual form. It was now firmly rooted in the Calvinist doctrine of the Fall. The prophet, a divine "instrument," stood apart; he viewed the world, as Knox wrote, in the "spirit of righteous judgment."

Denunciation made judgment a possibility; it had broken the link between divine command and earthly event. Although the theology of the Genevans remained strictly predestinarian, their rhetoric actually shifted the ground of argument. As is often the case with prophets, their polemical tongues and pens were bolder and more inventive than their theological minds. The prophet announced the effective and independent power of the devil. He could not, of course, fit such a power into his conception of God's omnipotence, but whatever the shifts to which he was driven, it was dramatically clear that with the devil in the field God's will was no longer revealed by what happened on earth.[106]

105 John Ponet, *A Short Treatise of Political Power* (1556), facsimile repr. in W. S. Hudson, *John Ponet, Advocate of Limited Monarchy* (Chicago, 1942), pp. 21ff., 95. On Ponet, see Hudson's introduction and Christopher Morris, *Political Thought in England: Tyndale to Hooker* (Oxford, 1953), pp. 152-155. Ponet's background was humanist and he apparently never adopted Calvin's theological doctrines. It is of little value, then, to suggest as Morris does that Knox was less "profound" than Ponet; in fact the basic assumptions of the two men were quite different, although perhaps equally profound.

106 See Goodman's discussion, *Superior Powers*, pp. 110, 133ff. "And in disobeying and resisting [tyrants and idolators] we do not resist God's ordinance, but Satan's."

Instead earth acknowledged another sovereign and the divine law existed in sharp and radical contrast to what were called the abominations of the world. Knox returned to the simplest sort of theodicy—as if Job had never been. To say that iniquitous kings were ordained by God, he wrote, would be to make God the author of iniquity.[107] Such a conclusion was impossible. Evil men might still be described as God's instruments, the whips and scorpions of divine punishment, but they were also God's enemies—a fact for which Knox found a novel corollary: "For all those that would draw us from God (be they kings or queens), being of the devil's nature, are enemies unto God, and therefore will God that we declare ourselves enemies unto them."[108]

III

The reality of Satan's power gave a new meaning to the usual Calvinist description of the warfare of saints and worldlings: it made the war a very immediate and practical matter. Indeed, the enlistment of soldiers became a prophetic task. "Our captain Christ Jesus and Satan his adversary are now at plain defiance. Their banners be displayed and the trumpets blow upon either party, for assembling of their armies. Our master calleth upon his own, and that with vehemence, that they depart from Babylon . . ."[109] Here was no merely defensive struggle. The prophet's denunciation of the world had made defense irrelevant; what was there left that might legitimately be protected? It had set the stage, instead, for transformation, for an all-out attack upon Satan, for the imposition of a new order upon the corrupted world.

Who would be the warriors in this struggle between Christ and Satan? In their "Letters of Admonition" during the early years of exile, the prophets were extremely cautious about recommend-

---

This should be contrasted with the older Protestant view of Tyndale: "Let us receive all things of God whether it be good or bad . . . and submit ourselves unto his nurture and chastising . . ." *Works of the English Reformers: Tyndale and Frith*, ed. Thomas Russel (London, 1851), I, 230-31.

107 Knox, *The Appellation, Works*, IV, 496.

108 Knox, *Godly Letter, Works*, III, 193. These lines appear in the mss. but not in the published version of the *Letter*. See also p. 198: "We are persuaded that all which our adversaries do is diabolical."

109 Knox, "Letter to Mrs. Anna Loch" (1559), *Works*, IV, 11; see also *Copy of an Epistle, Works*, V, 478.

ing any form of political activity; they preached a purely divine
destruction. In the last of his letters, Knox had prayed that God
raise up a Jehu "to execute his just judgement against idolators."[110] But he had gone no further; he had not called upon any
of the faithful to enact Jehu's part. He only asked that they do
what he himself had done: "avoid and flee, as well in body as in
spirit, all fellowship and society with idolators . . ."[111] But if exile
was the end of one fellowship, it was also the beginning of another. It set men free, as has been seen, from convention and law,
from the political passivity taught by English tradition. It brought
them together to consult and plan for war. And in their later
tracts, after years of discussion and argument in German and
Swiss towns, the prophets urged that godly men act to overthrow
the English idolator—and that they act immediately, forcefully.

In conventional Protestant fashion, Knox and Goodman turned
first to the magistrate, but their manner with magistrates was
significantly abrupt. They had no very elaborate view of constitutions or of legal order, and surely no reverence for either. They
viewed magistracy less as a constitutional office, formed by law and
custom, than as a single unmediated divine command: "that you
. . . with single eye do study to promote the glory of God." God
alone had made some men magistrates whom nature had not made
unlike their subjects: "for in conception, birth, life and death,
you differ nothing from the common sort of men."[112] Magistrates
and noblemen had no rights beyond the performance of their
godly duty and no rights at all short of that. With far greater forcefulness and freedom, Knox expressed a view not very different
from that of the later Huguenots: "Your subjects, yea your
brethren are oppressed," he wrote to the Scottish nobility in 1557,
"their bodies and souls held in bondage, and God speaketh to
your consciences (unless you be dead with the blind world), that
you ought to hazard your own lives (be it against kings or emperors) for their deliverance; for only for that cause are you called

---

110 Knox, *Faithful Admonition, Works*, III, 329.
111 Knox, *Godly Letter, Works*, III, 166 and 194.
112 Knox, *The Appellation, Works*, IV, 480, 481. Knox obviously saw no need for
such elaborate legal constructs as the two covenants of the *Vindiciae contra
Tyrannos* nor was he interested in historical and constitutional speculation like
Hotman's *Franco-Gallia*.

princes of the people . . . not by reason of your birth and progeny
. . . but by reason of your office . . ."[113]

In radical contrast with the Huguenots, however, Knox's view
of office was not constitutional. His appeal to the magistrate was
only the beginning of his prophetic activity. As his denunciation
had reached beyond the limited political audience of his day, so
his search for godly "instruments" moved outside the circle of officialdom and nobility; it was, so to speak, socially outward and
downward. In the course of this search, the prophet was driven
to an explicit denial of two traditional political ideas: that the
magistrate was the only public person and that private men were
politically irresponsible. "If they rule well, we shall fare the better;
if they be ungodly, they have the more to answer for their ungodli-
ness. What have we to do with their matters?"—so Christopher
Goodman represented the conventional speech of a private man.
And he commented: "Thus do all sorts of men . . . slip their heads
out of the collar."[114] Goodman would have fastened that collar
firmly around their necks. The magistrate, Knox also insisted, assumed no singular responsibility; obedience to kings did not
exonerate guilty subjects. Instead, the equality of all men before
God enforced an equal political responsibility, despite the social
hierarchy. "If you think you are innocent," Knox wrote in his
Letter to the Commonality, "because you are not the chief authors
of such iniquity, you are utterly deceived." God would damn also
the "consenters to iniquity."[115]

Let all men, therefore, seek political understanding. They are
"charged by God's word to know what [magistrates] command
. . . and not to do it except it be lawful . . ." The magistrate would
have no secrets; the prophets urged the social possession of knowledge in terms which went far beyond the medieval requirement
that law be publicly proclaimed. Being a man of enthusiasm,
Goodman was willing to suggest that the prophet would have no
secrets either: "for these are the days whereof the prophet Joel

---

113 Knox, Letter to the Scottish Nobles (1557), Works, I, 274.

114 Goodman, Superior Powers, p. 146. The traditional view is stated by
Shakespeare in Henry V, IV, 1: ". . . for we know enough if we know we are the
king's soldiers. If his cause be wrong, our obedience to the king wipes the crime
of it out of us."

115 Knox, A Letter Addressed to the Commonality of Scotland (1558), Works, IV,
535.

spoke, when all should be prophets and see visions . . . [when] all things [should be] as plain and evident to all sorts of men and women . . . as before . . . they were to the prophets themselves."[116]

Whether knowledge was, in fact, universal or particular, it was to culminate in action. He had only scorn, Goodman wrote, for those who preferred "to place themselves in corners, where they may be quiet and at ease," who thought it sufficient "if they have a little exercise in their houses in reading a chapter or two of the Scriptures." You cannot be a "manful soldier of Christ," he insisted, "except you resort where his banner is displayed and his standard set up . . ."[117] In this way would the army gather, exhorted by the prophets; and if the magistrate failed in his duty, it would enter the fray. "There is no remedy," wrote the unsympathetic Hooker, "all must come by devolution at the length . . . unto the godly among the people."[118] Hooker was accurate enough, for Knox and Goodman were no longer describing a circumspect and lawful resistance; they were describing revolution, and that with considerable prescience.

Failing in their duty, rulers and noblemen would "be accounted no more for kings or lawful magistrates, but as private men: and to be examined, accused, condemned and punished by the law of God . . ."[119] Goodman thus described what would become the key symbolic moment of revolution: the judicial murder of the king. The king would not be judged by his own laws, but by an entirely different law; nor would he recognize his judges for they would be new men who became public at the same time as the king was "accounted" private. And at their first appearance, these new men justified their politics by pointing not to their human rights but to their divine duties. Like the prophet, the revolutionary viewed himself as an instrument of God; in Calvinist ideology, then, he found an identity fortifying enough to permit him to act in a world temporarily devoid of conventional authority and routine procedures.

[Doubtless it is] a great discouraging to the people [wrote Goodman]

116 Goodman, *Superior Powers*, pp. 167, 169.
117 *Ibid.*, p. 226f.
118 Richard Hooker, *Ecclesiastical Polity, Book VIII*, ed. R. A. Houk (New York, 1931), p. 249.
119 Goodman, *Superior Powers*, p. 139. He advocated the execution (but not the assassination) of Mary Tudor, p. 99.

when they are not stirred up to godliness by the good example of all
sorts of superiors [and] magistrates . . . Nevertheless all this can be
no excuse . . . And though you had no man of power upon your
part, yet it is a sufficient assurance to you to have the warrant of God's
Word . . . who willeth not only the magistrates and officers to root
out evil from amongst them . . . but the whole multitude are there-
with charged also to whom a portion of the sword of justice is committed.[120]

For a time, Knox offered the people only a limited revolutionary
program. They were to work for reformation "according to the
vocation of every man." But if the reformer thus paid tribute to
the social hierarchy, he went on to overthrow it. "You, although
you be but subjects, may lawfully require of your superiors . . .
that they provide you true preachers . . . And if your superiors be
negligent . . . most justly may you provide true preachers for yourselves." Subjects might also withhold from their superiors "the
fruits and profits which [they] most unjustly receive of you . . ."[121]
Goodman forsook even such lingering caution and gave warning of
more violent things to come; he wrote a prophecy of Cromwell:
"And though it appear at first sight a great disorder, that the people should take unto them the punishment of transgression, yet
when the magistrates and other officers cease to do their duty,
they are as it were without officers . . . and then God giveth the
sword into the people's hand and he himself is become immediately their head . . ."[122] And even Knox's social conservatism
faded before his prophetic fury. It was the duty of the nobility and
the people, he wrote, "not only to have againstanded Mary that
Jesabel . . . but also to punish her to the death . . ."[123] Tyrannicide
was no longer the special mission of an inspired man; it had become the ordinary vocation of any man who would assume it.

But not of every man—only of a man who understood the ordinary vocation of a saint. With reason enough, for example, the
English Mary might have been murdered by someone greedy for
church lands (and not for the "Lord's hill"), or she might have
been assassinated as a bastard queen or a Spanish wife. Knox, who

120 *Ibid.,* pp. 179-180.
121 Knox, *Letter to the Commonality, Works,* IV, 534.
122 Goodman, *Superior Powers,* p. 185.
123 Knox, *The Appellation, Works,* IV, 507.

would doubtlessly have applauded the event, insisted nevertheless that every political act have a religious intention, that murder, whatever its manner, be a conscientious act. And despite Goodman's enthusiastic vision of a universe of prophets, Calvinist activity could hardly be universal. For it would then be dependent upon the affections and understandings of fallen men. Knox quoted with scorn the argument of moderate and gradualist reformers: "When the people be better instructed, then may we proceed further, etc." It was the doctrine, he wrote, of men "who are neither hot nor cold."[124] Revolution could not wait upon majorities; Knox described instead the political privileges of a small minority, a revolutionary elect "to whom God granteth knowledge."[125] Political right "devolved" only to the godly among the people: the prophet enlisted the saints.

For such men law and casuistry would have little application. They would not be bound by elaborate rules or careful, painstaking distinctions. The application of conscience to its cases was not for them a matter of endless debate and discussion as it was for Huguenot intellectuals; it was a matter of practical activity. The self-confident saint, intimately acquainted with God's Word, legitimized his every act by his divine intention. Prophet and saint thus shared a special political character, summed up most dramatically by Knox. "God's word draweth his elect after it," he wrote in a discussion of the slaughter of the golden-calf worshippers in Exodus 32, "against worldly appearance, against natural affections and against civil statutes and constitutions."[126] The privileges of the saint thus extended as far as his power might reach. Later in his life, when Knox was asked whether godly subjects might overthrow an ungodly prince, he answered briefly, raising no legal or moral problems: *if they are able.*[127]

[124] Knox, *Copy of an Epistle, Works,* V, 515-16.
[125] Knox, *Godly Letter, Works,* III, 199.
[126] Knox, *Faithful Admonition, Works,* III, 311-312. Exodus 32 was cited frequently during the English Revolution by preachers calling for a "purge" like the one which Moses carried out at the very foot of Sinai. It does not seem ever to have been cited by the leading Huguenot writers, though Calvin discusses the passage in a manner similar to Knox's; see *Sermons on the Fifth Book of Moses* (London, 1583), p. 1203.
[127] See Knox, *History of the Reformation of Religion in Scotland,* ed. Cuthbert Lennox (Edinburgh, 1905), p. 323.

IV

The saint was a new political man, different alike from the feudal officer and the "providential avenger." His duty did not stem from constitutional office nor from divine inspiration; his activity was neither resistance nor assassination. Resistance was a form of collective social defense by prescribed officials of recognized public and legal character. Assassination was the act of a private person, infused with grace, who sacrificed himself in a sudden, unpredictable burst of enthusiasm. The saint, however, was a revolutionary: a private man in the old order and according to the old conventions, who laid claim to public status upon the basis of a new law. He would not resist the king, but overthrow him; he would not assassinate the king, but put him on trial. His activity was systematic and organized; in some fashion he was already obedient to the discipline of the new order he envisioned.

In the old political order, the saint was a stranger. It was appropriate, then, that he be the creation of an intellectual in exile. The cleric, disillusioned with the old world, alienated from a conventional and routine obedience, turned upon England with his "spiritual hatred"—a hatred deepened and given intellectual form by Calvinist theology. Physically exiled, he had moved outside the world of political limitation and into the new world of self-control. His new freedom made radical aspiration and exploration possible; it also made fanaticism possible—and even necessary. An old-fashioned activity like piracy required only an adventurer, but revolution needed, perhaps, men made of "sterner stuff." By calling himself elect, the saint specified his exclusive allegiance to God's Word and (presumably) to the community of the future, when men would live in fellowship on the "Lord's hill." But for the present it was warfare and not fellowship, military order and ideological discipline, and not Christian love that occupied his mind. In order to produce a revolutionary, the prophet had set God against the devil's world and then the saints against the worldlings. Revolution in its origins was only a particular form of this eternal warfare, the continuation, it might be said, of religious activity by military means.

The rhetoric of opposition and struggle thus played an important part in the development of the idea of revolution. As rhetoric it was not, of course, new with the Calvinists. Warfare was much more ancient than political theory and its imagery had often been appropriated by the theorists. Since the time of the Greeks, for example, the warfare of body and soul had been a continually interesting theme and one which often came to suggest the actual struggles of groups of men. Medieval papalists vigorously insisted that the secular body politic must be dominated by its Roman soul, to which every member owed unquestioning obedience.[128] But there is a significant difference between the opposition of body and soul and that of saints and worldlings: for the latter terms are stripped of all organic connotation; they directly describe individual men; they are inclusive in a different way, suggesting anything from a mob to a party or an army, but never so closely articulated an entity as a body. Saints and worldlings would not be so limited in their activity as were the functionally ordered members of a body politic. Their warfare, then, while probably no more profound in its meaning, was likely to be far more extensive in its effects. And the warriors were likely to be more inventive, dangerous in new ways, continually moving beyond the limits of their traditional status or their prescribed social function.

Resistance in the Middle Ages had usually been viewed as a defensive struggle against a tyrant guilty of acts of aggression upon the political order. Defense was a temporarily necessary form of legal violence, ending as soon as order was restored.[129] But the permanent warfare of saints and worldlings set legality and order aside. The devil might be expected to use every imaginable form of wiliness and surreption, the saints would continually test his power and rise up whenever they found him weak. They would obey him, as Goodman wrote, only "in captivity and thraldom," never willingly, passively or in a routine fashion. They would dis-

128 See Walter Ullmann, *The Political Theories of the Medieval Canonists* (London, 1949) , pp. 81-83.

129 *Cf.* St. Thomas Aquinas, *Summa Theologica,* 1a 2ae, Q. 42. The same view was reasserted in early modern times by Suarez who treated resistance under the general heading of war and called it "just" whenever the king was a tyrant and therefore an "aggressor." Francisco Suarez, *Selections from Three Works* (Oxford, 1944), vol. II: *An English Version of the Texts,* trans. G. L. Williams, A. Brown, and J. Waldron, pp. 854-855 (Disputation XIII, in *A Work on the Three Theological Virtues*).

obey and rebel whenever it was possible, for it was their "bounden duty" to "maintain the cause of God with all [their] might."[130] In the history of political thought, this Calvinist idea of permanent warfare lies between the theory of resistance and that of revolution, and mediates the transition from one to the other. As Calvinism produced a new kind of army, so it discovered in warfare a new politics. The saints were soldiers, subject to an almost military discipline; the minister was "captain of the Lord's host"; together they fought in enemy territory where they were strangers, without earthly allegiance or sympathy.

v

Calvinist politics in France was aristocratic in character, tending however uncertainly toward a reorganization of the governmental functions of the upper classes. It was marked by the idea of the saint-in-office. Huguenot intellectuals like de Mornay sought anxiously to transform the old feudal lord into a conscientious magistrate possessed by a totally impersonal zeal for his official duties. Their theory of resistance depended finally upon the existence and activity of such magistrates. Among the Marian exiles, deprived of all official functions, another modern figure was being shaped: the saint-out-of-office, the oppositional man, the political radical. These two figures had something in common—above all, their participation in nonfeudal forms of organization grounded upon public service and ideological commitment. In and out of office, the saint was a man subject to discipline, ready to move beyond the range of familial connection, capable of making lasting alliances with men to whom he was not related, with whom he shared only opinions.

In France and among the exiles, these two men appeared in isolation. The French in the sixteenth century did not produce a band of radical intellectuals; in the long run, for all the tension between them, the ministers deferred to the nobility. On the other hand, the exiled English gentlemen in Geneva never had a chance to exercise their piety in office; they deferred instead to the angry ministers. But in England, in the years before the revolution, pious gentlemen and radical intellectuals coexisted. Over a con-

130 Goodman, *Superior Powers*, pp. 135-136.

siderable period of time, saints in and out of office worked together
and influenced one another. Their coexistence and cooperation
gave rise to new amalgams, new political types that were to play
their parts in the revolutionary period. In a sense, modern politics begins in England with the return of the Genevan exiles.

The beginning was not easy, least of all for the returning ministers themselves. Exile was a hothouse: they had moved far in
advance of their fellow countrymen; their ideas found little immediate sympathy. Indeed, John Knox was for the rest of his
life *persona non grata* in England and Christopher Goodman
fearfully delayed his return for many years. For some decades after 1559, the other Puritan ministers were isolated and alienated
even at home. Somewhat nervously, they pursued their godly
warfare, gradually transmuting it into the forms of oppositional
politics, searching continuously for lay allies. But it was not until
the 1640's that a man like John Milton, the product, in part, of
this Puritan search, could look back and acknowledge Knox,
Gilby, Goodman, and Whittingham as "the true Protestant divines of England, our fathers in the faith we hold."[131]

[131] Milton, *Works,* ed. F. A. Patterson, et al. (New York, 1932), V, 52.

CHAPTER FOUR · THE PURITAN
CLERGY: MODERN POLITICS
AND RADICAL INTELLECTUALS

"Had it not been much better," asked Thomas Hobbes in 1668, "that these seditious ministers, which were not perhaps one thousand, had been all killed before they had preached? It had been, I confess, a great massacre, but the killing of 100,000 [in the civil wars] is a greater one."[1] Half seriously, Hobbes proposed what may be called the classical solution to the problem of agitation. More than half seriously, he suggested that clerical agitation had been the mainspring of the English Revolution. The obvious reply—that the success of an agitator is entirely dependent upon the existence of men open to his ideas—may for the moment be laid aside. Hobbes' suggestion has in it a considerable truth. The English Revolution can only be explained in terms of the impact of the Puritan ministers and their ideology upon the gentry and the new merchant and professional classes. Had that impact, for whatever reason, never been made, social and economic forces might have produced many different forms of conflict and even of civil war in England; they would not have produced a revolution.

The Puritan clergy played a part quite different from that of the Huguenot ministers: its influence upon the political classes of the country was far more profound, its ideology far more radical. This was because the clergy itself formed for a time an independent and cohesive social force; its members, freed from feudal connections, anticipated in their own lives the politics of the revolution. In France, the Calvinist ministers had no such independence and no comparable influence; they were bound, for reasons of patronage and protection, to a nobility whose mind they never dominated. The greatest of the Huguenots were themselves aris-

---

[1] Thomas Hobbes, *Behemoth*, in *English Works*, ed. W. Molesworth (London, 1839-1845), VI, 282.

tocrats and though they occasionally served as ministers and more often as lay elders of the reformed church, their closest social connections and deepest political sympathies were with the old feudal families—and their behavior most often was after the old feudal fashion. The lower levels of the clergy never assumed great importance in the French wars of religion, except briefly, and then only in the Catholic League. Although ex-priests and monks, mendicants and schoolteachers were among the earliest converts to Protestantism, the League was the only political movement in which "the revolt of the clerical third estate" found real expression.[2] Hence the democratic radicalism of the Catholic preachers, which was never equaled among the Huguenots and which served to reinforce the hold of Catholicism in the major cities and among the urban poor. French Protestantism remained an aristocratic movement, shaped only up to a point by the religious impulse that came from Geneva and never under the control of its clerical adherents. Partly for this reason, the French civil wars were never transformed into a revolutionary struggle.

Puritanism, on the other hand, was from its beginning a clerical and evangelical movement. From the days of the Marian exile, the minister was its central figure. He had both patrons and allies among the gentry and even among the great noblemen, but Puritan ideology was entirely a clerical creation. Until the 1630's no important lay authors can be counted among the English Calvinists.[3] There was no English equivalent of de Mornay, no equivalent even of such secular Huguenot intellectuals and men of action as La Noue and de Rohan. In part, this was because of the political weakness of the English nobility after the fifteenth-century wars and the long series of petty revolts and conspiracies against Tudor government. By the 1580's the politically significant aristocracy was already a court aristocracy, caught up in the cult of Gloriana—whatever misgivings some of its members must have

2 Charles Labitte, *De la democratie chez les predicateurs de la ligue* (Paris, 1841), p. xxv.
3 Martin Marprelate is probably an exception to this general rule; J. E. Neale has identified him as Job Throckmorton, a country gentleman. See Neale, *Elizabeth I and Her Parliaments: 1584-1601* (London, 1957), p. 220. (Note that the term "Puritan" is used in this and the following chapters to refer only to those English ministers and laymen who adopted some recognizable form of Calvinist ideology; the range of opinion extends from "Scottish" Presbyterians to some of the more independent of the Independents, but not beyond.)

had. Courtiers like Leicester sought Puritan support and claimed to represent a militant Protestantism, but they were in no position to act consistently against the wishes of the Queen. The ministers were forced to act on their own.

An energetic lay Calvinism was also precluded by the sheer ambiguity of Elizabethan Anglicanism: the style of the new establishment was definitely Protestant, but it was also tolerant and politic, with little in it of Genevan or Jesuit zeal. The settlement of 1559 made religious persecution and religious warfare, suffering and enthusiasm, equally unlikely. The vision of a Protestant nation presided over by an elite of godly aristocrats waging chivalric warfare for God's glory, born in the mind of a man like Sir Philip Sidney, had no chance of realization in Elizabeth's England. Some of the privateers, perhaps, gave it a kind of outlaw expression. Other men made what compromises they could. But had there been a Catholic prince, there might after all have been a band of Protestant nobles; Leicester or Hastings or the brooding Earl of Essex—though none of these possessed a suitable territorial base or private army—might have played the Bourbon.[4] Sidney or Francis Walsingham might after all have been an English de Mornay. Calvinism might have served as the organizing center of aristocratic ideas, the church become one of the key forms of aristocratic association, and the ministry a noble career.

As it was, the tightly-knit band of clergymen, almost all of them commoners, who returned to England in 1559, never felt entirely at home there. Even an Anglican bishop, who had made his peace with Elizabeth's system, still remembered the exile in terms which suggest a kind of spiritual alienation from England: "Oh Zurich, Zurich, I think more of Zurich in England than ever I thought of England while I was in Zurich."[5] The Puritan ministers remained, despite considerable support from titled families and encouragement from members of the Privy Council, an isolated group. The tone of their literature and the modes of their association, at

4 Essex, perhaps, had something like this in mind. A small number of Puritan ministers gathered in his London house in the exciting days of late 1600 and early 1601; they are reported to have preached the Huguenot doctrine of the rights of the lesser magistrates. See G. B. Harrison, *The Life and Death of Robert Devereux, Earl of Essex* (New York, 1937), pp. 278-279.

5 J. Jewel to Peter Martyr in 1559, *Zurich Letters*, second series, ed. and trans. H. Robinson (Cambridge, 1842-1845), p. 23.

least until the 1590's, were those of a radical intelligentsia, narrowly constituted, totally committed, doctrinaire, with what must have seemed the most tenuous of connections to Renaissance England.

II

The early Puritan ministers had lived in the centers of Protestant intellectual life, in Germany and Switzerland, outside the range of traditional connection and authority. They had settled for a time in cities ruled by ministers like themselves and by godly, sober laymen whose authority was founded neither on blood nor on the mysteries of crown and order. The exiled ministers had themselves drafted the constitutions of their tiny independent churches. In these temporary communities of uprooted teachers, students, and young gentlemen, power depended largely upon intellectual talent, upon the ability to manipulate Scripture, to interpret the Word. The ministers in Geneva had preached and written with the ideological recklessness of exiles uncertain whether or not they will ever go home; exile had intensified their commitment to the new faith.[6]

They returned to an England where the decadence of the old church had resulted only in state action and state control—"the king's book and the king's proceedings"—but in no socially based reform movement in which they might participate. They could not expect to be patronized in any systematic fashion by an organized aristocratic opposition; nor were there as yet substantial groups of men to whom they might relate in the new ways they had learned in their exile.[7] The essentially equalitarian relation of an elected minister and his godly congregants, for example, was not immediately available to them. Indeed, the traditional

[6] The significance of time spent abroad—especially in Germany, Switzerland, and Holland—is noted by Knappen: "Protestants with any foreign experience almost always attached themselves to the Puritan party." This was true of diplomats as well as of exiles, but obviously there would be special factors at work among the exiles. See M. M. Knappen, *Tudor Puritanism: A Chapter in the History of Idealism* (Chicago, 1939), p. 232.

[7] The extent of Puritan isolation in Elizabethan England has been a matter of dispute. A radical statement of the argument that Puritans found little lay support is to be found in R. G. Usher's *The Reconstruction of the English Church* (New York, 1910), I, 244ff., especially pp. 280-281. Cf. Knappen, *Tudor Puritanism*, pp. 333ff. and *Letters of Thomas Wood, Puritan, 1566-1577*, ed. Patrick Collinson, Bulletin of the Institute of Historical Research, Special Supplement no. 5 (London, 1960), Introduction.

church with its hierarchical system of authority had never yet been decisively challenged. Before leaving Geneva, the more radical ministers had drawn up a letter urging just such a challenge: ". . . that we may altogether teach and practice that true knowledge of God's Word which we have learned in this our banishment . . . wherein no doubt we shall find many adversaries and stays . . ."[8] They encountered instead the amorphousness of Anglicanism. The Elizabethan establishment was incapable of winning their allegiance, as it was incapable of educating and disciplining the English people in the reformed manner. Yet it provided no such focus for opposition as had Mary's Catholicism. And then its indecisive and politic governor, Elizabeth herself, emerged in the 1580's as the Protestant champion. The Spanish war and the accompanying patriotic fervor forced the Puritan ministers to play a kind of double game, insisting honestly enough upon their political loyalty and yet simultaneously experimenting with the new, subversive politics of radicalism and reform.

The thrust of Puritan doctrine, for all the evasiveness of the ministers, was clear enough: it pointed toward the overthrow of the traditional order. The returning ministers attacked first the "dregs of popery" still to be found in the established church—the ceremonies, ritual ornaments, and priestly gowns—for these, they thought, were concessions to the traditional mentality, ambiguous reminders of the old mysteries. The Anglican bishop John Aylmer thought no differently when he described the surplice as "the Queen's livery," but he was no opponent of such ecclesiastical feudalism.[9] Knox's friend Anthony Gilby, on the other hand, condemned the surplice as "the defiled robe of Antichrist" because it confused "weak consciences" and prevented a final break with "idolatry."[10] "What reason is there," another of the Puritan writers demanded, "that the fashion and form of ministers' attire should be different from other men's?"[11] In fact,

8 William Whittingham, *A Brief Discourse of the Troubles Begun at Frankfurt in the Year 1554,* ed. John Arber (London, 1908), p. clxxxvii.

9 Quoted in William Pierce, *An Historical Introduction to the Marprelate Tracts* (London, 1908), p. 78. The best source of information on the Vestiarian Controversy of the 1560's is John Strype, *The Life and Acts of Matthew Parker* (Oxford, 1821).

10 Anthony Gilby, *To My Loving Brethren that is Troubled About the Popish Apparel, Two Short and Comfortable Epistles* (n.p., 1588).

11 Quoted in A. Tindal Hart, *The Country Clergy in Elizabethan and Stuart Times, 1558-1660* (London, 1958), p. 13.

of course, these costumes and ceremonies symbolized Elizabeth's determination to maintain the old habits of reverence and deference, the old distinctions of ranks and orders. This was also the reason for the absence of any very great anxiety at court or in the Privy Council about the ignorance and "superstition" of the rural clergy, another survival of the old order.[12] The Puritans, however, mercilessly attacked the country priests, who almost never preached, whose authority had once rested on their performance of the miracle of the mass and perhaps rested still on its memory, and who now proved themselves "time-servers" by adopting the Anglican prayer book.[13] These men reflected the backwardness of many rural areas, especially in the North and West, but they often served their parishioners well enough. Their successors, Anglican or Puritan, were not always welcomed. "True reformation" would have required coercion, which the Puritan intellectuals were quick to advocate and the Queen reluctant to adopt.

Above all, the Puritans demanded the replacement of the sacramental priesthood by a preaching ministry, and that necessarily meant a ministry of educated men. The preacher was the hero of sixteenth-century Puritanism, endlessly exalted in its polemical tracts: ". . . the Lord hath tied the food of understanding and knowledge," wrote the Welsh evangelist John Penry, "unto the mouths of those pastors who . . . in regard of gifts are according unto his own heart." The minister was the oracle of the church, taught Walter Travers, and this no man could be "without a great and excellent knowledge of the Word of God. . ."[14] The crucial distinction among men was between those who possessed this knowledge and those who did not. Dudley Fenner, one of

[12] Knappen, *Tudor Puritanism*, p. 253, who is possibly unfair to the Queen. Many of the bishops, themselves Calvinists and but recently exiles, strove to improve the position of the clergy. Elizabeth's position is best revealed in her rebuke to Grindal, *ibid.*, pp. 256-257.
[13] See especially the two *Admonitions to Parliament*, 1572, repr. in *Puritan Manifestoes: A Study of the Origin of the Puritan Revolt*, ed. W. H. Frere and C. E. Douglas (London, 1954). Also, *The Seconde Part of a Register*, ed. A. Peel (Cambridge, 1915), I, 189.
[14] John Penry, *An Exhortation unto the Governors and People of Her Majesty's Country of Wales* . . . (n.p., 1588), p. 9; Walter Travers, *A Full and Plain Declaration of Ecclesiastical Discipline Out of the Word of God and of the Declining of the Church of England from the Same*. Trans. from the Latin by Thomas Cartwright (n.p., 1574), p. 97.

the most intelligent of Puritan writers in the 1580's, made the point very clearly: "the prophetical power . . . of interpreting the Scriptures, to show the meaning the truth of God," he argued, belonged exclusively to ministers. Contrasted with this was the lesser power of "common spiritual men . . . enlightened . . . by the preaching of the Word."[15] Obviously it was the ministers who should rule the church: "Seeing there is so great art required to the government of the church . . . no men ought to have the guiding therof committed to him but that he is expert and cunning . . ."[16]

A government of Puritan experts, however, would have been very different from the traditional order—and this not only because the episcopal hierarchy, as the more popular Puritan writers were quick to point out, was hardly a hierarchy of intelligence. Martin Marprelate had riotous fun with the bishops.[17] What was more important was the fact that Puritan knowledge was not a matter of customary formulas and was not subject to traditional controls. The exiles had already experimented with book smuggling and illegal publishing. Their learning had been independently, often painfully, acquired—sometimes at foreign Protestant universities—and it led them to strange and novel pretensions. As they refused to reverence the appointed bishops, so they refused to read the appointed prayers. Puritan preachers claimed not to be bound "to any set form of prayers invented by man," but rather "as the spirit moved them, so they poured forth hearty supplication to the Lord."[18] This, indeed, was the difference between delivering a sermon and reading a homily—the latter favored by the Queen, who sensed the dangers of clerical invention. The Protestant autodidact would find no place in a traditional society: he would require a totally different system.

Hence the attack upon the bishops: it was made by educated (or self-educated) and aggressive men who wanted a voice in church government, who wanted a church, in effect, open to talent. And it was accompanied by a series of radical proposals

15 [Dudley Fenner], *A Defense of the Godly Ministers Against the Slanders of D. Bridges* (n.p., 1587), sig. ff$_2$.

16 Travers, *Ecclesiastical Discipline*, p. 98.

17 See *The Marprelate Tracts: 1588, 1589*, ed. William Pierce (London, 1911), *passim*.

18 *An Admonition to Parliament*, in *Puritan Manifestoes*, p. 11.

for a new church "discipline." By the 1570's the Puritan ministers were openly demanding parity, the abolition of the hierarchy and its replacement by a series of clerical conferences headed by no one more majestic than an elected moderator.[19] Decisions would be made by prolonged discussion and mutual criticism, and finally by a show of hands. Somber, undecorated clothing would suggest the supremacy of the mind. In their local churches the new ministers would no longer rule as priests, possessing a special ceremonial role, but as scriptural experts, through the sheer force of their talents. This was the view of ministerial position that the exiles had brought back from the continent; they taught it now to young and ambitious university students.

III

The Puritan ministers provide, perhaps, the first example of "advanced" intellectuals in a traditional society. Their exile had taught them the style of free men; its first manifestation was the evasion of traditional authority and routine. The doctrine of the objective Word reflected the new style; exclusive reliance upon the Word symbolized the intellectuals' escape from the corporate church, in effect, their self-reliance, for the Word was self-taught. It was lawful for men "to try whether the church's determinations be according to the Word and to reject them if they be otherwise."[20] The consequence of such a trial, however, was not mere personal eccentricity; the radical intellectuals did not disperse, but rather formed new associations. The Word gave birth to the Cause, and it was as representatives of a Cause that the returning exiles confronted corporate and feudal England.[21] The effect of this new role was to depersonalize political conflict

[19] The new discipline is described in the *Second Admonition* (n.p., 1572), p. 31ff; see also Walter Travers and Thomas Cartwright *A Directory of Church Government* (written 1587, printed 1644; facsimile repr. with intro. by Peter Lorimer, London, 1872).

[20] John Penry, *A Brief Discovery of the Untruths and Slanders . . . Contained in a Sermon by D. Bancroft* (n.p., 1588), p. 35.

[21] The manner in which intellectuals "objectify" social conflicts, intensifying the struggle by depersonalizing its purposes, is discussed by Lewis Coser in *The Functions of Social Conflict* (Glencoe, Ill., 1956), pp. 111-119. It is only necessary to add that this seems the achievement specifically of *modern* intellectuals, and that it is especially significant when they are attacking a society in which personal and corporate connections play an impoitant part. Ideological commitment is a powerful solvent of traditional order.

and to challenge the traditional forms of organization: the clique, the entourage, familial connection. In dramatic fashion, the preacher John Penry publicly announced the impersonal character of his devotion to the Puritan cause. In the late 1580's a warrant was issued for his arrest; he immediately published a treatise defending not himself but the reformation for which he labored. Had the accusation "reached no further than my own person," he wrote, "it were my duty in regard of the quietness of our state to put it up"—that is, to yield silently. "But seeing that *it doth not touch me at all* . . . and wholly striketh at that truth, in the defense whereof it pleased the Lord to use my weak and polluted hands," he fled the Queen's police and published his defense.[22]

In England many of the exiles found themselves once again members of some near-feudal entourage, caught up in an intricate system of connection and loyalty. Some of them, including the well-known Anthony Gilby, were protected by the Huntingdon faction; others discovered patrons in Lady Bacon's circle of friends and relatives. Leicester offered valuable support and, though the Genevan exile Thomas Wood told him bluntly that he was not sufficiently wholehearted, most of the ministers would gladly have accepted a reformation wrought by his hands.[23] There were later to be saints who connived at a reformation wrought by the even less godly hands of Essex and Buckingham. Despite all this, however, Protestant aristocrats never assumed such importance among the Puritans as did their French counterparts among the Huguenots. Nor were the ministers ever entirely satisfied with the comfort and assistance they found within the old order—not least, of course, because the assistance was never sufficient for their purposes.

Their own associations were not feudal factions at all, but gatherings of men familiar less with each other than with Scripture. Only such associations, argued two of the ministers, were

---

22 John Penry, *A Treatise Wherein is Manifestly Proved That Reformation and Those That . . . Favor the Same Are Unjustly Charged to be Enemies Unto Her Majesty and the State* (n.p., 1590), sig. 4 verso.

23 *Diary of Lady Margaret Hoby, 1599-1605*, ed. Dorothy M. Meads (London, 1930), Introduction, pp. 5ff.; A. F. Scott Pearson, *Thomas Cartwright and Elizabethan Puritanism: 1535-1603* (Cambridge, 1925), p. 345; *Letters of Thomas Wood*, pp. 18-22.

truly safe. The old ties of neighborhood and kindred, they warned, would fail, but allies chosen for their "virtue and godliness" could be trusted. "Be faithful," wrote Thomas Taylor some years later, "especially in the fellowship of the gospel."[24] Insofar as Puritanism spread among the gentry, the old feudal ties were supplemented by the new gospel fellowship. Thus Sir Richard Knightley writing to Leicester: "You have . . . gotten you such friends as would be ready to venture their lives with your lordship *in a good cause,* even such as would not do it so much in respect of your high calling . . ."[25] But such "friends" were still relatively rare among laymen; it was more significantly among the ministers that ideological commitment replaced personal loyalty. And the clerical saints came to identify their new *impersonal* organizations as the necessary forms of English life. Instinctively, as it were, with the sensitivity of hostile strangers, they pointed to the decay of the traditional order and suggested alternatives.

They were estranged not only from the corporate church and the feudal system, but also from the rapidly developing secular and aristocratic culture of London. For, in fact, these two coexisted without undue tension. Renaissance exuberance, in and of itself, did not involve any significant attack upon the traditional order of the church (or of the state); it did not provide any basis, surely no programmatic basis, for religious reconstruction or social discipline. It seemed, indeed, to intensify the disorder which attended the gradual decline of the traditional political and religious worlds; it symbolized the breakdown of the old norms and gave expression to the brilliant, often "fantastical" and bizarre individuality which that breakdown permitted. But the exciting and open city did not point the way, as the ministers sought to do, toward a new discipline.[26] No revivifying morality,

24 See John Dod and Robert Cleaver, *A Plain and Familiar Exposition of the Thirteenth and Fourteenth Chapters of the Proverbs of Solomon* (London, 1609), p. 119; Thomas Taylor, *The Progress of Saints to Full Holiness* (London, 1630), p. 341.
25 Quoted in *Letters of Thomas Wood*, p. xxviii (emphasis added).
26 The enthusiasm of Renaissance writers for the London underworld may have led them to exaggerate the viciousness and disorder which prevailed in the city. See, for example, George Whetstone, *A Mirror for Magistrates of Cities* (London, 1584) and Thomas Dekker, *The Seven Deadly Sins of London* (London, 1606). A Puritan version of this sort of thing, without the enthusiasm, is Philip Stubbes, *The Anatomy of Abuses* (1583; repr. by F. J. Furnivall, London, 1879).

no stream of selfless men flowed from London to the country. The movement of men was in the other direction, toward what Puritans felt was the decadence and corruption of the swelling, prosperous city. Their anxious response to the pleasure-seeking urban crowd is apparent in the attack upon the theaters, more so in the fierce condemnation of Renaissance extravagance in dress.[27] The purely individual preoccupation with fashion and style, the new interest in conspicuous consumption—these were worries also of traditional moralists, but Puritan concern was more nervous, more intense. The ministers constituted, as it were, an advance guard in the middle-class repudiation of Renaissance sensuality and sophistication.

Themselves the members of a clerical third estate, the Puritan ministers tended to anticipate the intellectual and social characteristics of a secular third estate. Their "plain speaking" and matter-of-fact style; their insistence upon education and independent judgment; their voluntary association outside the corporate church; their emphasis upon methodical, purposive endeavor; their narrow unemotional sense of order and discipline —all this clearly suggested a life-style very different from that of a feudal lord, a Renaissance courtier or even an Anglican archbishop. This new style was first developed and tested on the margins and in the interstices of English society by men cut off from the traditional world, angry and isolated clerics, anxiously seeking a new order. It was by no means the entirely spontaneous creation of those sturdy London merchants and country gentlemen who later became its devoted advocates; it was something they learned, or rather, it was something some of them learned. The automatic burgher values—sobriety, caution, thrift—did not constitute the significant core of Puritan morality in the seventeenth century; the clerical intellectuals had added moral activism, the ascetic style, and the quality of high-mindedness and taught these to their followers.[28]

27 "Attacks upon plays as such may be regarded as little more than skirmishes in the larger campaign against audiences." Alfred Harbage, *Shakespeare's Audience* (New York, 1941), p. 11. On the new styles in dress, see Stubbes, *Anatomy*, p. 34, discussing "gorgeous apparel" and concluding: "This is a great confusion and a general disorder: God be merciful unto us!"

28 Much of the literature cited by Louis Wright in his *Middle-Class Culture in Elizabethan England* (Ithaca, 1935) suggests that the immediate tendency of new

In politics, too, the "advanced" intellectuals, committed representatives of a Cause, developed a new style and taught it to those who came after. Years before English merchants and gentlemen were ready for an independent venture in politics and religion, the ministers had arrived in the political world and were already active, energetic, creative.[29] Their earliest organizations were made up almost entirely of clergymen; it was some time before Puritanism spread into the country and the clerical saints found themselves saddled with powerful allies. In this interval they experimented with many of the techniques of what came to be called modern politics; the politics of free assembly, mass petition, group pressure, and the appeal to public opinion. All this was illegal or at best semilegal in Elizabethan England; political experimentation required then, as it often has since, a willful disdain for lawful procedures. It was precisely their disdain which turned the "advanced" intellectuals into successful entrepreneurs. The methods with which they experimented were determined in part by their situation as political outsiders; in larger part, perhaps, by the new ideas that they had brought home from exile. While friendly but hesitant gentlemen held back, ardent Puritans were already insisting that politics was a public business and that the public was a great impersonal association of saints.

A group as small and as isolated as this radical band of clerics, however, can rarely play an important part in political history. A certain balance of social forces made Puritan innovation possible; it turned the disdain of the "advanced" intellectual into an effective political method; it set the saints free. In a society where the old feudal aristocracy no longer dominated political life, in which the patronage of intellectuals was no longer an exclusive prerogative of king's court, noble house or corporate church, and yet in the absence of well-established, politically sophisticated professional and commercial classes—in such a society the influence

---

gentlemen and merchants was toward an imitation of the old aristocracy; see especially pp. 138-139. It would appear that Puritanism had a major part in establishing a new and alternative style; see Ruth Kelso, *The Doctrine of the English Gentleman in the Sixteenth Century*, University of Illinois Studies in Language and Literature (Urbana, Ill., 1929), vol. XIV, no. 1-2, p. 107.

29 See the description of the country gentlemen in Parliament under Elizabeth, in W. M. Mitchell, *The Rise of the Revolutionary Party in the English House of Commons, 1603-1629* (New York, 1957), p. 2ff.

and power of an intelligentsia possessed with new ideas was quite out of proportion to its possession of land and wealth. "The elite of the word tries to establish its ascendancy where there is no elite of any other kind"[30]—or, for this was the situation in England in the late sixteenth century, where the decay of the old elite and the immaturity of a new one, result in a certain tense equilibrium. Until the gentry had seized secure hold of the House of Commons, there was no energetic, clearly dominant social group that could give a decisive lead to the creation of new forms and institutions. Social stalemate temporarily freed the men of ideas from their usual role as spokesmen and apologists for one or another established power.[31]

A closely united group of intellectuals—like the Puritan clergy —could then move into those social interstices where power and prerogative were indeterminate. The Puritans were protected by dissident elements in the aristocracy, but they never became dependent members of a feudal entourage, defended, as Wycliffe was, by such an "overmighty subject" as John of Gaunt. For they also found shelter, and then disciples, among the politically untrained and unorganized members of new and growing social groups. In contrast to the poor priests of the Lollards, for example, Puritan ministers moved easily among the merchant classes of the towns and among the country gentry.[32] Their ideas were adopted and helped eventually to form strong men, confident enough to challenge the old order. In its search for support, a radical intelligentsia may thus help to organize the inchoate

30 Suzanne Labin, "Advanced Intellectuals in Backward Countries," *Dissent* 6:240 (1959).

31 For the "usual role," see Karl Marx, *German Ideology* (New York, 1947), p. 39. Karl Mannheim's picture of the intelligentsia as a "socially detached stratum" would seem to describe its position only at particular and relatively rare historical moments. Even at such moments, it is doubtful that the intellectual achieves any sort of "objectivity." (See Mannheim, *Ideology and Utopia* [New York, n.d.] pp. 156ff). At any rate, objectivity could hardly be claimed for the nervously self-regarding Puritan minister. He does achieve *originality;* he can be an innovator— in the absence of a superior social force. The introduction of new political ideas by the clerical exiles may be paralleled by the introduction of new economic techniques by Flemish and Dutch Protestant refugees; see F. A. Norwood, *The Reformation Refugees as an Economic Force* (Chicago, 1942). For a comprehensive view of Elizabethan England as a "backward" society, open to foreign inspired innovation, see Thorstein Veblen, *Imperial Germany and the Industrial Revolution* (New York, 1942), ch. iv.

32 Cartwright provides a useful example; see Scott Pearson, *Cartwright*, pp. 168ff., 345, and *passim*, for the social connections of the sixteenth-century Puritan leader.

political forces of the classes to which it makes its appeal. For
the moment, however, neither the Merchant Adventurers of London, nor the godly members of the country gentry, nor even the
Puritan "chorus" in the House of Commons could compromise
the resolute independence of the ministers.

The demands they made were on their own behalf, developed
in direct proportion to their isolation and independence—which
is to say, to that superiority over their contemporaries that their
"advanced" ideas led them to claim. Clerical pretensions were
therefore greater among the English ministers of the sixteenth
century than they were in the seventeenth, when Puritanism had
far more support in the country at large and the ministers had
to reckon with the lay saints. They reached their highest point
in both periods among the Scottish Presbyterians who lived in
one of the most backward of European societies.[33] Before merchants and gentlemen could demonstrate their social power, the
ministerial mind constructed a Calvinist hierocracy, a tightly disciplined social order, dominated by the "elite of the word," ruled
according to those objective and absolutist criteria which appealed
to the new intellectual. The ministers were, in a sense, the predecessors of those merchants and gentlemen, but at the same time
their would-be rulers.

IV

In the course of the last three decades of the sixteenth century,
the Puritan ministers attained a surprising independence in both
organization and ideology, and developed a radical and innovating
politics. They continued the work of the Marian exiles—John
Field, one of their leaders, was Knox's literary executor in England[34]—but the revolutionary quality of their thinking was
blunted against the amorphous Protestantism of the Elizabethan
establishment. The ministers admitted that salvation was possible

[33] For examples of Presbyterian pretension, see W. L. Mathieson, *Politics and
Religion: A Study in Scottish History from the Reformation to the Revolution*
(Glasgow, 1902), I, 265 and *passim*. Cf. H. R. Trevor-Roper, "Scotland and the
Puritan Revolution," in *Historical Essays: 1600-1750: Presented to David Ogg*,
ed. H. F. Bell and R. L. Ollard (London, 1963) pp. 82-83.

[34] *The Seconde Part of a Register*, Introduction, p. 15. See Field's eulogy of
Knox: "so worthy and notable an instrument of God ... what a heroical and bold
spirit he was . . ." Knox, *An Exposition upon Matthew IV* (London, 1574),
Introduction, p. 91.

in the new English church; they even accepted Anglican benefices. But they were never integrated into the establishment and they continually sought to evade its discipline: ruse and deceit were among the first weapons of the radical. The returning exiles and their followers continued to associate—openly whenever possible, secretly whenever necessary—outside the church and to maintain among themselves the discipline that the Queen abhorred. The "prophesyings," held for mutual edification and criticism, kept alive their party spirit. They constituted an exile, so to speak, at home—and if this were true then the later "conferences" might well be called an underground organization.[35]

These secret clerical meetings represent an early form of the voluntary association. They indicate the tendency of Puritanism to set men outside the conventional patterns of Elizabethan England, much as it had set them outside the actual boundaries of Marian England. The "conferences" were planned in the form of a loose Presbyterian system: ministers met together in their local areas, and several times sent representatives to London for a "national synod." The synods were timed to coincide with parliamentary sessions—thus forming a kind of ministerial lobby. The various meetings throughout the country were informally coordinated by John Field, who served as secretary for the Puritan ministers in the 1580's. Field collected large amounts of written material, apparently planning some sort of propaganda campaign. His "registers" have survived and suggest the extent of the clerical effort: they include drafts of parliamentary bills, broadsides and pamphlets, political doggerel, and numerous examples of "supplications" (petitions) drafted by the ministers and circulated among country gentlemen. In the conferences themselves, the ministers debated fine points of theology and casuistry, but they also discussed parliamentary matters and the more secular aspects of their own affairs: money, relations with parishioners, troubles with bishops. The movement was, in effect, a substitute establishment, "in which things were compassed, which legally were never conceived."[36] "They have combined themselves together into a

---

35 See Neale, *Parliaments: 1587-1601*, pp. 18ff. The "prophesyings" were described by the contemporary minister William Harrison; see *Harrison's Description of England in Shakespeare's Youth*, ed. F. J. Furnivall (London, 1877), I, 17ff.

36 R. G. Usher, ed., *The Presbyterian Movement in the Reign of Queen Elizabeth*

strange brotherhood," wrote the future archbishop Richard Bancroft; "they challenge to their unlawful and seditious assemblies the true and most proper name of the church . . . For a full conclusion of their attempts [they] will take upon them . . . to discharge the estate of bishops and to direct their commissioners to her most excellent majesty . . ."[37]

Bancroft, the alarmed conservative, was probably right. The political activity of the ministers was marked by an extraordinary carelessness about the established channels and procedures of Elizabethan government.[38] Church convocation was avoided altogether after 1563. Contrary to all custom, the ministers discussed parliamentary affairs in their conferences; proposals and petitions were adopted and sent on to London. And at the London sessions of the House of Commons the ministers explored the techniques of lobbying: "[they] were wont . . . to attend the House of Commons door," a contemporary writer reports, "making legs to the members *in transitu,* praying their worships to remember the Gospel."[39] An effort was also made to organize public pressure upon the members of Parliament. The clerical conferences compiled a parish by parish survey of the established church, itemizing its supposed deficiencies; they published it for the parliamentary session in 1584 and circulated it along with numerous petitions from sympathetic gentry. It was an attempt, writes Neale, to create the appearance, at least, of "spontaneous, widespread discontent."[40] These efforts to influence parliamentary decisions and even to organize a following in the Commons represent a

(London, 1905), Introduction, p. xxiii. This book contains the "Minute Book of the Dedham Classis," which is the best source of information on the clerical conferences. On Field see Patrick Collinson, "John Field and Elizabethan Puritanism," in *Elizabethan Government and Society: Essays Presented to Sir John Neale,* ed. S. T. Bindoff, et al. (London, 1961).

37 Bancroft, *Dangerous Positions and Proceedings* (London, 1593), pp. 126, 127.

38 Frere and Douglas, *Puritan Manifestoes,* Introduction, p. xiv. Knappen treats Puritan parliamentary tactics as "ordinary"—excluding from this category, however, the appeal to public opinion (*Tudor Puritanism,* p. 234). In fact, these tactics were quite unprecedented—this was apparent to men like Bancroft and of course to the Queen, as it is today to conservative historians like J. E. Neale.

39 Quoted in Irvonwy Morgan, *Prince Charles' Puritan Chaplain* (London, 1957), p. 111. For another description of lobbying, see Thomas Fuller, *Church History of Britain* (London, 1845), V, 83.

40 Neale, *Parliaments: 1584-1601,* p. 61. See *Seconde Part of a Register,* for copies of the petitions.

major development in English political history. Many of the tactics of the lay saints and parliamentarians of the 1640's were anticipated and tested by the ministers of the 1580's.

v

Radical innovation was a function of the Puritan's detachment
from conventional and customary procedures, of his exile and
his isolation. The minister returning from Geneva and the young
student ambitiously pursuing his godly career amidst the "cor-
ruptions" of Anglicanism felt alike a sense of alienation. "Paradise is our native country," wrote the preacher Richard Greenham, and he meant *not England*. "We dwell here as in Meshech
and as in the tents of Kedar, and therefore we be glad to be at
home."[41] In a sense, radicalism was the politics of exile, of men
not at home in old England, and Calvinism was the ideology of
exiles, of men who had abandoned "father and fatherland" to
enlist in Christ's army. This was an army capable of making war
ruthlessly, because it had nothing but contempt for the world
within which it moved. It was only the Word which secured the
righteousness of the saints, and they set the Word in opposition to
all the "man-made" customs and comfortable traditions of their
native land. "Let them chant while they will of prerogatives,"
wrote Milton in 1641, "we shall tell them of Scripture; of custom,
we of Scripture; of acts and statutes, still of Scripture."[42] This was
precisely the view of the associated Puritan ministers and it freed
them from traditional restrictions upon political activity. It might
even make possible the boldest politics of all: "Tush, Mr. Ed-
monds, hold your peace," John Field told a worried colleague
after the parliamentary maneuvers of the 1580's had failed, "seeing we cannot compass these things by suit or dispute, it is the
multitude and people that must bring the discipline to pass which
we desire."[43]

Something of this same contempt for English law and custom
might well have marked the Elizabethan Catholics; their isola-

41 Richard Greenham, *Works* (London, 1612), p. 645; quoted in Knappen,
Tudor Puritanism, p. 350.
42 John Milton, *Works*, ed. F. A. Patterson, et al. (New York, 1932), III, part I, 246.
43 Quoted in Neale, *Parliaments: 1587-1601*, p. 145; see Bancroft, *Dangerous
Positions*, p. 135, for a slightly different version.

tion was surely far more cruel than any endured by the reformed saints. A close comparison of Puritan and Catholic politics, however, would probably reveal the superior entrepreneurial talents of the Puritans. More opportunities, of course, were open to them: they acted with a greater sense of the possible; they were largely untouched by the romance of martyrdom. At the same time, significant parallels exist between the two groups of outlaw clerics. The Catholic priests had also endured exile, had cut themselves off from their "fathers according to the flesh" in order to follow "the call of God and Holy Church."[44] After the failure of the loyal nobility in 1569, the priests had taken the lead in the Catholic struggle and their new power—somewhat like that of the Puritan clergy—was related to the collapse of the traditional lay leadership. Among the Catholic clerics, the Jesuits especially resembled the Puritan ministers, both in their impatience with episcopal control and their willingness to experiment politically. Robert Parsons, the Jesuit leader, assembled a kind of synod in London in 1580, and managed that same year to set up an illegal printing press.[45]

Among Catholics, however, the experience of exile was not enhanced, as it were, by a radical ideology. It seems clear that the courageous priests who crept into England, often to die there, were closely bound to the traditional social order and were most often willing to work within the limits of the feudal connection of lord and chaplain. The ultimate effect of their labor was to create a pariah culture, an enclave of secure traditionalism. Terribly handicapped by their connections in both Rome and Spain, they failed to generate any significant Catholic political organization in England. Catholic priests and laymen, engaged in political activity, tended in their tactics toward assassination plots and old-fashioned conspiracies revolving around great noblemen. Puritans, on the other hand, tended toward underground organization, or at any rate toward organization outside the traditional

44 A. O. Meyer, *England and the Catholic Church under Queen Elizabeth,* trans. J. R. McKee (London, 1916), p. 133.

45 J. H. Pollen, "The Politics of English Catholics during the Reign of Queen Elizabeth," *The Month,* in six parts (January-August 1902), XCIX, 147; E. L. Taunton, *The History of the Jesuits in England, 1580-1773* (Philadelphia, 1901), pp. 8, 55ff., 69; Meyer, *Catholic Church,* p. 201.

structure of authority, placing less emphasis upon great person-
alities and disavowing, even during their revolutionary period,
the technique of assassination.

Catholic politics was ultimately determined in Rome; English Jesuits did their lobbying at the papal court.[46] The Puritans,
faced with exile or imprisonment, turned in upon themselves;
their resort was to introspection and conference. Their politics,
then, derived directly from their experience and their ideology;
it was unmediated by any corporate body. The sources of Puritan
political innovation, of the tactics of the associated ministers, of
Field's revolutionary proposal, must be sought in that experience
and in the state of mind that it engendered. Most briefly, the lives
of the clerical saints were marked by a sporadic persecution and
a continual harassment—the price of their "advanced" ideas—
which effectively taught the techniques of evasion, mockery and
withdrawal; which often required rapid and sudden movement;
which induced a kind of nervous tension and a constant feeling
of "unsettledness"; but which rarely invited martyrdom. All this
recapitulated the experience of exile in which Puritanism had
been born, and then, as has been seen, the ministers reestablished
the organizations of the exile and readopted its style. Their
sense of superiority and strangeness was confirmed by the very
men who sought to impose conformity upon them.

The "desertion of the intellectuals"—to adopt Crane Brinton's
phrase—was at times a disorderly flight to the continent and at
times a most unwilling procession to the Clink. Field and Wilcox
spent many months in prison after they had illegally published
and distributed the *Admonition to Parliament*. Cartwright lived
for a year in Ireland in the 1560's, spent another in Geneva after
losing his lectureship at Cambridge and several more in the
Netherlands. Along with Udall, Snape, and others, he was imprisoned in the 1590's, after the collapse of the "conference"
movement; he spent his old age not in England but on the isle
of Guernsey.[47] Walter Travers was also a latter-day exile in Geneva and much later in Ireland; he and Dudley Fenner both

---

[46] Meyer, *Catholic Church,* pp. 420ff. Much Catholic political energy was
consumed in Roman intrigue and many of the polemical efforts of the priests were
written in Latin; see titles in Meyer, p. 432 and 432n.

[47] Scott Pearson, *Cartwright,* pp. 20, 150ff., 373. Other information in this
paragraph from the *DNB*.

served for several years as ministers or lecturers to the English church in Antwerp.[48] John Penry fled to Scotland after the Marprelate affair and was hung when he ventured to return. Waldegrave, the Puritan printer, lived for years in Huguenot La Rochelle and then in Edinburgh. The more radical separatists, like Browne and Harrison, spent much of their lives in Holland. Many more examples could be given; sixteenth-century Puritans were as familiar with the continent as many of their seventeenth-century counterparts were to be with the new world.

Even if he did not flee, however, the Puritan intellectual was not secure and at his ease in England. Archbishop Whitgift cruelly charged Cartwright with being a vagabond—homeless, he ate at other men's tables.[49] And, in fact, there was always something of the mendicant in the Puritan: even in the seventeenth century he lived off his lay supporters as best he could and was rarely financially secure within the established parish system. Nor was the Anglican Church capable of offering adequate spiritual or even material incentives to the educated and proud Puritan minister. His ambitions reached their highest point just when he was least likely—given the intellectual decadence and economic weakness of the establishment[50]—to realize them within the traditional order. So long as he stayed in England, however, he could not entirely escape that order. It was in the nature of his "advanced" ideas to alienate him from the routine of church life, but not to free him from an authority he no longer respected and which, deprived of respect, sought at least occasionally to be feared. Hence his own stubborn refusal to conform and hence the harassment to which he was subjected; hence again the willingness of so many to experiment with exile or to risk imprisonment.

The result of all this was to fix firmly in the Puritan mind that strange sense of "unsettledness" which was inculcated also by Calvinist theology. The ideas and the intellectual mood which

---

48 S. J. Knox, *Walter Travers: Paragon of Elizabethan Puritanism* (London, 1962), pp. 25-53.

49 Scott Pearson, *Cartwright*, p. 66.

50 The best descriptions of the condition of the Elizabethan Church are to be found in Usher, *Reconstruction*, I, 205ff., and in Christopher Hill, *Economic Problems of the Church: From Archbishop Whitgift to the Long Parliament* (Oxford, 1956).

originally made the Puritans outsiders in England were in their
turn intensified by Puritan experience. Thomas Taylor summed
up the lessons of that experience: "The more grace, the more
trouble," he wrote in 1618; when a man becomes a saint, he
knows "that bonds and imprisonment abide him everywhere."[51]
This same feeling was exemplified perfectly in the diary of Richard Rogers, full of pious worry and tense "watchfulness."

Rogers' self-esteem, the Puritan intellectual's sense of superiority, required an anxious avoidance of "common courses." Even
the routine of pastoral life dulled his saintly fervor: "we wandering by little and little in needless speech, somewhat of my former
fervency was abated."[52] Rogers prayed that "I may ever have . . .
watchfulness as a companion with me"—for the devil waited
only for a moment of carelessness, an abatement of zealous devotion. Rogers' spiritual uncertainty reflected, in a sense, his uncertain position in the church. Thus, in 1588, he visited the
prisoners at Bridewell and went home disturbed, "troubled in
thinking I am like to lose my liberty." In an entry made the
following year, he reported himself "not so cheerful nor of so
good courage as to be readily disposed to duty, and that by reason of my great likelihood of suspension . . ." Facing simultaneously the onslaught of the devil and the bishops, he was thrown
back upon the "good company" of his fellow Puritans. "The sixth
of this month [December 1587] we fasted betwixt ourselves, ministers, to the stirring up of ourselves to greater godliness." It is
worth noting that Rogers' sense of "good company" had little in
it that was familial or neighborly; when he urged upon his visit-
ors "the necessity of covenant making," he was suggesting a new
form of association—of "brethren" rather than kinfolk. It was
precisely with this sort of organization that the Puritans entered
the political world; for several years Rogers was active in the Dedham Conference. Celebrating fasts with his fellow ministers, praying with them for the King of Navarre, working himself up to a
pitch of piety—thus, though he did not actually go into exile,

---

51 Taylor, *Christ's Combat and Conquest* (London, 1618), pp. 4, 9.

52 *Two Elizabethan Diaries*, ed. M. M. Knappen (Chicago, 1933), p. 58. See also
Taylor, *Progress of the Saints*, who urges a "separation from the common courses,
unto special service," p. 216.

he avoided the common course in his "wary walking with the Lord."[53]

VI

Richard Rogers was the son of a carpenter,[54] Cartwright the son of a yeoman, Travers of a goldsmith. Fenner's family was apparently well-to-do, but in general the Elizabethan Puritans, like the ministers among the Marian exiles, were of common birth. This was most likely true of both Field and Wilcox, the authors of the *Admonition,* though little is known of their early years; their very obscurity argues the absence of gentility. Usher counts some three hundred Puritan ministers in 1603, and virtually all of these were commoners, hardly a third with university educations—the rest presumably self-taught.[55] And such men were unlikely to advance socially; clerical income was small and during the sixteenth century ministers were hard pressed to find lay benefactors. In their conferences the Puritan saints complained of "lack of maintenance."[56] By and large, the prejudice of the age prevented them from marrying well and thus securing a fortune that would free them from worldly concerns. Parson's wives, still the victims of scurrilous gossip, were "kept discretely in the background of their husband's lives." Such a dim existence was not what a gentleman or a prosperous merchant would seek for his daughter.[57]

A small group of relatively high-born clergymen, most of whom came into prominence only after the collapse of the conference movement, mark the transition to the next century. Laurence Chaderton, master of Emmanuel College, Cambridge, for nearly forty years, came from one wealthy family and married into another. John Dod was a gentleman's son, though the youngest of seventeen children. Henry Smith was of gentle birth, "heir to a large patrimony." Arthur Hildersham, incumbent at Ashby-de-la-Zouche from the early nineties until 1632, and suspended seven

53 *Ibid.,* pp. 67, 69, 77, 92.
54 *Ibid.,* p. 17ff. Other information in this and the following paragraphs, unless separately noted, is from *DNB* entries, or from Benjamin Brook, *The Lives of the Puritans,* 3 vols. (London, 1813).
55 Usher, *Reconstruction,* I, 250-252.
56 Usher, *Presbyterian Movement,* p. 43.
57 Hart, *Country Clergy,* p. 33f.

times during that period, was a distant relative of the Earl of
Huntingdon.

Among the Puritan brethren of the seventeenth century were
many men socially connected with the gentry and the urban upper
classes. Lower social groups, of course, continued to supply many,
probably most, of the important ministers: the popular lecturer
Richard Sibbes, for example, was the son of a wheelwright and
Stephen Marshall, the great parliamentary preacher of the 1640's,
was the son of a glover. John Preston, the only minister to play at
court politics, was the son of a farmer—presumably a yeoman,
though perhaps a decayed gentleman. Baxter's father, too, was a
"mean freeholder, called a gentleman for his ancestor's sake."
But William Gouge came from an old gentry family, not decayed;
his father had married the daughter of the wealthy and Puritanical London merchant, Nicholas Culverwell. Thomas Gataker was
the son of a clergyman, who had been himself the younger son
of a gentleman. Joseph Mead, the scholarly Cambridge don whose
treatise on the apocalypse inspired the radicals of the 1640's, came
from a gentry family with connections among London's merchants. Calybute Downing, who preached sedition in 1641, was
of gentle birth; the revolutionary pamphleteer Herbert Palmer
was the son of Sir Thomas Palmer; the staunch Presbyterian
minister Cornelius Burges came from an old and wealthy family
—he was able to advance 3500 pounds to the Long Parliament.
Hugh Peter, who preached before the King's execution in 1648,
was the younger son of a prominent Cornwall family.[58] Many
more ministers were closely connected with the ruling classes of
the towns. John Davenport's father had been mayor of Coventry;
William Whately's father had similarly presided over Banbury,
whose Puritanism Samuel Butler later made famous. The father
of the talented theologian Thomas Taylor was for many years re-
corder for the town of Richmond in Yorkshire. Preston was sent
to college by his mother's uncle, mayor of Northampton.

A good marriage was also easier in the seventeenth century than
it had been in the sixteenth. Thus the preacher Robert Bolton
married "a gentlewoman of an ancient house and worshipful
family in Kent." The Smectymnuans, Matthew Newcomen and

[58] R. P. Stearns, *The Strenuous Puritan: Hugh Peter, 1598-1660* (Urbana, Ill.,
1954).

Edmond Calamy, both found wives among the daughters of
Robert Snelling, who had been M.P. for Ipswich in the last several
parliaments of James I's reign. John Owen, the leading Independent minister of the 1640's and '50's, the son of an old Welsh
family, married the widow of an English gentleman and with her
acquired a considerable fortune. His colleague Thomas Goodwin
married the daughter of a London alderman. Thomas Case,
whose radical calls for reformation have been quoted above, married the daughter of a prominent and wealthy Manchester
burgher; his daughter in turn married a gentleman. The wife of
the moderate Presbyterian Stephen Marshall, "a gentlewoman of
considerable fortune," had been, it is said, "ravished with the
zealous delivery of his sermons."[59] It is significant that the daughters of the seventeenth-century gentry were susceptible to such
extraordinary ravishment.

The changing social character of the Puritan clergy between,
roughly, the 1570's and the 1640's entailed a gradual shift in
ideological emphasis. The "disciplinarian" doctrine of Cartwright
and his followers, developed in the earlier period, Presbyterian
in character, was the ideology of a clergy almost entirely made
up of commoners, socially and intellectually isolated in their
native land. It laid such tremendous stress upon the importance
of the ministry, that its literature can be comprehensively interpreted as a piece of clerical special pleading. Despite the powers
attributed to the eldership, Presbyterianism in its pure form was
a system of clerical domination.[60] If all the nervously insistent
proposals of sixteenth-century Puritans with regard to the ministry—its pay, status, power—were gathered together, this domination would be conclusively demonstrated. A section of the *Second
Admonition* designated in the margin, "the way to bring the
ministry into credit and estimation," may serve as an indication
of the anxiety and aspiration of the early Puritans. The congregation ought to know, the text explained, that "they [that is, the
ministers] are jewels of God bestowed upon his church."[61] Disciplinarian ambitions also took a more material turn. Walter

59 E. Vaughan, *Stephen Marshall* (London, 1907), p. 15.

60 The best treatment of disciplinarian ideology is Scott Pearson, *Church and
State: Political Aspects of Sixteenth Century Puritanism* (London, 1928).

61 *Second Admonition*, p. 22.

Travers ardently urged the inadequacy not only of Elizabethan esteem for the clergy, but also of Elizabethan maintenance. "The Lord did appoint it," he wrote, "that they which preach the Gospel should also live off the Gospel." The minister "ought to be liberally provided for by the churches lest they be compelled most injuriously by reason of their need and poverty to distract their studies."[62]

Throughout the early seventeenth century, the tendency of Puritan thought and practice was toward an independent position—whatever name the ministers themselves gave to their ecclesiology. Independency was the natural doctrine of a clergy which was growing into closer and closer rapport with the lesser gentry and the urban upper classes, and which included members of both in its ranks. There was much less in it of the anxiety and compulsive over-organization that characterized Presbyterianism. It was more relaxed about money; some of its more radical adherents were even willing to forego tithes altogether and rely for their support on an agreement negotiated between minister and congregation. The forms of independency were more open both to local and lay influence. In the town lectureships, in the contracts of special preachers with urban congregations, and in the positions provided in the country by gentry patronage, something of independency was being tested and worked out. At the same time, the increasingly friendly cooperation of ministers and parliamentary gentlemen was undercutting the demand for a centralized and powerful clerical organization. Even in the sixteenth century, many members of the Puritan "chorus" in the House of Commons doubtlessly saw themselves as godly elders dominating the local branches of a reformed church. The real home of clerical power and independence was Scotland, where the Protestant ministry, recruited from the towns and among the petty lairds of the countryside, waged a long and bitter fight against the feudal nobility.[63] And it was only in Scotland that a Presbyterian assembly carved out a powerful position for itself, alongside the older parliament.

This success contrasts sharply with the failure of the English disciplinarians. In the 1590's the conference movement was

62 Travers, *Ecclesiastical Discipline*, pp. 112, 113.
63 Mathieson, *Politics and Religion*, pp. 100, 160, 200ff.

broken up by Bancroft's police and the clerical underground was never reconstituted. From then on, clerical association was less rigidly structured, clerical activity less independent, less creative and less politically interesting. In the Feoffees of Impropriation —an illegal corporation established in the 1620's to buy up church livings and lectureships—Puritan ministers, merchants, lawyers, and gentlemen worked closely together.[64] The ministers, Gouge and Davenport, involved in the work, were already members of the same social class as their lay colleagues. On the local level, the congregation with its elders replaced the clerical conference as the key form of Puritan organization. The ministers settled down in the country, often in close harmony with the educated members of the local gentry. The transition from disciplinarian Puritanism to the congregational forms of the seventeenth century paralleled the rapid development of gentry sophistication and self-confidence. The two processes, indeed, were closely interrelated, for Puritan intellectuals shaped and directed (up to a point) the enthusiasm of the new class and the Puritan congregation provided a field for its exercise. The result, however, was a certain loss of ministerial freedom; the clerical third estate merged with and was carried along by the larger movement of the Commons. The ministers became the chaplains and tutors of the gentry, the actual teachers of its sons in the universities, their preachers in the Inns of Court.

Now at last the Puritan intellectuals lived off the gospel they preached, outside the system of benefices and at least partially outside the jurisdiction of the bishops. Their lectureships were supported by popular subscription; the contracts they signed with urban corporations usually brought them more money than tithes and the old dues brought the beneficed clergy. The freewheeling radicalism of the earlier days was replaced by a new alliance with energetic and ambitious laymen in town and country. The more sensitive among these gentlemen, lawyers and merchants undertook a spiritual journey with the ministers. At its end lay sainthood and revolution—but not such a revolution as Field had once envisioned. The new possibilities were admirably summed up in the person of a man like Cromwell, loyal not only

[64] Hill, *Economic Problems*, ch. xi; I. M. Calder, *Activities of the Puritan Faction of the Church of England, 1625-1633* (London, 1957).

to the idea of a reformed church but also to the vision of a holy commonwealth, both to be governed by the godly ministers, but only in subordination to such lay saints as himself.

VII

The career of a seventeenth-century Puritan minister, and of an increasing number of Puritan gentlemen, usually began at one of the universities. Cambridge and Oxford came to provide, less an education, than a crucial bit of social space where the alliance of ministers and lay saints could be worked out. It was at school that the saint's "spiritual struggle" and final conversion took place, though more often under the impact of town preaching than of university teaching. As among other groups of "advanced" intellectuals, a more important education was offered by the institutions and publications of the Cause than could yet be secured in the universities. The curriculum at both Cambridge and Oxford continued through the early seventeenth century to follow the old scholastic pattern. Ramus, perhaps, had replaced Aristotle for many of the tutors in logic, and the new categories may have lent support to Calvinist theology. But it is hard to discover anything in the subject matter of an academic education in the seventeenth century that would have turned a careless young man into an ardent Puritan. Perhaps the mere fact of an university education speeded the transformation, for Calvinism undoubtedly encouraged the pretensions of the newly educated, and English society was hardly ready to accommodate those pretensions or to provide some outlet for the ambitions of the godly graduate.[65]

The sudden influx of gentlemen's sons into the universities in the late sixteenth and early seventeenth centuries helped to free the Puritan dons and divinity students from Anglican discipline and to provide an alternative source of patronage and support. Men like Chaderton and Preston, masters of Emmanuel, trained a whole generation of young ministers and godly gentlemen. Among the pupils of Preston were many future members of the

---

65 Mark Curtis, "The Alienated Intellectuals of Early Stuart England," *Past and Present*, no. 23 (November 1962), especially pp. 27-28. On university life in general, see William Haller, *The Rise of Puritanism* (New York, 1957), ch. ii, and Mark Curtis, *Oxford and Cambridge in Transition: 1558-1642* (Oxford, 1959).

Long Parliament and a number of officials of the Protectorate.[66] In the university such men associated more or less freely with the future ministers—especially when their social status was the same—establishing connections often maintained for many years. Students boarded together at the home of a Puritan tutor, studied together and undoubtedly exchanged information as to their respective spiritual conditions. Or, they indulged together in that "wildness" and "dissipation" that were conventionally supposed to precede conversion. The influence of such associations can hardly be weighed; what is clear is that something of the style of the future ministers was acquired by men who looked forward to secular careers.

The alienation from the traditional forms of English life which the ministers had long felt, now came to be shared by many young gentlemen. They too learned to behave in a somber, unemotional fashion according to the dictates of the objective Word; they adopted the ascetic style and carried it outside the church; they devoted themselves to the Cause with a resolute high-mindedness. From among these university students came the first Puritan lay intellectuals. Milton, for example. attended Christ's College in Cambridge during the 1620's. He had planned to enter the church; instead, as Haller writes, he was one of the first to bring to the profession of letters an evangelical sense of commitment and activism.[67] Men like Cromwell—who had been tutored by the Puritan minister Thomas Beard before he came to Cambridge—carried this same commitment into politics. It brought with it that freedom from convention and routine that had previously been imparted to the ministry by the self-confident possession of "advanced" truths.

In a letter of 1638, Oliver Cromwell described his condition before the spiritual crisis of his final conversion. He had led, it should be said, an ordinary enough existence, undistinguished at the university and occupied thereafter with his lands and his family. "You know what my manner of life hath been," he wrote to his cousin, the wife of the lawyer St. John, "Oh, I lived in and loved darkness and hated light; I was a chief, the chief of sinners."

[66] Morgan, *Prince Charles' Puritan Chaplain* (a life of John Preston), pp. 28-40.
[67] Haller, *Rise*, pp. 293ff. See Milton's own statement of his commitment in his *Second Defense* (1654), *Works*, VIII, 119ff.

There was a certain perverse egotism in this, though Cromwell was undoubtedly sincere. That the most usual forms of English upper-class life suddenly seemed monstrous—this was a function of the enormous distance the reborn Oliver felt he had traveled. Now, he went on, "my soul is with the congregation of the first-born, my body rests in hope; and if here I may honor my God either by doing or by suffering, I shall be most glad."[68] But there was as yet no opportunity for godly "doing" in England; the high-mindedness and self-importance of the lay Puritan led only to frustration and bitterness. And so Cromwell's spiritual journey was a kind of internal emigration, a withdrawal from old England. It recapitulated the actual experience of the clerical intellectuals, an experience that had already become a part of Puritan imagery, and in whose terms many young gentlemen had been taught to think.

"Alas poor souls," one of the ministers had written, "we are no better than passengers in this world, our way it is in the middle of the sea."[69] The earthly home of the "first-born" was not yet determined. Cromwell would have deserted an England in which Laud was finally triumphant; many others fled a land in which he seemed to triumph— they turned their spiritual alienation into a physical withdrawal. The persecution of the 1630's reproduced, to some extent, the conditions of the Marian exile; this time, however, not eight hundred but more than twenty thousand fled England's shores. Between 1629 and 1640 some one hundred Cambridge men emigrated to New England; thirty-three of these were Emmanuel bred. Another thirty-two emigrants came from Oxford.[70] These were the intellectual and political leaders of the rush to America; they continued the sixteenth-century tradition of exile and escape. The long effort to transform the old order seemed now to have failed and the Calvinist sense of "unsettledness" deepened into that profound pessimism which characterizes the Caroline period. "I saw the Lord departed from England . . . and I saw the hearts of most of the

68 Thomas Carlyle, ed., *Oliver Cromwell's Letters and Speeches* (London, 1893), I, 79-80.

69 William Perkins, *Works* (London, 1616), I, p. 398; quoted in H. C. Porter, *Reformation and Reaction in Tudor Cambridge* (Cambridge, Eng., 1958), p. 312. .

70 S. E. Morison, *The Founding of Harvard College* (Cambridge, Mass., 1935), appendix B, pp. 359-410.

godly set and bent that way [toward the new world]," wrote
Thomas Shepard in his *Autobiography,* "and I did think I should
feel many miseries if I stayed behind." His view was shared by
such a pious gentleman as John Winthrop. "All other churches
of Europe are brought to desolation," he wrote to his wife, "and
it cannot be but a like judgment is coming upon us."[71] With the
dissolution of Parliament in 1629, the last channels of opposition were closed; the choice of ministers and lay saints was between radical conspiracy and emigration. Why should they stay,
engaging in illegal activity and filling the prisons, asked Shepard,
"when a wide door was set open of liberty otherwise?"[72]

Emigration was but one outcome of the Puritan's spiritual
estrangement from old England; revolution was another. Not
until 1640 did the Lord open the second "door." But even before
that date the lay Puritan, trained by the godly ministers, had begun his own revolutionary career. Alongside the large-scale emigration, there reappeared in the 1630's (for the first time since
the 1580's) the whole apparatus of radical politics: the illegal
press, organized book smuggling, a rough underground network.
Ministers like Henry Burton participated in the new illegal
Puritanism, but increasingly leadership fell into other hands. The
emergence of Prynne, Lilburne, and Bastwick—lawyer, cloth-
merchant's apprentice, and physician—opened a new era in
political history. Soon Cromwell and his friends would honor
their God "by doing."

VIII

Puritan literature explored in detail the themes of pilgrimage
and conflict, of exile and warfare.[73] It thus reflected the experience
of its clerical creators; it was first of all the product of their self-
consciousness, the collective record of their grace and their trouble.
At the same time, however, it sought to establish the forms within
which all experience was to be understood, to lay down the basic
patterns of the godly life. Despite their isolation, their exclusive-

71 Shepard, *Autobiography* (Boston, 1832), pp. 42-43; quoted in H. W. Schneider,
The Puritan Mind (Ann Arbor, 1958), pp. 78-79; on Winthrop see E. S. Morgan, *The
Puritan Dilemma: The Story of John Winthrop* (Boston, 1958), p. 40.

72 Quoted in Perry Miller, *Orthodoxy in Massachusetts 1630-1650* (Boston,
1959), p. 100.

73 The best study is Haller, *Rise*; for the themes of "wayfaring and warfaring"
see especially pp. 147ff.

ness and their introspective devotion, Puritan ministers wrote
and preached with an intense awareness of an audience—an audience different in size and kind from that which they might have
reached through the customary channels. Indeed, they consciously
aimed to shape other men to their own godly purpose, to proclaim
the Word in such a way as would best arouse and mobilize all the
potential saints for the "exercises" of spiritual warfare and pilgrimage.

In the sixteenth century, Puritan writing was polemical—as
befitted the disciplinarian venture into politics—and the polemic
was most often academic, turgid and verbose, the work indeed of
socially isolated intellectuals. The Presbyterian discipline was
turned by writers like Cartwright and Fenner into a series of
syllogistically proven propositions, defended in a dull and grace-
less prose which rarely resembled the vigorous language of the
English Renaissance—though Cartwright, in his heavy, academic
fashion, was capable of a Ciceronian period.[74] The dialogues of
Anthony Gilby and John Udall were early attempts at a more
popular style—harking back to the colloquial prose of the great
reformation preachers—and the Marprelate tracts were an extraordinary success in a similar effort.[75] But all these, whatever the
maladroitness of the polemic, aimed at influencing public opinion. Even Cartwright wrote, and knew that he wrote, for men
who had never before been called upon to consider such a question as the proper government of the church.[76] In this sense, the
Admonition to Parliament of 1572, one of the best of the sixteenth-century pieces, was a political pamphlet in the modern
style.

After 1590 a Puritan literature of theological tracts and casuistry was developed, primarily by pious academics like William
Perkins and William Ames. Ames, an exile for most of his adult
life, wrote in Latin, but Perkins, who taught for many years at

---

[74] C. S. Lewis, *English Literature in the Sixteenth Century* (Oxford, 1954),
pp. 441ff.

[75] Gilby, *A Pleasant Dialogue Between a Soldier of Berwick and an English
Chaplain* (London, 1581); Udall, *The State of the Church of England Laid Open in
a Conference* (London?, 1588?).

[76] See his elaborate apologia, in *A Reply to an Answer*, in John Whitgift, *Works*
(Cambridge, Eng., 1851-1853), I, 79f.; also Cartwright's defence of ministerial
election, I, 370ff.

Christ's College in Cambridge, wrote in a "plain" English, and
his treatises enjoyed an unprecedented popularity.[77] His books
were among the first to be carried to the new world. Perkins' success marked the Puritan breakthrough, for the earlier polemical
tracts—with the exception of those of Martin Marprelate—had
never sold well. Though the Puritan don had little of the subtlety
or precision of Calvin, whose teaching he had wholeheartedly
adopted, his writings began the long process in which Genevan
theology was turned into English experience and practice. Perkins and his followers produced for the first time in England a
popular casuistry aimed at the layman rather than the priest and
providing the set rules of godly conduct.[78] Often deprived of the
actual cure of souls in the established church, the Puritans turned
preaching and publishing into a kind of alternative cure. Freed
from the corporate church, they experimented with the typical
forms of modern intellectual activity and sought to organize men
around the Word.

The duty of the preacher, Perkins wrote, was "to apply (if he
have the gift) the doctrines rightly collected [out of text] to the
life and manners of men in simple and plain speech."[79] Standing
with his Bible before the assembled congregation, the Puritan
minister never doubted the sufficiency of his text. He drew from
it a long series of "practical" applications: he taught the "method"
of warfare and pilgrimage. This was his art: the preacher dramatized his theology by setting men on God's stage as travelers or
soldiers, there to fight off the attacks of Satan or to journey, never
without difficulty and hardship, toward salvation. And this was
his purpose: he taught the need for introspection and self-control,
for sustained devotion to the Cause. He did not aim at inspiration;
he did not seek to produce religious ecstacy; the sermon in his
hands was transformed into "a manual of spiritual technology."[80]
"If we would not quench the spirit," wrote Thomas Taylor in
1630, "then must we observe and carefully mark, not only the

77 On Perkins, see Haller, *Rise,* pp. 64ff. and Porter, *Reformation and Reaction,*
pp. 288ff.
78 Perkins, *The Whole Treatise of the Cases of Conscience, Works,* II.
79 Perkins, *Art of Prophecying, Works,* II, 673.
80 W. Fraser Mitchell, *English Pulpit Oratory from Andrewes to Tillotson. A
Study of its Literary Aspects* (London, 1932), p. 114.

presence, but the work of the spirit . . . Examine thyself in regard of good duties . . . Examine thyself in respect of sin . . ."[81]

Casuistry, practical theology, the sermon: these typical forms of religious literature, replacing the earlier clerical polemics, appealed to the new generation of godly and educated laymen. The sermon was the most popular of all; printed in pamphlet form, collected in thick quarto volumes, sermons account for an astonishing proportion of the published literature of the seventeenth century. The rise of the sermon as a popular literary genre symbolizes the appearance of an audience far larger than the Elizabethan Puritans had ever known. Now the ministers, continuing the work of Cartwright and his colleagues but no longer isolated socially or intellectually, began to educate a national public. They adopted their style to the capacities of the new public, attacking at the same time the metaphysical "wit" of the Anglican court preachers. His "manner of delivery," wrote Thomas Wilcox, would be "plain and short . . . serving for the more simple sort of people . . . [and] such as cannot or will not allow themselves leisure to read long commentaries." He would speak, said Taylor, "to the meanest capacity." Puritan ministers even sought to spread their own specialized knowledge, breaking down the exclusiveness not only of the schools but of the clerical brotherhood itself. Why should not all men glean, Fenner had asked in the 1580's, even in fields proper to the doctors? Theology was probably the first technical field of knowledge thus to be vulgarized.[82]

Puritan literature belongs, of course, to the category of the "higher vulgarization"—for though the saints might "be called sheep in respect of their simplicity," Cartwright wrote, "yet are they also wise as serpents in the wisdom especially which is to salvation."[83] Fenner's gleaning consisted of a highly technical handbook of Ramist logic; Wilcox's "short" commentary was 447 closely printed folio pages in length. Perkins' casuistry was dense and difficult. These men were, in fact, aiming at a relatively small public—by modern standards. What is most important,

81 Taylor, *Progress of the Saints*, p. 30.
82 Thomas Wilcox, *Works* (London, 1624), sig. A₆; Taylor, *Progress of the Saints*, epistle; Fenner, *The Arts of Logic and Rhetoric, Plainly Set Forth* (n.p., 1584), sig. B₂ verso.
83 Whitgift, *Works*, I, 372.

however, is that insofar as they reached this public, they undermined their own special position. The diligent listeners who took notes at sermons and later reviewed the argument in their diaries would shortly begin to argue with the ministers.[84] And one day a lay intellectual like Milton would produce his own theology. The specialized knowledge upon which Dudley Fenner based ministerial superiority grew less and less significant as gentlemen (and gentlewomen), merchants, lawyers, eventually artisans as well, roamed ever more widely in their gleaning. But, in a sense, this was the intention of the ministers themselves—those of them, at any rate, who transcended the nervous self-regard of the returning exile. They sought support, and support is what they found. They explored the new careers of pilgrim and soldier and they trained other men to follow. They taught the twin ideas of parity and plainness upon which a new social order was to be founded, and they raised up a generation of godly laymen who made the authority of the ministerial brethren superfluous. And this was precisely their revolutionary role: "the role of the intelligentsia is to make special leaders from among the intelligentsia unnecessary."[85]

[84] There is a discussion of note-taking in Mitchell, *English Pulpit Oratory*, pp. 31ff. See the diaries of John Manningham, ed. John Bruce (Westminster, 1868), and of Lady Margaret Hoby for examples.

[85] The quotation is from Lenin, *What the "Friends of the People" Are* (1894), p. 286 in the 1951 Moscow edition.

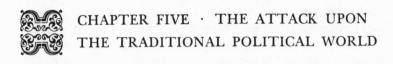

CHAPTER FIVE · THE ATTACK UPON THE TRADITIONAL POLITICAL WORLD

The attack upon traditional order often appears to men as a struggle for freedom: thus the deliberate choice of exile or evasion, the experiments with voluntary association, the entrepreneurial politics of the Puritan ministers. With all this the radical intellectual is familiar; this freedom is his element. But it is by no means an immediately comfortable element; the social breakdown and disorder which make possible the activity of the Puritan minister also produce in his mind and soul that strange "unsettledness" which has already been described. The minister is tormented by his anomalous social position, his permanent insecurity, his frequent poverty. He becomes, as Haller suggests, one of those sensitive men who embodies and articulates the stress of a changing society.[1] His "advanced" ideas give him a good conscience; his day-to-day experiences give him bad nerves. Something of both is present in his moral indignation, his extraordinary self-righteousness and pretension, his laborious introspective search for certainty. These doubts, worries, and aspirations have a political outcome: the intellectual seeks to build upon the newly won freedom from custom and personal connection a disciplined social order.

But it is not always easy to grasp the precise shape of that order from Puritan writing. The saints were quick to deny that any easy analogies could be drawn between their ecclesiology and their conceptions of society and polity. They piously insisted that King James' maxim "no bishop, no king" had never occurred to *them*. And this was probably not deception, or not mere deception. The saints worked out their freedom and sought their new order on the deepest levels of thought and expression and they rarely felt much hesitation about reiterating the political platitudes of their time. But these platitudes did not represent the

1 William Haller, *The Rise of Puritanism* (New York, 1957), p. 39.

thrust of their thinking—which in fact carried them further and further away from the manifest content of traditional doctrine and further and further also from the experience of freedom and unsettledness. Discipline and not liberty lies at the heart of Puritanism, and King James was not wrong to argue that Puritan discipline was incompatible with his ancient authority.

In order to understand the nature of godly discipline, it is necessary first to examine closely the ways in which the clerical intellectuals dissociated themselves from the three crucial forms of traditional relationship: hierarchy, organic connection, and family. For in the images of political fatherhood, body politic, and great chain, the old order found its symbolic expression and made its appeal for the emotional loyalty of its members.[2] The Puritans refused that loyalty and sought other symbols. Long before they launched a frontal assault upon political orthodoxy, then, they had undermined its foundations in feeling and thought. In a sense, their intellectual activity paralleled their underground politics. Subtle but significant shifts in imagery, style, and mode of argument provided the basis for a radically new way of talking about the political and social worlds. The language of the 1640's has a history, which can only be searched out by looking backwards; hindsight, for all its dangers, is here a form of insight.

Whereas Anglican preachers worked within a long literary tradition, so that their words carried meanings and intonations that they could neither discard nor deny, Puritans worked with new symbols and were quite capable of denying, perhaps even to themselves, their most apparent meanings.[3] For the saints, simile and metaphor were frequently means of concealment. Nevertheless, the central images of their literature suggest clearly enough the new politics. The soul's torturous progress toward salvation, the bitter and prolonged struggle with Satan, the voluntary covenant with God, all these might readily describe, indeed, were eventually used to describe, revolution as well as salvation. "A good heart will walk to heaven alone," wrote Thomas Taylor,

2 For a general discussion of these images, see E. M. W. Tillyard, *The Elizabethan World Picture* (New York, n.d.).

3 For some examples, see Thomas Cartwright, *The Rest of the Second Reply* (n.p., 1577), pp. 64-65; Dudley Fenner, *A Defense of the Godly Ministers* (n.p., 1587), sig. D.; William Stoughton, *An Assertion for True and Christian Church Policy* (London, 1604), pp. 20, 359.

"if it cannot get company; [but] it would rather have company."[4] Might not that company, someday, include all England? During the 1640's, personal and national regeneration were constantly linked together: the individual's covenant with the covenant of a nation reborn, the saint's private warfare against satanic lust with the collective warfare against Satan's cohorts.[5] The career of the lonely heart and of the regenerate nation were rooted in the same structure of feeling and expressed in the same language. And if this is true, it is not farfetched to suggest that the national covenant and the civil war were there, so to speak, all along, revealed in the imagery of the ministers before they ever became the subject matter of political debate.

A close investigation of the curious Puritan texts on angelology reveals a shared view of hierarchy: it is in effect a critique of the great chain of being and it has enormous political significance. Similarly, the images and metaphors of Puritan political sermons are so many clues to a slow movement away from organicist thought, a movement whose full meaning is not clear until the revolution. And again, the lengthy treatises on family government argue a new view, not yet applied politically, of authority and social connection. This is not to suggest that a fully developed political system already existed in the ministerial mind, but was only occasionally and artfully displayed. There was understatement, adjustment, and compromise not only in the published writings but, undoubtedly, in the private reflections of the ministers. Whatever limits they set themselves, however, consciously or unconsciously, the clerical saints did in fact work out a new description of God and the cosmos, of man and his earthly sojourn —a description radically different from that, for example, of Hooker and the Anglican preachers, and one which carried along with it political implications that might be denied but could never entirely be escaped.[6] Nor, indeed, when the test came, did most of the ministers seek an escape.

4 Thomas Taylor, *The Progress of Saints to Full Holiness* (London, 1630), p. 250; *cf.* Richard Sibbes, *The Complete Works*, ed. A. B. Grosart (Edinburgh, 1863), II, 232.

5 These parallels are used over and over again by the parliamentary preachers of the 1640's. See especially the sermons of Simeon Ashe, William Bridge, Edmund Calamy, Thomas Coleman, Thomas Goodwin, Stephen Marshall, John Owen, Thomas Temple, Henry Wilkinson, cited below (and in Chapters VII and VIII).

6 A very different view of Puritan politics is taken by Perry Miller, both in

PURITANISM AND THE GREAT CHAIN OF BEING

Calvin's polemic with the Anabaptists had led him to place an enormous emphasis upon the wickedness of men and to develop fully the political implications of original sin. This involved a harsh attack upon the role of reason and natural impulse—as well as of uncontrolled enthusiasm—in political life and suggested a narrow but highly "civic" view of the state as a disciplined, covenanted community. The necessities imposed by a polemic with more radical Protestants, however, were not central to the development of Puritan thought. The long quarrel with the Separatists concerned very specific questions of church government, and the further implications of the disagreement were not pursued. The more important object of Puritan attack in the sixteenth century, and again in the ten years before the revolution, was the Anglican hierarchy. This struggle too was waged largely over various technical questions of church government and scriptural interpretation. But it had its echoes in other areas of thought, for the bishops to most of their contemporaries were but parts of an universal system of order. And the world view of the Puritans may most conveniently be explored in terms of an attack upon this system, a critique of the traditional idea of hierarchy.

It is a commonplace of political history that despotism often plays an important part in clearing the way for democracy. A despot destroys the structure of intermediate powers and makes possible a politics based on individual interests. He overcomes the feudal baronage, breaks down the highly developed system of clan and tribal loyalties, attacks regional separatism and local privilege. He imposes uniformity and a kind of rough equality: he levels the political universe. Something of this same

---

Orthodoxy in Massachusetts, 1630-1650 (Boston, 1959), ch. i, and in his brilliant study *The New England Mind: The Seventeenth Century* (Cambridge, Mass., 1954), especially ch. xiv. Miller concentrates heavily on Puritan academic literature and it was precisely among the academics that the process of compromise was carried furthest. For this reason, perhaps, he emerges with a portrait of Puritanism as highly conservative; many of the ministers seem hardly to disagree with Aquinas. Puritan popular literature is surely very different. Nor is the state of mind of the preachers and diary-writers comprehensible if their ideas are assumed to be traditional. The argument of the following pages is that their ideas do, in fact, represent a major break with tradition—an argument which Miller himself has suggested: see *The Seventeenth Century*, p. 399.

role is played by the Calvinist God; his very existence endangers the medieval hierarchy of orders and powers. He establishes his own omnipotence by leveling the cosmos, by destroying the intermediate power of the angels, of the Blessed Virgin and the saints, of the pope, the bishops, and finally even the king.

This God, this arbitrary and willful, omnipotent and universal tyrant, shaped and dominated the Puritan conscience. But if he required an obedience so precise and total as to be without precedent in the history of tyranny, he also freed men from all sorts of alternative jurisdictions and authorities. The medieval universe had been pluralist. Angels and stars in the celestial spheres, popes and kings on earth, occupied places that were fixed in nature and linked in an harmonious fashion with the rest of the cosmic order. They were not generally subject to divine interference or perpetually dependent upon the divine will. They were sought out by men as alternative objects of loyalty and affection or as intermediate sources of power and fortune. Calvin's God, on the other hand, reigned over a single, unified domain; all powers held from him directly and owed nothing to nature. All men were his instruments, and whether they allied themselves with his sovereignty or rebelled against it, he imparted to them all something of his own willfulness. Men in themselves stubborn and scrupulous, independent among their fellows, precise in their activity, absolutist in their judgments—such were the bearers of the Calvinist "tender conscience."[7] And the tyrant to whom alone they bowed overthrew kingdoms at a stroke, sent churches into precipitous decline, waged war against rebellious angels, and bore the claims of no man—bishop or pope or king—to stand above his equals and to mediate between them and himself.

II

The defense of episcopacy by Elizabethan Anglicans—who knew something, after all, of this Calvinist God—was largely secular and utilitarian. They urged nothing more than the queen's

---

[7] The word "tender" in this important phrase does not mean "easily injured" or "sensitive," but rather "scrupulous," "exacting." The Puritan conscience does not so much receive God's imprint, as reproduce his tyranny and willfulness. *Oxford English Dictionary, s.v.* tender.

prerogative and the necessity of order and subordination.[8] But this defense was early seconded and reinforced by a religious, but pre-Protestant, view of the cosmos as a vast hierarchy stretching from God down to the smallest stone. This hierarchy was the great chain of being, and whatever their mere secular usefulness, it was difficult to keep archbishops out of the chain. Surely it was natural, and not merely a matter of Elizabeth's politic piety, that the order of the church should parallel the order of the universe. And the idea of the cosmos as a hierarchy of essence and degrees was a sixteenth-century commonplace, readily available even to the ordinary mind.[9]

The great chain derived originally from neo-Platonic theory, and though it had never been absent from medieval thought, the Platonists of the Renaissance brought it forward with a new vividness and intensity.[10] The chain was presided over by a God of enormous fecundity and goodness, whose creation of the world seemed less the result of an arbitrary command than the outcome of a kind of inevitable productivity. Out of himself, this God had shaped every possible form of existence, in every possible degree of excellence, down to the inanimate rock of the physical and the godless Satan of the moral universe. Driven by sheer goodness or inexorable necessity, he had filled every vacant place in the cosmos. Every created species and every inanimate form found its precise place in the great chain: angel, man, animal, plant, and stone—and each of these was divided once again into superior and inferior members. Long ago, bishops and kings had been fitted into this hierarchy; it lent to them, as to all creation, an aspect of natural inevitability.[11]

[8] This is most clearly true of John Whitgift, himself a good Calvinist. Throughout his polemic with Cartwright, Whitgift argued essentially that church government was a "matter indifferent" to be worked out in the interests of good order. See, for example, *Works* (Cambridge, 1851-1853), I, 176.

[9] Tillyard, *Elizabethan World Picture*, pp. 25ff.; Hardin Craig, *The Enchanted Glass* (New York, 1936), especially pp. 11ff.; Theodore Spenser, *Shakespeare and the Nature of Man* (New York, 1949), ch. i.

[10] A. O. Lovejoy, *The Great Chain of Being: A Study of The History of an Idea* (Cambridge, Mass., 1936), especially ch. iv. Lovejoy's views underlie virtually everything that has been written on great chain theory since his book first appeared in 1936.

[11] The comparison between the angelic and ecclesiastical hierarchies was already made by Dionysius in his two books *On the Heavenly Hierarchy* and *On the Ecclesiastical Hierarchy;* see Tillyard, pp. 42-43.

Toward this theory of cosmic hierarchy Christianity had certain basic antipathies which had been muddled and compromised by the theorists of the later Middle Ages, but which were reasserted by Calvinist writers. The God of Genesis with his command "Let there be!" was reconciled only with difficulty to the Divine Source who presided over the chain. And as with a willful God, so with his great enemy: the drama of Satan's rebellion could not readily be fitted into the chain of being theory. According to neo-Platonic thought, Satan's godlessness was a necessary aspect of his very existence: he was evil in precise accordance with his remoteness from God.[12] The Christian view of Satan's deliberate resistance to God was obviously very different from this; it suggested precisely that willfulness which ultimately destroyed the chain. The opposition of God and Satan was not precluded by the theorists of the great chain; it was turned, instead, into a mere function of the enormous, unbridgeable distance between them. But the warfare of God and Satan, involving attack, military engagement, strategical maneuver and retreat—this was inconceivable.

In the absence of war and will, the chain of being suggested an harmonious, ordered universe, in which each link found its place, adjusted perfectly to its intellectual and moral capacities. "For we see the whole world and each part thereof," wrote Hooker, "so compacted, that as each thing performeth only that work which is natural unto it, it thereby preserveth both other things and also itself."[13] Hooker's view of a hierarchy of laws, corresponding to the various intelligences of the creatures, was readily merged with chain of being theory. The fecund God of the neo-Platonists became the lawgiver of the Christian Aristotelians, and the harmony of the cosmos was made reasonable as well as natural. But once again there was no room for the outlaw Satan. Only in a Calvinist system could Satan be viewed dramatically as a rebel against the arbitrary sovereign of the universe.[14]

12 Robert West, *Milton and the Angels* (Athens, Georgia, 1955), p. 10.

13 Richard Hooker, *Works*, ed. John Keble, 7th ed. revised by Church and Paget (Oxford, 1888), I, 237.

14 This is the view taken by Milton in *Paradise Lost*; thus Satan's first speech: ". . . since he/ Who now is Sovran can dispose and bid/ What shall be right: fardest from him is best/ Whom reason hath equald, force hath made supream/ Above his equals" (I, lines 245-249).

Degree in the great chain, then, was a matter of being rather than behavior. Even an unusually energetic link in the chain could not hope to climb nearer the divine source: the toad would never be a lion; the lion would never be a man; Satan would never sit on God's throne. For man alone, a few writers thought, there was some hope; he might enter the "corporation" of the angels, but only after death had freed him from his body, that is, had altered his being. So far as this life was concerned, angels were above men in the chain and exercised a certain dominion over them. Henry Lawrence, a Puritan writer—one of Cromwell's officers—described the difference in traditional terms: "the angels which are invisible spirits, and are all spirits, have an influence upon men, which are partly spirits and partly bodies."[15]

But when hierarchy and dominion were repeated among men, they were no longer entirely a matter of nature and being. In nature, bishops could not be distinguished from their fellows; they had no less body and no more spirit. And the same could be said of kings. Even Anglican preachers grew eloquent when they touched upon the commonalty of the grave and invoked the power of the great Leveller before whom all men were equal. Yet in some sense, the relation of fallen man to fallen man—with sin and death the inevitable fate of both—was said to resemble the relation of eagle and sparrow or cherub and angel. Men were similarly different in kind, distinguished by their contrary "virtues" as the others by their contrary natures. Nobility, wrote Thomas Elyot, was the "surname of virtue" and it was the clear implication of his thought, for all its emphasis on education, that this virtue was inbred. But it was never entirely or exclusively so, and some men, lowborn, might rise to a place which would be *achieved*—even if it were, given their virtue, a proper place in the social hierarchy.[16] Neither the lion nor the cherub ever needed to make the effort necessary for such an achievement.

In any case, men were known to be unequal and their inequality was most often described in direct analogy to the cosmic

[15] Henry Lawrence, *Militia Spiritualis* (London, 1652), p. 23.
[16] Thomas Elyot, *The Book Named the Governor* (1531), Everyman's ed. (London, n.d.), p. 126; see discussion of social mobility in John Ferne, *The Blazon of Gentry* (London, 1586), pp. 12ff.

hierarchy. Within the great chain there were discovered a whole series of lesser chains—the animal hierarchy, presided over by eagle and lion; the nine angelic orders; the greater and lesser stars—and these were held to correspond closely to one another. The idea could hardly be avoided that such a lesser chain, corresponding to the order of animals and angels, existed also among men. Was not the society of men "even the diminutive and model of that wide-extending universe?"[17] Indeed, the feudal hierarchy of status and degree seemed to imitate perfectly the great chain.

The complex system of analogies up and down the chain cannot be taken entirely literally, nor can it be understood as a mere convention, a useful and pleasing metaphor. For the traditionalist writer Edward Forset, the universe and the human body, macrocosm and microcosm, were alternative "patterns" according to which the state might be framed by human "art and policy." The art of politics was the imitation of nature. At the same time, however, Forset insisted that the whole system of analogies was the creation of God and that the work of men was only "to find out the well-agreeing semblances . . ." The correspondences were by no means artificial; they had a real existence prior to their recognition by men. And neither recognition nor imitation were at all voluntary—for there were no alternative patterns. "To disjoin the well-coupled from their lovely analogy of each to other, is a violent divorce and distraction . . ."[18]

It is clear that for most Anglican preachers the degrees of the great chain were quite simply repeated among men, establishing in human society precisely the same order and harmony which prevailed in the universe. God "hath made in heaven angels and archangels," preached Thomas Hurste in 1636, "in the firmament the king the sun, the queen the moon and the common people the stars; in the air the eagle and the fly; in the sea the whale and the herring; upon earth the lion and the grasshopper . . ." The same God, he went on, had made men unequal. In the "body celestial," similarly argued Francis Gray, there was a hierarchy of cherubim, seraphim, archangels, and angels; in the "body astronomical" "one star differeth from another in glory;"

---

17 Edward Forset, *A Comparative Discourse of the Bodies Natural and Political* (London, 1606), "To the Reader."
18 *Ibid.*, sig. A.

in the "body natural" all members were guided by the head; in the "body economical" there were gold and silver, but also baser metals. And similarly in the "body politic" there were kings and lords and subjects. Even the Calvinist Joseph Hall suggested the same correspondence, though in a curious fashion he reversed the argument: "Equality hath no place, either in earth or in hell: we have no reason to seek it in heaven."[19]

For popular preachers like Hurste and Gray, the universe was of a piece. Its substance was not identical throughout—else there could have been no chain of being—but its formal structure was repetitive and within the recurring forms there was often glimpsed some mysterious but substantial likeness. Whatever there was in cherub and in gold, for example, in the sun or in the head, that made them superior, something of that was also in the king and the bishop—some special infusion of divine grace, some added wisdom or mystical insight, some distinction in natural make-up. The divinity that "hedged" a king "hedged" his person rather than his throne and obviously suggested some magical powers. The more strident of the Anglican preachers argued for a natural superiority in the king and carried their argument far beyond a mere assertion of his virtue. "Honor the king . . ." wrote Henry Valentine in 1639, "for there is nothing more great in all created nature." The king was a royal fountain much as God was a divine source; he "animates and informs the whole collective body of the people." "Nature herself," John Rawlinson had declared twenty years earlier at Paul's Cross, "hath made the physiognomy of princes to be such as strikes an awful fear and reverence into as many as behold them." He meant this literally, and as the king's face was fearful so his work must be mysterious. "None may, nor can search into the high discourse and deep counsels of kings," wrote Roger Maynwaring, "seeing their hearts are so deep, by reason of their distance from common men, even as the heavens are in respect of the earth."[20] The notion

19 Thomas Hurste, *The Descent of Authority: or, The Magistrate's Patent from Heaven* (London, 1637), p. 2; Francis Gray, *The Judge's Scripture or, God's Charge to Charge-givers* (London, 1637), p. 4; Joseph Hall, *The Invisible World Discovered to Spiritual Eyes*, in *The Works* (Oxford, 1837), VIII, 366-367.

20 Henry Valentine, *God Save The King* (London, 1639), pp. 9, 17-18; John Rawlinson, *Vivat Rex* (Oxford, 1619), p. 9; see also William Dickinson, *The King's Right* (London, 1619) sig. C_2 and Gray, *Judge's Scripture*, p. 5; Roger Maynwaring, *Religion and Allegiance* (London, 1627), first sermon, p. 17.

of the king as a special man with unique capacities who tended
the political *arcana* paralleled the much older idea of the priesthood. To Puritans, indeed to Protestants in general, the two
smacked alike of magic.

Analogical reasoning did not require charisma or natural superiority in political and ecclesiastical princes, though it surely
suggested their likelihood. The correspondence of the king to the
sun, the highest angel and the lion might be nothing more than
a formal and precise way of defining his personal status. It
fitted him into the social order, which paralleled the cosmic order, and it indicated the sphere in which he was to move. It
placed his person and it fixed the relations he would have with
other persons. These relations might be as precise and delicate
as were the harmonies of the heavens; they might require the
pomp and grandeur that poets saw in the sun; or kings might
need to roar like lions and inspire fear in all about them.[21] All
this was the artfulness of correspondence. Even for such a sophisticated Anglican as Hooker, however, the king's place seemed
entirely natural: order among men had to be hierarchical because
there was no other kind. "If things or persons be ordered, this
doth imply that they are distinguished by degrees. For order
is a gradual disposition."[22] The lives of men were determined
by status and degree: only within the forms of this determination
might they live together and relate to one another with certainty
and peace.

At the same time, however, these determinations were not so
inevitable as were those of angels and animals. Angels moved by
perfect intelligence and animals by perfect instinct; but men
possessed neither. They followed the correspondences, half rationally, half naturally, but they walked always on the very brink
of chaos and disorder. Sixteenth-century Englishmen were extraordinarily preoccupied with the historical fact of social mutability. Their concern gave a new urgency to the theory and
application of correspondence. But it also called the whole harmonious and hierarchical world view into question. Rebel,
usurper, conqueror, tyrant—all were objects of sixteenth-century

21 "Apparel may well be a part of majesty," wrote Elyot; *Governor*, p. 124.
22 Hooker, *Ecclesiastical Polity, Book VIII*, ed. R. A. Houk (New York, 1931),
p. 168.

speculation and dramatic representation.[23] The great chain could hardly account for them; they were unnatural and monstrous, yet all human history taught their reality. The son might kill his father and subjects assassinate their king. Hooker's notion of a common rationality—"an inbred inclination to the accomplishment of man's proper acts and ends"—and his refusal to dwell upon the calamity of the Fall served to mitigate these dangers.[24] But the Calvinist emphasis upon human wickedness brought them once again to the fore. Puritan writers, employing many of the old images but enlarging upon the idea of sin, produced descriptions of chaos which sounded very much like Hobbes' view of nature.[25] And if chaos were natural, there was no great chain.

For both Hobbes and the Calvinists, the antidote to wickedness and disorder was arbitrary power. But the most striking thing about chain of being theory was precisely that it had no room for arbitrary power; the idea of domination was foreign to it. For Anglican writers, the incredible variety of God's creation did not necessarily produce a permanent clash of interests and wills and hence did not require sovereign power as a remedy. Instead it resolved itself naturally into a gradation of degrees. Men of different degrees in the body politic related to one another in terms not of command and obedience, but rather of authority and reverence. Hierarchy depended upon a mutual recognition of personal place. The men of power were still "lords" and not yet "governors." But as magistracy replaced lordship and impersonal power replaced personal status, as repression and control replaced humility and subordination, the chain of being and the system of correspondences became less and

[23] Marlowe's *Tamburlaine* is perhaps the great example: "Nature, that fram'd us of four elements/ Warring within our breasts for regiment,/ Doth teach us all to have aspiring minds." Like Milton's Satan, Tamburlaine could hardly be contained within the hierarchical order.

[24] The quotation is from the seventeenth-century Anglican preacher Anthony Fawkner, who restated in popular fashion Hooker's view of natural law; *Nicodemus for Christ, or the Religious Moot of an Honest Lawyer* (London, 1630), p. 6.

[25] See Robert Bolton, *Two Sermons Preached at Northampton* . . . (London, 1635), p. 10. Bolton's long description is virtually quoted from Hooker, *Ecclesiastical Polity*, Book I, III, 2 (*Works*, I, 207-208), but with several significant changes. Hooker says nothing of chaos in human society whereas Bolton dwells at length on "murder, adulteries, incests, rapes," and so forth. And Hooker looks for an end to chaos in obedience to natural law, Bolton in the exercise of divine power.

less useful in descriptions of political life. Order became a matter of power and power a matter of will, force, and calculation. The changing nature of the political world was, however, paralleled by changes in the conception of the cosmos—so that it was some time before analogical reasoning was entirely discarded. These changes in the view of God and his universe had many sources; Calvinism was among the most important.

III

That Calvin and his theological heirs did not live in an harmonious universe may be readily understood if nothing more than the theory of the Fall is considered. The French Calvinist Lambert Daneau in a book on natural philosophy, translated into English in 1578 insisted that the Fall had corrupted not only human nature, but nature in general: it was the cause of the appearance of plague and poison, "of deadly herbs, so many serpents," and so on. But even the original creation had not been a world of harmony and corporate integration such as Hooker described. The "fellowship" of angels with men, upon which the great Anglican dwelt so happily, had after all been preceded by the terrible war of angels with angels, which he hardly mentioned. God had, indeed, created "opposition and contraries"— hot and cold, wet and dry, dark and light, "that one should be a let, bridle and temperament to the other." Daneau went on to describe the universe, not as a natural hierarchy, but in terms of the social organization of a city, where there were many different men "of divers state and unlike callings, and many also of contrary . . ."[26]

Confusion and contradiction would obviously be intensified by human wickedness. While a few Puritan writers adopted some version of Hooker's Aristotelianism, most of the brethren were of Calvin's mind and thought harmony and peace to be hardly imaginable without rigorous discipline: "that there should be order amongst such multitudes of persons, is more than miracle," wrote one Puritan preacher, "there are so many millions of men in a nation, all of various opinions and affections . . . generally disobedient, deceived, serving divers lusts and pleasures . . .

26 Lambert Daneau, *The Wonderful Workmanship of the World*, trans. Thomas Twyne (London, 1578), p. 83, 85 recto and verso.

they are like the waters gathered together in the seas, an unquiet and restless element . . ."[27] This was a view of the world which fitted Puritan experience far more closely than did Hooker's. The sense of "unsettledness" and danger that marked the clerical saints, their tense awareness of opposition and enmity—all this found expression in a cosmology emphasizing the continual need of divine power and in a catastrophic universal history emphasizing the ever-present Satanic threat. Only God's command, only the perpetual struggle of his saints, imposed some minimal order on earth. Similarly, Daneau's analogy suggested that the unity of the universe was imposed from above and was neither natural nor inherent; it too depended directly and continuously upon the commands of God, imagined as the chief magistrate of a cosmic city.

The extraordinary transformation that divine command and Satanic threat worked upon the great chain of being was revealed with especial clarity in the new Puritan view of the angels. "Angelology" was still considered a science in the sixteenth century and its study was still a matter of profound human concern. The bright angelic "squadrons," thought Hooker, corresponded to the multitudes of men: "such correspondence there is, as maketh it expedient to know in some sort the one for the other's more perfect direction."[28] Eventually philosophers and scientists would turn away from such analogies and dispense altogether with the population of the heavens. But there was a previous shift in intellectual outlook by which the angels, still thought to be of great importance, were nevertheless removed from any part in the day-to-day proceedings of the physical world. This was the work of Protestant writers engaged in developing and explicating the idea of God's absolute sovereignty. Their work may well have helped prepare the way for the Royal Society. More immediately, however, it turned the attention of men away from nature altogether and concentrated it instead upon the divine will.[29]

In any ultimate sense, of course, Anglicans as much as Puritans placed angels at the command of God. But the Anglicans, follow-

27 John Ward, *God Judging among the Gods* (London, 1645), p. 23.

28 Hooker, *Works*, I, 281; see also pp. 212-213.

29 For a discussion of the connection of Puritan thought on the angels and modern science, see West, *Milton*, pp. 14-15. West's fine exposition of seventeenth-century angelology has been followed closely throughout this section.

ing scholastic and Jesuit writers, were far more interested in the intermediate realm that the angels occupied, a realm where the harmonious functioning of the universe made continual divine intervention unnecessary and invited the imaginative investigations of men.[30] Angels were viewed as the powers that moved the stars and the planets, thus maintaining the intellectual character of the celestial spheres (and keeping them above men in the great chain). Among Catholics, angels were frequently venerated along with saints as mediating creatures who might intercede with God. But above all, they were thought of as other *beings,* higher created forms, who shared the intellectual universe with men. There was an insatiable curiosity about the detail of angelic existence: did angels age, how did they know one another, could they take on bodies, what were their ranks and orders? The crucial question for chain of being theory was obviously the question of hierarchy. Here the mystical writings of the pseudo-Dionysius represented the acme of medieval wisdom and their doctrine of the nine angelic orders had become commonly accepted. It underlay, for example, the exotic but tedious pageantry of Thomas Heywood's *The Hierarchy of the Blessed Angels,* published in 1635.[31] At this point the Puritans, not likely in any case to admire exoticism, began their disagreement.

Calvin had called Dionysius' notions "mere babbling"; in his many *Commentaries,* he repeatedly criticized medieval angelology.[32] He did not simply reject the ancient science, however, but took refuge in pious ignorance, and the plea of ignorance was the stratagem of his Puritan followers when they in their turn confronted the hierarchy of angels. "What that order is," wrote Richard Sibbes, "I confess with St. Austin is undetermined in Scripture; we must not rashly presume to look into these things." Men are "too curious and bold," wrote William Gouge, who divide angels into nine orders. That there was some kind of hierarchy, William Perkins did not doubt, "but it is not for us to search

---

[30] The best Anglican text on angelology is John Salkeld, *A Treatise of Angels* (London, 1613).

[31] Tillyard, pp. 41-42, 52, 88; Thomas Heywood, *The Hierarchy of the Blessed Angels* (London, 1635). Salkeld does not accept Dionysius' hierarchies—presumably because he sought the approval of King James who had Calvinist views on these matters; see the discussion in West, *Milton,* pp. 50-51.

[32] West, *Milton,* pp. 13-14; cf. *Institutes of the Christian Religion,* I, xiv, 44.

who, or how many be of each order; neither ought we curiously to inquire how they are distinguished, whether in essence, gifts, or offices . . ."[33] In part, this was only another aspect of the Calvinist campaign against theological curiosity. But it was also a conscious effort to minimize the role of angels, as of all other intermediaries —hence the unabashedness of the Puritan ignorance. Whatever the ranks of the angels, they were not to be too greatly admired. "God does not make them the ministers of his power and goodness," wrote Calvin, "in order to divide his glory with them . . . Let us take our leave, therefore, of that Platonic philosophy which seeks access to God by means of angels . . ."[34]

Despite their reticence, Puritans did have a notion of angelic order different from that of the chain of being theorists. They required, quite simply, that the rank and power of the angels not derogate in any way from the absolute sovereignty of God. But that meant that before an omnipotent God angels would have no power, and in their impotence they would be equal to one another. Even the cherubim were not excluded, therefore, when John Preston wrote of all God's creatures: "We say that they are nothing because they are at his command." "All the creatures of God in this world (let a man cast his eye upon the whole universe) they are all but as so many servants." Puritans tended to praise the angels not for their purely intellectual being, but only for what Sibbes called "the quick dispatch of the angels in their business." They "are so prepared for the performance of God's commands," Calvin had declared, "that he has no sooner signified his will than they are ready for the work." Angels were superior to men, Perkins suggested, because they obeyed more willingly and more speedily; they were more "serviceable."[35] Among Puritans it was behavior rather than being that determined status.

Henry Lawrence, who has been quoted above describing the relations of angels and men in traditional terms, will also serve to indicate the modifications that tradition had undergone. Among

[33] Sibbes, *Works*, VI, 319; Gouge, *The Whole Armour of God* (vol. II in *Works*) (London, 1627), p. 42; Perkins, *Works* (London, 1616), I, 16-17.
[34] Calvin, *Institutes*, I, xiv, 12.
[35] John Preston, *Life Eternal, or a Treatise of the Knowledge of the Divine Essence and Attributes* (London, 1634), p. 138; cf. also *The New Covenant, or The Saint's Portion* (London, 1629), p. 48; Sibbes, *Works*, VI, 320; Calvin, *Institutes*, I, xiv, 5; Perkins, *Works*, III, 133-134.

the angels, he wrote, there was to be found a certain "division of work"; the division was neither necessary nor natural, but "these are God's ways of administration, his ordinances of which we can give no account, he useth this chain and subordination of which one link toucheth another . . ."[36] The chain was thus no longer the inevitable form of cosmic order; it had become for Lawrence, nothing more than a convenient means for God's administration of the universe. And in this administration angels were a species of heavenly civil servants, divine instruments. They were no longer in any sense intermediate powers; they had no independent sphere of action. They were responsive to command, but no longer knew with perfect intelligence the laws that governed their activity. "There is not any creature in heaven or earth," wrote Preston, "that stirreth without a command . . . if he do command them they go; they are ready and nimble to do any service."[37]

By the time Milton wrote his *Paradise Lost,* Puritans had produced a considerable literature on the angels. Several major treatises appeared during the revolutionary period and angels continued to be a topic of much speculation for some years after, though by the end of the century, with the impact of Royal Society science, interest had largely abated. Even before the scientists set to work, however, Calvinist writers had removed angels almost entirely from the physical world. The nature of their own interest can be seen in the titles of two of their most important books: Lawrence's *Militia Spiritualis* and Isaac Ambrose's *War with Devils and Communion with Angels.*[38] According to these Puritan texts, angels carried out God's commands in the perpetual war against Satan. The angelic armies were the guardians of the elect—so important was this function to Puritan writers that they tended to ignore all other angelic activities and to forget the ancient curiosity about angelic nature. Lawrence and Ambrose had little to say about the intelligence of the angels or their ranks and orders; the two books, in fact, were not concerned with the ancient science of "angelology," but were rather manuals of

36 Lawrence, *Militia Spiritualis,* pp. 48-49.
37 Preston, *New Covenant,* p. 33.
38 Lawrence's book was first published in 1646, reissued three times by 1652; Ambrose's work appeared in 1662. See also Robert Dingley, *The Deputation of Angels* (London, 1654), and Christopher Love, *Ministry of Angels* (London, 1657).

edification, calls to spiritual warfare, treatises on the temptations of Satan and the godly strength of the heavenly "battalions."

Most important of all, perhaps, both Puritan writers tended to deemphasize the role of angels in the routine of nature. Cooperating with God as secondary causes, they would inevitably, Puritans thought, usurp something of his glory. And, indeed, angels could not easily be made the mere instruments of God's will, for traditional theory had made them so much more. "God, which moveth mere natural agents as an efficient only," wrote Hooker, "doth otherwise move . . . his holy angels . . ." "Rapt with the love of his beauty" they freely imitate him and "do by all means all manner good."[39] Such independent goodness Calvinists could hardly tolerate; they preferred to ascribe all natural events directly to God, who worked in ways "best known to himself." They denied, then, that the stars were animated or moved by free intelligence; the arbitrary, impersonal force of an inscrutable God was sufficient.

When God used angels in the spiritual warfare, he chose them without reference to any preexisting hierarchy. He did not recognize their status, Puritans insisted, rather he appointed their offices. This opinion was apparently adopted by Milton, for all his fascination with traditional angelic lore. Though he felt the ancient hierarchical terms necessary for his poetic purposes, he used them "virtually without hierarchical meaning."[40] The old titles distinguished offices rather than degrees. Milton followed in a line of Protestant thinkers that had probably begun with Bullinger in the sixteenth century. The Zurich reformer held that angels were called archangels only when they "were sent in message in God's greatest matters." The same idea was obviously repeated in Lawrence's "division of work." Again, the Puritan William Gouge claimed that angels differed only in their functions and not in their natures; they occupied "distinct and several offices"— "for if all should do the same thing," he sensibly reasoned, "how should the other things be done?"[41] For most Puritans, employment determined status and employment was at the will of God.

39 Hooker, *Works*, I, 212.
40 West, *Milton*, p. 133-136.
41 Gouge, *Armor of God*, p. 30.

The independent sphere of angelic activity had vanished. A system of temporary offices had replaced the old hierarchy; the chain of being had been transformed into a chain of command.

IV

The relation between God and man was governed by a similar structure of command and obedience. In human society, as among the angels, God's sovereignty destroyed the old hierarchy of degree. "Calling" was a form of office. Though the idea may have served at particular historical moments to reinforce status, God's call was in fact a command, and was so described, with characteristic imagery, in Perkins' important *Treatise of the Vocations*: "For look as in a camp, the general appointeth to every man his place and standing . . . in which he is to abide against the enemy . . . even so it is in human societies: God is the general appointing to every man his particular calling . . ." John Preston, speaking to a Cambridge audience in the 1620's, suggested what might happen if men disobeyed the general: "they may be sure to find God ready to destroy them."[42] Preston went on to develop the metaphor of the instrument, which is thrown away when it is no longer fit for use. So men may be discarded by God. This metaphor was commonly used in late medieval and early modern polemical literature to attack the old hierarchy of personal status: for if man was only a tool of God, he had no personal, no hereditary claim to his place or power. Savonarola had employed the same figure in his struggle with the pope. God moves all men, he claimed, "as the saw is moved by the hand of the craftsman." The man who disobeys is "thrown down among the broken tools."[43] It was a figure that would naturally appeal to a Calvinist preacher. The image of the divine instrument was so frequently used in Puritan literature that it came near to replacing the much older image of man as God's child.

But if God used men as instruments, they obeyed him as saints and here lay a certain difficulty. Obedience among men was an act of the will. They did not follow divine commands with a perfect insight into divine purposes as did the angels nor was their

---

42 Perkins, *Works*, I, 750; Preston, *Life Eternal*, pp. 146-147.
43 Roberto Ridolfi, *The Life of Girolamo Savonarola*, trans. Cecil Grayson (New York, 1959), p. 218.

obedience instinctual. God did not simply "use" his saintly instruments; in some sense their activity had to be deliberate. Given the Calvinist insistence upon man's moral impotence, however, it was extremely difficult to see what part his deliberation could play. Between the command of God, his predestinating decree, and the activity of fallen men, there was a great gap, a vast, uninhabited, unmediated distance which stretched from heaven to this "molehill" earth. A way had to be found for men to respond to God and simple submission was not an adequate response. The resigned passivity and quietism which predestination might induce were dangers of which Calvinist theologians and preachers were nervously aware. God's command sought out not only pious acquiescence, but a kind of eager consent, a response registered, so to speak, not in the mind or the heart so much as in the conscience and the will. Men must make themselves "serviceable"; God's willfulness required human willingness. The two came together, finally, in the Puritan idea of the covenant.[44] Enabled by God's grace, the saints volunteered to be God's instruments; command and consent met, and terms were drawn up. Human consent did not, of course, limit divine sovereignty. The covenant was a way of activating men and not of controlling God. Nor was that consent a matter of free choice, for grace sought out the saints and no man earned salvation by volunteering for it. What the covenant did was to suggest a disciplined and methodical response to grace, a new, active and willing obedience to command—and these were the major themes of Puritan "practical" theology during the seventeenth century.

The intricacies of covenant theology cannot be discussed here. It is important, however, to say something of the relations between God and man that the covenant suggested and also of the imagery with which they were described in the popular literature. For God's sovereign will and man's willing obedience were two as-

---

[44] The best treatment by far of covenant theology is that of Perry Miller, *The Seventeenth Century*, ch. xiii. On the dangers of passivity and the need for spiritual "exercise," see Taylor, *Progress of Saints*, pp. 12ff, and *Christ's Combat and Conquest* (London, 1618), p. 213; also Preston, *A Sermon Preached at a General Fast* (London, 1633) (printed with *The Saint's Qualification*), p. 285; and *New Covenant, passim*. Some Puritan ministers (including Paul Bayne, Samuel Ward and Thomas Twisse) rejected covenant theology because they thought it limited God's sovereignty; J. D. Eusden, *Puritans, Lawyers and Politics in Early Seventeenth Century England* (New Haven, 1958), p. 29n.

pects of that universal voluntarism which destroyed the great chain. The covenant emphasized once again the abolition of the older connections founded upon creative love, filial humility, and the merciful intercession of saints and angels.[45] An agreement between God and man whose terms were supposedly written out in Scripture, it symbolized perfectly the artificial nature of all relations. Through the covenant men became the "bondsmen" of God —not the children—and the image implied the voluntary recognition of an existing debt, a legal or commercial obligation. God was the creditor of all men, but some were enabled by his grace to acknowledge the debt and, through obedience, in part to repay it. This acknowledgment was precisely that act of the will which God required of his saints: "you must covenant knowingly . . . conscientiously . . ." Simeon Ashe told the burgesses of London at the renewing of the Solemn Oath and Covenant in 1646, "our vows are deliberate . . . before witnesses."[46] "Deliberate" vows could hardly have had a place in the chain of being, nor are they usually required between father and child.

The bargain between God and man was sometimes discussed in terms which suggested a kind of "spiritual commercialism": for so much obedience there would be so much grace.[47] More often, however, the analogies were political and social. Covenant theology had its source in the solemn promises made by God to the Israelites and it was in the form of a national covenant that the contractual idea first entered Protestant minds. The practical culmination of covenant theology can be seen in the collective commitments undertaken in the 1630's and '40's by both the Scottish and English nations. Here the overriding Puritan concern for discipline and social order was most dramatically revealed. Even the private contract between an individual saint and his God, however, was described in imagery that suggests a smaller version of the collective agreement: the terms were most fre-

---

45 It is, of course, only God's love that makes the covenant available to men, but in general any very forceful or passionate emotion has been removed from the relationship—as the imagery discussed below suggests. See also Miller, *The Seventeenth Century*, pp. 381ff.

46 Simeon Ashe, *Religious Covenanting Directed* . . . (London, 1646), pp. 7ff; see also Edmund Calamy, *The Great Danger of Covenant-Refusing* (London, 1646).

47 The term is Miller's; *The Seventeenth Century*, p. 389.

quently those of master-apprentice and captain-soldier.[48] Significantly enough, the connection between lord and man, the old
feudal oath so often invoked just a quarter-century earlier in Huguenot literature, was not employed in Puritan writings. Probably
the feudal connection was too personal, but another possible reason for its absence is worth noting. Feudal bonds, like the relations among men suggested by great chain theory, were lifelong
and even hereditary, whereas the connections of master-apprentice and captain-soldier were only temporary, though subject to
renewal. Puritan "method" required a constant reaffirmation of
the covenant, after each engagement with Satan, after each temptation, even regularly on fast days and solemn occasions. Similarly,
the idea of divine calling, in contrast to that of natural hierarchy,
did not necessarily suggest a permanent social position: "when God
doth lead us to more free and comfortable conditions," wrote the
Puritan Paul Bayne, "we are rather to use them."[49] Periodic self-
examination was a feature of the Puritan life, for will and conscience could never be permanently bound; unlike the bonds of
nature and blood that of consent must on occasion be renewed
or else it lapses.[50]

The connection of captain and impressed soldier might well
figure that of God and predestinated man, but the enlisted soldier
was similar to the man of the covenant, taking deliberate vows.
God had his chosen instruments, but the sign of their choseness
was the act of volunteering. In these terms did the Puritan governors of New England advertise for settlers: "Christ Jesus . . . stirs
up his servants as the heralds of a king to make this proclamation
for volunteers . . ."[51] But the volunteer was obviously no private
soldier; he enlisted in an army or he joined a new political community. In either case his choice was also an agreement to be obe-

48 Calamy, *Great Danger*, passim; Joseph Caryl, *The Nature, Solemnity, Grounds,
Property and Benefits of a Sacred Covenant* . . . (London, 1643), p. 42.
49 Paul Bayne, *A Commentary upon the First Chapter of the Epistle of St. Paul*
(London, 1618), pp. 8-9.
50 See the radical opinion of Buff-Coat (Robert Everard) in the Putney Debates:
"Whatsoever . . . obligation I should be bound unto, if afterwards God should
reveal himself, I would break it speedily, if it were an hundred a day . . ."
Puritanism and Liberty, ed. with an intro. by A. S. P. Woodhouse (London, 1938),
p. 34.
51 Quoted in H. W. Schneider, *The Puritan Mind* (Ann Arbor, 1958), p. 8.

dient. Indeed his very consent made the agreement more far-reaching—much as the citizens of Geneva bound themselves to an extraordinarily rigid discipline through their covenant. Contract might establish connections neither permanent nor hereditary; but it also created bonds in many ways more intensive than those of blood and nature. Even the private covenant of the individual saint exposed him to the discipline and bound him to the religious exercises of the church; voluntary allegiance led him to a collective discipline. It was the constant tendency of Calvinism to turn the theology of salvation into a sociology: "holy societies," wrote Richard Baxter, "honor our maker more than holy separate persons." Or, in the more appropriate imagery of military life: "The Apostle joys to see the saints' close order . . . not only in watching as single professors, but in marching orderly together as an army with banners."[52]

Among Puritan writers the terms of the covenants of private men and nations were virtually interchangeable—so little did they care for the utterly personal quality of religious ecstasy. Personal salvation and national reformation were both aspects of that divine politics that sought to establish order and discipline among men. They were explored by the same writers and preachers who conceived the cosmos as an urban agglomeration of disparate and contrary elements, who imagined the angels to be divine civil servants and the devil an omnipresent threat, who transformed the chain of being into a chain of command and the harmonious universe into a world of strife and contention. In human society, they replaced the old hierarchy with a collective discipline, shaped by command and covenant, a new order not natural and inevitable but artificial and purposive. God "associated" himself with his saints, but the association was narrowly political (or military), involving less of paternal affection than of deliberate alliance for a purpose. The cosmological chain of command thus found earthly expression as James I had feared: in a militant congregation of saints, led perhaps by generals and colonels but not by kings. The magic of priesthood was gone and all hierarchies were called into question. Covenant and command turned men into instruments; calling and office took the place of birth and status. The shattering

52 Richard Baxter, *A Holy Commonwealth* (London, 1659), p. 14; John Owen, *The True Nature of a Gospel Church* (London, 1689), preface.

of the old order might have set men free, but the will of God and their own godly consciences bound them more tightly than ever before.

FROM BODY POLITIC TO SHIP OF STATE

The idea of the state as a body politic, a living organism, was probably as common in the sixteenth and seventeenth centuries as was the notion of the great chain. The two were, in fact, part of the same world view, for the whole of the chain of being might be imagined as an immense organism, animated by its divine source.[53] This was the macrocosm, the universe in its organized form, harmonious in all its parts, alive, compacted as Hooker said, so that all things within it hung together in mutual dependence. Man was the microcosm, the model of the universe, "even a very world in himself." Standing midway, as it were, in the great chain, part soul, part body, he was constituted from the same elements as was the cosmos, on a vastly smaller scale. The relation of microcosm and macrocosm was probably the most important of the correspondences. Human society corresponded to the two alike, but the analogy with the microcosm was both more easily understood and politically more useful. "The head represents the prince . . . ," wrote the Anglican preacher Robert Sibthorpe in a typical development of the image, "the trunk the commonwealth or people; and as in the body natural . . . so in the body politic, every one of the . . . members hath his duty to perform . . . and his due to receive of others."[54]

The use of organic analogy in political thought is undoubtedly very old. Its tremendous importance in late medieval and early modern times, however, had a particular reason and history. The image of the body politic derived much of its emotional power from the parallel conception of the church as the visible body of Christ. For the medieval community of Christians was no mere society of men; through a mystery akin to transubstantiation in the eucharist, it was revealed as the bodily half of an organism that had God himself at its head.[55] Image and metaphor were

[53] Tillyard, *Elizabethan World Picture*, pp. 83ff.
[54] Robert Sibthorpe, *Apostolic Obedience, Showing the Duty of Subjects to Pay Tribute and Taxes to Their Princes* (London, 1627), p. 10.
[55] Gerd Tellenbach, *Church and Society at the Time of the Investiture Contest,*

thus originally sacrament and undoubtedly sacramental thinking
lent a peculiar vividness and persuasiveness to subsequent analogical reasoning.

It is certain that for many Anglicans in the early seventeenth
century elements of mystery lingered in the old images. But it is
the papalist literature of the eleventh and twelfth centuries that
suggests the real force of this imagery—and its historical function.
Ecclesiastical spokesmen drew upon the organic idea to support the
unity of the church and to attack its various feudal connections.
They described the integration of the church into the feudal order
as an illicit sexual assault upon Christ's body. A church properly
married to its divine or its popish husband—this was an alternative image serving the same purpose—would necessarily be free
of all worldly (adulterous) entanglements. The organic conception of the state provided a similar argument against the feudal
pattern of local and private relations. And this was the key reason
for its systematic exploitation throughout the later Middle Ages.[56]
From John of Salisbury onward, the analogy of the bodies natural
and political served to emphasize the interdependence of all the
members of a society and to suggest the necessity of a single
"head." The organic analogy was an argument for unity and monarchy; as such it was still employed in the sixteenth century and
even with especial force after the depredations of "bastard feudalism."

Though Suarez in the early seventeenth century was still able
to describe the political community as a "mystical body," the mystery of the organic analogy had actually been rejected in the
thirteenth century by Aquinas. The great Catholic rationalist
had recognized that the individuality of the human members of
the body politic made them vastly different from the organs of the
natural body. Nevertheless, society was not merely a company of
men. There were natural connections among its members and
there was also a functional integration at least similar to that of an
organism. Thus the government of men required that the king
be to the kingdom what the soul was to the body, and the de-

trans. R. F. Bennett (Oxford, 1940), pp. 126ff.; Otto Gierke, *Political Theories of the
Middle Ages*, trans. with intro. by F.W. Maitland (Boston, 1958), p. 132 n77.

56 John of Salisbury, *Policraticus*; partially repr. by John Dickinson, *Statesman's
Book* (New York, 1927). See Dickinson's Introduction, pp. xix.

fense of the state required that some men function as its "arms."[57]
In these terms did Hooker defend monarchy and even Bodin,
who relied largely on other arguments, did not forget that "all
the laws of nature point toward monarchy, whether we regard the
microcosm of the body, all of whose members are subject to a
single head . . . or whether we regard the macrocosm of the world,
subject to one almighty God."[58] Such writers no longer applied the
organic analogy strictly, but its actual denial awaited the pamphleteers of the English Revolution. The apparent meaning of
Bodin and Hooker was that reason or art might reproduce the
forms of organic connection. Bodin's English translator, Richard
Knolles, argued in 1606 that the purpose of political speculation
was

to find out a good and reasonable means, whereby such multitudes of
people, so far differing in quality, estate and condition, and so hardly
to be governed might yet into one body politic be in such sort united,
as that every one of them should . . . together with the common good
(as members of one and the self-same natural body) have a present
feeling of others good and harms . . .[59]

But this sophisticated view had a more popular rival. In the
same year that Knolles published his translation, Edward Forset
brought out his *Comparative Discourse of the Bodies Natural and
Political,* developing the analogy in some detail and implying that
deviation from it was not merely a lapse of art or reason, but
a disease.[60] Forset's book was probably the last systematic exploration of the organic idea, but the analogy pervaded the popular literature of the next forty years. And the key to its popular
use was the widely shared notion that society naturally and
inevitably fell into organic form and that any alternative form
would be "monstrous" if not impossible: "as in the natural body,
so it is in the body politic," declared John Rawlinson in 1619, "if

[57] Aquinas, *Selected Political Writings,* ed. with intro. by A. P. D'Entreves
(Oxford, 1954), pp. 67, 191-193; Francisco Suarez, *Selections from Three Works*
(Oxford, 1944), vol. II: *An English Version of the Texts,* trans. G. L. Williams,
A. Brown and J. Waldron, p. 375. But note that Suarez is speaking of "moral" and
not physical unity.
[58] Bodin, *Six Books of the Commonwealth,* abridged and trans. M. J. Tooley
(Oxford, n.d.), p. 199. Hooker, *Book VIII,* pp. 195ff.
[59] Richard Knolles, "Epistle to the Reader," in Bodin, *Six Books . . . done into
English* (London, 1606).
[60] Forset, *Comparative Discourse,* pp. 62ff.

the body be without a head it presently falls to the ground."[61]

Like the great chain, the organic analogy described an harmonious order: the members of the body politic were bound together by mutual concern and a common sense of self-preservation. This harmony was also a hierarchy—one not different from the hierarchy described by John of Salisbury. "Shall the foot be permitted to partake in the point of pre-eminence with the head?" asked Forset, "or were it seemly for the head leaving his state to abase himself to a toil . . . in the trading business?" Rather, he thought, "should the meaner and ministering sort run the race and catch the goal to them proposed . . ."[62] Though Anglican preachers used the image of the head (or the heart or soul) to glorify the king, the organic idea excluded domination quite as much as did the theory of the chain. It also, of course, excluded rebellion: thus a royalist pamphleteer during the revolution insisted that the body politic might wage war "against an outward power, but not (as now) by one part of it set against the head . . . for that tends to the dissolution of the whole."[63] At its best, the organic analogy described a commonwealth where rebellion would be quite inconceivable, a society having but one soul though its members had many separate bodies. "And from this conjunction," preached Thomas Foster at the Devon assizes in 1630, "must grow a community: from the unity of affections, a community of charitable actions." "You are one another's members," Foster told the judges, "knit together by the sinews of policy, to one monarchical head; let it be your care to study the welfare of him and one another."[64]

The most significant implication of the organic analogy was the idea of the *member* as a man with a fixed function and no capacity for independent activity. A Puritan minister described functional inequality as nothing more than a necessary division of labor: "If the whole body were an eye, where were the hearing . . . ?"[65] But Anglicans usually dwelt insistently upon the spe-

61 Rawlinson, *Vivat Rex*, pp. 9-10.

62 Forset, *Comparative Discourse*, p. 50. Compare Salisbury, *Statesman's Book*, pp. 64ff.

63 The Royalist pamphleteer was Henry Ferne; he is quoted in [Herbert Palmer] *Scripture and Reason Pleaded for Defensive Arms* (London, 1643), p. 14.

64 Thomas Foster, *The Scourge of Covetousness: or, An Apology for the Public Good, Against Privacy* (London, 1631), pp. 15, 22.

65 John Ward, *God Judging*, p. 9.

cial talents of the various members and especially of the head. Forset discussed at length the secrets which the rational head might
keep from the unreasoning body; the search for political knowledge he treated as a form of rebellion.

> . . . when this searching and piercing presumption shall get up to
> the highest step, and fall to pry into the prince himself, to make dis-
> coveries and divulgings of his dispositions, intentions, affections, qual-
> ities, weighty business and serious actions, then it hath a resemblance
> . . . [to] the sly surreption of Prometheus . . .[66]

It was most important that every member keep his place and
perform his duties. The disorder of the parts was anarchy and
personal ambition or intellectual doubt was the beginning of disorder. Innovation of any sort was the greatest possible danger to
the delicate health of the political body.[67] Following the organic
analogy, only growth, among all the forms of change, might be allowed. And growth, Anglican writers stressed, was so gradual as
to be hardly noticeable. "There must be a leisurely and advised
proceeding in every alteration," wrote Forset, "nature hath left
us a pattern . . . we must let it grow by degrees . . ."[68] In precisely
such a fashion, Hooker thought, had law arisen, supported by custom, ratified by the wisdom of the ages. That this view of change
as growth could not possibly encompass Puritan reformation was
recognized at the time. Reform, Calybute Downing argued, would
"necessarily induce an alteration in the profession and practice of
the laws, which by reason of their long use, are . . . naturalized
into the manners and disposition of our nation." They are like
the habits of the body, difficult to break. Nor, once established,
should they ever willfully be broken; for they are grafted into
that natural order which, as Maynwaring said in his famous sermon
Religion and Allegiance, "gives to everything its proper place and
so procures and preserves rest and quiet thereunto . . ." And when
the body is sick, Downing went on, rest and quiet are its surest
cure. "Now all stirring changes are dangerous, especially when
the body of the commonwealth is full of diseases."[69] The only dras-

---

[66] Forset, *Comparative Discourse*, p. 99.

[67] Gervase Babington, *Works* (London, 1622), p. 296ff. (third numbering).

[68] Forset, *Comparative Discourse*, pp. 62, 64.

[69] Calybute Downing, *A Discourse of the State Ecclesiastical* (Oxford, 1634), pp.
14-15. Downing later reversed his position and supported Parliament in the civil

tic change was death itself and in the harmonious order of nature
even death came slowly, with age and gradual decay.

II

Puritan preachers could hardly avoid the imagery of organism;
it was common, easily understood and therefore of some use in
their "plain speaking." Nevertheless, the systematic development
of the image in a sermon is an almost sure sign of an Anglican
preacher. Organism did not fit readily into Puritan doctrine. The
relations that it suggested seemed mysterious, not easily described
in terms of command or discipline. Nor could Calvinist activity
and reform easily be defended in organic terms. In his *Appeal to
Parliament* of 1628, Alexander Leighton attempted the analogy:
he called upon the members of Parliament, as the "eyes, ears, and
hands" of the kingdom, to become "men of activity." "What can
the head do," he asked, "if the hands deliver not?" But he apparently did not dare reverse the order of the members and ask
an even more obvious question. As it was, the metaphor was
clearly inappropriate and Leighton did not develop it. Instead,
he began again: "You are the physicians of the state; up and do
your cure . . . it were happy for the king and us, if you knew
your power practically."[70]

Significantly enough, the only aspect of the organic image that
appealed to Puritan preachers was the idea of disease—they veiled
their demand for reformation in the metaphor of treatment and
cure.[71] This did not involve the full acceptance of the organic
analogy, for the magistrate-physician, upon whom Puritans placed
such great emphasis, was not a member of the body at all. And
the cure which Puritans urged was far more drastic than Calybute Downing's rest and quiet. Medical terminology provided one
of the key themes of the revolutionary period: "you are physicians
to the state," Francis Cheynell told the Commons in May of 1643,
"and these are purging times; let all malignant humors be purged

---

wars; he preached an important sermon, favoring rebellion, in 1640; see *DNB*.
Maynwaring, *Religion and Allegiance*, Sermon II, p. 9.

70 Alexander Leighton, *An Appeal to Parliament* (n.p., 1628), pp. 173-174, 208-209.
Cf. Sibbes, *Works*, VI, 89.

71 See examples cited in M. A. Judson, *The Crisis of the Constitution: An Essay
in Constitutional and Political Thought in England, 1603-1645* (New Brunswick,
N.J., 1949), pp. 343ff.

out of the ecclesiastical and political body."[72] But since the purpose of treatment could not be anything else than the restoration of some previous state of normality and health, even this form of the organic analogy did not ultimately suit the Puritan preachers. During the revolution the theme of treatment was gradually replaced by the theme of reconstruction. Several of the parliamentary preachers elaborated an historical analogy between the work of the M.P.'s and the rebuilding of the temple by the returning Babylonian exiles. The imagery of reconstruction obviously opened a much clearer path to fundamental reform than did that of treatment. "Take heed of building upon an old frame, that must be all plucked down to the ground," a minister told the Commons only five months after Cheynell had preached, "take heed of plastering when you should be pulling down."[73] Thus the revolution required not the curing of an old body, but the construction of a new building. Puritan purposes could not be served by the health and harmony of the ancient political organism.

III

According to the Christian Aristotelians, the purpose of politics was the good life; men naturally came together in society, Hooker wrote, seeking "a life fit for the dignity of man." Aquinas used the image of a ship of state to suggest that politics was teleological: "Now when something is ordered to an end which lies outside itself, as a ship is to harbor, it is the ruler's duty not only to preserve its integrity, but also to see that it reaches its appointed destination."[74] The organic analogy did not suggest the same teleology, but after the civil wars of the fifteenth century many men apparently came to feel that the integrity and health of the body politic was more important than any outside end. Life itself—the harmony of the organs, the balance of the humors, the

---

[72] Francis Cheynell, *Sion's Momento and God's Alarum* (London, 1643), p. 19. One of the best of the sermons demanding a "purge" is Samuel Faircloth, *The Troublers Troubled, or Achan Condemned and Executed* (London, 1641), especially pp. 22ff. On the magistrate-physician, see Robert Harris' address to the judges of Oxford: "You are called *healers;* would God you would go to the quick . . ." *Two Sermons* (London, 1628), p. 21.

[73] Henry Wilkinson, *Babylon's Ruin, Jerusalem's Rising* (London, 1643), p. 26; cf. Thomas Goodwin, *Zerubbabel's Encouragement to Finish the Temple* (London, 1642).

[74] Hooker, *Works*, I, 239; Aquinas, *Selected Writings*, p. 73.

conformity "of each degree . . . to its own duties"—became the only purpose of politics. The image of the ship of state did not reappear in Hooker, and, common as it had been in classical literature, was rarely invoked by the "elegant" Anglican preachers.[75]

For them, the individual Christian had an end outside the body politic and that end was heaven; but there was no haven for the ship of state, no harbor that was anything more than a peaceful anchorage. Indeed, the organic analogy suggested that the only end of political life was political death. The history of the state presented by most Renaissance writers, and developed in detail by Bodin and Le Roy in France, was the ancient cycle of rise and fall.[76] Although the evidence of the two French writers was chiefly historical, the idea of the state as a political body undoubtedly provided the formal structure of the cycle. And so long as this structure was accepted, it was difficult to suggest a completely voluntaristic politics. In effect, the skill of the ruler could only speed up or slow down the organic and inexorable time schedule of history.

But the politics of the Calvinist God was purely willful; he had his own purposes not connected with the organic cycle and the laws of nature were no bar to his arbitrary power. In 1642, Stephen Marshall explicitly rejected the cyclical idea. That nations "have their youth, their strength and after a time their declination . . ." he wrote, was not a "certain rule." History, instead, was in the hands of God: "whensoever the sins of any church, nation or city . . . are come to full measure, then God infallibly brings ruin upon them . . ."[77] The same notion was common among the Puritan preachers; God acted suddenly, either without warning or after sending prophets; he used the whip of a conquering nation, or he sent plague and flood, or he stirred up ambitious men to wage

---

75 For the classical use of the image, see Plato's *Republic* as cited by Sir John Eliot, *The Monarchy of Man*, ed. with intro. by A. B. Grosart (London, 1879), II, 22ff; and Horace, *Odes*, Book I, 14.

76 See Bodin, *The Method for the Easy Comprehension of History*, trans. by B. Reynolds (New York, 1945), pp. 235, 300; and discussion in E. L. Tuveson, *Millenium and Utopia: A Study in the Background of the Idea of Progress* (Berkeley, 1949), pp. 56ff.

77 Stephen Marshall, *Reformation and Desolation* (London, 1642), p. 29. Bodin also says that the precise duration of empire is fixed by God, but he does not believe that God violates the cyclical pattern, *Method*, p. 236.

civil war.[78] Looking upon political history, Puritans would hardly have agreed with Bodin that the activity of God was organic in its character, accomplishing all things slowly, one step at a time. "God causes a tall and spreading tree to spring from one small seed, but always by imperceptible degrees," wrote the French philosopher. "He unites extremes by their mean, putting spring between winter and summer, and autumn between summer and winter."[79] Puritan rhetoric was far less gentle than this; when the revolution came it was readily adapted to the announcement of God's "fearful shakings and desolation."

The imagery and similitudes of Puritan rhetoric suggested another view of history, a view more readily expressed in terms of the ship of state than through the organic analogy. Once again, the preachers tended to generalize and socialize the themes of their theology. The idea of the ship of state was closely related to the Puritan view of life as a voyage. That metaphor was perhaps best developed in a sermon of Thomas Adams entitled *The Spiritual Navigator Bound for the Holy Land,* published in 1615.[80] For Adams the world was a sea and man a traveler encountering sea-dangers; heaven was the promised land. The image was as old as Christianity, but the Puritans made it their own, elaborating details of the voyage and emphasizing far more the "progress" of the Christian pilgrim than his heavenly destination.

A few years after Adams delivered his sermon, the country preacher William Pemberton, speaking at the Hartford assizes, developed the same image politically. Magistrates, he said, are "masters and pilots in the ship of the commonwealth, who sit at the stern and guide it forward through their wisdom and fidelity . . . unto the desired haven of peace and prosperity . . ."[81] Judging from the text of his sermon, Pemberton was a very moderate Puritan; the political goal he suggested was not different from that implied by the organic analogy and his use of the ship

[78] See especially the enormous compilation of examples by Thomas Beard, *The Theater of God's Judgments,* 3 ed. rev. (London, 1631).

[79] Bodin, *Six Books,* p. 127.

[80] Thomas Adams, *The Spiritual Navigator Bound for the Holy Land* (London, 1615); see also Anthony Nixon, *The Christian Navy: Wherein is Plainly Described the Perfect Course to Sail to the Heaven of Eternal Happiness* (London, 1602).

[81] William Pemberton, *The Charge of God and the King* (London, 1619), p. 24.

image was unimaginative. But when Puritans actually began to sail, not toward "peace and prosperity," but rather toward "the place where the Lord will create a new heaven and a new earth, in new churches and a new commonwealth together," the metaphor rapidly took on a new meaning. The storms of politics became increasingly important, worth enduring and worth analyzing, once the sailors had set out for a new world. The image was entirely compatible (as the organic analogy was not) with the notions of reform, movement, and progress.

The power of the ship of state image can best be seen in the excited sermon which Stephen Marshall preached to the Commons in June of 1643: "the glory of Christ, the establishment of this church and kingdom, yea, the welfare of all Christendom," he cried, ". . . are all embarked in that vessel the steering whereof is in great part committed unto you." The pilgrim had become an enthusiast and the preacher a revolutionary. As the ship of state moved away from the shores of the old world, neither of these figures had any time for regret. "The welfare and good success of religion," Marshall went on, "in which cause you are properly engaged . . . I hope is dearer to you than ten thousand Englands."[82]

IV

The ship of state appeared frequently in Puritan sermons of the 1640's and in those years of war against the king it played a significant role in intellectual history. For if the body could not make war upon its head, the mariners of a ship could certainly depose a captain drunk or mad. That might be mutiny, but it was justifiable mutiny and conceivably the very opposite of suicide. So the image of the ship of state was used to justify the English Revolution. When Anglican pamphleteers invoked the organic analogy, Puritans replied in two ways. First, they denied the validity of the analogy: "The natural body can do nothing but by the guidance of the head," wrote Herbert Palmer on behalf of "divers reverend and learned divines." "But a body politic is a company of reasonable men, whose action may be divided from their politic head, and yet be rational and regular." "The head natural is not made a head," Rutherford pointed out, "by the

82 Marshall, The Song of Moses . . . and the Song of the Lamb (London, 1643), p. 37.

free election and consent of arms, shoulders, legs, toes, fingers, etc." Hence these members cannot resist their head, "but the members of a politic body may resist the politic head."[83]

The second Puritan reply ignored the organic image altogether and developed instead the idea of ship and captain. William Prynne did this as early as 1642 and John Goodwin repeated his argument in 1649, defending the purge of Parliament and the trial of the king.

> When the pilot or master of a ship at sea, be either so far overcome and distempered with drink, or otherwise disabled . . . so that he is incapable of acting the exigencies of his place, for the preservation of the ship, being now in present danger . . . any one or more of the inferior mariners, having skill, may, in order to the saving of the ship and of the lives of all that are in it, very lawfully assume, and act according to the interests of a pilot . . .[84]

This was a defense of revolution in terms of secular necessity alone—although the notion of the "inferior mariner" had its Calvinist antecedents. There was necessarily a third, less direct, Puritan reply to the Anglican attack: this was simply to insist that the saints acted at the command of God, that they were his instruments, even that revolution was their political calling. This position will be discussed below. But given the significant qualification that God's command bound all men to obedience, the analogy of the ship involved a long step toward a free-wheeling politics.

The ship of state still implied a close political unity and a mutual concern: "For in reason we see, the safety of every man's cabin in a ship, consists in the safety of the ship . . . if the ship sinks, what will become of his cabin?"[85] But the image also suggested that the members of the crew had "signed on" (for they had surely not been born sailors) and it suggested too that the ship of state had had its shipyard and its time of construction. It had even had, perhaps, its craftsmen. The idea of building and especially of building upon "new foundations" was very old in

---

[83] Palmer, *Scripture and Reason Pleaded*, p. 14; Samuel Rutherford, *Lex Rex, or The Law and the Prince* (London, 1644; repr. Edinburgh, 1843), p. 71.

[84] John Goodwin (citing William Prynne), *Right and Might Well-Met* (London, 1648), pp. 9-10.

[85] David Cawdry, *The Good Man a Public Good* (London, 1643), p. 38; note that Cawdry is arguing against "neutrality" in the civil wars.

Puritan thought. It obviously was antithetical to the Aristotelian notion of the state as the natural product of human sociability (the idea of the magistrate as a craftsman was Platonic). It was related instead, however distantly, to the Renaissance sense of political artfulness and calculation. Aquinas, who occasionally used the image of the ship in attacking the magical doctrine that the commonwealth was a real body, denied, at the same time, that the construction of the state could be compared "to the mechanical art of the smith and the shipwright." Rather it belonged to the "moral sciences."[86] For the sixteenth-century Puritan Thomas Cartwright, however, God had solved all the moral problems and had left men nothing more to do than to follow blueprints. Nothing that might pertain to the "building of the church" or to "the form and fashion of it" had been left out of God's Word. And "as the hangings are made fit for the house," Cartwright argued, "so the commonwealth must be made to agree with the church . . . as it [is] the foundation of the world, it is meet that the commonwealth, which is builded upon that foundation, should be framed according to the church."[87] Precisely the same idea was proclaimed by John Owen during the revolution, some seventy years later. The civil constitutions of all nations, he insisted, were not yet in order for the bringing in of Christ. They would have to be "shaken, broken . . . and turned off their old foundation." Only then could the new church and commonwealth be constructed, with a truly Christian "frame."[88]

Puritans could hardly develop the secular implications of this kind of political thinking. It represented a sharp break with the organic analogy and with the idea of functional integration and harmony. It suggested that there were goals quite apart from the preservation and health of the body politic, goals that made men into instruments and changed politics itself from a self-sufficient organic existence into a means, a method, and a purposive discipline. For the Puritans these goals would be fixed by God, just as the terms of the contract to which they consented had been

86 Aquinas, *Selected Writings*, p. 197.
87 Thomas Cartwright, *A Reply to an Answer* (1573), in Whitgift, *Works*, III, 189.
88 John Owen, *The Advantages of the Kingdom of Christ in the Shaking of the Kingdom of the World* (London, 1651), p. 9; and *The Shaking and Translating of Heaven and Earth* (London, 1649), in *Works*, ed. W. H. Goold (Edinburgh, 1862), VIII, 256-257.

drafted in heaven. So the member of the body politic, like the
link in the great chain, when he became a saint, was freed from
his old connections and yet not set free.

POLITICS AND THE FAMILY

There was a third traditional way of establishing political life
within the natural world: this was to study the commonwealth
as a family and the king as a father.[89] For Aristotle and again for
Aquinas and Suarez, there was, of course, a qualitative difference
between the family and political society. The family, wrote
Suarez, was the most immediate product of human nature; it was,
however, "imperfect from a political standpoint" because it could
never achieve self-sufficiency. But the historical progression from
family to *civitas* which the Spanish Jesuit went on to describe
demonstrated the naturalness of both: sociability led men alike
to the "fellowship" of husband and wife and to the political
commonwealth. Suarez suggested, too, that analogical reasoning
from one to the other was perfectly proper. The basis of the
analogy was the idea that in the development of the political
world certain key elements of familial life had not been lost. It
was thought possible, for example, to rediscover the natural authority and the affectionate concern of the father in political
form. Something of both, in fact, was read into kingship and then
the subject was made to share the sweet incapacity and trustful-
ness of the child.[90] Familial imagery intensified political bonds
and suggested the mystical cult of the political father.

All this could be carried considerably further than the Christian Aristotelians would have thought appropriate. For while
they might have tempered their rational view of politics by urging
paternal benevolence upon the king, they had little taste for
mystery. Indeed, the familial analogy was one of the means by
which the Thomist attack upon political magic was blunted and
turned away from its goal, which was a secular and naturalistic
(if still pious and exalted) view of the state. The denial of any
sacramental value in the annointing of a king, for example, successfully pressed by papalist theoreticians, would prove a very in-

---

[89] See Peter Laslett's introduction to Robert Filmer, *Patriarcha and Other
Political Works* (Oxford, 1949).
[90] Suarez, *Selections from Three Works*, II, 364-366, 371, 378.

complete triumph if the king could still be annointed intellectually, as it were, with a mystical fatherhood. For then the king's
subjects would still stand in awe of his person and not merely of
his office. The relationship between political father and political
children would plausibly be described in terms of love alone and
by no means as a rational and necessary form of subordination.
And law-making would be a matter of paternal concern and not
of the searching out of the natural law. For these reasons, perhaps,
the imagery of family and patriarchy was not common in either
Aquinas' or Hooker's work. In discussing political order and
subordination the "judicious" Anglican preferred cosmological
to familial reference—most likely because the cosmos did not
require the same emotional ties as did the family.[91]

But among more popular Anglican writers the family was a
common "pattern" for political life. Preachers and publicists suggested quite clearly that political bonds were natural, if not actually physical. They paid tribute to the king as the husband of
the kingdom and the father of its members and they clearly implied that his benevolence was to be relied upon and never
doubted.[92] The contrast between this reliance and mere political
subjection was presented in typical fashion by the Elizabethan
writer Geoffrey Fenton: political society, he wrote,

is . . . as a general family or household wherein good governors do
put on the same careful affection to the advancement of their subjects, which wise and dear fathers use to their entirely beloved children . . . Let then wisdom, love and zeal of magistrates . . . surmount
their authority in commanding . . . And let humility, frank obedience
and perfect love be greater in the subjects than their civil subjection.[93]

Mutual love would thus transform both authority and subjection.
Sovereign will became paternal wisdom and obedience became
humility, when political society was seen as a true family.

In the late sixteenth and early seventeenth centuries, however,
there was developed a very different view of the family that cor-

91 See Aquinas' reluctant admission that there is a "certain similarity" between
kings and fathers, *Selected Political Writings*, p. 9. Hooker calls the king only a
"brother . . . unto whom all the rest of the brethren are subject." *Book VIII*, p. 283.
92 See Babington, *Works* (third numbering), p. 291; William Goodwin, *A Sermon
Preached before the King's Most Excellent Majesty* (Oxford, 1614), pp. 22-24;
Rawlinson, *Vivat Rex*, pp. 10-13; Maynwaring, *Religion and Allegiance*, I, 2-3; II,
24-25; Hurste, *Descent of Authority*, p. 24.
93 Geoffrey Fenton, *A Form of Christian Policy* . . . (London, 1574), p. 13.

responded to a very different view of the state. Originally, this was the work of Bodin, who reacted in practical fashion to the same political disorder that was so much a part of the Calvinist world view. Bodin revived the old Roman notion of the *pater familias*—an idea in which love and concern were entirely replaced by legal sovereignty. Rather than seek a father in the state, the French *politique* sought a sovereign in the family. While still recognizing the differences that generation and love might make, Bodin insisted that Aristotle had been wrong to divide "economy" from "politics." Instead, "the well-ordered family is a true image of the commonwealth, and domestic comparable with sovereign authority." The logic of this identification forced Bodin to give the father the same power of life and death that the king possessed. And he refused to the child, as to the subject, any right "to defend himself and resist [an] unjust attempt at coercion."[94]

Bodin's view represented a new departure, but it was integrated readily enough with the popular forms that the old analogy had taken; these had always tended toward a simple identification of king and father, turning political society into a vast patriarchy: "he is the father of the families, upon whom the whole household depends." In England this integration was definitely achieved by Robert Filmer, whose *Patriarcha* was the last systematic exploration of the familial conception of the state, much as Forset's *Comparative Discourse* was the last significant development of the organic analogy.

The tendency of Bodin's writing was to politicize the family in the interests of an absolutist state. This same tendency appeared in Calvinist thinkers whose interest in God's sovereignty paralleled the new secular concern with political power. Their conception of the family as a political rather than a natural or sacramental community culminated eventually in civil marriage among Protestants and in the radical views of Milton on divorce. It led also to Hobbes' insistence that the family was ultimately founded upon conquest and to the characteristically different

---

[94] Bodin, *Six Books*, pp. 6-11. The idea that fathers should have power of life and death over their children was endorsed by the Anglican convocation of 1606— the same year that Knolles' translation of Bodin appeared. See *Bishop Overall's Convocation Book, 1606* (1690, repr. Oxford, 1844), pp. 22-23.

view of Puffendorf, that it was founded upon consent.[95] But Filmer, while adopting the Bodinian notion of sovereign power, returned to the older view of political society as an enormous family and did not imitate the significant reversal of this analogy that was being discussed in the work of his contemporaries. He thus made the family into a justification for royal absolutism without really altering the traditional nature of familial ties: "If we compare the natural duties of a father with those of a king, we find them to be all one, without any difference at all but only in the latitude or extent of them . . . all the duties of a king are summed up in the universal fatherly care of his people." And the Anglican preachers similarly compounded new sovereignty with old paternity; they stretched fatherhood to an overbearing absolutism, but did not cease to urge the necessity of mutual love between subject and king.[96]

II

Familial imagery appeared frequently in Puritan sermons and treatises, but the notion of political fatherhood was never developed so vividly or so naturalistically as in Anglican literature. Puritan ministers continued to believe, as Christians had believed for centuries, that the fifth commandment was an injunction to political obedience. The Denham preacher, Robert Pricke, produced a treatise of great length expounding *The Doctrine of Superiority and Subjection Contained in the Fifth Commandment.* But Puritans were unlikely to revere a purely natural relationship and it was the divine commandment rather than its familial content that they respected. Hence Pricke dealt with the *duties* and *office* rather than the love of political fathers.[97] And

95 Hobbes, *Leviathan*, II, xx; but note that for Hobbes the family can also be founded on a contract. Puffendorf, *On The Law of Nature and Nations*, trans. by C. H. and W. A. Oldfather (Oxford, 1934), pp. 914-915; see p. 911f. for discussion of Hobbes' views.

96 Filmer, *Patriarcha*, p. 63; *cf.* Rawlinson, *Vivat Rex* p. 13 and King James himself, *The Political Works of James I*, ed. C. H. McIlwain (Cambridge, Mass., 1918), p. 61. This was the view of kingship that the future Earl of Strafford expressed in his first speech as president of the Council of the North: "Princes are to be the indulgent nursing fathers to their people . . . Verily these are those mutual intelligences of love and protection descending and loyalty ascending, which should pass . . . between the king and his people." Quoted in C. V. Wedgwood, *Strafford* (London, 1935), pp. 74-75.

97 Robert Pricke, *The Doctrine of Superiority and Subjection* (London, 1609), esp. sig. C_8-D_1.

his colleagues among the brethren insisted that even paternal authority must be tested by the Word of God. Indeed, the Puritan critique of custom often led the ministers to question radically the authority of fathers: if men had "earnest minds," wrote John Stockwood, "they would not be blinded with those vain shadows of fathers, times and customs, but would measure the truth of religion by the square of the Word."[98] The traditional arguments that Stockwood was attacking—"our fathers, our rulers, our ancients . . . thus they think, thus they do"—rested on a system of historical connection, which was summed up in paternity and generation. Ideals and values were inherited—found, that is, and not agreed to. Such a system was not acceptable to Puritan scruples; writing in the 1640's, Herbert Palmer effectively turned it upside down: "as for inheritance," he wrote, "it is nothing but a succession of consents."[99] The natural connection was thus made subject to human will, as it was already subject to God's Word.

Puritans similarly disapproved of any reliance upon that other form of connection, which was not backward in time, but outward, so to speak, in space and which was summed up in local loyalty, kinship, familial alliance, and marriage.[100] "Vicinity and neighborhood will fail," wrote the preachers Dod and Cleaver, "and alliance and kindred will fail but grace and religion will never fail. If we adjoin ourselves unto [godly men] for their virtue and goodness, they will not separate themselves from us for calamities and trouble."[101] The critique of local and familial connection thus suggested the new forms of association with which the ministers were already experimenting. But it also involved a transformation of the family: a free alliance "for virtue and goodness" was exactly what Milton thought marriage was.

Men who shared the Calvinist distrust of nature, however inarticulately, were not likely to defend kingship by referring to the

[98] John Stockwood, *A Sermon Preached at Paul's Cross* (London, 1578), 55-56.

[99] Palmer, *Scripture and Reason Pleaded*, pp. 38-39.

[100] For the importance of local connection in the seventeenth century, see R. H. Tawney, "Introduction," in D. Brunton and D. H. Pennington, *Members of the Long Parliament* (London, 1954), p. xvii; also J. H. Hexter, *The Reign of King Pym* (Cambridge, Massachusetts, 1941), pp. 75-88.

[101] Robert Cleaver and John Dod, *A Plain and Familiar Exposition of the Thirteenth and Fourteenth Chapters of the Proverbs of Solomon* (London, 1609), p. 119; quoted in Christopher Hill, *Economic Problems of the Church: From Archbishop Whitgift to the Long Parliament* (Oxford, 1956), p. 23.

natural monarchy of the father. Instead, the tendency of Puritan thought was to turn fatherhood into a political sovereignty and the family into a "little commonwealth." The brethren produced a fairly large literature on family life, but they rarely discussed the traditional themes of alliance and misalliance and they dealt curtly with the degrees of natural affinity that made marriage impermissible.[102] In their treatises, neither nature nor love played much of a part. Their concern was almost entirely with the "government" of the household; they wrote prolix chapters with such titles as "How women ought to be governed," and "How children owe obedience and honor to their parents." Like the state, the family was viewed as a divine institution, established at God's preemptory command, which men entered by contract. The contract produced a society "by the good government whereof, God's glory may be advanced."[103]

The family, as it appeared in seventeenth-century social thought, was actually an establishment of considerable size, including a wide range of kin and a large number of servants, apprentices, and even hired workers. This establishment was probably the most significant corporate body in traditional English society; indeed until the industrial revolution it determined the most crucial loyalties of ordinary Englishmen.[104] Nevertheless, Puritan domestic literature represents the beginning of a movement away from this extension of familial ties and from the forms of authority that it imposed. Puritanism heralds the shift, which takes place in the next two hundred years, from the patriarchal to the conjugal family, that is, to the family centered on the married couple. This transformation in the nature of family connection parallels and supports the rise of secular political sovereignty. At the same time, it is secular authority that frees individuals from the bonds of the corporate family and enables them to enter voluntarily into the marriage contract. First in Calvinist Holland, next in Cromwell's England, this contract was made a matter of public

102 See C. L. Powell, *English Domestic Relations, 1487-1653* (New York, 1917), p. 123.

103 Robert Cleaver and John Dod, *A Godly Form of Household Government*, (London, 1621), sig. A₇.

104 Peter Laslett, "The World We Have Lost," *The Listener*, April 7, 1960, pp. 607-609.

record and secular regulation.[105] The conjugal family, formed by a civil agreement and shaped at least in part by the Puritan concept of household government thus became, in effect, the local unit of the sovereign state. It was as a member of this family— obedient child or stern husband and father—that modern man was integrated into the new political order. The child of the patriarchal family, bound within the old kinship system, committed in advance to the family allies and followers, was not so susceptible to political control: a loyal son, he was less likely to become a good citizen.

Puritan writers tended to restrict the size of the household, largely because of their intense dislike for the undisciplined semifeudal entourage. Thus Dod and Cleaver, in the key Puritan text on family government, denounced the "companies of idle serving-men" maintained by the great families—such men were not subject to religious (or political) control. They might win trust and affection from the family patriarch; they deserved only his suspicion. "Except you have rare servants, such as truly fear God . . . trust them not further than you see them except necessity drive you."[106] This Puritan view needs to be contrasted with the more traditional outlook which was forcefully expressed by the Jacobean moralist and playwright Thomas Dekker: "Remember, O you rich men, that your servants are your adopted children; they are naturalized into your blood, and if you hurt theirs, you are guilty of letting out your own . . ."[107] Puritan uneasiness with the traditional notions of connection, loyalty, and service militated against this kind of naturalization just as it did against the naturalization of laws and customs into the "disposition" of the body politic. Puritans kept servants, of course, and presumably worked them hard so as to save them from the sin of idleness; but it is worth noting that Dod and Cleaver thought it better if husband and wife saved themselves by doing much of their own work. The good Puritan draper, William Scott, added that it was better for business as well as for the soul: "let him that

[105] See G. E. Howard, *A History of Matrimonial Institutions* (Chicago, 1904), I, 404ff.

[106] Dod and Cleaver, *Household Government*, sig. B₇.

[107] Dekker, *The Seven Deadly Sins of London* (first published in 1606); quoted in L. C. Knights, *Drama and Society in the Age of Jonson* (London, 1937), p. 230.

takes the profit, take the pains . . . that man may blush for shame, who puts off his business to servants doing nothing himself, but by thoughts and verbal directions."[108]

III

The dangers of idleness and disorder required that all the members of the household be under the vigilant eye of its "governor" —much as they also required that all the members of the commonwealth be subjected to the political sovereign. And Puritan fearfulness determined the nature of the governor's authority as of the sovereign's. In a passage that was only a logical development of the Calvinist doctrine of the Fall, Dod and Cleaver argued the need for a virtually absolute power:

> The young child which lieth in the cradle is both wayward and full of affections; and though his body be but small, yet he hath a great heart, and is altogether inclined to evil . . . If this sparkle be suffered to increase, it will rage over and burn down the whole house. For we are changed and become good not by birth but by education . . . Therefore parents must be wary and circumspect . . . they must correct and sharply reprove their children for saying or doing ill . . .[109]

The father was prince and schoolmaster, minister and judge in his house, but none of these were functions of his affection so much as they were duties of his office. Natural feelings played little part; they were indeed to be consciously repressed so that evil children not be spoiled by affection. The need for government was overriding and Puritans did not distinguish to any significant degree between fathers and legal guardians or, for that matter, between children and servants: "children while they be under government . . . differ nothing from servants." Household government had been instituted by God and could not therefore be a purely personal or a purely emotional matter. "A conscionable performance of household duties," wrote William Gouge, "may be accounted a public work."[110] Like the magistrate, the father commanded an unruly multitude; natural wisdom would not suffice for his task; he would require both "civil" and "godly"

108 William Scott, *Essay of Drapery* (London, 1635), p. 104; Dod and Cleaver, *Household Government*, sig. F$_8$.
109 Dod and Cleaver, *Household Government*, sig. S$_8$ and S$_8$ verso.
110 William Gouge, *Of Domestical Duties* (London, 1622), pp. 18, 442.

understanding. Fatherhood was thus a political office and also a calling and in that office and calling a man possessed something very near to sovereignty. "The man must be taken for God's immediate officer in the house, and as it were the king in his family . . ." And this kingship, wrote William Perkins (who probably did not know Bodin's work), meant that "the father hath authority to dispose of his child . . ."[111]

Familial sovereignty must not, of course, interfere with the power of the actual political sovereign. It was not akin to the lordship of feudal times, when a baron or earl played the king on his own lands. The father of the Puritan family was not a lord over vast territory; he was instead a magistrate who ruled over men and he ruled less in the interests of his family—so the theory went—than as an instrument of God and the prince. He raised his sons to be saints and citizens. Here Puritanism paralleled the older humanism, for Renaissance thought had also tended toward the idea of a "civil education."[112] The broader meaning of such a training was probably obscured by both the secular theorists of absolutism and the Calvinists, the chief interest of both being obedience; but their aim was similarly "civic." Bodin insisted upon granting the power of life and death to fathers because "children who stand in little awe of their parents . . . readily set at defiance the power of magistrates."[113] Puritan writers viewed the family as a training ground for religious discipline and also for political obedience. The two, in fact, went together: "a family is a little church and a little commonwealth," wrote Gouge, ". . . whereby trial may be had of such as are fit for any place of authority . . . Or rather it is a school wherein the first principles and grounds of government and subjection are learned . . ."[114] The idea of the family as a school, like that of the state as a ship, reveals once again the overbearing Puritan sense of purpose, directed toward ends beyond or, at any rate, not identical with, the needs and feelings of ordinary men.

The stern paternal commitment to these divine purposes was

111 William Whately, *A Bride-Bush, or A Direction for Married Persons* (London, 1619), p. 89; Perkins, *Works*, II, 269; see also Gouge, *Domestical Duties*, p. 263.

112 See J. H. Hexter, "The Education of the Aristocracy in the Renaissance," in *Reappraisals in History* (New York, 1963), pp. 45-70.

113 Bodin, *Six Books*, p. 13.

114 Gouge, *Domestical Duties*, pp. 17-18.

softened somewhat by maternal solicitude—though mothers, too, were required to discipline their children: "The gentle rod of the mother is a very gentle thing, it will break neither bone nor skin: yet by the blessing of God with it . . . it would break the bond that bindeth up corruption in the heart."[115] Puritan literature suggests a certain sentimentalizing of the role of the woman both as wife and mother. One example, perhaps, is the insistence that women nurse their children.[116] The probable effect of the new view, as of the emphasis on paternal sovereignty, was to bind the basic family unit more closely together. These are, of course, things which it is not possible to measure; moreover, Puritans were extraordinarily reticent and cautious even on the subject of maternal love. It was necessary to keep a "due distance," warned one of the ministers, between parents and children; "fondness and familiarity breeds . . . irreverence . . ."[117]

But fondness and maternal solicitude, in another sense, were aspects of repression, softening its impact, perhaps, but deepening its effects. The connection between the two is best suggested by a series of letters written by the Puritan Lady Brilliana Harley to her son at Oxford between 1638 and 1643. Lady Harley is endlessly apprehensive about the health of her son; she urges medicinal syrups upon him, hopes that he will exercise diligently (but not tire himself), wishes helplessly that he would avoid London: "my thoughts are much with you; be careful to improve your time. London is a bewitching place." Throughout the letters, her one ambition is that Ned be a "good boy"—and that is the occasion for all her solicitude. "My dear Ned, keep your heart above the world." "Tie yourself to a daily self-examination; think over the company you have been in." "Be careful to keep the Sabbath." All this was discipline and preparation, as this intelligent mother well knew; it directly paralleled the schoolmasterish role of the Puritan father. And in it one can even detect, sadly, the same suspicion. It was a more "gentle rod" but it served the same purpose: the "good boy" would grow up to be a good citi-

115 John Eliot, *The Harmony of the Gospels* (1678), quoted in E. S. Morgan, *The Puritan Family* (Boston, 1944), p. 57.

116 Dod and Cleaver, *Household Government*, sig. P₃ verso.

117 Thomas Cobbett, *A Fruitful and Useful Discourse Touching the Honor due from Children to Parents and the Duty of Parents towards their Children* (London, 1656), p. 96.

zen. "I pray God bless you," wrote Lady Harley, shortly before her son entered the Parliamentary army, "that you may be very able to do your country service."[118]

IV

A woman who thus directed her son might also direct her husband. Puritan writers insisted upon the inferiority of the female, but nevertheless recognized in her the potential saint: "Souls have no sexes," wrote Robert Bolton. "In the better part they are both men."[119] Marriage between two saints would be a "spiritual union" and not, in Milton's terms, "the prescribed satisfaction of an irrational heat."[120] The new Puritan view of the woman, then, entailed a new view of marriage. Founded on a voluntary contract, it was directed in some fashion toward "healthful pleasures and profitable commodities."[121] This was to make the choice of a partner far more important than it had ever been before—and a bad choice, as Milton was to learn, far more disastrous.

Puritan writers continued to stress, but at the same time subtly to undermine, the authority of parents in determining this choice.[122] Increasingly, marriage was presented as a voluntary agreement between two individuals, each, as it were, appraising the other's potential godliness. The agreement was a "civil contract" and a "public action." It was no longer a sacrament; the civil ceremony replaced the religious mystery. Emphasis upon the secular, contractual bond tended to move the two individuals most involved outside the range of extended familial connection. The new, primarily legal relationships among the members of a family did not generate the same sense of permanence and stability as had the sacramental tie and the system of patriarchal con-

---

[118] *Letters of the Lady Brilliana Harley*, intro. by T. T. Lewis (London, 1854), pp. 8, 69, 101, 178, 180.

[119] Robert Bolton, *The Works* (London, 1631-1641), IV, 245-246.

[120] Milton, *Works*, ed. F. A. Patterson, et al. (New York, 1932), III, part II, 394.

[121] Dod and Cleaver, *Household Government*, sig. K$_{5-7}$.

[122] See Lawrence Stone, "Marriage among the English Nobility in the Sixteenth and Seventeenth Centuries," in *Comparative Studies in Society and History* 3:182-206 (1961). Stone argues that Puritanism was in part responsible for the increasing freedom of children. At the same time, he stresses the "bitter family struggles" which accompanied the change (pp. 183-187). In general, Puritan writers tended to grant parents considerable authority, but to reserve at least a veto for children; see, for example, Thomas Gataker, *A Good Wife God's Gift* (London, 1637), p. 138.

nection. There were obvious differences between an alliance of families and a marriage of individuals and the chief among these was the sharp decline in kinship obligations in the second case. All this made it possible, indeed, necessary, to discuss marriage in terms of original and eventually of continuing consent. Contracts must be voluntary—and voluntary marriage shortly enough produced the romance of married love. "There must and ought to be a knitting of hearts before a striking of hands."[123] Love would reinforce the legal tie between husband and wife, but it need be extended no further.

All this obviously called into question the political sovereignty of the father. The preachers thus suggested one of major themes of the middle-class novelists, who are in a way their successors. Pamela and Clarissa, as yet unknown, were the true subjects of the tedious treatises on family government. The plight of true love was already described in the seventeenth century by the Puritan poet George Wither:

> Can there be any friend that hath the power
> To disunite hearts so conjoined as ours?
> Ere I would so have done by thee, I'ld rather
> Have parted with one dearer than my father.

So sang the heroine of Wither's *Fidelia*. Her feelings undoubtedly made the old forms of familial diplomacy increasingly difficult; willful children had not had to be reckoned with before. Or, their willfulness had never before been so reinforced by piety.

> For though the will of our Creator binds
> Each child to learn and know his parents' minds,
> Yet sure am I so just a deity
> Commandeth nothing against piety . . .
> And though that parents have authority
> To rule their children in minority,
> Yet they are never granted such power on them
> That will allow to tyrannize upon them . . .[124]

The critique of the patriarchal conception of family unity thus

---

123 Dod and Cleaver, *Household Government*, sig. V₅ verso. On romantic love as the "ideology" of the conjugal family, see Talcott Parsons, *Essays in Sociological Theory Pure and Applied* (Glencoe, Ill., 1949), p. 241.

124 *The Poetry of George Withers*, ed. Frank Sedgwick (London, 1902), I, 121; the poem is discussed in H. J. C. Grierson, *Cross-Currents in Seventeenth Century English Literature* (New York, 1958), pp. 150-151.

made the romance of individuals possible. And for the moment, the dangers which romance posed for Puritan family discipline were hidden from the ministers by their idealized conception of love. "Fond he or she may be that pray not among themselves," wrote one preacher, "but loving they cannot be."[125]

The same religious idealization was at work in Puritan descriptions of master-servant relations. The suggestion of well-meaning preachers that servants choose godly masters and withdraw from ungodly homes opened another field for minor social conflict, similar to that already opened by the pious willfulness of children. Puritan discussion of these problems must have seemed a little whimsical in the seventeenth century; most servants probably had little choice as to their masters. Still, if the household was to be a "little commonwealth" and a "little church," its members would necessarily possess those same rights of emigration and separation that many Puritans already claimed in the larger society. So Dod and Cleaver suggested that servants ought "to be very wary and careful that they do not place themselves with any such . . . as are profane and wicked."[126] And masters too, if they were Puritan, were to be on guard against profane and wicked servants. It is difficult to imagine lord and man thus exchanging pious references. The search, the wary investigation, the decision: all this is quite new. Milton, with his heavy moral seriousness, might well have turned courtship into a similar procedure.

Among Catholics, marriage, celebrated as a sacrament, was an indissoluble bond. Physical union was mystically compared to the union of Christ and his church. Protestants generally, denying the sacrament, urged the possibility of divorce at least for adultery and desertion. These two broke the natural bond and effectively ended the union. The real test of the Puritan view of the family as a society and a "little commonwealth," however, was divorce for incompatibility—for that broke only the social bond. On this delicate point, most of the brethren took a conservative position: their intense fear of disorder persuaded them

125 Whately, *A Bride-Bush*, p. 51.
126 Dod and Cleaver, *Household Government*, sig. Aa₇ verso. See also the advice of the Puritan minister Nicholas Byfield to a young man apprenticed in London: that he might refuse to run errands for his master on the Sabbath; the boy's uncle disagreed. The case is cited in Louis Wright, *Middle-Class Culture in Elizabethan England* (Ithaca, New York, 1935), p. 267n.

that the social connection must be permanent even if it was unpleasant. "If they might be separated for discord," wrote Henry
Smith, "some would make a commodity of strife; but now they
are not best to be contentious, for the law will hold their noses
together 'til weariness make them leave struggling . . ."[127] But the
position at which Milton finally arrived was anticipated in the
late sixteenth century by William Perkins. The great Puritan
casuist argued that divorce was possible for "malicious dealing"—
that is, if "when dwelling together, they require each of other,
intolerable conditions."[128] This did not, by any means, permit
divorce wherever there was lack of love, but it was a step in that
direction. A few Protestant writers cautiously suggested that
divorce might also be possible if religious differences arose between husband and wife: this presumably broke the spiritual bond.
The godly member of the married pair must strive for his companion's salvation, but he need not strive indefinitely.[129]

   In effect, such views turned the family into a voluntary association, though Perkins still clung to an Aristotelian definition of
this "first society in nature" and, to compound the confusion,
insisted upon the ordinance of God as the only source of the
father's authority. But contract and divorce made the family free
and did so—at least in theory—some fifty years before the theoretical reorganization of the state reached a similar point. It would be
much longer than that, however, before the theory was worked
out in practice.

v

   The Puritan transformation of the family remained incomplete:
so long as children were born, instead of appearing voluntarily
like colonists in a new country, the family could not become a
purely political society. The connection of parents and children,
at least, was a natural connection and even Milton, the great
theorist of legal divorce, treated nature awkwardly. But if the
Puritans thus failed to transform the family into a little common-

<hr />

127 Quoted in Powell, *Domestic Relations*, p. 75.

128 Perkins, *Works*, III, 688. Note also Perkins' insistence that divorce can be
required by the man *or* woman "because they are equally bound each to other . . . ,"
p. 690.

129 Milton took this position, but carefully noted the disagreement of Theodore
Beza, *Works*, III, part II.

wealth founded entirely on command and consent, they also made it impossible to imagine the state as an old-fashioned family founded on nature and love. When the revolution came and royalist pamphleteers urged the mystical fatherhood of the king, Puritans replied with an abrupt denial: "A father is a father by generation . . . and is a natural head and root without the free consent and suffrages of his children," wrote Samuel Rutherford, ". . . but a prince is a prince by the free suffrages of a community."[130] Herbert Palmer went further, arguing from freedom in marriage to freedom in politics: "Marriage is God's institution; . . . yet are not all of mankind bound to marry, but for their own good and comfort . . . So it is with power or government political."[131] There could not be a more complete reversal of the terms of Filmer's argument. Men are born free, thought Palmer, not subject to political fathers and not even bound to establish governments.

But Palmer, in 1643, had moved considerably beyond the scope of the Puritan family literature. The older ministers always insisted upon the enormous significance of family ties; they sought only to refashion them somewhat, to establish their new discipline in the home itself. They urged every man to marry so that no one would live outside the range of household government. Wandering beggars, wrote William Perkins, were "an unfaithful and ungracious generation." As they wander "the curse of God pursueth them . . . for they range not themselves into any families . . ."[132] The stress of the Puritan literature on household government was on religious duty and, once again, on political order. The "mutual duties of husband and wife," the "duties of parents toward their children"—these were the themes of the ministers. Love itself could hardly have lightened the ponderous moral tone of Puritan family relationships.

Yet there was one man whom Puritans would have freed from necessary membership in a family and he was, in fact, a wanderer. This was the saint-in-exile, the gospel-seeker who broke all the old ties and left father and fatherland behind. Such a figure ap-

130 Rutherford, *Lex Rex*, p. 63. See also Milton, *Works*, VII, 45, 279, on the metaphor of fatherhood, better left "to the muses."
131 Palmer, *Scripture and Reason Pleaded*, pp. 30-31.
132 Perkins, *Works*, III, 71, 191.

peared in Puritan writings, as he had in the work of Calvin and Beza, as a "stranger and pilgrim"—never at home on earth, traveling toward his heavenly country. He is Christian, the hero of Bunyan's epic, who follows after the shining light: "his wife and children . . . cry after him to return; but he put his fingers in his ears, and ran on, crying, Life! Life! eternal life!"[133]

But if Calvinists described this "stranger" with considerable emphasis and literary skill, they were extraordinarily uneasy with him in practice. His only home might be in heaven; he might be free indeed from the old bonds: this was nothing more than the immediate result of the Puritan critique of hierarchy, organism, and the extended family. But freedom, it must be said again, was not the Puritan purpose and the "unsettled" saint was not the Puritan hero. He represented, so to speak, only the starting point of godly activity—just as Hobbes' "masterless man" represented the starting point of late sixteenth- and early seventeenth-century social legislation. Religious discipline, household government, the holy commonwealth: all these were presented as substitutes for the traditional forms of order and relationship. The stranger and the pilgrim were once again to be bound up and compelled as saint and citizen to glorify God.

The forms of traditional society had all existed, or been thought to exist, by nature. The Puritan substitutes, on the other hand, had all to be created. Calvinist cosmology and sociology thus committed the ministers and their lay followers to the hard and often dangerous work of political invention. Their own experience drove them, as will be seen, to the same work.

133 John Bunyan, *Pilgrim's Progress*, ed. J. B. Wharey (Oxford, 1928), p. 11.

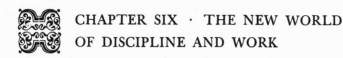 CHAPTER SIX · THE NEW WORLD
OF DISCIPLINE AND WORK

At the time of the Puritan attack, the traditional political ideas of hierarchy, organism, and patriarchy did not accurately describe English government or society. A long process of social and economic change—in which Puritanism itself played a part—slowly made the old ideas and symbols irrelevant. The civil wars of the period of "bastard feudalism," the development of Tudor absolutism, the destruction of the Catholic Church, the gradual but continuous progress of enclosure, the rapid economic growth of the later sixteenth century, the revolution of the seventeenth—these were so many stages in the transformation of traditional feudal society into a modern social order. In the course of this transformation, men faced dramatic new problems, symptoms of the collapse of old beliefs and the dissolution of old bonds. These can be summed up most sharply in the appearance of the "masterless man," alien from the feudal world, vagabond and criminal, hero of the new picaresque. In the eyes of their sober, prosperous and fearful fellows, these uprooted peasants, disbanded soldiers, and discharged retainers were the most hated villains of the age, carriers of the social diseases of violence and crime.[1] Taken together, however, their desperation, the cruel difficulty of their lives, their riotous and occasionally rebellious activity, did not produce at any single moment a total crisis. Throughout the long period of social transformation there was a strong undercurrent of more routine activity, of accumulation and minor loss, of complacent and self-righteous prospering. The routine was maintained, to be sure, at some cost to the nerves; Tudor government was as watchful and tense as any of the Calvinist saints might have

---

[1] See C. J. Ribton-Turner, *History of Vagrants and Vagrancy* (London, 1887); Sidney and Beatrice Webb, *English Local Government: English Poor Law History: Part I. The Old Poor Law* (London, 1927), pp. 23ff., 42ff.; W. K. Jordan, *Philanthropy in England 1480-1660* (London, 1959), pp. 78ff.

wished. The new problems required a continual vigilance; they burst into view in a long series of minor crises, resulting chiefly from agrarian dislocation, which prompted the sporadic legislative efforts of the early Tudors and led eventually to the great compilations of Elizabeth's reign. Increasingly, an order still defended as natural was buttressed by legislation and governmental force. These served, however, as a more or less stable framework within which the slow processes of social change continued to work their way.

In the literature of the age, there was an intense awareness of mutability, danger and—by the Jacobean and Caroline periods —decay. While the preambles to Tudor enactments stressed the ever-present threat of social disorder, writers and dramatists explored with a new forcefulness the vicissitudes of private life— for now that life was lived largely outside the stable country world of the old order. In such a midsixteenth-century collection as the *Mirror for Magistrates,* the wheel of fortune seemed to turn only for the few: those born to power and princely status on the one hand, bold usurpers on the other.[2] Private men might still live quietly for all the dramatic struggles of princes and pretenders. But this was not so a half century later; the wheel turned for everyone, Ben Jonson thought:

> We see these changes daily: the fair lands
> That were the clients, are the lawyer's now;
> And those rich manors there of goodman Taylor's
> Had once more wood upon them, than the yard
> By which they were measured out for their
>   last purchase,
> Nature hath these vicissitudes.[3]

Such descriptions probably tended to exaggerate the changes actually taking place, but they were themselves an important element in the whole long process of transformation.

The social problems most immediately relevant to the study of Puritanism were of four sorts. First, the problem of rural "depopulation," vagabondage, and extensive (one modern historian

2 *The Mirror for Magistrates,* ed. L. B. Campbell (Cambridge, Eng., 1938), p. 87: "In greatest charge cares greatest do ensue./The most possessed are ever most annoyed,/In largest seas sore tempests lightly brew,/The freshest colors soonest fade the hue . . ."

3 Ben Jonson, *The Devil is an Ass,* II, i.

writes "Asiatic") poverty.[4] Perhaps caused as much by rapid population growth as by enclosures and sheep-farming, the dislocation
of men from the old rural society set thousands of beggars wandering the roads. For more than a century these beggars quite
literally formed a distinct social group, completely alienated from
the work-a-day world on whose fringes they dwelt, raising children
who would make the best of their misfortune and turn begging
(to the horror of the godly ministers) into a profession and a way
of life. Other men, driven from the land, poured into the cities
and boroughs where they were newly subject to the calamities
of depression and urban unemployment.[5]

Secondly, then, the problem of rapid urbanization (if only in
London) with its intensification of the dangers of plague and
fire and its even more important effects upon medieval corporatism,
upon the old, highly integrated and well-governed burgher community. London's population grew enormously, probably trip-
ling, between the accession of Elizabeth and the death of James;
at the latter date it certainly exceeded 300,000 souls. This dramatic burgeoning of the ancient city took place despite the great
plagues of 1603 and 1624 when—in the two years together—more
than 65,000 men and women died in the city.[6] The entire population increase, and more, was the result of emigration from the
country. It brought new men into London who could not be
absorbed by the existing civic institutions. Many of them settled
in the suburbs and outparishes of the old city and were free of
the London magistrates and the powerful Livery Companies (but
also less protected than London citizens in time of depression,
famine, or plague). Crime flourished in the suburbs, flourished,
judging from the literature, to a greater degree than Londoners
had ever known before. The suburbs are "no other but dark dens
for adulterers, thieves, murderers and every mischief worker,"
wrote Henry Chettle in 1591. And in the rapidly expanding city
all the forms of urban exploitation, rack-renting, and profiteering

[4] R. H. Tawney, *The Agrarian Problem in the Sixteenth Century* (London, 1912).
On "Asiatic" poverty, see Peter Laslett, "The World We Have Lost," *The
Listener*, April 14, 1960, p. 649.

[5] There is an especially fine summary of the existing material on urban poverty
in the sixteenth century in Jordan, *Philanthropy*, pp. 66ff.

[6] F. P. Wilson, *The Plague in Shakespeare's London* (Oxford, 1927), appendix
II, pp. 209ff.

were already well known. Indeed, Thomas Hobbes thought urban life and its dangers a sufficient validation of his doctrine of
the war of all against all.[7] Yet Puritanism flourished also in the
city and especially in the suburbs: in the records of the bishop's
court recent immigrants turn up often as members of sectarian
religious groups.[8] Deprived of village solidarity, disoriented in
the great crowds, many men must have found solace in Puritan
faith and even in Puritan discipline. Other newcomers, however,
wandered more vaguely through the crowded city, the permanent
basis of a mob, the permanent concern of the traditional authorities, who sought sometimes to drive them out of the city, sometimes to prevent their coming in.

There was, thirdly, the problem of the religious vacuum left
by the slow decay and then the abrupt collapse of the old church.
At a fairly early point, both in London and the country, this
vacuum began to be filled by Puritanism. Nevertheless, well into
the seventeenth century and despite what one writer has called the
"reconstruction" of Anglicanism there were many parishes without ministers and with churches in disrepair, many thousands
of men deprived both of spiritual leadership and traditional
religious activities. Throughout the later sixteenth and early
seventeenth centuries, there was apparently a slow eclipse of the
once vigorous parish social life—the feastings, dances, and church-
ales—due in part to the disappearance of the old faith, but also
to the Tudor transformation of the parish into an administrative
unit.[9] Once again, for many men, Puritanism provided an alternative set of social and spiritual activities.

Finally, and in a way including all the rest, there was the basic
problem of social organization, raised by the dissolution or disruption of the manorial and parochial systems, the end of rural "housekeeping," the disappearance of the urban confraternities and the
weakening of guild ties, the increased rate of social and geographic
mobility, the creation of the urban crowd and the urban under-

7 Valerie Pearl, London and the Outbreak of the Puritan Revolution: City
Government and National Politics, 1625-1643 (Oxford, 1961), pp. 13-23; Chettle is
quoted on p. 38. Thomas Hobbes, Leviathan, ed. Michael Oakeshott (Oxford, 1960),
pp. 82-83.
8 Champlin Burrage, The Early English Dissenters in the Light of Recent
Research: 1540-1641 (Cambridge, 1912), II, 27; Pearl, London, pp. 40-42.
9 Sidney and Beatrice Webb, Old Poor Law, pp. 11ff; Mildred Campbell, The
English Yeoman Under Elizabeth and the Early Stuarts (New Haven, 1942), p. 301.

world.[10] How were men to be reorganized, bound together in social groups, united for cooperative activity and emotional sustenance? It was in response to such questions that there emerged, in the course of the sixteenth and seventeenth centuries, so many new forms of organization and relationship, so many theories of contract and covenant. Debate over the precise nature of the new organizations—and especially of the Puritan congregation—makes up a considerable part of the tractarian literature of the period. The intensity and detail of the discussion and the fervor of the polemic seem pedantic and even foolish today; they suggest, however, the revolutionary character of the debate, in which the most important matters seemed at stake, no distinction was too fine to be made and every point required an equally total commitment.

From Thomas More's *Utopia* to the utopian and millenarian tracts of the revolutionary period, these problems were the major concern of social and religious thinkers. Statesmen, theologians and then "mechanic preachers" sought to solve them in one way or another and, of course, sought also to take advantage of them. Puritan literature represents one of the most significant efforts to do both: "God's people, as well as worldlings, have their times to fish in troubled waters." And the first effort of the saints was a radical and sustained polemic in defense of a new "discipline"— which suggests very quickly the nature of the troubled waters in which God's people hoped to fish. "Those who know Calvin only as a theologian," wrote Rousseau in *The Social Contract*, "much underestimate the extent of his genius."[11] The same can be said of the Puritan preachers: they too were would-be legislators, and like both Calvin and Rousseau their legislative effort had as its goal the replacement of a decaying order and the regeneration of "wicked" men.

If their constructive plans, however, were a response to social and economic change, they did not make up, in modern terms, a theory of society and economy. Puritans confronted a disorder and confusion whose particular, material causes they hardly

10 On the decay of "housekeeping," see the contemporary tract by Gervase Markham (?), *A Health to the Gentlemanly Profession of Servingman* (London, 1598), repr. in Roxburghe Library, *Inedited Tracts* (London, 1868). On the guilds, see George Unwin, *The Guilds and Companies of London* (London, 1909).

11 Jean-Jacques Rousseau, *The Social Contract*, trans. G. D. H. Cole (New York, 1950), p. 39n.

needed to know: they expected nothing else; organic harmony was never their presupposition. Calvinist theology already mirrored the new social reality and suggested a general explanation: nothing but disorder could possibly follow from the activity of fallen men, restless, lustful, and disobedient. When a Puritan looked about him in the sixteenth or early seventeenth centuries, he saw everywhere the work of the old Adam: strife, confusion, movement, contradiction, riot, fraud, greed. This at any rate was the world he described and with an anxiety and fearfulness that carries conviction even today. The same fearfulness set off the Hobbesian search for absolute power. But the Calvinist God already exercised such power and exercised it as jealously as the God of the Jews. Puritans searched instead for obedient and conscientious subjects, regenerate men, the willful saints of the covenant. And it was in part their success in finding, or creating, such men that made Hobbesian power unnecessary in England.

II

Nothing is more common, or finally more tiresome, in the sixteenth and seventeenth centuries than the moralizing treatise or sermon (or play) in which the sins of contemporary Englishmen are balefully itemized—and only rarely successfully satirized. It was not a complacent age, though it might well be objected that the descriptions of London vice are a little too vivid and enthusiastic to be taken seriously as morality; they had a commercial value as well. In sum, however, the literature was serious enough, even pious and occasionally, as in the sermons of the early Protestant preachers, powerful and moving. The burden of the criticism is well-known: bold evangelists like Latimer and Hooper preached against enclosure and rack-renting, against what they claimed was the new acquisitiveness of the landlord;[12] commercial pamphleteers like Greene and Marston "scourged" the gamblers, prostitutes, pimps, and confidence men of the London underworld;[13] Jacobean dramatists attacked the ambitious schemes of the "projector"—the new capitalist with his "city doctrine"—

---

[12] Helen C. White, *Social Criticism in Popular Religious Literature of the Sixteenth Century* (New York, 1944), especially chs. iii and iv.

[13] Greene, *A Looking Glass for London and England* (London, 1594, repr. Oxford, 1932); see also his "cony catching" books. Marston, *Scourge of Villainy* (London, 1599).

Nature sent man into the world (alone),
Without all company, but to care for one,
And that ile doe.[14]

Virtually all the critics mourned the increased mobility of the
lower orders and mocked the ostentation of the *nouveau riche* and
the effeminate and mannered elegance of the court.

This steady stream of mournful criticism, sometimes brilliant
invective, sometimes naïve analysis, most often, perhaps, only a
kind of conventional chatter, paralleled the legislative activity
of the Tudors. In common with the less enforceable sections of
sixteenth-century legislation, the moralistic literature was marked
by a tendency to harken back to the stable and benevolent world
of tradition. Against all the sins of their contemporaries, the new
greed, the racking of the poor, the lust after titles, the pursuit of
fashion, the writers, preachers, and lawmakers raised the image
of an older England in which paternal lords and sturdy but
deferential yeomen lived in harmony and alms flowed freely.
The medieval England of conservative mythology had its origins
in the sixteenth century; its appearance at that time already indicated a considerable failure of memory, which suggests in its
turn a fairly long period of social change.

The myth of the good-days-gone-by is probably the most naïve
form of social criticism; for that very reason, it is subject to a wide
range of interpretation and use. Even Puritan writers, for example, indulged their fancy with the new mythology, though in
their hands traditional society took on an unlikely Spartan hue.
Men in former times, thought Philip Stubbes, were "ten times
harder than we . . ." With their rough garments and simple fare,
they were healthier and stronger than the degenerate subjects of
Elizabeth.[15] Conservative writers more often emphasized the benevolent and kindly features of the old hierarchical order: the
true love of masters and servants, the generosity and liberality
of the country gentry, and the loyalty of the yeoman.[16] Among all

[14] Thomas Dekker, *If it be not Good, The Devil is in it*, in *Dramatic Works*
(London, 1873), III, 324; quoted in L. C. Knights, *Drama and Society in the Age of
Jonson* (London, 1939), p. 243.
[15] Stubbes, *Anatomy of Abuses* (London, 1583), repr. by F. J. Furnival (London,
1897), p. 54.
[16] Markham (?), *A Health*, p. 113; Anon., *The English Courtier and The
Country Gentleman* (London, 1586), repr. in Roxburghe Library, *Inedited Tracts*
(London, 1868), pp. 34ff.

writers the theme of primitive simplicity and goodness was pervasive; it prevailed even in the aristocratic genre of the pastoral,
though once the impact of French and Italianate styles had been
felt, rural simplicity became something of a convention, itself
paradoxically elaborate and artificial. In Puritan hands, once
again, it came to describe a new kind of rigor and virtue. The
earlier tradition may be summed up in the words of an anonymous
writer of 1568; it used to be the custom of gentlemen, he solemnly
declared,

> to feed many and be themselves fed of few, to seek London seldom
> and at their own houses often to be sought, to have their smoky kitch-
> ens replenished with victuals, their stables with horses, their ward-
> robes rather with harness than silk garments, their halls with men,
> their chambers with plenty of fuel and few perfumes.[17]

Puritan ministers joined eagerly enough in the attack upon
silk and perfume. They even joined in the traditional moralists'
critique of private wealth and of men who "think they may do
with their own what they list." Once again, however, the tone of
the indictment was changed; the myth of old England was transformed from a tale of jovial hospitality to one of stern and
patriotic virtue. Thomas Scott, that original and industrious
warmonger, who published some twenty-three pamphlets in five
years (1620-1624) in a determined effort to force a renewal of the
struggle with Spain, saw old England as the home of selfless
warriors. These were men different indeed from "the monopolists
and improvers of our land and the irreligious impropriators who
prey upon church and state." Today, Scott wrote, "all our private
wealth swarms with such monsters and their breed is from the
lazy scum of counterfeit gentility, who bearing those arms idly
which their diligent predecessors have purchased as badges of
some honorable achievement, do thereby disgrace their originals."
A true gentleman would rather fight than "live idly acquainting
[himself] with all effeminate fashions and mollifying pleasures . . .
where no other counsel is called for but the page, the footboy
and the coachman, no other action exercised but court-wars . . .
no other enemy seen but what the stage presents."[18]

---

17 Anon., *The Institution of a Gentleman* (London, 1568), sig. C_1.
18 Thomas Scott, *The Belgick Pismire* (London, 1622), pp. 27-28; cf. Scott, *The Highways of God and the King* (London, 1623).

In such criticism, elements of the old and the new were inextricably entangled—suggesting, by their very confusion, the dilemma of men caught up in a process of rapid social change. A kind of nostalgic utopianism jostled along in Puritan writing with the zeal for reformation—or, as in Scott's case, for godly warfare. Nowhere were nostalgia and zeal more perfectly confused than in Henry Crosse's *Virtue's Commonwealth* (1603), whose title suggested the future Puritan state. Crosse himself was a conservative, specifically disavowing "those that carp at the present discipline," but his ideas may safely be labeled puritanical.[19] *Virtue's Commonwealth* was a dissertation upon the dangers of wealth, the typical product of a moralist responding unhappily to the sudden affluence of his society. Money and the greed for money, Crosse thought, set men in motion, drew them from their ancient homes and their fixed vocations, lured them to the corrupting cities. Too many men "leave the limits of their calling . . . and either fall into a loitering life or attempt that wherein they have no skill . . ." "We see how men of good place and reckoning will hide themselves in corners, live privately . . . crowd into cities [and] boroughs . . . roll up and down from one lodging to another . . ." He evoked once again the image of a stable country society in which "men dwelt upon their own . . . kept good houses and were no small stay to the places where they lived."[20]

"Out of our conceptions of the past," wrote Thomas Hobbes, "we make a future."[21] But Crosse's conception was not equal to the task. The virtue he demanded, like the moral reformation of the Puritan ministers, required more than the hospitality and "good houses" of the country he remembered. And in fact, Crosse's primary concern was not with the decay of the old order. It was with the harsh and contemporary fact of disorder: it was not nostalgia but anxiety that pervaded his work. He was as worried as any of the ministers when he confronted the exuberance, the despair, and the free-wheeling energy of the Renaissance city. Thus he joined in the Puritan attack upon the theater not so much be-

19 Crosse, *Virtue's Commonwealth* (London, 1603), sig. N_3 verso.
20 *Ibid.*, sig. I and I_4 verso.
21 Thomas Hobbes, *Behemoth*, in *English Works*, ed. W. Molesworth (London, 1839-1845), VI, 259.

cause the plays were "scandalous" and immoral, but because their
showing was an occasion for riot and their audiences were "for
the most part the lewdest persons in the land . . . an unclean
generation . . ." They were the very same people who were incapable of attention "at a lecture and holy exercise." Similarly,
Crosse followed the Puritan ministers in their denunciation of the
great feudal and Renaissance houses. Parents who "put their children to be servingmen," he thought, did them a great disservice;
among courtiers and pageboys they learned only vices, they did
little work, carousal was their only recreation. Crosse held up
instead the image of the Puritan family where the father sternly
trained his sons in the habits of work. "Everyone ought to betake himself to some honest and seemly trade, and not suffer his
senses to be mortified with idleness . . ."[22] This was hardly an
invocation of traditional country life.

Crosse's views were fairly typical; in one form or another they
were repeated by other men, moderates, who were not ready to
identify themselves with the Puritans. They found their echo, for
example, in King James' *Basilikon Doron,* a book whose somewhat strenuous tone hardly suggests the future Cavalier—hardly
suggests, indeed, James' own courtiers. The king's insistence upon
the necessity of physical exercise and industry "to banish idleness"
touched the central theme of Puritan social criticism and emphasized once again the nature of Puritan uneasiness with afternoons
spent at the theater, with days of lounging and "waiting" in the
great households.[23] But the Puritan ministers carried this sort of
thing much further. They sought a more rigid discipline than
King James could have imagined and this very rigidity cut them
off from any nostalgia for the old ways. They came, in fact, to see
that the idleness they hated so much had been a disease of the
old order itself and so they turned their backs altogether on the
traditionalist mythology. Idleness was the mark of the feudal
houses and the Catholic Church as well as of the growing city of
London. The habitual indolence of monks, servants, and gentlemen "wholly given up to hunting and hawking" had only been

22 Crosse, *Virtue's Commonwealth,* sig. P_2, S_3 and S_3 verso.
23 *The Political Works of James I,* ed. Charles McIlwain (Cambridge, Mass., 1918),
pp. 48-49. See discussion of this literature in W. L. Ustick, "Advice to a Son: A Type
of Seventeenth Century Courtesy Book," *Studies in Philology* 29:409-441 (1932).

supplemented by the new "chaos" of beggars, vagabonds, and the unemployed or underemployed poor. These were all men who did not "betake themselves" to honest work; Crosse's phrase suggests the voluntaristic nature of the Puritan ideal and sets that ideal clearly apart from the more natural, essentially sentimental behavior urged by the traditional moralist.[24]

The Puritan demand for continuous, organized, methodical activity—to banish idleness—was a reaction to the breakdown of country stability and (as in Crosse) to the sudden appearance of the mobile urban man. But it was not a reaction in traditional terms. It was in fact part of the complex process by which contemporary Englishmen adjusted to the changes taking place in their society. While the moralists dwelt with morbid fancy upon the inevitability of vicissitude and decay and recalled sadly the old virtues of moderation and degree, Puritan writing took another turn. The ministers suggested the literal possibility of "opting out" of the world of idleness and confusion. Their emancipation from nostalgia made possible a direct and personal confrontation with the visible signs of disorder: men without work in the cities; noisy, jostling crowds; vagabonds on country roads; great houses filled with idle, merry men. With the intense moral discomfort of the righteous and the high-minded, Puritans sought desperately to separate themselves from the chaotic sinfulness that they imagined to surround them.[25] This indeed was the central purpose of their self-discipline and their search for "good company." But they wished also, with a fervor that clearly surpassed that of Crosse and King James, to create a society in which godly order would be the rule and sin not a possible activity. The Puritans sensed in themselves, saints that they assuredly were, men of substance that they often were, the strength and energy to control human wickedness even as they transcended the world of sin and distinguished themselves from its less fortunate members. They sought to create a new discipline through three different methods of social control. These need now to be considered in

---

[24] For a summary of the work of the Jacobean moralists, see Knights, *Drama and Society*.

[25] The idea of separation from the wicked pervades even the literature on marriage and friendship: see, for example, Baxter on the theme "Beware of the company of the ungodly" in Richard Baxter, *The Saints' Everlasting Rest* (New York, n.d.), pp. 188ff.

some detail: the first of them is revealed in the Puritan doctrine
of vocation, the second in the congregational system, the third
in the theory of magistracy.

III

After having recalled the warrior virtues of the medieval English, Thomas Scott turned abruptly to the more contemporary
virtues of the Calvinist Dutch. He emphasized their *industriousness:* the word had only recently taken on an almost religious
tone suggesting zealous and painstaking application.[26] "There
are none or very few beggars," wrote Scott. "For indeed every man
works and depends upon himself . . . their diet is but homely,
every day is not a feasting day . . . Yea their whole life seems
nothing but a fast from superfluity." The image of the industrious
Dutch—their praises sung by many an exiled minister—gradually
replaced that of the patriarchal lord and sturdy yeoman. Puritans
discovered a utopia of men without leisure. The businesslike behavior of Dutch merchants and artisans (one writer included the
"diligent" fisherman) not only insured the stability and order of
their society, but also set them apart as a godly people.[27]

The new view of work and the rhetorical violence of the accompanying critique of idleness formed the concrete basis of the
Puritan repudiation of the old order. God honored men as he
honored angels: in proportion to their "serviceableness"—that
is, to their zealous application, their skill, and their effectiveness.
And he organized men as he organized angels: through a division
of labor, in a chain of command. *All men must work,* gentlemen
and commoners alike. The sons of the gentry, untrained in a
"good occupation," wrote the ministers Dod and Cleaver, were
the "seedmen of all mischief in our country."[28] Idle men were
rebels and in the houses which sheltered them, family government did not exist and God was not served. "Honor and worship
resteth not in keeping many servants," Crosse had written, "or

26 *Oxford English Dictionary, s.v.* industry, industriousness.

27 Scott, *Belgick Pismire,* pp. 5off., 75, 80. On Holland as a model, see Raymond
Stearns, *Strenuous Puritan: Hugh Peter, 1598-1600* (Urbana, Ill., 1954), pp. 307,
309-310, 370-371; also Stearns, *Congregationalism in the Dutch Netherlands* (Chicago,
1940), p. 76. The tribute to the Dutch fishermen is found in Tobias Gentleman,
England's Way to Win Wealth (London, 1614), pp. 10-11.

28 Robert Cleaver and John Dod, *Household Government* (London, 1621), sig.
P_6 verso and P_7.

[in] riding with a great troop . . .''[29] The theme was often repeated in Puritan literature; it was a far cry from the happy memory of the anonymous writer of 1568: stables full of horses, halls full of men. Inevitably, Puritans found themselves caught up in a sharp attack upon the leisured classes and their traditional ideas of service, honor, and recreation. The industrious saints tended to set themselves apart from both the idle rich and the men whom the rich supported: servants, ex-soldiers, actors, beggars, and the multitude of urban poor who sought occasional employment— grouped together they made up Crosse's "unclean generation."[30]

Puritans discovered in work the primary and elemental form of social discipline, the key to order, and the foundation of all further morality. William Whately stressed the importance of keeping busy if one was to avoid committing adultery: "for pains in a calling will consume a great part of that superfluous nourishment that yields matter to this sin. It will turn the blood and spirits another way . . ."[31] But work was something more than this obvious and inadequate form of domestic discipline; it was also the self-affirming activity of the godly. The saints were distinguished from the disorderly mob of worldlings by their industry and diligence: their industry *revealed* their saintliness—to themselves as well as to their fellows. The old Catholic theory of good *works* was here transformed into a Protestant theory of good *work:* the difference lay not only in the question of the efficacy, but more significantly in the question of the nature of the required activity.[32] Man's *work,* wrote the Puritan minister Samuel Hieron, is "the testimony of his religion." He was discussing continuous labor in a calling and not occasional good deeds. "He that hath no honest business about which ordinarily to be employed,"

[29] Crosse, *Virtue's Commonwealth*, sig. S₈.

[30] See Richard Baxter's list of the men who supported the king in 1642: gentlemen, beggars, and servile tenants; *Reliquiae Baxterianae*, ed. M. Sylvester (London, 1696), p. 30.

[31] Whately, *A Bride-bush* (London, 1619), p. 9.

[32] The classic discussion of this point is Max Weber's *The Protestant Ethic and the Spirit of Capitalism*, trans. Talcott Parsons (New York, 1958), esp. pp. 109ff. Weber emphasizes the role of work in the individual's pursuit of salvation; the ability to work hard and achieve success, he argues, was seen as a sign of grace. But the stress of the preachers is most often on the social and moral effects of hard work and not on its spiritual significance. The new ethic is at least as much a response to the overriding problem of social order as it is to the individual's anxiety with regard to his fate in the life to come.

he went on, "no settled course to which he may betake himself, cannot please God."[33] "Business" like "industry" had taken on a new meaning in the course of the sixteenth century: to a word which originally meant merely occupation or trade, but which until the 1580's also carried the implication of mischief and impertinence, there had been superadded a sense of diligence and systematic activity.[34] It was this new meaning that was intended by Hieron and many other Puritan preachers; they taught men "to make a conscience of their calling." Work—and magistracy, warfare, philanthropy, and religious exercise were but different aspects of this general theme—was to be systematic and sustained; any sort of sporadic or spontaneous activity had to be rigorously avoided. So William Scott's "complete citizen" worried over his occasional afternoon naps and worried most of all because they came at "unaccustomed times"—they were unplanned.

If a man should at every week's end consider with himself how he hath spent it, how many hours might he reckon up which he cannot tell how he bestowed, besides eating and drinking? How many needless items would he find given to sleep? Item, seven nights; item perhaps seven half-afternoons, besides half-hours and quarters at unaccustomed times . . .[35]

The two implications of Puritan labor—social discipline and self-affirmation—were brought together by the ministers in the theory of the calling. As presented by William Perkins in his *Treatise of the Vocations,* the theory suggested a new order among the saints replacing the forms of organic connection and hierarchy. Puritan calling closely paralleled the Huguenot idea of political office, but its social extension was far more wide. Whereas the Huguenots sought chiefly to reorganize and discipline a feudal nobility, the Puritan effort would have included nobility and commoners alike; it would have turned politics from an aristocratic duty into a kind of work and made work in general the religious duty of everyman. Given this wider range, however, the two ideas were strikingly similar; like the Huguenot doctrine of office and obligation, Puritan calling opened the way to responsible and impersonal commitments among men. Obligation in the

---

33 *All the Sermons of Samuel Hieron* (London, 1614), pp. 245-247.
34 *Oxford English Dictionary, s.v.* business.
35 Scott, *Essay of Drapery* (London, 1635), p. 101.

work-a-day world formed the basis for a wide network of contractual arrangements.

In a Puritan society, the scheme of human relations would be
effectively determined by the scheme of human employment. The
saints would come together almost exclusively in the course of
their work. "Honest business" would fill their lives and absorb
all their enthusiasm.[36] Such relations as they then established
would be contractual, that is, entered into voluntarily by formally
free men, whose calling was sufficiently certain and whose activity
was sufficiently sustained for them to make long-term promises and
agreements.[37] This was the obvious social meaning of those "settled courses" which Hieron urged upon all who sought to please
God: "settled courses" made men dependable. Perkins repeated
the older idea that men of divers callings were bound together
by love; but in fact love played little part in the Puritan theory of
social organization. "It is necessary my citizen defend himself,"
wrote the draper Scott, "by this buckler: distrust, which is a great
part of prudence . . ." Nor was it any act of charity for Perkins to
exclude beggars from civil society: they "are as rotten legs and
arms," he wrote, "that drop from the body." Great lords, then,
might no longer recruit loyal followers from among the multitude
of vagabonds and beggars; the ministers even urged that the army
not be filled with such men, "tattered jailbirds and masterless
vagrants." "It is no Christian policy to choose such sinful instruments for such a serious action."[38] Civil society, contractual relations, trust and responsibility existed, Puritans thought, only
among those who had already submitted to the discipline of a
"particular office."

This submission was an act of the will, a voluntary act that
belied the organic imagery Perkins occasionally employed. Men
must choose their offices for themselves, he insisted, responding to

[36] Six hours, Baxter thought, was the maximum amount of sleep that healthy
Christians might allow themselves; even prayer, he argued, must not be prolonged;
God was a hard master demanding long hours and strict attention to business. See
discussion and many citations in Richard Schlatter, *The Social Ideas of Religious
Leaders* (London, 1940), especially pp. 190ff.

[37] For a somewhat different discussion of Puritanism and the idea of contract,
see Christopher Hill, *Economic Problems of the Church: From Archbishop Whitgift to the Long Parliament* (Oxford, 1956), pp. 184-185, 346-347.

[38] Perkins, *Works* (London, 1616), I, 755; Scott, *Essay*, p. 137; Thomas Palmer,
Bristol's Military Garden (London, 1635), p. 21.

an inner call that was also a divine command. They must examine themselves, study their affections and gifts: "he that is fit for sundry callings must make choice of the best." Similarly in the political world, where groups of men acting as "instruments of God" choose officers from among their fellows: they must examine their gifts, they must choose the best man. "Thus may a private man become a magistrate." All this implied not only a formal freedom, but a formal equality; all men might not have equal gifts, but all would be "examined." Puritans went on to suggest that there was a kind of spiritual equality among the callings. Before God all callings were equal, wrote Perkins, "though it be but to sweep the house or keep sheep . . ."[39] The idea was hardly new, but Puritans gave it a new importance. Application and diligence in *any* vocation was a tribute to God and an effective guarantee of social order. Whatever the rank of the saints, then, they must be drawn into the discipline. "The great and reverend God," wrote Dod and Cleaver, "despiseth no honest trade . . . be it never so mean, but crowneth it with his blessing, *to draw all good minds to his holy ordinance*."[40] Men accepted the discipline and received in return, as it were, a godly sense of self-importance.

They then entered into agreements with their fellows. The value of such agreements was obviously enhanced by the formal equality and spiritual self-esteem of the saints. A contract, for the first time, was clearly seen as an agreement between equals, unmarked by deference or humility on either side, fully voluntary and unforced on both sides and a matter not of personal loyalty or fear, but of conscience. "Natural necessity destroys the very nature of a covenant," wrote one Puritan minister, for it must be "a voluntary obligation between persons about things wherein they enjoy a freedom of will and have a power to choose or refuse." Given this freedom, the crucial feature of the contract was the mutual recognition of honest intention: "the form doth require," wrote the casuist William Ames in his *Cases of Conscience,* "internal and essential, the upright dealing of the contractor to be true and sincere."[41] Spiritual equality was the basis of this mutual recognition

39 Perkins, *Works,* I, 756-762.
40 Dod and Cleaver, *Household Government,* sig. P$_6$ and P$_7$.
41 Quoted in Perry Miller, *The New England Mind: The Seventeenth Century* (Cambridge, Mass., 1952), p. 375.

of good faith. Even the covenant between God and fallen men, thought John Preston, "implies a kind of equality between us."[42] Some sensitivity to the human dignity implied in this notion of a contract underlay Puritan ideas of master-servant relations and even, as has been seen, of the marriage bond.

The ideas of self-examination and free contract required Puritan writers to come to grips not only with equality, but also with social mobility. Choice would have to be left free, in politics and in business, if men were to "choose the best." Perkins recognized that mistakes might be made, even by parents with regard to their children; the ear was not always attuned to the call.[43] But so long as free choice was accompanied by painstaking introspection, he had little to fear from the disruption of the hierarchical world. There would still be no freedom for "masterless men." The saints were masters of themselves and claimed only the privileges that their "pains" had earned, and beggars and vagabonds were simply expelled from the vocational world, cut off like rotten limbs because, thought Perkins, they took no pains at all. Eventually, the painful diligence of the saints would require also a kind of peace with material success and affluence, but on this point the earlier Puritan writers were extremely hesitant. It was not intended that work should bring wealth; the ministers had little sense of the possibility of rapid increases in productivity. Instinctively, they tended toward a kind of economic restrictionism. Men should be content, Perkins wrote, "if they have as much as will provide them food and raiment, and thus much lawfully may they seek . . ."[44] For the moment the emphasis was on the lawful seeking—"skill and labor in a good occupation"—and not on its possibly dangerous results.

IV

That the Puritan theory of the calling involved a radical social criticism has already been suggested. Its nature was made clear by Perkins when he listed four groups of men who possess "no particular calling to walk in," who live outside the vocational

[42] Preston, *The New Covenant* (London, 1629), p. 331.

[43] Perkins, *Works*, I, 758. The Puritan defense of mobility ought not to be overemphasized; nevertheless Perkins' voluntaristic vocabulary—*examine, choose*—is significant.

[44] Perkins, *Works*, I, 769.

world. The list included: 1) rogues, beggars and vagabonds; 2) monks and friars; 3) gentlemen who "spend their days in eating and drinking"; and 4) servants—"for only to wait . . . is not a sufficient calling."[45] All these were dangerous men, thought Perkins, because they were not subject to control and discipline. Some were wanderers with no fixed dwelling: they slipped in and out of parish, city, and shire "so avoiding the authority of all." "It is no good token, but an ill sign," wrote the Puritan theologian, "for a man to be uncertain in his dwelling."[46] Others had no honest business, no settled courses. "An idle man's brain," thought the ministers Dod and Cleaver, "becometh quickly the shop of the devil . . . Whereof rise mutinies and mutterings in cities against magistrates? You can give no greater cause thereof, than idleness."[47] Here was the source of riot and rebellion, of theater crowds and crowded brothels and of everything else that the godly identified as the work (or the play) of the damned.

There was no salvation in idleness or in vagabondage. The lazy multitude was always inclined, Perkins thought, to popish opinions, always more ready to play than to work; its members would not find their way to heaven. A careless, hand-to-mouth existence almost certainly precluded the sustained effort that salvation required. Poverty might, of course, be the fate of the saints: "The state of God's church and children in this world, for the most part, is to be afflicted and poor in their outward condition."[48] But this was a godly poverty, the poverty of the "industrious poor" that led neither to disorder nor discontent. The saints would find the world sufficient; they would ask but little and that would be granted: "Set thy heart to seek God's kingdom," wrote Perkins, "follow the Word and labor therein for regeneration and doubt not, but if thou be upright and diligent in thy lawful calling. thou shalt find sufficient for this life."[49] The complacent piety of Perkins' statement seems hardly compatible with the discovery of his contemporaries that idleness and unemployment were often involuntary. It reflected, however, a signif-

45 *Works*, I, 755-756; see discussion in Christopher Hill, *Puritanism and Revolution* (London, 1958), p. 226.
46 *Works*, III, 71.
47 Dod and Cleaver, *Household Government*, sig. X_3.
48 Richard Sibbes, *Complete Works*, ed. A. B. Grosart (Edinburgh, 1863), VI, 236.
49 Perkins, *Works*, III, 191; see Hill, *Puritanism and Revolution*, pp. 215ff.

icant Puritan judgment upon the capacities of willful, godly men. When the same judgment was made by the poor themselves, it may be regarded as the very perfect ideology of pious poverty.

At the same time, the growing awareness of human helplessness did produce—and especially among Puritans—a new kind of philanthropy directed more or less exclusively at these very same godly poor. Wealthy Puritans, tutored in part by the ministers, sought to provide not only direct relief, but also educational opportunity and apprenticeship training and sometimes capital or materials for men who were willing, in effect, to become saints. Administered privately, outside the traditional channels, most often by laymen acting as trustees of substantial funds, Puritan philanthropy was deliberately discriminating and purposive. It was directed less toward the relief of beggars than toward the transformation of a selected number of religious paupers into self-sufficient and presumably self-disciplined men.[50] The ministers carefully and correctly distinguished such charity from that casual, indiscriminate, and spontaneous alms-giving that constituted what Perkins called a "very seminary of vagabonds."[51] Puritan philanthropy was a school of a different, undoubtedly a more rigorous sort. Like much of the legislation of the Tudors, though perhaps more effectively, it aimed at creating a disciplined, methodical worker, a man who could be trusted by his employer—the employer might well be the same person as the Puritan philanthropist—and who need not be feared.

But there was another kind of poverty bred in the disorder of the times and Puritan ministers almost invariably described its victims with nothing but hatred and dread. This was the poverty that beset hundreds and thousands of countrymen who wandered into the city, never found work and learned to live haphazardly as best they could.

A man, as he goes along in the streets [wrote Richard Sibbes], shall hear a company of poor that are the greatest rebels in the world against God; that blaspheme and swear, that rail against magistrates

---

50 Jordan, *Philanthropy*, pp. 240ff., for the impressive record of sixteenth and seventeenth-century philanthropy, much of it Puritan; for a discussion of Puritan intentions, pp. 143ff. W. T. MacCaffrey, *Exeter 1540-1640: The Growth of an English Country Town* (Cambridge, Mass., 1958), provides a particular example of the changing nature of philanthropy, p. 109.

51 Perkins, *Works*, II, 144-145; see also Hieron, *All The Sermons*, pp. 388-389.

and governors. They are the most unbroken people in the world, the poorest and beggarliest, the refuse of mankind. As they are in condition, so they are in disposition.[52]

The last sentence strikes the typically Calvinist note. The most hopeless forms of idleness and poverty could only be the products of fallen nature, of the "disposition" of corrupt men. The same judgment was rendered by Perkins: beggars, he wrote, were "an unfaithful and ungracious generation . . . [they] live liker brute beasts than men . . ."[53] They were without a calling and were not members of a particular congregation or a settled family. They had not undertaken the systematic labor through which ordinary men might transform themselves into saints; they were, indeed, most unwilling to work. That essential voluntarism which underlay all Calvinist thought made any understanding of the utter helplessness of these uprooted people impossible. Work was a test for which men must volunteer; their failure to volunteer was evidence that they had not been called.

Puritanism was in a sense the religion of the sociologically competent, of those who *had* been called. In the seventeenth century anti-Puritan publicists were quick to say that it was the religion also of the economically prosperous—a judgment at least partially true. Philanthropy might seek bravely to widen the area of competence, but in a fundamental sense those men who were most hurt in the long period of social dislocation and disorder were least willing, or rather least able, to join in Puritan discipline, introspection, and self-affirmation. Puritans, in their turn, called only those men saints who could, in the words of a modern writer, "conduct themselves as energizing centers of ethical action."[54] This sort of voluntaristic doctrine came down hardest on the poor, though few of the preachers forgot to include the idle or old-fashioned rich in their invective. But while the rich were convicted only of wickedness and pride—and found both still pleasurable—the poor were blamed for their very helplessness and misery and denied the balm of self-respect. Puritan ministers would have subjected them without hesitation to the violence of the

---

52 Sibbes, *Works*, VI, 238.
53 Perkins, *Works*, III, 71, 191; see discussion in Hill, *Puritanism and Revolution*, p. 227.
54 Gertrude Huehns, *Antinomianism in English History* (London, 1957), pp. 66-67.

magistrate. And from an "ungracious generation" the saints would have separated themselves, both in their everyday work and in their religious exercises.

v

Religious exercise was the second aspect of Puritan social order; alongside the discipline of work stood the discipline of faith. Both were open to all men willing to submit and take pains. Man's work, wrote Perkins, was his "particular calling." God had also proclaimed a "general calling" which all Christians shared: they must labor for "the building of [his] church." In the church, as in the economy, all the saints were to be methodically active. "Though men . . . fondly imagine that this duty is proper to the ministers, yet the truth is, it belongs not only to them, but to everyone."[55] The building of the church was carried on in hundreds of local congregations where the saints struggled for power, harassed the sinful and zealously strove for such a "reformation of manners" as might please their exacting God. As work had been made a matter of choice and self-affirmation, so religion was now made a matter of self-government (though not democratic government). And as work in one's chosen calling was harder, more regular and assiduous than work had ever been before, so Puritan self-government was more systematic and repressive than government had ever been before.

Local self-government by the godly: this was the creed of the sixteenth-century "disciplinarians," first proclaimed by Thomas Cartwright in the 1570's.[56] Seventy-five years later it was still the creed of moderate Presbyterians and Independents like Richard Baxter and John Owen. And whether they accepted every detail of Cartwright's system or not, it is clear that Puritans of the revolutionary period still shared the high hopes that he had placed in godly self-government. John Milton summed up those hopes at the very beginning of the revolution: discipline, he wrote was the key to every "sociable perfection in this life, civil or sacred . . ." It was "not only the removal of disorder, but . . . the

55 Perkins, *Works*, I, 753.

56 On "disciplinarian" Puritanism, see Marshall Knappen, *Tudor Puritanism* (Chicago, 1939); Donald J. McGinn, *The Admonition Controversy* (New Brunswick, N.J., 1949); A. F. Scott Pearson, *Church and State: Political Aspects of Sixteenth-Century Puritanism* (London, 1928).

very visible shape and image of virtue." Cartwright had only been more specific in 1573 when he argued that congregational discipline would restrain stealing, adultery, and murder; even more, it would "correct" sins "which the magistrate doth not commonly punish"—he listed lying, uncomely jesting, choleric speeches. John Penry included poverty in the list: "there lacketh that orderly seeing to the poor which [is] expedient . . . by idleness and liberty great poverty [is] among us . . . which might very well be amended by Christ's discipline."[57] After the inevitable and lengthy citations of Scripture, arguments of this sort were perhaps the major theme of Puritan polemic: the new structure of church government was advocated as a panacea for social disorder. Francis Walsingham described the disciplinarian position as it had been presented to him (or, perhaps, as his agents had heard it argued in the streets): "Because multitude of rogues and poverty was an eyesore and a dislike to every man, therefore they put it into the people's head that if discipline were planted, there should be no vagabonds nor beggars . . ."[58]

This was to put the Cartwrightian position in its starkest and most practical terms; the same point might be made differently: the purpose of the discipline was to teach and enforce Christian standards of behavior. Enforcement was to be local, by the saints themselves; mutual control was the method of the new discipline. Church government by ministers, elders, and deacons, wrote Field and Wilcox in the *First Admonition,* was "an order left by God unto his church, whereby men learn to frame their wills and doings according to the law of God, *by instructing and admonishing one another,* yea, and by correcting and punishing all willful persons and contemners of the same."[59]

Not only Christian behavior, but also a new kind of Christian fellowship was to follow from the discipline. In an age when many ministers drew income from parishes that they rarely visited, Cartwright stressed the "four-fold cord" of pastoral duties that

57 Milton, *Works,* ed. F. A. Patterson, et al. (New York), III, pt. I, 185; Thomas Cartwright, *A Reply to an Answer* in Whitgift, *Works* (Cambridge, 1851-1853), I, 21; John Penry, *An Humble Motion with Submission* [Edinburgh, 1590], p. 72.
58 Quoted in Hill, *Puritanism and Revolution,* p. 234.
59 Field and Wilcox, *An Admonition to the Parliament,* in *Puritan Manifestoes: A Study of the Origins of Puritan Revolt,* ed. W. H. Frere and C. E. Douglas (London, 1954), p. 16.

bound the minister to his congregation: preaching, examination, admonition, and "dissolving of doubts."[60] Similarly, though the congregation was founded neither on neighborhood (for only local *saints*, as will be seen, were admitted to communion) nor, properly speaking, on love, the connection of its members was very close. They examined and admonished one another. The saints were thus bound together in a close system of collective watchfulness, which might occasionally turn into a kind of spiritual terrorism. In his Kidderminster parish, Baxter reported, the enforcement of the moral discipline was made possible "by the zeal and diligence of the godly people of the place, who thirsted after the salvation of their neighbors, and were in private my assistants."[61]

Congregational unity approached the intense collectivism of the sect; the disciplinarians transformed the local church into a voluntary association of the holy. Among the separatists an actual covenant was signed confirming the sectarian organization.[62] Covenant and discipline alike were made possible by the long-term commitment of the saints to their "general calling." The two may be said to parallel the contractual relations made possible by commitment to a "particular calling." The sectarian covenant was a voluntary agreement undertaken among equals; the Puritan discipline a common regiment to which all the saints equally submitted. As the parity of ministers made possible an alliance founded on ideology alone, so the equality of lay saints was the basis of local and national Puritan endeavor. "How vile account soever you will make of them," wrote Cartwright of the Puritans, "they are the people of God and therefore spiritual and forthwith those of whom St. Paul saith, 'The spiritual man discerneth all things.' "[63] Such a view provided the basis for a religious organization which was not a mysterious union but a willful association of saints, working together on the basis of their own *word* and of their recognition of each others' right to make promises and capacity to keep them.

Both Cartwright and his chief disciple Walter Travers often re-

60 Whitgift, *Works*, I, 517.
61 Baxter, *Reliquiae Baxterianae*, p. 87.
62 See Champlin Burrage, *The Church Covenant Idea: Its Origins and Development* (Philadelphia, 1904); Ernst Troeltsch, *The Social Teaching of the Christian Churches*, trans. by Olive Wyon (London, 1931), II, 590ff.
63 Whitgift, *Works*, I, 372.

ferred to the new community as a "commonwealth," thus stressing its essentially political nature. Close association might help the godly, as ministerial conferences helped Richard Rogers, to maintain a pitch of fervor and self-confidence, but its main purpose was social control. Godliness was the *civisme* of the tiny parish commonwealth and the elected elders were its special agents, a kind of moral police.[64] Travers compared them to the civil officers in Athens—"which had care to see the laws kept"—and to the censors of Rome.

For although after a sort it is all men's duty to bring him into his way which goeth astray, yet better and more diligent heed is taken that offenses arise not in the church, when every part of the church have their watchmen assigned to them to whose office especially it should belong to mark, oversee, and examine all men's manners.

The elders, then, were magistrates of a sort and it was surely the Puritan intention that some men should double in the two roles and serve both as church elders and justices of the peace. The congregation would have been the local unit of the "holy commonwealth" much as the parish was of the Elizabethan state.

But the congregation would not include all the residents of the parish—as the old church had done. That would make godliness a matter of geography, said the ministers, and turn the church into "an inn to receive whoever cometh."[65] Instead, participation depended upon behavior and behavior presumably upon will. Puritans therefore required a careful testing of all who desired entrance into the parish commonwealth, an inquiry, as it were, into the patriotism of future citizens. They claimed the right to exclude even neighbors and kinfolk from the communion in order to maintain a clear distinction between the godly—who lived in pious and sober order—and the sinners—who "rioted" in uncleanliness. "There is something generally in the dispositions [of the religious sort]," Baxter argued, "which inclineth them to dissociate from open ungodly sinners, as men of another nature and

---

[64] See Cartwright's arguments for the election of ministers and elders, Whitgift, *Works*, I, 370ff. Also Walter Travers, *A Full and Plain Declaration*, pp. 57-58, 156, 160-161, 177, 191. The quote that follows is from Travers, p. 156.

[65] See discussion of Puritan exclusiveness in H. H. Henson, *Studies in English Religion in the Seventeenth Century* (London, 1903), esp. pp. 116-119. Quotation is from Cartwright, *Reply*, in Whitgift, *Works*, I, 139.

society."[66] In Baxter's own parish, some two-thirds of the people were excluded from communion; "all the parish kept off, except about six hundred communicants." The other twelve hundred declined to accept the moral discipline and were, in Baxter's eyes, no longer members of his reformed church. "The church severeth those," Cartwright had written, "which being of the parish, are none of the church."[67]

Those who remained were drawn into the strange, time-consuming activities of the Puritan congregation: diligently taking notes at sermons, attending endless meetings, associating intimately and continuously with men and women who were after all not relatives and, above all, submitting to the discipline and zealous watchfulness of the godly. Puritanism required not only a pitch of piety, but a pitch of activism and involvement. Baxter's description of his weekly round is instructive: he preached twice, on Sundays and Thursdays; Thursday evenings he met with those of his congregants who "were most desirous and had opportunity," to discuss the sermon; on Saturday nights he met with the "younger sort" to "prepare [them] for the following day"; once in every few weeks, he celebrated a "day of humiliation" with his congregants and whenever one of the women of Kidderminster gave birth he kept a "day of thanksgiving" with some of the neighbors—"instead of the old feastings and gossipings"; two evenings every week he and his assistant met with fourteen families "for private catechizing and conference"; the meeting of church elders for "parish discipline" was held every first Wednesday of the month; and finally, the ministers' meeting for "discipline and disputation" was held on the first Thursday. Puritanism, like Oscar Wilde's socialism, took too many evenings. Yet Baxter's sermons and meetings must have been attended; he kept them up for many years.[68]

The ungodly twelve hundred presumably held off from all this; yet their severance was not an entire separation. The Puritans, unlike the sectaries, were not interested simply in saving themselves, but in bringing every Englishmen under the vigilant eye of minis-

[66] Baxter, *Reliquiae Baxterianae*, p. 91; for another example of "separation" within the parish, see Joseph Hunter, *The Rise of the Old Dissent Exemplified in the Life of Oliver Heywood* (London, 1842), pp. 99-105.

[67] *The Second Reply of Thomas Cartwright* (n.p., 1575), p. 146.

[68] Baxter, *Reliquiae Baxterianae*, p. 83.

ters and elders. The parish for them was still a community, but once they had seized control, it was transformed into a community at war within itself. Led by their minister—"chief captain of the Lord's army and conductor of his host"—the godly did battle for the souls of the local worldlings. But if they were to battle for the souls, they would have to have access to the bodies: they would have to compel catechism, religious education, and attendance at sermons. Most Puritans unhesitatingly called upon the Christian magistrate, hopefully he was also a church elder, to provide the necessary coercive force.

> They may be of and in the commonwealth [wrote Cartwright] which neither may nor can be of nor in the church; and therefore the church having nothing to do with such, the magistrate ought to see that they join to hear sermons . . . and cause them to be examined how they profit, and if they profit not, to punish them . . .[69]

The magistrate, wrote Baxter some eighty years later, must force all men "to learn the word of God and to walk orderly and quietly . . . till they are brought to a voluntary, personal profession of Christianity."[70] Joining the congregation would thus remain a voluntary act and Puritan Christianity an extremely strenuous form of self-government, but the men who refused to govern themselves would have to be governed nevertheless—until, in effect, they could be forced to be free.

VI

The saints would work voluntarily much as they would walk to heaven alone, but even the saints preferred company in their pilgrimage and might require encouragement in their diligent labor. Other men would need not only encouragement and company, but coercion and control, direction and domination, if they were to honor God in their everyday behavior. It was not with love but with material force that the Puritans sought to respond to the sin-

---

69 Cartwright, in Whitgift, *Works,* I, 386.

70 Baxter, *Holy Commonwealth* (London, 1659), p. 274. The extent of congregational discipline and the limits of state coercion were, of course, crucial points of difference during the revolutionary period. These disagreements cannot be considered here. But it is important to stress the general Puritan commitment to moral discipline and reformation, a commitment shared even by men who disagreed on the precise roles of church and state. See William Lamont, *Marginal Prynne: 1600-1669* (London, 1963), pp. 157-174.

fulness of an "ungracious generation." The men who governed
themselves would also govern the others, nervously calling upon
the magistrate, aggressively exploring the uses of sovereignty. Cartwright described "two kingdoms"—one was the congregation, a
world of self-control; the other was the state, a world of external
coercion. The men who refused the discipline of work, the men
who "kept off" from the discipline of the congregation: these were
subjected entirely to the secular power and controlled violence
of the state.

During the years of change and dislocation, Calvinism was one
of the ideologies that legitimized the aggrandizements of state
power. Puritan ministers, extraordinarily sensitive to the dangers
of disorder and wickedness, developed the moral authoritarianism
of their theology into a theory of secular repression. From the beginning, Calvinists had been advocates of regulation and control;
the Genevan system was constructed so as to maximize both—a
task that involved the steady extension of secular authority at
the expense of the lax and inefficient ecclesiastical courts. In Puritanism the same tendency was clear. The saints demanded that
the state replace the corporate church in caring for the poor, in ad-
judicating wills and contracts, in regulating marriage and divorce,
even in enforcing much of the moral law. "There is no crime,"
wrote William Stoughton in 1604 in a treatise dedicated to the
lawyers of the London Inns, "respecting any commandment contained within either of the two tables of the holy law of God but
that . . . hath been evermore and is now punishable by the king's
regal and temporal jurisdiction." Stoughton went on to discuss
adultery, perjury, heresy, and absence from church; he had already
argued that "all and singular matters of espousals and marriages"
should be determined by civil tribunals.[71] Here was a jurisdiction
virtually coextensive with conscience and an authority—the modern state—far more efficient than the old priest-confessor or the
bishop's court. Much of the repressive activity of the revolutionary
Rump and the Cromwellian major-generals was anticipated in the
work of Puritans like Stoughton. Only repression, the fearful

---

[71] William Stoughton, *An Assertion for True and Christian Church Policy*
(London, 1604), pp. 78ff., 85, 116-117. See also Cartwright, in Whitgift, *Works*, I, 267,
and Penry, *A Brief Discovery of the Untruths and Slanders* . . . [Edinburgh, 1590],
pp. 50ff.

ministers believed, could lead to that significant increase in the intensity and security of social control which they so ardently desired. The "reformation of manners" was, or rather would have been, had it ever taken place on the scale which the ministers intended, the Puritan terror.

The need for secular regulation was one of the recurrent themes of Puritan literature. Philip Stubbes, for example, reiterated with what was for him extraordinary precision, Calvin's position on usury. Before God, he wrote, the taking of interest was simply unlawful; "but seeing how much [usury] rageth, lest it should rage further and overflow the banks of all reason and godliness . . . they [i.e. the magistrates] have limited [it] within certain meres and banks . . ." The purpose of such legal limitation, he continued, shifting his metaphor, was to enclose "within the forest, or park, of reasonable or conscionable gain, men who cared not how much they could extort . . ."[72] Long after the publication of Stubbes' *Anatomy of Abuses*, Puritan preachers continued to denounce the usurer and his trade, devoting to the attack all the rhetorical vigor which the sin required. In large part, however, this was mere self-indulgence for Puritan purposes were achieved by governmental regulation. Casuists like Ames and Baxter made more careful distinctions: the saints were not to charge interest on loans to the needy; they were not to press the borrower in time of misfortune.[73] But what was most important was that the ministers left the state to fix the legal limits and set the legal rates.

William Perkins treated the idleness of beggars much as Stubbes had treated the greed of the usurer: he defended ardently the principles of secular regulation and punishment set forth in Elizabeth's poor laws. "And therefore the statute made the last Parliament [1597] for the restraining of beggars and rogues is an excellent statute, and being in substance the very law of God, is never to be repealed."[74] The cruel punishments for vagrancy were, perhaps, less important to the Puritan ministers than the

72 Stubbes, *Anatomy*, pp. 123-124.
73 R. H. Tawney, *Religion and the Rise of Capitalism* (New York, 1926), pp. 180, 185f. But Charles H. George argues that many of the ministers reneged on Calvin's position and were absolute opponents of usury; see "English Calvinist Opinion on Usury, 1600-1640," *Journal of the History of Ideas* 18:462-471 (1957).
74 Perkins, *Works*, I, 755.

extensive and minute control to which the poor were subjected in the "houses of correction." Of course, the numerous instances in which men and women "strong and fit for labor, but having neither masters nor lawful vocations whereby to get their living" were ordered to be whipped and then "burnt through the gristle of the right ear" must have had their emphatic approval.[75] Godly magistrates would not be lax in seeing such punishments carried out; the ministers called upon the J.P.'s vigorously to enforce the new law. They were especially concerned, however, with the close supervision of the workhouses.[76] And here they did not differ from such an intelligent advocate of secular authority as Francis Bacon. "I commend most," Bacon wrote, "houses of relief and correction . . . where the impotent person is relieved and the sturdy beggar buckled to work, and the unable person also not maintained to be idle, which is ever joined with drunkenness and impurity, but is sorted with such work as he can manage and perform."[77] Some of the ministers went further than this and suggested that beggars might even be saved—turned into industrious men. But whether they were saved or not, they would be subject to control—like usurers in the closed "park of conscionable gain"—and no longer free to wander on the open road.[78]

The limitation of usury and the repression of beggary were only two features of the secular controls that the Puritans sought. Their legislative demands would have involved far more regulation, even of activities which other of their contemporaries regarded as harmless enough: bear-baiting, dancing, swearing, Sunday sports, church-ales, and so forth. Puritan M.P.'s introduced one bill after another aiming at the governmental repression of vice, and even attempting to make the local justices responsible for the enforcement of church discipline. Among the papers of the young John Winthrop, who never entered Parliament, is a draft

---

[75] E. P. Cheyney, *History of England* (London, 1926), II, 333.

[76] See the views of Nicholas Bownde, quoted in Knappen, *Tudor Puritanism*, p. 413; also Perkins, *Works*, III, 539. In the seventeenth century, the minister William Gouge is said to have maintained a small workhouse out of his own pocket, employing the poor in the manufacture of cloth; in the Puritan tradition he wrote savagely of men who would not work; Schlatter, *Social Ideas*, p. 142.

[77] Quoted in Sidney and Beatrice Webb, *Old Poor Law*, p. 85.

[78] Charles H. and Katherine George, *The Protestant Mind of the English Reformation* (Princeton, 1961), pp. 156ff.

bill against drunkenness. Both his unofficial concern and his official cure must have been typical of the Puritan gentry.[79]

Puritan demands for secular control find a pale reflection in Tudor and Stuart statutes such as those of James I for the regulation of ale houses.[80] But these laws were so ill-enforced that during the civil wars Richard Baxter could suggest that every drunkard was a royalist: "Every drunken sot that met any of the [godly] in the streets would tell them: we shall take an order with the Puritans ere long . . . And when the wars came almost all these drunkards went into the king's army, and were quickly killed."[81] The statutes for the relief of the impotent poor and the punishment of lusty beggars, the very laws of God, were no better administered. Baxter was certain that beggars also fought for the king. Indeed, the king, who ought to have crowned the whole system of repression, seemed almost to patronize its potential victims. To the pious horror of the ministers, James even encouraged the traditional Sunday revels.

The passage of laws was not enough; there must also exist a will to enforce them. Secular regulation required secular regulators, and if the purposes of the regulation were ultimately Christian, who would be more likely to carry it through successfully than the lay saints? William Stoughton's program for the expansion of state power in fact depended, whether he knew it or not, upon the appearance and activity of godly laymen. For this very reason, Puritan reformation was incompatible with Tudor and Stuart absolutism. Elizabeth and her successors were utterly unwilling to authorize that independent and godly magistracy which alone could have made the discipline a reality. Insofar as they set goals for themselves, they aimed rather at a restoration of traditional order, with the newly sovereign monarchy capping a paternalistic and hierarchical system. In their government they employed a set of instruments appropriate to the world they hoped to restore. And from their subjects they asked only those "easy, dull and drowsy performances" that Puritan activists so vigorously

---

[79] J. E. Neale, *Elizabeth I and her Parliaments, 1587-1601* (London, 1957), pp. 58-60, 99, 394, 396-397; E. S. Morgan, *The Puritan Dilemma: The Story of John Winthrop* (Boston, 1958), p. 26.

[80] 1 James I.c.9; 4 James I.c.5; 21 James I.c.7.

[81] *Reliquiae Baxterianae*, p. 42.

denounced.[82] They had little use for the gratuitous zeal of a John Winthrop.

Jacobean Privy Councillors were, of course, quick to complain of lax administration and willing enough to mock "the new and young knights who come in their braveries" to the Quarter Sessions and "stand like idols to be gazed upon and do nothing."[83] But they were never authorized by their royal master to begin the recruitment of a new magistracy. Kings still relied upon

> The primogenitive and due of birth,
> Prerogative of age, crowns, sceptres, laurels.

Puritan reformation, on the other hand, required a different kind of secular power. It required the replacement of birth, age, and honor by ideological commitment and administrative diligence. This the saints came gradually to understand. Just as the Puritan emphasis upon sustained and methodical endeavor was carried over from the economy to the church (from the particular to the general calling), so it was imported also into the political world. Repression and control would have to become the work of pious magistrates before the king's temporal jurisdiction could be extended to the two tables of the moral law. And magistrates unwilling to be pious, "idols" who did nothing, would have to be overthrown—though, for the moment, that was left to God. "In you it is now to cleanse, to free your country of villainy," Thomas Reeve told the Norwich judges in a typical example of Puritan assize preaching, ". . . consider your power to reform . . . if you be faithful and God's power to revenge if you be faithless."[84] The saints were eager to extend the power of the state only for the sake of reformation, which is to say, only because they hoped one day to exercise that power themselves. And that, indeed, was to be God's revenge on old England.

VII

Despite the well-known intentions of the Puritan Deity and the providential victories of the New Model army, however, the

[82] Sibbes, *Works*, VI, 309.

[83] Quoted in Webb, *Old Poor Law*, p. 94.

[84] Thomas Reeve, *Moses Old Square for Judges* (London, 1632), pp. 98-99; cf. Baxter, *Holy Commonwealth*, pp. 274-78, and the parliamentary sermons cited in Chapter VII.

revolutionary effort to establish a holy commonwealth in England failed. The rule of the saints was brief; the new forms of repression were never enforced through the decisive activity of a state police. Those Englishmen who entered the world of Christian discipline and work did so voluntarily, and their numbers were relatively small. A way of life resembling Puritan repression in some of its features spread more widely, but its adherents were not marked by the fervent willfulness of the saints. With them discipline became a dull routine. It is very difficult to judge the precise role of Puritanism, alongside so many other factors of social and economic history, in creating that new routine. For the moment it is enough to suggest that the transition from a traditional to a modern society was in some fashion mediated by the self-government of the Puritan saints, by their industriousness and their "settled courses," by the dependability of their contractual relations, the effectiveness of their "mutual surveillance," and their sustained commitment to the cause of reformation. The cause was never won, but the struggle undoubtedly had its effects.

Karl Marx suggested another cause of the new disciplinary routine. In the sixteenth and seventeenth centuries, he wrote, beggars and vagabonds, driven from the land, were "whipped, branded, tortured by laws grotesquely terrible, into the discipline necessary to the wage system."[85] But this is not a sufficient explanation. There are in fact very few social transformations in which men can be described so simply as the objects of disciplinary activity. They are also the subjects. And the more successful they are as subjects, the smaller the part played by governmental force. Marx's description is true only because the mass of rural laborers and the multitude of vagabonds and beggars were not yet ready to become the subjects of a systematic self-control. But for that very reason, they were not taught the "discipline necessary to the wage system." They were brutally repressed, but they were not yet morally or psychically transformed and they were not yet integrated into a modern economic system. The making of the English working class came much later, and along with it came ideologies parallel to that of the saints, similarly inculcating self-discipline and teaching a religious or political activism.

85 Karl Marx, *Capital* (Chicago, Ill., 1932), I, 809.

It was not the workers who were being disciplined and who were disciplining themselves in the seventeenth century. That was the pious labor of the saints, who usually occupied a different place in the economic system. The saints had originally planned to extend their control throughout society. But perhaps as they won their inner battles—however paltry the victories—and established their new routines, the "visible disorder" of the "unbroken poor" became less and less a personal threat. After the Restoration, at any rate, separatism put an end to that parish civil war to which the Puritans had been committed. The struggle between saints and worldlings that, according to Baxter, "was begun in our streets before the king or Parliament had any armies," was not resumed after the armies went home.[86] The most difficult stage in the social transition was over—at least for crucial sectors of the population.[87] The fearful Puritan demand for total, state-enforced repression was slowly forgotten. And "the poorest of the people whom the others call the rabble" were pushed into those dim and ugly regions where the whip and the branding iron do their ineffective work. Methodism and the factory, socialism and the unions would one day bring them back into the world of saints and citizens.

[86] Baxter, *Holy Commonwealth,* p. 457.
[87] See Christopher Hill, *Puritanism and Revolution,* p. 235, for a roughly similar view.

CHAPTER SEVEN · PURITANISM AND
THE GENTRY: POLITICS AS A VOCATION

In 1659, John Eliot of Roxbury, Massachusetts, the "apostle to
the Indians," drafted a proposal for a Christian commonwealth
and dispatched it to England, to "the chosen and holy and faithful who manage the wars of the Lord against Anti-Christ . . ."
The American apostle made no effort to describe the political
experience of his fellow colonists or the tribal organization of the
Indians. Instead, he worked out the presumed implications of the
eighteenth chapter of Exodus and called for a new constitution
founded on the ten and the hundred. "God hath commanded that
ten men should choose unto them a ruler of ten." Eliot would
have maintained Puritan family government; in his tens he
counted neither women nor servants nor children, but only "public
free-men." He obviously believed, however, that the ten was a
more important political unit than the household, providing just
the right "compass" for the administration of discipline and making possible those "choices" that Puritans thought so important to
moral life. As soon as children were old enough, he wrote, they
would leave their father's house and ten: "then are they capable
of and bound personally to act, in the choice of their public rulers . . ." This system, Eliot claimed, was already in use among the
angels, and in heaven as among so numerous a people as the English, it required an ascent in numerical order to the myriad and
million, each with its component tens and hundreds and its elected
rulers.[1]

Social discipline was the purpose of Eliot's system, in which a
tenth of all adult males (excluding servants, a category he seemed
to define very narrowly) would become magistrates. Strange utopia
which needed so many governors! But their presence was necessary

[1] John Eliot, *The Christian Commonwealth: or, the Civil Policy of the Rising
Kingdom of Jesus Christ* (London, 1659), sig. A₃, pp. 5-6, 8, 28ff.

to guarantee the development in detail of a godly politics, to insure "the orderly and seasonable practise of all the commandments of God, in actions liable to political observation." "Sin will grow apace," Eliot warned, "like ill weeds if it be not always watched and often weeded out." So the activity of governors must be constant, regular, systematic, "speedy." And the governors themselves, like those Puritan church elders whom they so much resembled, must be pious and knowledgeable, "skillful in the Scriptures . . . that thereby they may be enabled to do their office faithfully."[2] Godly activity and scriptural expertise: these were the key elements in that conscientious magistracy with which Puritans sought to replace the older political fatherhood.

In the sermons and treatises of Eliot's counterparts at home, even the glory of the ministry faded before that of the new officialdom, the lay saints. By the 1640's, the minister had become the adviser and exhorter of the gentleman-in-office, training him in the style and method of conscientious activity. The new clerical function is best exemplified in the revivalist sermons preached to the Long Parliament. Even earlier, Puritan political sermons had emphasized the godly significance of magistracy: preaching at court sessions, at city elections, and occasionally before the king, the ministers had glorified the officer and his "charge" almost to the exclusion of the prince and his prerogative. So they sought to generate that diligent activism which their program required. Christian conscience, they insisted, enforced the charge of God to magistrates. It was the "divine deputy"—"that little God of thy conscience," so William Pemberton described it at the Hartford assize in 1619, "who will sentence thee secretly if thou do amiss."[3] At the Oxford assize in 1628, Robert Harris presented an elaborate picture of the soul as a legal system in which conscience sat as the Lord Chancellor, obliging men to forget if necessary every human tie and do their political duty for God's sake. He warned the judges not to conceal any transgression, not to favor any man.

Now speak, now commence it, spare none. What? Shall I indict my friend?—No, nor foe neither, unless conscience binds thee; if [so],

---

2 *Ibid.*, pp. 11-12, 21.

3 William Pemberton, *The Charge of God and the King, to Judges and Magistrates for Execution of Justice* . . . (London, 1619), p. 70.

present him, whatever he be.—What, a neighbor?—A neighbor.—A kinsman?—A kinsman.—A justice?—A justice.—My landlord?—Thy landlord.[4]

The justice of the saints would thus be impersonal and universal, enforced without favor or feeling. In carrying out the duties of their office, Pemberton told the judges, they must lay aside all "unquiet passions"—he preached against "love, friendship . . . rash zeal."[5] "As they must be godly . . . so they must learn to deny themselves," Stephen Marshall told the members of the Long Parliament in 1641, "they must be taken off from all private self engagements . . ."[6] Men who thought in these terms began in the 1630's and '40's to develop a conception of public service very different from that strong sense of personal loyalty to the king which underlay Tudor and Stuart absolutism and which was not incompatible, because of the nature of the system, with other loyalties to friends and relatives. Conscience required entirely new commitments difficult to reconcile with courtly intrigue or familial aggrandizement. It required above all a commitment to divine purposes that undoubtedly reinforced (but also transformed) the older humanist devotion to the common good; here as in other areas Calvinist godliness is related to the traditions of "civility." But godliness was probably even more important than civility in undercutting and corroding traditional loyalties. The modern notion that a public servant must divest himself of all private connections —which, strictly applied, would have seemed absurd in the sixteenth century and is by no means established doctrine in the twentieth—was enormously strengthened by the Puritan association of sainthood and magistracy. The outcome was suggested in the aphorism of a secular writer in 1654: "Public persons with private aims are monsters in church and state . . ."[7]

4 Robert Harris, St. Paul's Exercise, in Two Sermons (London, 1628), pp. 5, 13.
5 Pemberton, Charge of God, pp. 46, 62.
6 Stephen Marshall, Meroz Cursed (London, 1641), pp. 33-34; see also Thomas Sutton, England's First and Second Summons (London, 1616); Stephen Denison, The New Creature (London, 1622); and John Lawrence, A Golden Trumpet to Rouse Up a Drowsy Magistrate (London, 1624).
7 R. Whitlocke, quoted in Sir George Clark, Three Aspects of Stuart England (London, 1960), pp. 49-50. On the gradual development of a new "mental attitude" toward public service and office-holding, see G. E. Alymer, The King's Servants: The Civil Service of Charles I, 1625-1642 (New York, 1961), pp. 464-465; also his discussion of attempted reforms in the period after 1642, pp. 433ff. The importance of Calvinism for this new "mental attitude" is discussed in C. J. Friedrich, "Introduc-

The social identity of these godly officials was the great dilemma of Puritan politics. Where in the old society, where within the intricate system of personal connection, would such men be found? The preachers called for a conscientious magistracy, but hardly discussed the mechanics of selection. Some of them did insist, however, that office could not be inherited, for "it is not the birth, but the new birth, that makes men truly noble."[8] If a few of the Puritan intellectuals still called magistrates "civil fathers," a larger number talked of them as political saints, elected indeed, but elected by God: "God hath lawfully called you together," preached Richard Byfield to the Commons in 1645, "legally established you, armed you with authority . . . seated you in the hearts of thousands."[9] And if "called" by God, they were transformed by the call: "Private persons are self-centered like clods of the earth," John Ward told the Commons that same year, "but public persons are turned into other men, and have a public spirit . . ."[10] This did not imply any personal superiority; it did seem to open magistracy to the same men who found sainthood available—that is, to open it without regard to social standing.

But this was not the original intention of the ministers. Most Puritans were at least in one crucial sense social conservatives: they believed in a strict and orderly subordination—devoid of mystery, without love or paternal concern, but a subordination nonetheless. And so they turned in their search for the pious magistrate to the already established nobility and gentry. Like the Huguenots, they were willing enough to take advantage of the existing social arrangements; at the same time they sought to rationalize those arrangements and make them purposive. You must act resolutely for God, they told the temporal lords, "not only in your own persons but you and your houses, you and your tenants, you and all that depend on you."[11] In order to do that, however, the lords would first have to turn their households into little

---

tion" to *Politica Methodice Digesta of Johannes Althusius* (Cambridge, Mass., 1932), p. lxxix.

[8] Thomas Adams, *The Holy Choice, in Three Sermons* (London, 1625), pp. 63-64.

[9] Richard Byfield, *Zion's Answer to the Nation's Ambassadors* (London, 1645), p. 8.

[10] John Ward, *God Judging Among the Gods* (London, 1645), p. 16.

[11] Edmund Calamy, *The Nobleman's Pattern of True and Real Thankfulness* (London, 1643), p. 51.

churches and holy commonwealths. They would have to submit to the rigorous discipline of conscience.

II

Change in the political order would require a parallel transformation in the character of the old nobleman—a transformation made possible by the collapse of the feudal order and the "rise" of the gentry and significantly mediated by Puritan ideology. The emerging forms can be traced in the literature of the period even before they make any dramatic appearance in day-to-day activity. Changes in character and politics were paralleled by the development of new ideal types, new models that men were trained to imitate at least in their more public behavior. The old knight and the Renaissance courtier gave way to the Christian gentleman and the pious magistrate.[12] For a time, however, this shift was incomplete and the character of gentry politics indeterminate; and then, as has been seen, the ministers, usurping some of the functions of their temporal lords, anticipated the new styles of behavior. This was a brief though significant moment in the long process out of which something like a modern political order would emerge. But the energetic clerics were no permanent substitute for aristocrats and gentlemen; the increasing political power and intellectual sophistication of the gentry eventually broke open the narrow and exclusive world of the ministers. The new order would require the lay saints—or rather, the lay saints, in the course of establishing their secular and spiritual positions, would create a new order.

In the sixteenth century the nature and meaning of gentility had been made the subject of a great debate, which reflected the gen-

12 The great controversy over the gentry begun by R. H. Tawney with his brilliant "The Rise of the Gentry," *Economic History Review* 11:1-38 (1941), might best be resolved by the argument that the term "rise" actually describes or ought to describe not the appearance of a *new* social class, but rather the transformation of an old one, a transformation which did not occur, for example, in France and which is best defined as an adjustment to modern politics and society. The complex set of changes in personal style, education, religion and economic and political activity *within* the landed classes, taken together, would seem to provide the firmest foundation for an explanation of the growth of parliamentary power, the spread of Puritanism and the seventeenth-century revolution—and this presumably was Tawney's purpose. See G. R. Elton, *England under the Tudors* (London, 1956), pp. 255-259 for a summary of the literature; also J. H. Hexter, *Reappraisals in History* (New York, 1963), chs. ii, iv, vi. That a major change in English character took place in the sixteenth and seventeenth centuries has recently been argued by Zevedei Barbu, *Problems of Historical Psychology* (New York, 1960), chs. v, vi.

erally uncertain position of the nobleman as the period of feudal warfare drew to a close and the sphere of feudal prerogative narrowed. Under attack from the theorists of royal absolutism, the aristocrat needed to reassert his social value if he was to retain some practical independence—as well, perhaps, as some considerable self-esteem. Hence the tendency of the debate was toward a "civil" view of nobility, emphasizing the public functions of gentlemen and aristocrats and deemphasizing their patriarchal responsibilities, their military prowess and their personal or familial loyalties.[13] The earliest Italian discussions of aristocratic "honor," for example, required that the political community always be given precedence over the family, the prince over a man's own father or brother.[14] Humanist writers, on the continent and in England, argued that education rather than birth was the key to true nobility, though they did not mean by this to encourage lower-class ambition. Their purpose was rather to elevate the ambitions of the aristocracy, even to raise learning and "civility" above breeding and heroism in the hierarchy of aristocratic values. Invariably, the writers praised achievement rather than ancestry and usually achievement in the public service. The long discussions of the value of universities, academies and law schools in the education of noble children reflected this new concern, as did the sharp decline, in England, in the number of young men raised as pageboys in the great feudal households.[15]

Both Machiavelli's citizen and Castiglione's courtier are examples of the new "civil" view of gentility, though the second of these suggests at the same time that narrowing of the political public from free city to royal court which marked the later Renaissance. In England, Thomas Elyot's *The Governor* similarly stressed the public role of the nobleman; the activity he envisioned for aristocratic young men was later made more explicit by the authors of

13 See Ruth Kelso's excellent monograph, *The Doctrine of the English Gentleman in the Sixteenth Century*, in University of Illinois Studies in Language and Literature (Urbana, Ill., 1929), vol. XIV, no. 1-2, especially pp. 11ff. There is a discussion of this point in Mark Curtis, *Oxford and Cambridge in Transition, 1558-1642* (Oxford, 1959), p. 267.

14 See F. R. Bryson, *The Point of Honor in Sixteenth Century Italy: An Aspect of the Life of the Gentleman* (Chicago, 1935), p. 108.

15 J. H. Hexter, "The Education of the Aristocracy in the Renaissance," in *Reappraisals*, pp. 45-70; Curtis, *Oxford and Cambridge*, especially chs. iii and iv. On the decline of the "gentlemanly profession of servingman," see J. E. Neale, *The Elizabethan House of Commons* (New Haven, 1950), p. 25.

the "character" books, discussing such figures as The Ambassador and The Counsellor.[16] These were not yet, however, prototypes of the Puritan magistrate. The emphasis of Renaissance writers on personal virtue set fairly clear limits to aristocratic politics, calling into question the impersonality of office. Political office and power were seen as the rewards of talent and audacity; they were pursued because they provided opportunities for the display of personal merit, for such deeds as poets and artists might record. Instead of the disciplined official, the Renaissance produced a political *virtuoso* for whom the state was indeed a work of art, but not yet a sphere of duty.[17]

The struggles of the *virtuosi* produced in their turn a new kind of political lore: the records of opportunities seized and missed, the history of political calculation, the beginnings of statecraft. Here, indeed, was a trade and a mystery which would quickly find its devotees. The combination of aristocratic honor and the ideology of *raison d'état* might even have provided a secular basis for that diligent magistracy toward which Puritan piety also tended. In fact this was the case only occasionally; the devoted and *serious* practitioners of statecraft usually found themselves engaged in an unending feud with the brilliant, but often politically incompetent, court favorites. Nor did the secular ideology of the statesmen provide sufficient force to reshape a nation, to organize the enthusiasm of large numbers of their fellows. The great majority of officials continued to work in the traditional manner, adjusting as best they could to court intrigue and carrying out their appointed functions with little organized or systematic sense of the public good.

Despite the experience of urban republics and royal bureaucracies, then, neither aristocrat nor courtier ever wholly adapted himself to impersonal administration or ideological conflict. In

16 The best study of the sixteenth and seventeenth-century character books is W. E. Houghton, Jr., *The Formation of Thomas Fuller's Holy and Profane States* (Cambridge, Mass., 1938), chs. iii-vii.

17 Jacob Burckhardt, *The Civilization of the Renaissance in Italy* (London, 1955), esp. part II; see also his description of the great despots, pp. 23ff. Some sense of what virtue meant is provided by Thomas Elyot, *The Book Named the Governor*, Everyman edition (London, n.d.), p. 121: In a governor of great authority, he writes, "the fountain of all excellent manners is majesty, which is the whole proportion and figure of noble estate, and is properly a beauty or comeliness in his countenance, language and gesture apt to his dignity, and accommodate to time, place and company . . ."

Italy, assassination, surely the most personal form of political attack and one specifically ruled out by most Calvinist writers, was used freely by both government and opposition. The assassin, if he was not a mere paid killer, "sought only to give vent to the universal hatred or to take vengeance for some family misfortune or personal affront."[18] The murder of Buckingham, the favorite of the English court, by an unimportant gentleman in 1628 might be similarly described. And in a sense, assassination was a proper response to the "fantastical" politics of self-glorification pursued by men like Essex and Buckingham; this was the very antithesis of statecraft, indeed, of any purposive, disciplined political activity. The persistence of nepotism and of the personal entourage in Tudor England and the continuous peculation by royal officials, though both can be explained in terms of the contemporary bureaucratic structure, demonstrate once again the absence of a conscientious self-discipline in public life. A detailed contrast of Elizabethan and Cromwellian warfare would probably suggest the considerable advance in efficiency, system, and routine impersonality that Puritanism helped effect.[19]

At the end of the sixteenth century, it seemed clear that the type of the courtier was at least temporarily dominant and in the close confines of the royal household politics tended to become almost entirely a matter of faction and intrigue. Elizabeth had brought the great Renaissance court to London, permitting the rise of accomplished courtiers like Leicester and Essex alongside such diligent civil servants as Burghley and Walsingham who had absorbed something of the new statecraft. King James' much beloved Buckingham dominated the politics of the early seventeenth century. All the extravagant vitality and the often bizarre brilliance which flourished amidst the decay of the old order was concentrated in the court circles. There personality triumphed; personal cultivation was the key to success—hence the significance of beauty, manners, costume, and wit.[20] The result was a growing

---

18 Burckhardt, *Renaissance*, p. 36.

19 C. G. Cruickshank, *Elizabeth's Army* (Oxford, 1946), pp. 132-133 and *passim;* Cyril Falls, *Elizabeth's Irish Wars* (London, 1950), especially p. 65; the author describes the "dishonesty running through the system," but argues that there was some improvement in the course of the reign. For Cromwell's wars, see Denis Murphy, S.J., *Cromwell in Ireland: A History of Cromwell's Irish Campaigns* (Dublin, 1883), especially ch. iii on preparations for the war.

20 Burckhardt, *Renaissance,* especially p. 223: "The demeanor of individuals, and

estrangement between those ideas relative to success at court and any impersonal religious or political purposes. The intense involvement of Puritan clerics and laymen in the continental religious struggles, for example, was never shared by the English court, not only because of King James' well-known predilection for peace, but also because of the absence of any ideological commitment. Thus a court poet writing during the Thirty Years' War:

> Let the German drum bellow, its noise
> Disturbs us not, nor should divert our joys.[21]

Courtly fashion tended toward increasing refinement and subtle elegance, producing an ever-more delicate and private style. Elizabeth's taste in clothing had been extraordinary both in its unselfconscious ostentation and its grand impracticality. James was already more sophisticated: the king, wrote a contemporary diarist, "doth admire good fashion in clothes . . . [he] is nicely heedful of such points."[22] The latest modes of courtly language, manner and dress were imitated, at some distance, in the Renaissance city of London—though with a growing sense of dissonance as the process of refinement continued. In the more simple countryside, refinement was often identified with vice and the effeminate behavior of the courtiers made the occasion for moral indignation. Nevertheless, Jacobean London became a center of consumption and display, where rural wealth was dissipated in vulgar imitation of courtly styles or in the search for influence and position.[23] The country squire or the squire's son, drawn to London by the court, was endlessly satirized on the Stuart stage. The pursuit of luxury and grace and the consequent decay of rural housekeeping and magistracy were the constant themes, as has been seen, of seventeenth-century moralists. "So should we be easily reformed, and

---

all the higher forms of social intercourse, became ends pursued with a deliberate and artistic purpose." There is an interesting discussion of the "baroque" character in Barbu, *Problems*, pp. 172ff. For a latter-day puritanical view of the court of James I (which is perhaps not so different from that of contemporary Puritans) see Lucy Aikin, *Memoirs of the Court of King James I* (London, 1822).

21 Quoted in Sir Charles Firth, *Oliver Cromwell and the Rise of the Puritans in England* (Oxford, 1953), p. 24.

22 Sir John Harrington, *Letters and Epigrams*, ed. N. E. McClure (Philadelphia, 1930), pp. 32-34.

23 F. J. Fisher, "The Development of London as a Centre of Conspicuous Consumption in the Sixteenth and Seventeenth Centuries," *Transactions*, Royal Historical Society, 4th series, xxx.

made to give over our superfluities," wrote the country gentleman and future royalist, Sir Henry Slingsby, in his diary, "if the
court did not give reputation to such things, and increase our longing by their practicing."[24] The effect of the "longing" created by
courtly splendor was obviously to challenge the stable values of
the country life that Sir Henry loved. But "reform" did not come,
as he would have wished, by example from above; it came rather
as a reaction from below to the courtly challenge and, even more,
to that breakdown of traditional norms that the court both reflected and helped effect.

III

Courtier politics was urbane and sophisticated, but it also was
unprincipled. Protestants like De Mornay in France and Sidney
in England were as frustrated and unhappy in the great northern
courts as they undoubtedly would have been in the south. The two
suggested a Renaissance ideal alternative to the courtier: animated
by a fine sense of personal virtue, they were conditioned at the
same time by a new Calvinist zeal. The court offered no arena
for their idealistic ambitions, yet both were drawn to it as the only
center of political life. Fifty years later, however, young men with
access to court circles—like the future Reverend Richard Baxter
and the future Colonel Hutchinson—would turn away and seek
careers elsewhere.[25] Puritanism on the one hand, and the new
forms of urban and rural life associated with the gentry and lawyers on the other, had come to provide alternatives to the world of
courtly fashion.

The various alternatives were joined, perhaps, in those strange
pieces of Protestant *pastorale* which appeared in the work of Calvinist poets like Du Bartas, Buchanan, and Milton.[26] These suggested a turning away from the court which—though it was con-

24 *The Diary of Sir Henry Slingsby*, ed. Rev. Daniel Parsons (London, 1836), pp.
25-26.
25 F. J. Powicke, *A Life of the Reverend Richard Baxter, 1615-1691* (London,
1924), pp. 18-19. Lucy Hutchinson, *Memoirs of the Life of Colonel Hutchinson*,
ed. by Julius Hutchinson, revised C. H. Firth (London, 1906), p. 47.
26 Milton's masque *Comus* is the finest of the pieces; see also George Buchanan,
Baptistes: A Sacred Dramatic Poem, trans. by Milton (London, 1641), and repr. in
Memoirs of the Life and Poetical Works of John Milton, ed. Francis Peck (London,
1741), and William du Bartas, *The Divine Weeks*, trans. Joshua Sylvester (first
published in installments in the 1590's), ed. by T. W. Haight (Waukesha, Wisconsin,
1908), p. 64-66.

ventional in Renaissance literature—might well have new purposes. Calvin's disciple Theodore Beza had rigorously excluded the pastoral element from his dramatic poem *The Sacrifice of Abraham:* he was responding to an image of country life which was at once simple and sensual, an image not very different from that which was to appear in the work of the Cavalier poets.[27] By the early seventeenth century, however, the dialogue between court and country, a common genre of both medieval and Renaissance literature, has come to suggest the future opposition of Cavalier and Roundhead. The countryman stood now for severity and virtue and he spoke up against the Italianate culture of the court:

. . . for kissing of the hand as if he were licking of his fingers, bending down the head as if his neck were out of joint . . . or leering aside like a wench after her sweetheart, or winking with one eye as if he were levying at a woodcock, and such apish tricks as come out of the land of Petito, where a monkey and a baboon make an urchin generation; and for telling of tales of the adventurous knight and the strange lady . . . for swearing and braving, scoffing and stabbing, with such tricks of the devil's teaching, we allow none of that . . .[28]

The figures in the frontispiece of Nicholas Breton's *The Court and the Country,* published in 1618, actually resemble the drawings which later appeared in revolutionary pamphlets. It was at least partly in the country that the frustrated idealism of the cultured Protestant aristocrat—and equally, of course, the resentment of the sturdy but boorish gentleman farmer—was turned into the stern duty and high-mindedness of the Christian magistrate and saint. Indeed, the revolution can be described in part as an encounter of court and country.[29]

A dialogue between *The English Courtier and the Country Gentleman,* which appeared in 1586 with a dedication to Walsingham, reveals the early stages of the coming conflict. The courtier argues that gentleman's sons should be brought up in the city, frequent the court and serve the king; they should cultivate "civility"—which is more important than "person . . . patrimony or . . . parents." "Husbandry, tillage, grazing, merchandise, buying

27 Theodore Beza, *A Tragedy of Abraham's Sacrifice,* trans. by Arthur Golding, ed. with intro. by Malcolm W. Wallace (Toronto, 1906), p. xlii.

28 Nicholas Breton, *The Court and Country* (London, 1619), sig. B verso.

29 See development of this theme in H. R. Trevor-Roper, "The General Crisis of the Seventeenth Century," *Past and Present,* no. 16 (November 1959), pp. 31-64.

and selling . . . [are] not one of them fit for a gentleman's exercise." The countryman is in some ways more traditional, in some more modern. He will send his sons to the university, "where many become so learned as they gain by learning their own living." "Some also we bring up in the Inns of Court, where if they profit we suffer them to proceed; if not, speedily revoke them from thence, lest they acquaint themselves too much with the licentious customs of the city . . ." "To serve in court, or follow the war, we account these lives rather lewd than laudable."[30] The distaste for the court and the city is a key to future Puritan attitudes. If some gentlemen came to London in eager pursuit of courtly splendor, others reacted to the "licentious customs of the city" with rigid distaste. There was always something in Puritansim of rural simplicity and plainness, of the countryman's dislike for the wicked city, England's Babylon or Nineveh. The godly discipline is not quite accurately described as the religion of the middle classes of Renaissance London; it was much more the religion of men newly come to the city, uneasy there, not yet urbane, not yet sharing the sophistication of the town dweller or the courtier. Such men, disoriented and unsure of themselves, responded to the intense moralism of the clerical saints; at the same time, the congregational discipline taught them an urban style, provided new standards of order and a new routine, set them apart from the motley population of the expanding city and eventually produced a new self-confidence. Indeed, Puritanism taught them a routine that has often and incorrectly been assumed to be that of the city itself.

The countryman of the dialogue of 1586 was himself uncultivated, defending the old rural pastimes and the traditions of hospitality. His sons, educated at the universities and the Inns of Court, would be different men. The Inns underwent an enormous expansion in the century after 1520; they came to provide a center of urban life where fashions often differed from those of the court and where countrymen might find a refuge from London's "licentiousness." By 1620 several of the leading Inns were Puritan dominated; there lawyers and students listened regularly to the sermons of ministers like Sibbes and Preston and absorbed something of the self-discipline and pride of the saint. The out-

---

[30] Anon., *The English Courtier and the Country Gentleman* (London, 1586), repr. in Roxburghe Library, *Inedited Tracts* (London, 1868), pp. 15, 16, 20, 68ff.

come of this training is suggested in the diary of Sir Simonds D'Ewes, associated for many years with the Middle Temple. In the 1630's, D'Ewes won some notice at court, but his interests already lay elsewhere: "I accounted all these aulical favors to be but sandy foundations, which could minister no solid content or satisfaction to a mind accustomed to the raptures and delights of study and knowledge." D'Ewes' scholarly inclinations were reinforced by his puritanical moralism; the two were both in evidence when he followed the king and queen to Cambridge in 1632, but declined to share in their entertainment: "Whilst they were at an idle play there, that gave offense to most of the hearers, I went to Trinity College library and there viewed divers ancient manuscripts . . ."[31]

Gentlemen who shared D'Ewes' tastes usually made their homes in the country, but they visited London, knew their way around the city and were acquainted with the leading merchant families. Already in Elizabethan times, groups of gentlemen—from the same county, with the same rural associations—met occasionally in London taverns to drink and talk together and of course to criticize the government.[32] The Society of Antiquarians apparently originated in informal gatherings of this sort. This important association of friendly scholars and lawyers, whose members included future parliamentarians, met to discuss such topics as the origin and nature of gentility, the antiquity of parliaments, the dignity of titles. "There are divers gentlemen studious of this knowledge," wrote Robert Cotton in 1603, ". . . which have of a long time assembled and exercised themselves therein . . ." James I prohibited them from associating in any formal fashion, but their "studies" were undoubtedly pursued both in the city and in rural retreat.[33] Discussion and study of this sort were so much

31 The following figures for the growth of Gray's Inn are cited in Fisher, "Development of London," p. 41; 200 students admitted in decade 1521-1530; 799 in 1591-1600; 1265 in 1611-1620. *The Autobiography of Sir Simonds D'Ewes,* ed. J. C. Halliwell (London, 1845), II, 67, 140.

32 Fisher, "Development of London," p. 47. There was apparently a particular Inn, in Whitefriars, where Puritan clergymen visiting London on "godly business" lodged; see Valerie Pearl, *London and the Outbreak of the Puritan Revolution: City Government and National Politics* (Oxford, 1961), pp. 179, 233.

33 Joan Evans, *A History of the Society of Antiquaries* (Oxford, 1956), pp. 7-13; also Vernon Snow, "Essex and the Aristocratic Opposition to the Early Stuarts," *Journal of Modern History* 32:226-228 (1960).

preparation for the diligent magistracy—the new civility—which was to be a kind of self-affirmation for both gentlemen and saints.

Sons educated in the universities and in London returned to the country with new interests in law, theology, and business. The children of lawyers and merchants established on the land were similarly disinclined to the old rural ways; the land for them was an investment in both profit and respectability. The scene of pastoral pleasure and peacefulness was invaded by a diligent activity. "Gentlemen," wrote Thomas Wilson in 1600, ". . . are now for the most part grown to be good husbands and know well how to improve their lands and to the uttermost . . ."[34] The new interest is best revealed in an entry in Slingsby's diary: "I am now about a new point of husbandry, new grown in fashion, of burning the swarth they mean to plow, the ashes whereof by experience they find to yield a greater increase of corn than any other manure . . . I will try it upon a piece of ground . . . being never before plowed . . ."[35] The keen sense of experiment here was not reflected in Slingsby's politics, which remained conservative. Nevertheless, intelligent husbandry formed one of the economic bases of the new gentry and for the class as a whole such serious endeavor had its political parallels. A fairly extensive literature explained the new techniques; Gervase Markham's *A Way to Get Wealth* published in 1625 and reissued several times in the thirties is a typical example. Markham had many experiments to suggest and his book—one of several that he wrote on similar topics— was clearly aimed at cultured men.[36] Yet in the years before the accession of James, only one among all the writers on gentility had admitted agriculture to be a gentleman's concern. This was the Puritan minister Lawrence Humphrey, who hated rural idleness.[37]

As a companion of new status and businesslike endeavor, a pervasive seriousness invaded the country. At Little Gidding it took an Anglican form; more often, perhaps, it was nourished

---

[34] Quoted in Maurice Ashley, *England in the Seventeenth Century* (London, 1952), pp. 18-19.

[35] *Diary of Sir Henry Slingsby*, p. 27.

[36] See Gertrude Noyes, *Bibliography of Courtesy and Conduct Books in Seventeenth Century England* (New Haven, 1937), p. 11 for discussion of new interest in husbandry; pp. 72ff. for list of books by Markham.

[37] On Humphrey, see Kelso, *English Gentleman*, p. 58.

by some sort of Puritanism. Though it probably affected only a
small segment of rural society, this seriousness, this atmosphere
of "savoury discourse and grave deportment," helped provide the
moral tone appropriate to the gradual consolidation of the country
gentry and the development of its peculiar style, reflecting the
long years of interaction with the city, the attractions and repul-
sions of the court.[38] London news circulated in the country and
London politics found, perhaps for the first time, a national response. The Suffolk vicar and Justice of the Peace John Rous
recorded the arrival of the latest "corantos" in his diary; he worried over the Montagu affair in the twenties and mourned Alexander Leighton's ears in 1630. Lady Brilliana Harley sent the
latest "foreign news" to her son at Oxford in 1639, "being still
desirous to have your mind keep awake in consideration of the
affairs abroad."[39] Such examples are by no means atypical and
the diaries record the arrival of sermon books as well as news-
letters full of gossip and court scandal. An extraordinary intellectual life grew up in the country. Sometimes it reflected the culture
of the court and the new Renaissance learning, and then a man
like Robert Filmer of Kent was its product. The antiquarian
D'Ewes or the earnest Colonel Hutchinson, poring over parliamentary speeches, were products of another sort. Among the
various groups which shared intellectual interests new forms of
affinity developed; manuscripts were circulated and opinions can-
vassed. The practice of countryhouse visiting, a modern historian
has suggested, reveals a new "lateral movement" in English society through which families in different parts of the country
were linked by friendship and politics.[40]

Status and seriousness were summed up in the Commission of
the Peace, which acquired an enormous prestige in the early seventeenth century. Here was the position around which the ideas of
pious magistracy first clustered. They reflected the ambition of
new men, who possessed the knowledge (or knowledgeability),
the professional style and the sense of dignity which the colleges

38 An excellent discussion of country life in the seventeenth century is to be
found in David Mathew, *The Age of Charles I* (London, 1951), chs. viii, x, xii, and
xix; see also Robert Ramsey, *Henry Ireton, 1611-1651* (London, 1949), p. 203f.

39 *Diary of John Rous*, ed. M. A. E. Green (London, 1856), pp. 31, 45-47, 53, 67;
Letters of the Lady Brilliana Harley, ed. T. T. Lewis (London, 1854), p. 51.

40 Mathew, *Charles I*, pp. xiii, xiv.

and the Inns of Court provided. The older Renaissance ideals—
prince, courtier, ambassador, counsellor—must have seemed distant to the country justices, either not within practical range or
newly undesirable because of their dislike for court intrigue. To
become Justice of the Peace signaled one's arrival in country
society. Equally important for ambitious men, the ministers made
the commission appear a dramatic opportunity for the exercise
of godliness. The idea of "reformation," so vividly acted out by
members of the Long Parliament, had for several decades before
1640 been associated—at least in the printed literature—with the
activity of the local J.P. It was among these country magistrates,
a recent writer has suggested (but also, it should be added, among
their counterparts and colleagues at the London Inns), that the
skills, the self-confidence, the resolute high-mindedness and the
actual opinions which made political opposition possible first appeared in lay society.[41]

IV

That general uncertainty as to the nature of gentility which
marked sixteenth-century thought went hand in hand with a considerable confusion as to the actual membership of the English
gentry. Several generations of economic instability—the result
of the price revolution and the extraordinarily active trading in
land which followed the confiscation of the monasteries—had
brought men of doubtful families into the country and forced
many children of gentle birth into "servile" trades in the city.
The most immediate result of status confusion of this sort was
status anxiety. And anxiety undoubtedly played an important
role in opening men for that character transformation with which
Puritanism has been credited. The literature of the late sixteenth
and early seventeenth centuries seems at times to suggest a kind
of status panic roughly analogous to the salvation panic often
induced by Calvinism. Clearly, the two forms of uneasiness were
related (and, clearly, the two have sometimes been exaggerated).
Their expression occasionally took on a similar tone, as in an
ostensible "apprentice's letter to his father" reprinted in a book
by the minor English writer Edmund Bolton in 1627. The letter

---

[41] Peter Laslett, "The World We Have Lost," *The Listener*, April 21, 1960,
pp. 700-701.

is well worth quoting for its obvious similarity to the religious introspection of contemporary diaries:

> . . . my mind and spirits . . . are very much troubled . . . [By] reading certain books, at spare hours, and conferring with some who take upon them to be very well-skilled in heraldry, I am brought to believe that by being a 'prentice, I lose my birthright . . . which is to be a gentleman, which I had rather die than to endure . . . This is my grief and this the cause why my mind is so troubled as I cannot eat nor sleep in quiet . . .

Bolton argued with considerable passion that apprenticeship did not involve bondage and hence did not require "the barbarous penalty of loss of gentry." If worry of this sort was serious and not mere affectation, it must have involved a considerable number of people; in London in the 1620's there were "many hundreds of gentlemen's children apprentices . . ."[42]

Similar doubts existed as to the gentility of the merchant; in the sixteenth century, at least, it was commonly denied. John Ferne, the best Elizabethan authority on heraldry, argued "that the practice [of trading] consisteth of most ungentle parts, as doubleness of tongue, violation of faith . . ."[43] Heralds, of course, had a vested interest in such distinctions, a vested interest indeed in anxiety itself and this especially in an age when merchants "often change estate with gentlemen, as gentlemen do with them, by a mutual conversion of one into the other."[44] In the early years of the seventeenth century, the position of Ferne was so vigorously attacked as to indicate that some doubts still remained, but the balance was clearly shifting. By the 1620's and '30's, London merchants, often themselves sons of country gentlemen, had developed a considerable if still uneasy literature of self-enhancement. Thus Lewis Roberts in one of the first systematic treatises on commerce, published in 1638, opened with an apology for his ungentle style—"had not my younger years been drawn by adverse fortune . . . from the study of arts to the study of

---

42 Edmund Bolton, *The Cities' Advocate* (London, 1629), sig. B verso; Bolton disputed the assertion of the Elizabethan writer Sir Thomas Smith that apprenticeship was a form of servitude, pp. 8-15; he argued instead that it was a "civil contract," p. 9.

43 John Ferne, *The Blazon of Gentry* (London, 1586), p. 7; see Bolton's disagreement, *Cities' Advocate*, p. 54.

44 William Harrison, *Harrison's Description of England in Shakespeare's Youth*, ed. F. J. Furnivall (London, 1877), I, 131.

marts, I myself . . . etc."—but proceeded to argue that the merchant was better prepared than any other man to perform the duties of a statesman.[45] It is significant that Roberts made this the test of gentility. "Worthiest of all immortal praise are these [merchants]," wrote Gerard Malynes in 1622, taking a different tack, "who can and do (by easy, just and politic means) enrich kingdoms and commonwealths."[46] The idea of the merchant as a public benefactor and a man well-prepared by travel and experience for public office took hold in the years before the revolution. But the new reputation attached securely only to the "merchant royal" whose trade was a "full fraught and free adventure" and not yet to "the hedge-creeper that goes to seek shelter from shop to shop."[47] "The merchant adventurer," wrote Thomas Wilson, "is and may be taken for a lord's fellow in dignity as well for his hardy adventuring upon the seas . . . as for his royal and noble wholesales . . ."[48] This was an attempt to assimilate the merchant to older ideas of nobility and therefore it excluded "retailers at home." Such distinctions only intensified ambition, for they already involved significant compromises.

In the sixteenth century, an effort was made with some success to revive the ancient College of Heraldry. The enormous expansion in the number of pedigreed families, of knights and esquires, which took place in the next seventy-five years, suggests the intense concern with status.[49] The new interest in heraldry provided a means at once of recognizing the newer members of the gentry and of maintaining the class's old and exclusive dignity. Armor and blazon, as Bolton remarked in an earlier book (*The Elements of Armory*, 1610), were "the marks by which gentlemen are known, first from the ignoble and then one from the other."[50] The heralds developed a curious mythology in which gentlemen were viewed as a race apart from ordinary men, a race possessed

45 Lewis Roberts, *The Merchant's Map of Commerce* (London, 1638), epistle and p. 2; see *DNB* for Roberts' social background.

46 Gerard Malynes, *The Maintenance of Free Trade* (London, 1622), epistle.

47 Thomas Powell, *The Art of Thriving* (London, 1635), p. 84; see Kelso, *English Gentleman*, pp. 60-61.

48 Thomas Wilson, *A Discourse upon Usury* (London, 1572), ed. R. H. Tawney (London, 1925), p. 203.

49 See Kelso, *English Gentleman*, p. 26; also Lawrence Stone, "The Inflation of Honors: 1558-1641," *Past and Present*, no. 14 (November 1958), pp. 45-70.

50 Edmund Bolton, *Elements of Armories* (London, 1610), p. 5.

of superior *virtue* and incorporated, as it were, under the law of arms—"begun before any law in the world but the law of nature, and before the Ten Commandments of God."[51] A group of English writers, Ferne among them, revived the medieval insistence that the distinction of noble and ignoble, of gentle and churlish, went back to Noah's sons and had been continuous ever since. This latter argument did not appear in seventeenth-century texts, but the treatises on heraldry continued to be popular right up to the revolution. There was, however, a subtle change in the tone of the books, due apparently to the realistic response of author and publisher to a changing audience. Ferne's *Blazon of Gentry,* printed in 1586, had been belligerently marked out "for the instruction of all gentlemen bearers of arms, whom and none else, this work concerneth." Bolton's *Elements,* published only twenty-four years later, was addressed to the "learner" without qualification. It concluded with "A short table of some hard words," for though he wished, wrote Bolton, "such a reader as need not an interpreter, yet I must not neglect such as I have."[52] Presumably his audience already included those merchants and apprentices whom he later defended.

One of the results of the confusion and anxiety over gentility was a series of books on how to be a gentleman. These reflected a desire to organize life in its smallest details, to achieve self-assurance by obeying rules. Richard Brathwait's *The English Gentleman* (1630) set out to present "the true and new art of gentilizing . . ." The chapter titles suggest the method and contents of the book: "How a gentleman is to demean himself in public affairs of state," "How a gentleman is to bestow himself in recreation," "What directions are to be observed in the choice of a wife," "Who are the best consorts to pray with, to play with, to converse or commerce with." The book would appeal especially

51 Anon., *The Gentleman's Academy* (London, 1959), pp. 43-44.
52 Ferne, *Blazon,* title page; Bolton, *Elements,* p. 202. A similar comparison may be made between *The Gentleman's Academy* (1595) addressed "To the gentlemen of England and all good fellowship of Huntsmen and Falconers," and a later reprint of the same book, *A Jewel for Gentry* (London, 1614), described as "a true method to make *any man* understand all the arts . . ." (emphasis added). The same shift may be seen in the books on horsemanship and soldiering—once thought "gentle" arts; see, for example, John Curso, *Military Instruction for the Cavalry* (Cambridge, 1632), which is written, proclaims the epistle, in the "bluntest and plainest" style, for the "tyro and untutored horseman."

to new men, for its emphasis throughout was on doing rather than being.[53] In the century before the revolution, a vast number of similar works appeared with the same emphasis, handbooks, compilations, almanacs of all sorts, all claiming to "lay forth a pathway so apt, plain and easy, to any learner's capacity." Publishers preyed on men's fear of betraying social inferiority; they printed treatises on letter writing, collections of pretty sayings, rules of behavior in every possible situation, "academies of compliments," and so on.[54] Like the Puritan popular literature, all this was vulgarization and yet it must have been the occasion for much labor as men sought anxiously to avoid gaucherie. It was not only the matter of good form, however, which made them buy the conduct and courtesy books; it was also a desire to convince themselves, so to speak, of their social merit.

Significantly, such books were similar in form and often in content to Puritan texts on godliness: social how-to-do-it found its parallel in spiritual method. The two were related in their purposes: they both helped men achieve a sense of merit. In the same year that Brathwait's book appeared, the Puritan minister Thomas Taylor published a treatise presenting the "means of attaining a full measure of holiness"—"To do this," wrote Taylor, "observe these rules." The preacher Paul Bayne suggested "how we may excite repentance" and prescribed a series of practical "exercises." In an assize sermon preached in 1623, Immanuel Bourne touched upon what was perhaps the most important problem: he offered "rules of counsel to get and preserve a good conscience."[55] Uncertain of his salvation, the saint was thus stirred to methodical and disciplined activity. Like Brathwait's gentleman, "he holds idleness to be the very moth of a man's time; day by day hath he his task imposed." For saint and gentleman alike life itself became a series of tasks, performed according to rules for explicit purposes. As the new gentleman was required to ride and hunt less for the pleasure and the "good fellowship" than for the

[53] Richard Brathwait, *The English Gentleman* (London, 1630), table of contents; on Brathwait see W. L. Ustick, "Changing Ideals of Aristocratic Character and Conduct in Seventeenth Century England," *Modern Philology* 30:153-157 (1932).

[54] This literature is described in L. B. Wright, *Middle Class Culture in Elizabethan England* (Ithaca, New York, 1935), pp. 126ff., especially pp. 136-137.

[55] Thomas Taylor, *The Progress of Saints to Full Holiness* (London, 1630), p. 259; Paul Bayne, *A Caveat for Cold Christians* (London, 1618), pp. 11-13, 19ff; Immanuel Bourne, *The Anatomy of Conscience* (London, 1623), p. 32.

exercise—and of course the display—so with the saint: religion was a method rather than a comfort.[56] "The health of the body is preserved by exercise," wrote Thomas Taylor, "so is the health of the soul by the exercise of grace." He went on to describe the arduous method of self-examination. "Sanctification is a continual act and proceeding . . ."—a continual effort. Similarly, grace was an exercise and not a pleasurable, soul-filling ecstasy.[57] Similarly again, gentility was no longer a status confidently assumed; there was the difficult matter of observing the proprieties and diligently, day after day, carrying out the correct tasks. The activity of the gentleman acquired a new precision at the same time as his person became more difficult to define. The same can be said of the saint; and in the amalgamation of sainthood and gentility can be seen that reinforcement of self-esteem and confidence which made possible (and which was expressed in) the diligently "re-forming" activity of the pious magistrate.

v

There were gentlemen enough, of course, who took their nat-ural superiority entirely for granted, without anxiety and with-out any noticeable diligence in their activity. Many country squires would have agreed with Viscount Conway's summary of their prerogatives: "We eat and drink and rise up to play and this is to live like a gentleman, for what is a gentleman but his pleasure?"[58] Nor did the social how-to-do-it literature require anywhere near so arduous a self-discipline as was demanded by the Puritan method. Brathwait, indeed, had a gift only for the platitudinous; his four-hundred-fifty page book makes Shakespeare's Polonius appear a model of wit. Along with a certain puritanical piety, he added only prolixity to the older humanist idealism; his real im-portance lay with his audience, assiduously gathering the elements of respectability from his text. There was an alternative outcome

56 Brathwait, *English Gentleman*, sig. Nnn; on the new, utilitarian view of physical exercise, see W. L. Ustick's discussion of King James' *Basilikon Doron* and of a letter of advice from Bacon to Buckingham, in "Advice to a Son: A Type of Seventeenth Century Courtesy Book," *Studies in Philology* 29:417-419 (1932).

57 Taylor, *Progress of Saints*, pp. 20-21, 202.

58 Quoted in Maurice Ashley, *England in the Seventeenth Century (1603-1714)* (London, 1952), p. 18.

of sixteenth-century humanism, however, even less compatible with Puritan discipline; this was best revealed in Henry Peacham's *Complete Gentleman* (1622), which may be taken as a character of the future Cavalier. Peacham emphasized the importance of education, but he had little to say about the practical activity of the gentleman; hence education for him culminated in external accomplishment and display rather than in humanist civility or in anything resembling Puritan magistracy. The object of learning was something very near to personal development; it quite clearly was not the service of God. More than this, it was a fine sense of personal worth and a trained capacity for adventure that he required of his complete gentleman and not a conscientious concern with duty—founded, as among the Puritans, upon a certainty of personal worthlessness or at least upon some more vague sense of social or spiritual inadequacy.[59]

Peacham's book dealt only briefly with the public role of the gentleman. In this sense, the Cavalier, for all his culture and accomplishment, was something of an anachronism long before the period of Jacobitism and romantic decline. For the aristocracy of the seventeenth century was increasingly defined by its public activity. This was the period of the rise on the continent, under the auspices of royal absolutism, of aristocratic military and administrative castes. And it was the period in England when the parliamentary gentlemen and the Justice of the Peace reached the peak of their importance. The Cavalier was too much a cultivated and adventurous individual to feel at ease in a world of prosaic or pious officialdom. He did have something in common, however, with the new ideal types of the continental aristocracy. At court and in the military castes a corporate sense of pride was cultivated which, in fact, closely resembled the Cavalier's more personal sense of honor and worth. In general, it may be argued that with Cavalier and army officer alike, honor took the place that conscience filled in the pure type of the Christian gentleman.[60] And honor was related only indirectly to civic or religious

59 Henry Peacham, *The Complete Gentleman* (London, 1622), *passim*: see also Ustick, "Changing Ideals," p. 153.

60 See discussion of honor morality in Kelso, *English Gentleman*, pp. 96ff. Burckhardt describes honor as "that enigmatic mixture of conscience and egotism

duty; it involved, instead, a personal, familial, or corporate sense of dignity and courage; it required the graceful display of those attributes conventionally assumed to belong to aristocracy. Conscience, on the other hand, dictated and presumably directed the acting out of inner goodness. The two were not, of course, entirely distinct: some sense of duty developed alongside the nervous egotism of the Renaissance courtier; and the reformed magistrate, for all his sober piety, did not surrender a certain pride of place and a considerable flair for self-dramatization. Conscience and egotism, piety and honor—all four had their place in the formation of the rigorous social and moral codes of the new administrative and military elites. This is especially evident in any examination of the continental officers' corps that had its origin in the seventeenth century.[61] However, the stereotyped honor of the court clique and the military caste did not make for independent political activity. Wounded honor was satisfied in the duel; injured conscience led to political opposition.

The Cavalier, in summary, was less a divine instrument than a courtly ornament and if at times an ornament of courage and prowess, then also an ornament of conversation, personal beauty, and erotic attraction. These last were simply ignored in the Puritan literature, which always disparaged the values of personality and wit. What is more important, they were absent also from the conduct literature in which the ideal of the Christian gentleman was developed. Throughout the pamphlets and treatises the impact of seriousness is apparent; it came eventually to be thought a character trait of the English. And seriousness combined with a peculiar style of personal effacement: "Let us therefore be persuaded," Stephen Marshall told the members of the Long Parliament at Pym's funeral, "to *use* men as God's instruments, but *build* nothing upon them . . ."[62]

which often survives in the modern man after he has lost . . . faith, love, and hope." *Renaissance*, p. 263.

61 See G. A. Craig, *The Politics of the Prussian Army, 1640-1945* (Oxford, 1955), pp. 11, 16. Craig quotes the following description of the officer corps under Frederick II, p. 16n.: The officers are always prepared for the "renunciation of all personal advantage, of all gain, of all comfort—yes! of all desire if only honor remain! On the other hand, every sacrifice for this, for their King, for their fatherland, for the honor of Prussian weapons! In their hearts, duty and loyalty; for their own lives, no concern!"

62 Stephen Marshall, *The Church's Lamentation for the Good Man's Loss* (London, 1644), pp. 9-10.

VI

The century before 1640 can be regarded as the time of the gentleman's education: in "city-arts," in "the new art of gentilizing," in the godly method and finally in "parliament-craft." Pym, Hampden, Cromwell—such men were the products of this education. The how-to-do-it books were a part of their training; so were the Puritan sermons; so, in fact, was the whole wide range of published works, so tremendously expanded by the early seventeenth century and including by 1620 the ancestor of the modern newspaper. Significantly, it was the new men and the saints who sought to know the "news." The readers of the weekly pamphlets of the twenties were characterized by an antagonistic court poet in a revealing bit of doggerel: ". . . the 'prentices, new maids, and rich, wealth-witi'd Loobies . . ."[63] Ben Jonson satirized the gentleman in search of information and gossip in his play *The Staple of News* and described the fledgling Puritan statesman in an epigram "The New Crie:"

> Ere cherries ripe, and straw-berries be gone
> Unto the cries of London Ile add one;
> Ripe statesman, ripe: They grow in every street.
> At sixe and twentie, ripe . . .
> The councils, projects, practises they know
> And what each prince doth for intelligence owe,
> And unto whom
> They carry in their pockets Tacitus
> And the Gazetti, or *Gallo-Belgicus* . . .
> . . . And they know,
> If the States make peace, how it will goe
> With England. All forbidden bookes they get.
> And of the poulder-plot they will talk yet.
> At naming the French King, their heads they shake
> And at the Pope, and Spaine slight faces make.
> Or 'gainst the Bishops, for the Brethren, raile . . .[64]

The *Gallo-Belgicus* was a yearbook reporting the news of the continental religious struggles; it was succeeded in the 1630's by the *Swedish Intelligencer* that retailed news of even greater inter-

[63] Abraham Holland, quoted in J. B. Williams, *A History of English Journalism* (London, 1908), p. 5. But the news letters in fact were read in families like Sir Robert Harley's; see *Letters of Lady Harley*, p. 19: ". . . and now the corantos are licensed again, you will weekly see their relations."
[64] Ben Jonson, *Poems*, ed. G. B. Johnston (Cambridge, Mass., 1955), pp. 43-44.

est to Puritan readers. Cromwell apparently conned his lessons in strategy from the *Intelligencer's* detailed accounts of Gustavus' German campaigns. This too was a form of education.[65]

Jonson was undoubtedly right to connect the "new statesmen" with the Puritan "brethren." Upstarts both, they were bound together by more than their mutual sense of newness. Puritanism was functionally related to the politics of public opinion, even when it did not provide its actual content. Like the handbooks and the compilations, but far more importantly, the literature of the clerical intellectuals taught the "new statesmen" a style. Serious endeavor and self-control, the intellectuals' response to disorder in the social and religious world, were the primary elements of this style and both were appropriate to men in the process of achieving a new place for themselves in the world of affairs— making their way through the universities, into the city, into Parliament. There is a close historical correlation between the political development of the English Commons and the spread of Puritan piety: the men who connived at the committee system, insisted on a say in foreign policy and fastened a hold on the national purse were above all *serious* men and serious in the Puritan sense, their egos and their consciences inseparable. They or their kin or their friends or their supporters—perhaps all together— took notes at sermons, consulted with the ministers, and recorded in their diaries their daily sense of accomplishment and failure. All this was education, too. Braced by their contact with Calvin's God, imagining themselves to be his instruments, country gentlemen and city merchants and lawyers learned to be parliamentary statesmen.

This process is crucially important and needs to be described in much greater detail than is possible here. In one sense, parliamentary politics was only the "reflex" of the solidity and seriousness of the new gentry. Just as the clerical saints imagined a church ruled by men like themselves, sincere, learned, conscientious intellectuals governing purely by the Word and not requiring the

[65] See the preface to the second part of *The Swedish Intelligencer* (London, 1632): the author writes that "God has begun to send a deliverer unto his people" and that to bring this news to "well-affected Englishmen . . . was next unto the preaching of the Gospel." On Cromwell, see Firth, *Oliver Cromwell*, pp. 29-30.

support of sensual garments, ritual or art, so the Christian gentleman constructed his politics from the elements of his character
and his interests. The pious magistrate was a rural judge or a
member of Parliament, raised up in the universities and preached
at endlessly in the name of God and public service. Soon enough
he produced a commonwealth governed by men like himself,
diligent parliamentarians, lawyers, and judges—and godly major-
generals—who did not require the symbolic accouterments of
power, for whom the book and the sword sufficed. Milton spoke
for both groups, ministers and gentry, when he denounced not
only the "costly and dear-bought scandals and snares of images,
pictures, rich copes, gorgeous altar cloths . . ." but also "the dis-
solute and haughty court . . . of vast expense and luxury."[66] Devotion and talent were best symbolized by a plain black suit and
a modest manner. Thus the older humanist tradition of civility
survived but was transformed by the impact of Calvinist piety
and discipline. Milton, in a way, was the embodiment of both.
It was the fusion of the two also in the character of the English
gentleman that provided the intellectual and spiritual basis for
political opposition.

But opposition in practice required something else, some more
special preparation—a peculiar certainty, a willfulness, almost a
fanaticism. This was exclusively a Puritan product, the result of
an intense, disciplined response to deeply felt anxieties, to some
secular form of the ministers' "unsettledness." When the gentleman's nervous self-esteem took the form of sainthood, when he
saw himself an instrument of God, then his pious willfulness set
him free from traditional political controls. So the ministers had
been set free in the 1580's and had laid the foundations of radical
politics. "In pursuit of their aims," writes J. E. Neale, "they
taught the House of Commons methods of concerted action and
propaganda. Indeed, the art of opposition . . . was largely learnt
from them or inspired by them."[67] By the 1640's, this art had been
widely diffused through lay society and the philosophical or
theological principles that might have limited its use had been

---

[66] Milton, *Works*, ed. F. A. Patterson, et al. (New York, 1932), III, Part I, 54; VI,
120.

[67] Neale, *Elizabeth I and Her Parliaments: 1584-1601* (London, 1957), p. 436.

worn away. More than this, a large number of laymen had been trained in the Puritan congregations who saw in the art of opposition an inescapable duty.

"If we have the honor to be God's instruments," Edward Corbett told the Commons in 1642, "we must do the office of instruments and be active . . . we must go along with Providence."[68] But the "office of instruments" included many duties which the office of a member of Parliament did not traditionally include. The persistent invasions of the royal prerogative by Puritan parliamentarians were probably the acts of instruments more often than of members—though for many men the two identities fused, each strengthening the other. Thus Peter Wentworth, a country gentleman from Northamptonshire imprisoned in 1591 for his attacks upon the Queen's prerogative, asked the privy councilors how else he could have behaved—"the Lord opening a clear view thereof to mine eyes, and I being a Parliament man?"[69] They had no choice, thought the Puritan member Dalton; they must "proceed orderly to the discharge of their own consciences in making law." And *let them care for the rest whom it behooveth.*"[70] Without some such attitude, radical politics is probably inconceivable. Oliver Cromwell at least would never have acted as he did—so he told the First Protectorate Parliament in September 1654—had God not again opened a "clear view." Not as a Cambridgeshire gentleman but only as a saint could he rule England. "I called not myself to this place." But the Lord had "most clearly by His Providence" put power into Oliver's hands and not until the providences were clear again could he yield it up.[71]

This extraordinary sense of religious vocation, reinforcing secular reasons for opposition to the crown, can be seen at work in three different aspects of parliamentary life: in elections, in political organization, and in the religious "exercises" that were so crucial to revolutionary activity in the 1640's. These can only be outlined here; they deserve to be examined much more care-

68 Edward Corbett, *God's Providence* (London, 1642), p. 28.

69 Quoted in Neale, *Parliaments: 1584-1601*, p. 261.

70 Quoted in Neale, *Elizabeth I and Her Parliaments: 1559-1581* (New York, 1953), p. 213 (emphasis added).

71 *Letters and Speeches*, III, 41, 46. Cromwell's sense of vocation is well described in R. S. Paul, *The Lord Protector: Religion and Politics in the Life of Oliver Cromwell* (London, 1955), pp. 148, 271-272, 386-389.

fully—perhaps through a number of biographical studies of the political saints in which the delicate task of weighing the impact of religious zeal might be undertaken. For the moment, it can only be suggested that in the sixteenth and seventeenth centuries radical innovation in politics (especially when this involved the cooperation of numbers of men) was inconceivable without the moral support of religion—and that religion probably provided the major incentive for innovation.

(1) *Elections.* Since the divine instruments (except for Oliver) were in fact elected by men, Puritan preachers tended to infuse the election process with a religious purpose. They appealed to the seriousness of the electors: the "holy choice" was to be made with "religious care," preached Thomas Adams, and only after a period of "public devotion." Adams' intention was to overcome or at least call into doubt the old ties of family and patronage. He could hardly have been successful in 1625; what is important is that the intention was present, working its way into the consciousness of the voters. The preacher warned against the casual assumption of office by the son of the previous incumbent: "Nature is regular in the brute creatures; eagles do not produce cravens . . . But in man she fails . . . Children do often resemble their parents in face and feature, not in heart and qualities . . ."[72] Similarly, John Preston insisted that "it is an error among men to think that in the election of burgesses . . . [they] may pleasure their friends or themselves . . ." Preston described the way instruments might be chosen who would be free, under God and the discipline of conscience, to act for the public good. The electors, he wrote, "ought to keep their minds single and free from all respects; so that when they come to choose, they might choose him whom in their own consciences and in the sight of God, they think fittest for the place . . ." Had he lived, the Puritan leader would undoubtedly have been pleased with the report that Isaac Pennington was elected to Parliament by the London Common Hall in 1640 because of his "known zeal, by his keeping a fasting Sabbath . . ." This was an election, presumably, in the godly manner—and it also suggests the nature of Puritan campaigning.[73]

---

[72] Adams, *Holy Choice*, pp. 56-57, 63.

[73] John Preston, *Life Eternal or, A Treatise of the Knowledge of the Divine Essence and Attributes* (London, 1634), Second sermon, p. 67. On Pennington, see Pearl, *London*, p. 179.

To insure such a choice as Preston described it was necessary to make the election a public proceeding and godliness a political issue. The Elizabethan Puritan Job Throckmorton told his constituents that he "would not have this matter [the parliamentary election] huddled up in a corner, as most of your matters be."[74] He would not, in other words, have elections settled through old-fashioned familial negotiation. In the seventeenth century the spread of political consciousness made it increasingly difficult to "huddle up" the choice of M.P.'s. Elections became instead occasions for the assertion by the gentry of their new public spiritedness and their new godliness. When John Pym rode through England in 1640 promoting the election of "puritanical brethren" he was acting out a conception of political activity that had had a long development. That same year the "ripe statesmen" whom Ben Jonson once satirized were vividly present at the London elections. The result of all this activity, a Puritan preacher suggested, was that the members of the Long Parliament represented "laconically and by way of abridgement, the piety and holiness . . . of a kingdom"—and not the leading subjects merely or the dominant interests.[75]

(2) *Political organization.* As familial and personal loyalties were not to influence elections, so hierarchy was not to limit the zeal of elected representatives. Only action, the ministers taught, "makes us instruments of God's glory." In order that action might be free, the parity of ministers found its political parallel in the equality of magistrates. "The conscience of the monarch and the conscience of the inferior judges are equally under subjection to the King of Kings," wrote Samuel Rutherford, "for there is here a co-ordination of consciences, and no subordination . . . it is not in the power of the inferior judge to judge . . . as the king commandeth him . . ."[76] This is another example of the leveling power of the Calvinist God. At the same time, it was exaltation indeed for rural J.P.'s, city aldermen and members of Parliament and it made possible new sorts of organization among them. Like the ministerial conferences and the Puritan congrega-

---

74 J. E. Neale, *The Elizabethan House of Commons* (New Haven, 1950), pp. 252-254.

75 Henry Wilkinson, *Babylon's Ruin, Jerusalem's Rising* (London, 1643), p. 30.

76 Samuel Rutherford, *Lex, Rex, or The Law and the Prince* (first published in 1644; repr. Edinburgh, 1843), p. 5.

tions, these new organizations were based upon the mutual recognition of equality and dignity. They committed men to coordinated activity and generated new patterns of trust and loyalty appropriate to the difficult and dangerous work of the lay saints.

Among the parliamentary Puritans of the seventeenth century there already existed a complex system of matrimonial alliances. In part, this system was the outcome of Puritan separatism: the saints would have nothing to do, and would permit their children to have as little as possible to do, with the ungodly. But, of course, the Puritan "party" was also, quite simply, an association of relatives and it was undoubtedly strengthened by familial loyalty. What was new about the Puritan parliamentarians, however, was that they were strengthened also in a very different way. Alongside the old-fashioned matrimonial alliances they developed associations more like those with which the ministers had experimented in the 1580's—just as, alongside the traditional parliamentary ritual, they produced new "exercises" of commitment which resembled the religious exercises of the Puritan congregation. The Solemn Oath and Covenant was typical of the new associations; it was conceived as a parallel to the Old Testament covenants that had been explicated in great detail by Puritan writers and preachers. Pym had actually proposed a version of such an association as early as 1621.[77] In 1628 the minister Alexander Leighton published an *Appeal to Parliament* in which he anticipated the coming revolution by suggesting a parliamentary covenant for "the breaking down of Babel," to last "'til God give the victory." Leighton would have required a commitment not to dissolve even at the king's command, an English Tennis Court oath: "No sure . . . except you keep the ship . . . neither king, you nor we can be saved."[78] The covenants urged by Pym and Leighton were paralleled by associations outside Parliament (like the Feoffees of Impropriation) and undoubtedly by many less formal alliances similarly rooted in religious zeal.

(3) *The "exercises."* The public fast was the most important of the religious "exercises" that Puritans turned into a kind of political propaganda. Pym moved a day of national fast at the

[77] S. Reed Brett, *John Pym, 1583-1643: The Statesman of the Puritan Revolution* (London, 1940), p. 42.

[78] Alexander Leighton, *An Appeal to Parliament* (n.p., 1628), pp. 330ff.

opening of Parliament in 1626, but the members voted the cele-
bration only for themselves. Even so, it was a significant act, a
deliberate effort to arouse emotion and already a feature of oppositional politics. Stephen Marshall in 1648 complained that
before the revolution "sometimes a dozen, sometimes more years
passed in this land and kingdom without any public fasts . . ."[79]
Throughout the revolutionary period fasts were held monthly
and were accompanied by sermons and prayer meetings.

Days of "solemn prayer" were also the occasions for public and
private "exercises" designed to stimulate religious zeal and political activity. Before going to London for the meeting of the
Short Parliament in 1640, Sir Robert Harley "kept a day" with
his family, praying for guidance. A short time later his wife reported again: "We at Brompton kept the day . . . to our God
for his direction of the Parliament. I believe that hierarchy must
down and I hope now."[80] Years later, in 1649, when monarchy
went down as well, the remaining parliamentarians (Harley not
among them), the army officers and the king's judges were stimu-
lated and sustained by days of "public humiliation," fasts, and
frequent prayer meetings. All this obviously tended to reinforce
devotion to the cause, to calm the consciences of men doing terrible and dangerous deeds. The Long Parliament carried on its
business in an atmosphere frequently marked by religious excitement and its accomplishments are hardly to be explained
without taking that excitement into account.

Puritan electioneering, the equality of magistrates, parliamentary association, and the religious "exercises"—these derived from
the conception of the official as an instrument of God. They illustrate the role of Puritan piety in the education of the parliamentary gentleman. Taken together, given their maximum impact, however, they clearly reach beyond the gentleman, for all
his serious ambition and his conscientious self-esteem. They suggest one of the most fundamental doctrines of radical politics:
that men unwilling to be instruments have no right—whatever
their social status—to be magistrates. Pym's Association of 1621

<hr>

79 Marshall, *The Right Way: or, A Direction for Obtaining Good Success in a
Weighty Enterprise* (London, 1648), pp. 30-31.
80 *Letters of Lady Harley*, pp. 87, 111.

would have excluded from office anyone who refused the prescribed oath. The parliamentary purges of the 1640's were undertaken in the same spirit: it was necessary, preached George Hughes
to the Commons in 1647, "to honor God's kingdom so much as to
make gross sin uncapable of membership among you."[81] Even in
Elizabeth's England, a daring Puritan preacher, the Welsh evangelist John Penry, had argued a similar doctrine. Addressing himself to the Queen's Lord President of Wales, Penry wrote: "If it
lie not in you to bring Wales unto the knowledge of God, or if
your leisure will not serve thereto, then be not the Lord President
thereof." It belonged to the "essence" of his calling, Penry went
on, to see the true religion preached. Men "have no allowance to
be rulers where the Lord is not served . . ."[82] This was surely no
more than a logical development of the Puritan doctrine of vocation; yet, just as obviously, it called the identity of gentleman and
saint into question.

The Commons, after all, was a class organization; the Christian
gentleman might expect to behave with all due piety when he was
a member and thus vindicate his gentility. He did not expect,
however he behaved, to be excluded from membership. The
purge of the Long Parliament and the dissolution of the Rump
were thus revolutionary acts; yet they were also acts of godly
gentlemen—functioning as instruments rather than as members.
At this point, however, the two identities could no longer be
joined and men had to choose. Those who were, in Cromwell's
words, "gentlemen, and nothing more" went home.[83] The places
left vacant had then to be filled with other men, saints without
breeding. When Lazarus Seaman told the members of the House
of Commons in 1644 that "the supply of our king's failings are
expected at your hands," he was stating a principle obviously
capable of extension.[84] So the supply of the aristocracy's failings
would be filled from among other social groups.

[81] George Hughes, *Vae-Euge-Tuba: or, The Woe-Joy Trumpet, Sounding the
Third and Greatest Woe to the Anti-Christian World* (London, 1647), pp. 29-30.

[82] John Penry, *An Exhortation unto the Governors and People of Her Majesty's
County of Wales* (n.p., 1588), pp. 26-28.

[83] *Letters and Speeches*, I, 135.

[84] Lazarus Seaman, *Solomon's Choice: or, A Precedent for Kings and Princes and
All that are in Authority* (London, 1644), p. 40.

VII

The initial Puritan effort had been to turn gentlemen and magistrates into saints "to convert great men." "If they were once converted, hundreds would follow their example." But in the course of the revolution this effort was at least partially reversed: in effect the ministers called upon the saints, gentle and ungentle alike, to become magistrates, to make themselves, like those Puritan angels, "serviceable to God." Sainthood blurred the distinction between public and private men, for the saint's conscience was God's writ and imposed public duties. "If you be of a private station," preached William Bridge in 1641, "yet you ought to be of a public spirit." There were many "wearisome tasks" to be performed; soldiers in the army and merchants in London alike had public roles to fill if God was to be served.[85] So the saints prepared. When the future Colonel Hutchinson of Cromwell's army heard of the quarrels between king and Parliament, he retired to his study and—so his wife relates—"applied himself to understand the things then in dispute, and read all the papers that came forth . . . besides many other private treatises . . . Hereby he became . . . convinced in conscience of the righteousness of the Parliament's cause . . ." The same papers and treatises that Hutchinson read in his country home were read also in the London rooms of the future Colonel Harrison; he was as convinced in conscience and as ready to act. But Harrison was not a gentleman.[86]

The consciences of the saints, like those of the godly magistrates, were equal and "co-ordinate"—"so shall not the conscience of him that commandeth be anymore a sovereign judge over him that obeyeth," wrote a "religious gentleman" in 1601, "then shall the conscience of him that obeyeth be sovereign judge over him that commandeth."[87] If this did not involve actual participation in decision-making, it obviously suggested the saint's right to know the grounds of decisions made and to be convinced. Like Jonson's statesmen, the saints sought knowledge; scrupulous consciences

85 William Bridge, *Babylon's Downfall* (London. 1641), p. 10ff.
86 *Memoirs of the Life of Colonel Hutchinson*, p. 78; C. H. Simpkinson, *Thomas Harrison: Regicide and Major-General* (London, 1905), pp. 2-6. Harrison believed himself an "instrument," see p. 33.
87 Anon., *Certain Demands with Their Grounds . . . Propounded in Foro Conscientiae by some Religious Gentlemen* (n.p., 1605), p. 41.

required information, discussion, and debate. Indeed, public discussion with the Puritans as with the Huguenots took the place of that older forum of conscience, the confessional. The anonymous gentleman's pamphlet of 1601 was entitled *Certain Demands with their Grounds ... Propounded in Foro Conscientiae*. Printed illegally, it was an appeal to opinion. And by implication it was an appeal for action: conscience, wrote William Perkins, was not concerned with "theoretical understanding." Hutchinson and Harrison alike read in order to act. "The things that conscience determines of, are a man's own actions . . . conscience meddles not with generals, only it deals in particular actions."[88] Inevitably then, Puritanism fostered the idea that every conscientious man was a godly instrument and at least potentially a magistrate, "a man of public employment." As men "crown Christ in their own hearts," preached Thomas Temple to the Long Parliament, so they must "help . . . to set his scepter over all the world." This was the usual Puritan argument from private religious experience to public duty. But Temple went on: "All persons are called into this work, people, ministers, magistrates, kings themselves . . ."[89] "There is neither man nor woman of us, neither young nor old," wrote John Goodwin, "but hath somewhat or other, more or less, a mite or two at least, to cast into the treasury of public safety." The Puritan emphasis on activity was so great that the clerical intellectual felt the need to justify himself: "Headwork is every whit as necessary in such a time . . . as handwork is."[90] The important thing was that all sorts of work might be done by all sorts of men, with godliness their only license.

To the mind of Cromwell, however, that godliness was the beginning at least of gentility. In his speeches the Lord Protector still occasionally connected honor and conscience: they belonged to the same sort of men. But if the first was not present, then the other was warrant enough. "It had been well that men of honor and birth had entered into these employments," he wrote of the parliamentary army (and in fact a high percentage of the New

88 William Perkins, *Works* (London, 1616), I, 517.

89 Thomas Temple, *Christ's Government in and over His People* (London, 1642), p. 30.

90 John Goodwin, *Anti-Cavalierism: or, Truth Pleaded as well as Necessity . . . for the Suppressing of that Butcherly Brood of Cavaliering Incendiaries* (London, 1642), pp. 3-4.

Model's officers' corps was drawn from the gentry). "But seeing it was necessary the work must go on, better plain men than none; but best to have men patient of wants, faithful and conscientious in their employment."[91] He was describing here the same ideal figure that had appeared so often in Puritan sermons as the pious magistrate, not the man of valor, magnanimity, or personal cultivation, but the man "conscientious in employment." In a sense, the revolution itself was the culmination of a historical process that had long tended toward the creation of such men and had steadily set them in opposition to courtiers and old aristocrats. When the struggle between these two groups finally broke out, leaders like Cromwell were faced with the need to recruit a new magistracy (and a new soldiery) for the reformation and purgation of the commonwealth. It was not to be a recruitment at random, for Cromwell thought the marks of the godly a "serious business," worthy of sustained intellectual consideration and even of definition. He came near to suggesting a heraldry for the saints: "May not this character, this stamp [of God] bear equal poise with any hereditary interest that could furnish, or hath furnished, in the common law or elsewhere, matter of dispute and trial of learning?"[92]

It was true, then, as a Puritan minister said, that the calling of the Long Parliament "opened many mouths."[93] It created new public men—though always from the ranks of those who had been shaped in the Puritan mold. For insofar as the new men became active in English politics, they adjusted themselves to the type of the pious magistrate. The typical revolutionary figure was still the magistrate and not yet the citizen; still the gentleman and not yet the *sans-culotte*. If proof were needed, the haste of the successful saints to buy land—not only for speculation but also in order to settle in the country and enter local gentry society —would be sufficient. Once established in the country, they undoubtedly thanked God for their triumph, worried in pious diaries over their worthiness, consulted a godly minister and ran for office. They conned Scripture for justification, attended the

91 *Letters and Speeches*, I, 140.
92 *Ibid.*, III, 52.
93 Henry Burton, *England's Bondage and Hope of Deliverance* (London, 1641), p. 14.

assizes and did their duty with methodical thoroughness.[94] They were only the latest in a long line of ambitious men, serious, self-absorbed, their backs turned to the court, their faces, so they thought, to the Almighty. From their ranks came "statesmen" capable of purging a Parliament and killing a king. But in all this their models were godly gentlemen and they were inspired and driven forward by pious divines like Hugh Peter—himself of gentle birth. After the clerical insurrection of the 1570's and '80's, it was nowhere true, except among the Levellers and the more extreme sects, that the ungentle took the lead or developed new political forms. It was rather men like Cromwell who felt most deeply the impact of Puritan thought. Such men combined their conscience and their office and became something very near to lay ministers. The saint was the gentleman's *alter ego* and even when he was in fact a different person, the connection was always close. In a nice comparison, Cromwell set the "courage and resolution" of the Cavalier gentry against the "spirit" of the Puritan saints. In battle, surely in politics, he thought, the men of spirit were "likely to go as far as gentlemen will go."[95] It was, indeed, for this very reason that England's revolution was also a fratricidal civil war.

[94] "And if once landlords," wrote Gerard Winstanley, "then they rise to be justices, rulers and state governors, as experience shows." Quoted in Christopher Hill, *Puritanism and Revolution* (London, 1958), p. 156. See the discussion on land purchase during the revolution, pp. 156ff., 181ff.

[95] *Letters and Speeches*, III, 249-250.

CHAPTER EIGHT · POLITICS AND WAR

The conscientious activity of pious magistrates often culminated in violence against godless subjects, heretical sovereigns, or the "popish power" of Hapsburg and Spanish kings. Warfare in all its forms was a common and accepted feature of sixteenth and seventeenth-century life. The use of force by magistrates and judges —or by torturers and hangmen—was equally accepted and similarly explained by the traditional theology of the Fall. But if among Christians the legitimacy of warfare and civil coercion had long been recognized, attempts had also been made to control their extent, to limit the violence they involved. Medieval casuists had developed a precise and detailed set of conditions under which war might legitimately be waged. These theorists of the "just war" had sought to impose, even upon the army with justice on its side, a "mournful" combat, to be fought without zeal or hatred. Conquest and indiscriminate slaughter were absolutely proscribed.[1]

Since warfare was only an aspect of the political behavior of fallen men, just-war theory had clear implications for domestic politics. In describing the necessary conditions for a civil war, it suggested circumstances in which the commands of kings might legitimately be resisted. In its terms tyranny came to be regarded as a kind of aggression against the established legal or moral order, an unjustified act of offensive war. Resistance, on the other hand, was described in terms of defense; the example of the Huguenots has already been given. Rebellion against a tyrant could thus be called *just* whenever it fulfilled the three traditional requirements of the just war: that it be truly defensive, fought at the command of a legitimate authority, and carried on in a restrained and more or less orderly fashion, without pillage, rape, or unnecessary murder.[2]

---

1 See Alfred Vanderpol, *La doctrine scholastique du droit de guerre* (Paris, 1919).
2 The connection of just war and resistance is explicitly argued in Francisco

Calvinist magistrates and noblemen, driven as in France to acts of resistance or rebellion, revived and elaborated this application of just-war theory. They sought to demonstrate the legality of their activity and uphold their authority over the religious insurrection. Theirs was the constitutional power that made the war just. But this was true only so long as the war was really defensive, fought to maintain life, property, and legal order. The medieval writers had recognized no just war for religion's sake. Warfare in their terms pertained only to the realm of fallen nature. It might have its reasons; it might be necessary and inevitable, but it could hardly be exalted. In any ultimate sense, warfare could not be said to have a *purpose*—no purpose, at any rate, beyond the temporary restoration of peace and the prewar status quo. Men may not fight on God's behalf, Suarez repeated in the seventeenth century. "War is permissible only that a state may guard itself from molestation."[3] For the reformers, however, war like politics did have a purpose; both were waged in the name of God. As the goal of the struggle there stood the reformed church, later the holy commonwealth and the New Jerusalem. In pursuit of these goals, Calvinist writers eventually found their way to the alternative medieval tradition of the holy war or crusade.[4]

By the time Aquinas codified the Christian view of warfare, the passion for crusading had almost died in the West. That it had been revived in more recent times is obvious enough; this revival first took place in the course of the sixteenth and seventeenth centuries. A crusade, in the Middle Ages, was a war fought for God's purposes; as it did not require secular reason, so secular authority was not necessary. The holy war was fought at the command of God or of his church, and it was led by the Lord himself—a man of war—as Urban told the crowd at Clermont. The crusading army was made up, in theory at least, not of feudal vassals and men-at-arms but of volunteers who had come forward

---

Suarez, *Selections from Three Works* (Oxford, 1944), vol. II: *An English Version of the Texts*, trans. G. L. Williams, A. Brown and J. Waldron, pp. 854-855 (Disputation XIII, in *A Work on the Three Theological Virtues*).

[3] *Ibid.*, p. 815.

[4] The terms of the argument in this chapter were first suggested by Roland Bainton in "Congregationalism: From the Just War to the Crusade in the Puritan Revolution," *Andover Newton Theological School Bulletin* 35:1-3 (1943).

"to take the cross." Shaped and dominated by their enthusiasm, such men might leave behind the motley order of the feudal band and experiment with a new discipline: the repression and self-control of the religious zealot. Such discipline was rare in the Middle Ages; marauding and butchery were common features even of wars called holy. But something of the new spirit was revealed in the semimonastic orders of crusading knights. There looting and rapine were banned and at the same time the knights dispensed with pious melancholy. The crusader's military style was described by St. Bernard in a sermon in praise of the Templars:[5]

A new sort of army has appeared . . . an army such as the world has never seen. It fights a double war; first, the war of flesh and blood against enemies; second, the war of the spirit against Satan and vice. Physical war is not rare or astonishing, spiritual war is a common thing among many monks . . . But it is not usual to see men fighting in these two ways at once. What can such soldiers fear, who have consecrated their lives to Christ . . . ? The soldier of Christ kills with safety; he dies with more safety still. He serves Christ when he kills, he serves himself when he is killed . . .

All this—including the double warfare—would be recapitulated in the hundred years of Protestant militancy that stretched roughly from the 1550's to the 1650's. The culminating point was reached in Cromwell's England. For if the political analogue of the just war was the limited act of legal resistance, then the analogue of the crusade—once the nation had replaced the world of Christendom—was revolution. Behind both crusade and revolution lay the idea of contention for a cause. It was at revolution that Calvinist thinkers finally arrived, by imposing their conscientious purposes upon the medieval notions of warfare.

II

In this same period of Protestant militancy, major changes took place in the technique of warfare, changes so significant as to make up what one writer has called a "military revolution."[6] Though its fundamental causes were to a large extent independent of religion, this was a revolution for which both the opportunity

5 Quoted in Vanderpol, *Droit de guerre*, pp. 204-206; see also Steven Runciman, *A History of the Crusades: The First Crusade* (Cambridge, Eng., 1957), pp. 109, 115.
6 Michael Roberts, *The Military Revolution, 1560-1660* (Belfast, 1956).

and initiative were often provided by Protestant radicalism. Here too, warfare and politics must be seen as aspects of the same thing —whether of the endless dissension of fallen men or the purposive pursuit of power and godliness. Changes in the idea of warfare paralleled and reinforced changes in the idea of political conflict. Before going on, then, to examine Puritan notions of the just war and the crusade, it is necessary to say something about certain aspects of military history.

In the feudal world the Christian limits upon warfare had never been more than precariously established. Neither kings nor bishops ever succeeded in imposing upon the feudal melee that discipline which both magistracy and religion required. The rise of "bastard feudalism" and the apppearance of the *condottieri* with their mercenary bands signaled the virtual collapse of the attempt. It had achieved no major institutional form, but had relied largely upon the impact of the chivalric ideal on the individual knight and upon the power of the confessional. The problem of military order, never really solved by the Church, would eventually be solved, up to a point, by the state. But between the failure of the Truce of God and the final establishment of the King's Peace, there was a period of intellectual and political confusion with regard to the idea of war. The conditions of warfare, the purposes for which and the methods with which it was carried on, the forms of cessation and peace—all were called into doubt. At times, as in the civil wars of the late medieval period, the melee seemed to become permanent; at times, as in the bloody battles of the Swiss mercenary pikemen, all conventions of humane conduct seemed forgotten.[7]

But political disorganization and the collapse of religious discipline might have other outcomes. Renaissance warfare, so often trivial in its purposes, lent itself to a kind of romantic elaboration, and at the same time invited the manipulations of businessmen. For the *condottieri,* as J. U. Nef has suggested, warfare was a combination game and business and in practice it was often less savage than even the Church had demanded.[8] In Italy, profes-

[7] Sir Charles Oman, *The Art of War in the Middle Ages* (Oxford, 1885), pp. 49-51, 73-87; Roberts, *Military Revolution*, pp. 9-11.

[8] J. U. Nef, *War and Human Progress: An Essay on the Rise of Industrial Civilization* (Cambridge, Mass., 1950), pp. 136-137.

sional soldiers are described fighting virtually bloodless battles; they were as unwilling to kill as to be killed, perhaps recognizing the considerable capital investment which each man represented. Nor were slaughter and the old-fashioned melee compatible with the new forms that chivalry took in the Italian and French courts or with the Renaissance sense of pageantry, romance, and adventure. "The young have been reading too many romances of reckless adventure, full of *amours déshonnêtes* and objectless fighting . . ." wrote the Huguenot warrior François de la Noue in the later sixteenth century.[9] Warfare for him was a serious matter. But in the years before the religious struggles, men in both France and Italy learned to find "delight" in battle—less perhaps in the actual fighting than in soldierly pageants and the rich ornamentation of weaponry. And the fighting itself was increasingly limited, since neither pageantry nor ornamentation made for ruthless efficiency. Aristocratic young men and mercenary captains together produced a kind of military stalemate, a considerable slowing down of the pace of battle, which served the purposes of them both and lasted until both were replaced by the political— or the religious—soldier. The classic symbol of the stalemate was the *caracole*, an elegant cavalry maneuver in which all direct contact was avoided. "Instead of relying upon the impact of the mass of man and horse," writes Michael Roberts, "the cavaliers of Western Europe were reduced, in battle, to the debilitated popping of pistols."[10]

A writer like Castiglione suggests the meaning of warfare as an aristocratic sport. It was indeed a more important sport than, for example, tennis: a far more significant occasion for honorable self-display and the public performance of "fine deeds."[11] But it was not different in kind—in seriousness—from any of the courtier activities. Some of the participants in the discussion over which Elisabetta Gonzaga presided even suggested that the bearing of arms was less important than other, more peaceful pursuits. Their

9 Quoted in Sir Charles Oman, *A History of the Art of War in the Sixteenth Century* (London, 1937), p. 396.

10 Michael Roberts, *Gustavus Adolphus: A History of Sweden, 1611-1632* (London, 1958), II, 180; for a description of the caracole, see J. R. Hale, "Armies, Navies and the Art of War," in *The New Cambridge Modern History*, vol. II: *The Reformation 1520-1559*, ed. G. R. Elton (Cambridge, 1958), pp. 483, 498.

11 Baldesar Castiglione, *The Book of the Courtier*, trans. C. S. Singleton (New York, 1959), pp. 73, 99.

goal was to turn a bright young man into a perfect ornament of courtly life, not into a butcher; what was wanted was renown, excellence and beauty, but not mere military effectiveness. If fighting was still reckoned by most writers as one of the essential. accomplishments of the courtier, then its violence would be limited by his culture and its zeal controlled by his "nonchalance."

Neither cultivation nor nonchalance, of course, were limits that could be relied upon. Machiavelli easily pushed them aside; he was not interested in the courtly or even the professional soldier. Equally important, he also pushed aside the older limits of religion and law. With the publication of his books it is possible to date the beginning of a new view of warfare. For him, conflict and battle were no longer merely the results of human sin, to be controlled and repressed like all sin; nor were they occasions for heroic exercise. They were studied, instead, as aspects of the pursuit of power. And this pursuit itself was no longer conceived in terms of the occasional pillaging or petty conquests of aggressive feudal princes or expansionist medieval towns. Instead, the pursuit of power was made a matter of permanent, systematic struggle and accumulation. This outlook was elaborated by the theorists of the new dynastic state, whom it obviously suited far better than Machiavelli's own Florentines. They defined ever more clearly the set of purposes to which warfare was now to be permanently connected. Before the end of the seventeenth century, the first standing armies had been created for the sake of these purposes.[12]

The pursuit of power was justified by the theory of "reason of state." This effectively placed both policy and warfare at the service of the new class of rulers and magistrates that had succeeded to the inheritance of feudal lords. Reason of state overrode the old Christian limits; at the same time the new rulers forsook Renaissance "delight." Expansion and aggrandizement became purposive and systematic, totally controlled by the same men who controlled the state. *"Le roi seul a droit de glaive."* Policy required discipline; no longer was there room for the independent

---

12 Niccolo Machiavelli, *The Art of War* (Albany, New York, 1815); Roberts, *Military Revolution*, p. 19; Sir George Clark, *War and Society in the Seventeenth Century* (Cambridge, 1958), p. 71. Roberts and Clark describe "the *étatisation* of war."

knight, the marauding baron with his feudal entourage, the
local war; the state strove to suppress even the duel. And eventually the mercenary captains were brought into its service,
morally transformed (up to a point) by the new aristocratic ethic
of honor and public duty. But the corollary of the King's Peace,
thus established, was the king's war.

The great religious communions of the sixteenth and seventeenth centuries also found the politic rationality of the new
doctrine attractive and useful. And as reason of state justified the
king's war, so reason of religion might justify the war of God.
The preservation of the church or the establishment of God's
kingdom on earth: these were occasions for warfare parallel to
the ever-threatened security of the dynastic state. Like the latter,
they too might call forth the wisdom of the serpent.[13] What is
more important, they would require, and produce, an organization
of power strikingly similar to that of the new kings. This is what
lay behind one of the most singular features of sixteenth and
seventeenth-century history—the appearance of voluntary associations, usually religious in character, which claimed the right to
organize politically and to wage war. The Huguenot churches,
the Catholic League, the Scottish Covenant are all early examples.[14] Their appearance parallels that of the dynastic states,
though in their later forms these independent political organizations often claimed a more far-reaching and total loyalty than did
the state and granted to their activists an even greater freedom
from casuistic restriction. The effect of these developments
quickly became apparent: the precisely defined and circumscribed idea of resistance gave way to the idea of revolution; the
tactical stalemate was overcome; the feudal melee was succeeded
by military discipline and international war.

In still another sense, Machiavelli had pointed the way to all
three of these changes with his suggestion that wars should be

13 G. L. Mosse, *The Holy Pretense* (Oxford, 1957), p. 62 and *passim*. See the
discussion of the Calvinist writer Althusius and reason of state in C. J. Friedrich,
Constitutional Reason of State: The Survival of Constitutional Order (Providence,
R.I., 1957), pp. 66ff; also Friedrich's elaboration of the idea of "reason of church,"
p. 61.
14 Clark, *War and Society*, p. 25; H. G. Koenigsberger, "The Organization of
Revolutionary Parties in France and the Netherlands during the Sixteenth
Century, *The Journal of Modern History* 27:335-351 (1955).

fought by citizen armies.[15] His reasoning was not merely utilitarian; it had its roots in the Renaissance revival of what might best be called classical *civisme*—a republican sense of patriotism and virtue. That a city should be defended by its own armed citizens was an old burgher notion; but that a citizen army might, like the legions of ancient Rome, be the basis of an offensive force was unimagined until the astonishing success of Sweden's national conscript army in the Thirty Years' War and of the New Model in the English civil wars. Major changes in discipline and morale underlay these successes; together they made possible a tactical revolution that produced for the first time something very much like modern warfare.[16] The new tactics were tentatively experimented with in the Huguenot and Dutch armies and were more fully developed by Gustavus Adolphus and Cromwell. Machiavelli's writings were only a distant anticipation of the forms of warfare later introduced in the north; for in the event, the emotions upon which they rested were neither classical nor civic. By and large, they were Protestant and national—and the combination was significant. More than any other factor, perhaps, it was the new confessional and patriotic ardor that ended the tactical stalemate and the highly civilized fashion of endless maneuver, and brought direct contact back into fashion. The cavalry onslaught was first revived by the Huguenots and the same reliance on the impact of man and horse was a feature of Swedish tactics.[17]

Experimentation took place largely (though not entirely) in the Protestant armies. Rebels, defying the traditional order, the Protestant commanders proved themselves more open to innovation than were their Catholic rivals. This was not only because of their rebelliousness, however, but also because of their more clear-cut sense of purpose, their more ruthless pursuit of definite goals. It was the Swedes who broke medieval precedent and first attempted to fight through the winter. And it was the English and Dutch who took the lead in getting rid of richly ornamented

[15] *The Prince*, chs. xii and xiii; *The Discourses*, book III, ch. xx; *The Art of War*, part I.

[16] The argument here and in the next several paragraphs follows that of Roberts, *Military Revolution;* see also Lynn Montross, *War Through the Ages* (New York, 1944), pp. 235ff.

[17] Roberts, *Gustavus Adolphus*, II, 245ff.

weaponry—thus clearly setting Renaissance "delight" apart from the serious business of war.[18] The most significant innovations were of this sort, as much social and political as military. Within the army itself, they consisted largely of changes in the nature of order and subordination and in the training and discipline of the soldiers. Perhaps the "military revolution" is best summed up by the introduction of uniforms and of marching in step, both in the early seventeenth century.[19] The models here were Roman, but the armies most often Protestant. The ideology of the continental officers was frequently some version of Stoicism (this was especially true of the men around Maurice of Holland), but Calvinist writers quickly developed ideas of discipline and exercise that were closely connected with the organization and drill of the new armies. In England, these ideas were especially significant, contributing to the remarkable power of Cromwell's cavalry. The immediate result of the transformation in tactics and discipline was a centralized army, composed of small, highly mobile units, capable in battle of rapid maneuver, attack, and orderly reformation. Despite the fact that there were no major technical advances in musketry during the period, the new drill produced a significant rise in fire-power.

Officers like Gustavus and Oliver Cromwell acted so as to increase the number of men participating in organized warfare and to intensify the involvement and activity of each individual soldier. In turn, these changes made army morale a more crucial factor than it had ever been before. Neither feudal loyalty nor mercenary calculation were sufficient to sustain the new warfare. The religious purposes that so often underlay the tactical innovations had to be made explicit. Fervor had to be encouraged even in common soldiers and war itself described as if it were a crusade.[20] The saint and the citizen were more likely than the vassal, the mercenary, or the kidnapped vagrant to commit themselves

18 Nef, *War and Human Progress*, pp. 95, 129.

19 Roberts, *Military Revolution*, p. 11; on marching in step, see Edward Davies, *The Art of War and England's Trainings* (London, 1619). Nef, *War and Human Progress*, p. 95, argues that uniforms for common soldiers were first introduced in Cromwell's New Model Army; but see Roberts, *Gustavus Adolphus*, II, 236, for an earlier example.

20 See, for example, *The Swedish Discipline, Religious, Civil and Military* (London, 1632), pp. 2, 3, 22. Gustavus is compared to Moses, organizing his army to fight the battles of God.

to a long and difficult struggle on God's behalf. "Here strive God and the devil," wrote Gustavus Adolphus. "If you hold with God, come over to me. If you prefer the devil, you will have to fight me first." This was a bit of Protestant bravado—not true, since Gustavus' war, financed by Richelieu, was hardly a crusade —but it indicated the way things might move. The war against Satan would absorb all other struggles: "all the wars in Europe are now blended into one," boasted the Swedish king.[21] And it would draw all godly men into the fray; shortly enough the preachers of the English Revolution would declare that there could be no neutrals. But those who fought for God would have to *know the reasons;* only then could army regulations and religious fervor come together in a new discipline.

The new ideas about warfare were readily transferable to politics. The religious soldier directly paralleled the pious magistrate. In politics too the conflicts engendered by social change or religious reformation would come to be viewed as continuous struggles of permanently rival forces. Men would turn away, at least in their rationalizations, from individual ambition and familial interest and would search for higher goals in politics and transcendent purposes in the state. And as politics became a serious and protracted struggle, so its "common soldiers," electors, parliamentarians, and minor magistrates, would commit themselves to the goals of the struggle and take on a new importance. The more sensitive and intellectual among them would understand that their goals could not be reached except by disciplined domestic armies. Politics like war would have to be waged through the winter and the morale of the saints sustained. These tendencies toward a military view of the political world are most noticeable among Puritan writers. Their elaborate use of warfare as an image of the Christian life suggests that the military outlook was entirely compatible with Calvinist theology.

III

Puritan writing about warfare is in the nature of an elaborate conceit, worked out in great detail, continually employed though with varying degrees of seriousness. It may be said that as the news

21 Quoted in Montross, *War*, p. 262 and Roberts, *Military Revolution*, p. 13.

of the Thirty Years' War circulated in England and as the time for
her own civil war drew near, the metaphor was used more and
more intentionally and its surface meaning became increasingly
significant. The "militancy" of the church and the spiritual warfare of godly men were ancient Christian themes. But they
achieved in the work of Calvin, in the combative ideology of the
Marian exiles and then in the vast popular literature of the Puritans a new power. If in some writers the themes remained literary—allusive and suggestive but very far from programmatic—
in others the Calvinist impulse to materialize and socialize the
intellectual world was often apparent. So the allegorical figure of
the Christian pilgrim became the very real and lifelike hero of
Bunyan's picaresque novel. And so the spiritual soldier finally
appeared on a real battlefield.

There are two elements in the Puritan use of war as a metaphor: the first is cosmological in its reference and the second
worldly and human. The figure is applied to God himself and
to his universe. "The Lord is a man of war." Not only the
Old Testament Jehovah, but even the merciful Christ was seen
as a "captain" by Puritan writers.[22] The angels were an army—
as they had often been in Christian literature—"a multitude of
heavenly soldiers." They fought against Satan and their war had
by no means ended with that astonishing battle which Milton
was later to describe. *"Satan never turns Christian."*[23] Tension and
struggle were permanent elements of the cosmic scheme. The old
harmony of the chain of being had been replaced by a universe
of "opposition and contraries" and this made necessary a military
chain of command. "The world is the great field of God, in
which Michael and his angels fight against the dragon and his
angels."[24]

The second element of the metaphor is equally significant. A
warlike God made warlike men; earth too was a field of war
which God overlooked and approved. "Above all creatures [God]
loves soldiers," proclaimed a Puritan preacher, ". . . above all
actions he honors warlike and martial design." "Whoever is a

22 See Thomas Adams, *The Soldier's Honor* (London, 1617), sig. A$_3$ verso;
J. Leech, *The Train Soldier* (London, 1619), pp. 25-26. Also *The Swedish Discipline*,
p. 22.
23 Stephen Marshall, *A Peace-Offering to God* (London, 1641), p. 7.
24 Thomas Taylor, *Christ's Combat and Conquest* (London, 1618), p. 8.

professed Christian," declared another, "he is a professed soldier; or if no soldier, no Christian . . ."[25] The godly must harden themselves to face the continual onslaughts of Satan and his allies. As there is permanent opposition and conflict in the cosmos, so there is permanent warfare on earth. "The condition of the child of God," wrote Thomas Taylor, "is military in this life." The saint was a soldier—but so was everyone else; Puritans did not recognize noncombatants. "All degrees of men are warriors, some fighting for the enlargement of religion and some against it."[26]

Puritan warfare consisted first of all in the struggle against temptation, the vigilant avoidance of evil company, the submission of the sinner to the discipline and exercises of the reformed religion. War described a state of mind, a degree of tension and nervousness. This tension was itself an aspect of salvation: a man at ease was a man lost. "The world's peace," wrote Thomas Taylor, "is the keenest war against God."[27] The saints were continually exhorted to be ready for battle, indeed, to begin the fighting. Satan was active, militant, industrious, and cunning; God would have his warriors be the same. "Consider of our enemy and of our danger by him, be the place never so secret, never so secure . . ."[28] To be aware of danger, to be on one's guard, to be at war: all this was a sign of grace. For the saints, the devil's attack could never be a surprise. And as they had experienced it in their personal lives, so they would be ready for it also in the world at large. Men who fought, in St. Bernard's words, "the war of the spirit against Satan and vice" were—whether they knew it or not —preparing themselves to fight "the war of flesh and blood against enemies."

Puritan use of the imagery of warfare seemed so extravagant that it became something of a joke. It was used still, however, and no less extravagantly: "A sacrament is a soldier's oath," proclaimed

[25] Thomas Sutton, *The Good Fight of Faith* (London, 1623), p. 7; Leech, *Train Soldier*, pp. 25-26. Cf. John Everard, *The Arriereban* (London, 1618), pp. 17-18.

[26] Taylor, *Christ's Combat*, p. 4; Sutton, *Good Fight*, p. 8; see also p. 9; "the life of every Christian man is a continual battalion and bloody skirmish . . . against the devil . . ."

[27] Taylor, *The Progress of Saints to Full Holiness* (London, 1630), p. 180. God's peace, on the other hand, is "a war against sin." The same sentiment is expressed by Everard in *The Arriereban*, p. 13: "War with Amalek is the condition of Israel's peace."

[28] Taylor, *Christ's Combat*, p. 20.

Simeon Ashe, "when we were baptized we took press money, and vowed to serve under the colors of Christ . . ." And at the very moment when the image seemed most absurd, it was most serious: Ashe was preaching in 1642 to "the commanders of the military forces of the renowned city of London" and the commanders would shortly engage the king. Christians fight first against "armies" of devils and lusts, Ashe suggested, but also "of men and women in the world, that do wage war with every Christian."[29] Since the 1620's the trend of Puritan preaching had been to suggest the reality of the Christian struggle and even to give it a political dimension. As the individual saint must never be at ease—"seeing in the way to heaven we live in the midst of enemies"—so the Christian commonwealth. To be unprepared for war, wrote the preacher Richard Sibbes, is to tempt God.[30] It was as dangerous for the state as for the soul to feel secure. For Thomas Adams, the two dangers were virtually the same. Writing in 1617, he urged military preparedness: "Bring forth that malefactor security, a rust grown over our souls, in this time of peace, and send him packing."[31] The Christian armor is spiritual, wrote William Gouge, but the enemies of Christ are flesh and blood. "Are spirits only our enemies? . . . Other men also are enemies: there are many adversaries, as infidels, idolators, heretics, worldlings, all sorts of persecutors, yea, and false brethren."[32] Gouge's book *Of Arming a Christian Soldier* was published fifteen years before Ashe preached his sermon and the civil war began.

IV

Since warfare was not entirely a metaphor, since English soldiers were already involved in the fighting in Germany, Puritan writers were forced to reexamine the idea of the just war. A major restatement of the traditional Christian position had been made in the early seventeenth century by Francisco Suarez and, Spaniard and Jesuit though he was, Suarez was the Puritan's major

29 Simeon Ashe, *Good Courage Discovered and Encouraged* (London, 1642), p. 8. That the military metaphors were sometimes ridiculed is suggested in W. Fraser Mitchell, *English Pulpit Oratory from Andrews to Tillotson* (London, 1932), p. 372n.
30 Richard Sibbes, *Complete Works*, ed. A. B. Grosart (Edinburgh, 1893), II, 282.
31 Adams, *Soldier's Honor*, p. 14; see also William Gouge, *The Dignity of Chivalry* (London, 1626), pp. 32ff.
32 William Gouge, *Of Arming a Christian Soldier*, in vol. II of *The Works*, titled *The Whole Armor of God* (London, 1627), pp. 27-28.

source. In their hands, however, the three elements of the traditional theory—the just authority, just cause, and just means—
all underwent a transformation. This work was not completed
by any one writer; there is no Puritan theorist comparable to
Suarez. As with so much else in Puritan thought, the outcome
was revealed only in practical activity. Until 1640 the changes
in the theory of the just war were hidden behind a veil of orthodoxy and evasion—and, it should be said, behind the reality of
a frequently genuine conservatism.

Catholic writers always insisted that a just war could be waged
only at the command of a prince: "only a sovereign prince who
has no superior in temporal affairs . . . has by natural law legitimate power to declare war."[33] Similarly the Puritan Richard
Bernard: the first mover in warfare must be the "supreme authority in the state." Bernard went on to accept Suarez's view of the
duty of subjects. "Private persons may not sit and judge of
princes' actions . . . a good man . . . may serve under a sac-
rilegious prince: for the unjust command shall bind the prince,
when the duty of obedience shall make the soldier free."[34] Only
princes might judge the justice of a war. No Puritan writer before
1640 dared deny this, though most avoided explicitly asserting
it. The strict Presbyterian Alexander Leighton did insist that
the authority which sent men into war must be "godly" as well
as legitimate. And Puritan ministers preaching before the voluntary "artillery companies" of London, Bristol, and Coventry emphasized "God's call" rather than the king's command.[35] But this
crucial feature of the royal prerogative was challenged only indirectly.

Throughout the 1620's Puritan ministers were interested in
bringing England actively into the European war.[36] They did not

33 Suarez, *Selections*, p. 805.
34 Richard Bernard, *The Bible-Battles, or The Sacred Art Military for the Rightly
Waging of War according to the Holy Writ* (London, 1629), pp. 57, 66-67.
35 Alexander Leighton, *Looking-Glass of the Holy War* (n.p., 1624), pp. 9-20;
see Samuel Buggs, *Miles Mediterraneus, The Midland Soldier* (London, 1622), p. 33:
"God calls you, the King allows you, the cause encourageth you . . . therefore be
ready."
36 See especially John Preston's dramatic sermons, *The New Life* (1626), *A
Sensible Demonstration of the Deity* (1627)—both published in *Sermons Preached
before His Majesty* (London, 1630). Also Preston's *The Breastplate of Faith and
Love* (a collection of sermons preached at Lincoln's Inn in 1625) (London, 1634),
especially the last sermon in the collection, pp. 211ff. (3rd numbering). See the

so much dispute the right of the king to require warfare from his subjects, then, as urge the right of subjects to require warfare from their king. This was at least equally dangerous to the prerogative. That remarkable pamphleteer, Thomas Scott, who rushed nine pamphlets through eighteen editions in the critical year 1624, all of them urging war with Spain, insisted that he possessed a lawful vocation for his (illegal) efforts. "The general calling of a subject and of a Christian," he wrote, "warrants any particular action which I do for the benefit of the state and church . . ."[37] Other preachers and publicists joined in the demand for war; the dedications of treatises and sermons urged King James to arms. Together with the Puritan campaign against the Spanish Match, this godly warmongering of the late teens and early twenties represents, as Godfrey Davies has suggested, "the first definite example of an attempt to marshall public opinion in opposition to the foreign policy of a government in England."[38] The war against Satan was much too important to be left to the king. And if subjects could decide when fighting was necessary "for the benefit of the state and the church," they might also decide when it was unnecessary or unlawful. For the saints, all this could depend only on God; here was the logical conclusion of their argument, nowhere made explicit until 1640. They did not need the king, Ashe then told London's commanders: "If the Lord please to beat up the drum; if the Lord please to bid them arm and come abroad, his call is sufficient."[39]

Puritans never adopted the Catholic insistence that war was essentially a secular affair, a matter of fallen nature, a limited, short-term response to a specific violation of peace and order. The cautious Bernard provided a long list of "lawful causes," most

discussion of these sermons in Christopher Hill, *Puritanism and Revolution*, pp. 249ff.

37 Thomas Scott, *Vox Regis* (n.p., 1623), p. 14. Also see Scott's *Votivae Angliae: or, the Desires and Wishes of England to Persuade His Majesty to Draw His Sword* (Utrecht, 1624), and *The Belgick Soldier . . . or, War Was a Blessing* (n.p., 1624). Scott's earlier anti-Spanish tract, *Vox Populi* (n.p., 1620) was approved, wrote Sir Simonds D'Ewes, "by all men of judgement that were loyally affected to the truth of the Gospel." *Autobiography*, ed. J. O. Halliwell (London, 1845), I, 158-159.

38 Godfrey Davies, "English Political Sermons," *Huntington Library Quarterly* 3:1-22 (1939). John Everard, who played a leading part in the Puritan campaign, still paid lip service to the king's prerogative in his sermon *The Arriereban*, pp. 30-32.

39 Ashe, *Good Courage*, pp. 6-7.

of them secular, but the dedication of his book was part of the Puritan campaign for military intervention on the continent: "The poor distressed churches cry aloud for help . . . Stand therefore (Oh King) in the forefront of the Lord's battles . . ."[40] To fight for God's glory on earth, for the advancement of the Gospel, to avenge God upon idolators—all these were legitimate reasons for warfare urged in Puritan sermons.[41] They pointed the way toward a war different in kind from anything contemplated by Suarez and the just-war theorists. They pointed toward the crusade, a struggle against external enemies as continuous and unrelenting as was the saint's war against sin. Suarez would have permitted only wars limited in their purposes and so in their length: the just war had a clear terminal point, ending as soon as aggression was repulsed and the prewar status quo restored. But the "Lord's battles" went on and on, so long as Satan survived and found allies among men.

Once war of this sort was being fought, casuistic distinctions as to means would most likely be pushed aside. To be sure, there were not many distinctions left to be made, once Suarez had applied his logical mind to the problem of means and ends: "if the end be permissible," he wrote, "the necessary means to that end are also permissible; and hence it follows that in the whole course . . . of the war hardly anything done against the enemy involves injustice, except the slaying of the innocent."[42] But the Puritan Bernard went further than this and managed to suggest the nightmare of total war. "In a just and necessary war, the conquered are in the hands of the conquerors . . . That state can no otherwise be weakened but in [its] subjects, the hands of all which, though they be not in war, yet are they in heart and contributing . . ."[43] Bernard's view clearly reflected the "military revolution" which had come about with the rise of modern states and reformed churches.

Puritan casuists examined the problem of means and ends and seem to have adopted some religious version of the doctrine of reason of state. Here they could pick and choose among Catholic

40 Bernard, *Bible-Battles*, dedication to Charles I.
41 *Ibid.*, pp. 38ff.; Sutton, *Good Fight*, p. 19; Adams, *Soldier's Honor*, p. 20.
42 Suarez, *Selections*, p. 840; see also the qualifications on p. 845.
43 Bernard, *Bible-Battles*, p. 71.

authorities, for the position is not quite so modern as its identification with Machiavelli suggests.[44] Nevertheless, Puritan writers went beyond the usual Catholic view to emphasize the extralegal privileges of the saints. Calvinist voluntarism provided a theological foundation for their position. Thus William Perkins repeated the radical argument of John Knox, though he hardly shared the temperamental radicalism of the leader of the Marian exiles in Geneva. "God is an absolute God," he wrote, "and so above the law; and may therefore command that which the law forbids." Joshua's stratagem in the battle for Ai, Abraham's failure to avow his wife before Pharoah, Rahab's lie to the king's messengers: all this might be justified by God's command. Rahab hid the spies, Perkins argues, "not in treachery but in faith."[45] As God's instruments men may sometimes act in ways to all outward appearances unjust. What was most important in the Puritan position, however, was not the extent of these special privileges. Even Alexander Leighton tended to be cautious here, though he allowed considerable latitude to the saintly spy: "he may conceal the truth, or some part of the truth, change his habit, make show of what he meaneth not to do. In all which he must take heed that [his lies] be not in matter of religion . . ."[46] The crucial point in the Puritan argument was that strategem and evasion were available equally to all men. Reason of state, on the other hand, had always implied a "ruler morality," that is, it had justified only the crimes of statesmen. And reason of church was similarly restrictive; both had in fact encouraged a double standard, policy and moral latitude for rulers, obedience and conventional morality for subjects. Such a distinction was not made by the major Puritan casuists.[47] The exercise of prudence, the pursuit of policy against a politic Satan—these were left open to God's instruments, whatever their social or political status. The king, in short, would not be alone either in declaring war or in directing

44 See R. H. Bainton, "The Immoralities of the Patriarchs according to the Exegesis of the Late Middle Ages and of the Reformation," *Harvard Theological Review* 23:39-49 (1930).

45 William Perkins, *Works* (London, 1616), III, 165, 171; see discussion in Mosse, *Holy Pretense*, pp. 49ff.

46 Leighton, *Looking Glass*, pp. 133ff. Compare Bernard, *Bible-Battles*, pp. 197-198.

47 Mosse, *Holy Pretense*, pp. 64-65, 87, 123.

it. If he had succeeded in overcoming the freelance knight, he now had to face the conscientious saint, permanently at war.

v

The Puritan development of just-war theory suggested a considerable increase in the participation of godly men in the politics of warfare. It was inevitable that the ministers should also urge participation in the actual fighting. Men should indeed labor for peace, wrote Alexander Leighton. "But we must understand with whom we live in this world, with men of strife, men of blood, having dragon's hearts, serpent's heads." It behooves the saints to "work with one hand and with the other hold the sword."[48] If actual fighting was nothing but unpleasant, Puritan preachers nevertheless insisted that drill was a godly discipline and the new army a highly commendable order. Without reviving the old feudal zest for combat, they labored to improve "the soldier's honor" and to create a new, Protestant version of the "dignity of chivalry."

The organization of the new army—as distinct from "the feudal collection of bellicose individuals"—had a special appeal to the Puritan mind: it was an order based on command and requiring a rigid discipline; it resembled the order that a sovereign God had established in his church. "The people of God . . . are beautiful," wrote Richard Sibbes, "for order is beautiful. Now it is an orderly thing to see many together submit themselves to the ordinance of God . . . An army is a beautiful thing, because of the order and the well-disposed ranks that are within it. In this regard the church is beautiful."[49] Protestants strove to introduce the discipline of the reformed churches directly into the army; this would serve to reinforce a system already parallel in its purpose and genesis, for the Calvinist discipline and the new army regulations were responses respectively to disorder and melee. Cromwell's request to Richard Baxter that he organize the East Anglia cavalry into a church is well known. The covenanted army of Scotland actually achieved such an organization, at least on paper. The first article of the Scottish *Military Disci-*

48 Leighton, *Looking Glass*, pp. 7-9.
49 Sibbes, *Works*, II, 232.

pline proclaimed "That in every regiment . . . there be an ecclesiastical eldership or high session, consisting of the minister . . . of the regiment and elders to be chosen . . ." The *Discipline* of the Swedish army, circulated widely in England during the 1630's, was similar in form.[50]

Their concern with "godly discipline" led the Puritan ministers to favor the volunteer over the impressed soldier. The discipline of an army, they thought, was evidence of the godliness of its members; conversely, a godly army could never be "gathered [out of the] riff-raff, the refuse and dregs of the people . . ." The perennial victims of the press were also the objects of Puritan attack: vagrants and vagabonds, the unemployed or idle poor—men, that is, not subject to discipline in civilian life. Since warfare was a "serious action" such "sinful instruments" would inevitably fail to realize its purposes. Nor would they make good soldiers; they would be unwilling at best, hapless, literally driven into battle without training or religious preparation. As an alternative to such men, Puritan ministers urged prosperous (and presumably godly) citizens to enlist in the volunteer companies that drilled and practiced arms in many of England's cities. "The distress of our brethren abroad," John Davenport told the members of the London artillery company, "should quicken us to the use of all means, whereby we may be enabled to help them."[51] Soldiering would have to be made, once again, a trade for gentlemen and also a vocation for the saints. Years before Cromwell recruited his East Anglia regiments from among "men of spirit," the idea of an army different in kind from the feudal band and the impressed horde was being circulated. Once again, the ministers were attacking traditional forms of loyalty and organization and recommending instead a modern discipline founded on ideological commitment.

Military drill was the exercise of the saintly soldiers. One pragmatic minister suggested its secular importance: it was no longer numbers or strength, he said, but "experimented order" that

---

50 *Articles of Military Discipline* (Edinburgh, 1639), p. 3 and *The Swedish Discipline* (second part).

51 John Davenport, *A Royal Edict for Military Exercises* (London, 1629), pp. 14, 16; Thomas Palmer, *Bristol's Military Garden* (London, 1635), pp. 20-21. Davenport's *Royal Edict*, Adam's *Soldier's Honor*, Leech's *Train Soldier*, Gouge's *Dignity of Chivalry*, Sutton's *Good Fight* and Ashe's *Good Courage* were all preached before the Honorable Artillery Company of London.

won battles.[52] This was an acute insight into the changed character of warfare. Generally, however, Puritan ministers did not talk so much of the military utility as of the spiritual value of the new forms of marching and drilling. Writing for the officers of the Dutch army, the neo-Stoic philosopher Lipsius had suggested that drill might be a means of inculcating Stoic virtues in the soldier.[53] In a similar fashion, Puritans found drill an aid to godliness and a useful exercise in the internal war of the saints against Satan. Even if there were no danger of external war, wrote John Davenport, military drill might well replace other recreations: "And in religious respects, since every man will have recreations, that be best which is freest from sin, that best which strengtheneth a man . . . then abandon your carding, dicing, chambering, wantonness, dalliance, scurrilous discoursing and vain raveling out of time, to frequent these exercises . . ."[54] The exercises were to be pursued even when their rational end, warmaking, was no longer apparent. Warfare, which in Renaissance Italy had been an aristocratic sport (symbolized in the tourney), would have become in a Puritan England a calisthenic for the saints (symbolized in the drill). "It is good to be doing something, that when Satan comes . . . he may find thee honestly busied . . . The exercises of war step in here to challenge their deserved praise . . ."[55]

Lipsius' argument for the new drill was part of a more general trend in neo-Stoical thought which eventually—in combination with elements of the old chivalric code—produced a kind of ideology for Europe's new officers' corps. Here again, Stoicism played a part, which may be compared with that of Calvinism, in creating royal office holders out of feudal lords and Renaissance *gentilhommes* and in this case in particular, in transforming "dying chivalry" into an official "military caste."[56] No similar transformation took place in England, though other, related effects of Puritanism upon the mind of the gentry have been suggested above. The extraordinarily low esteem into which soldiers had fallen in the last half of the sixteenth century (when England was ruled by a woman) was not raised significantly in the early seven-

52 Palmer, *Military Garden*, pp. 26-27.
53 Roberts, *Military Revolution*, p. 7.
54 Davenport, *Royal Edict*, p. 18.
55 Adams, *Soldier's Honor*, p. 18.
56 Roberts, *Military Revolution*, p. 26.

teenth. Nevertheless the excitement caused by the Thirty Years' War did lead to a noticeable increase in the number of men choosing arms as a profession in the 1630's.[57] During the period immediately preceding the revolution a group of Puritan preachers, speaking before the voluntary artillery companies, urged young gentlemen and merchants' sons to become "men of war." Elaborating on the "honor" of the soldier, apparently a matter of considerable anxiety, the ministers argued not only the lawfulness of the profession and the manliness and virtue of the exercise, but also the religious necessity of warfare itself. They boldly contrasted the "effeminateness" of the courtier who dances and woos, with the "nobleness" of the soldier who trains and exercises.[58] Like the Puritan assize sermons, this too was an aspect of the education of the gentry and its urban counterparts, a training in duty and in a kind of Protestant *civisme*. As the magistrate was told to be ever-vigilant against sin, so the future soldiers were warned again and again that England had enemies who, like Satan himself, were "daily plotting and contriving." Military honor, like religion, "calls for all to be ready."

The intense seriousness of the men in training for politics and warfare set them apart in old England. It isolated them especially from the company of nobles, writers, and clerics who were patronized by the court. There war was viewed only as an aristocratic sport or a matter of state policy. And the king, despite the popular pressure that the Puritans were able to generate though not yet to organize effectively, was a man of peace. Writing of the German wars in 1622, the Anglican minister Robert Willan made no

57 That such an increase took place is suggested by a statistical study in Robert Merton, *Science, Technology and Society in Seventeenth Century England,* in *Osiris,* IV, part 2 (Bruges, 1938), pp. 372-373, 393, 395. On the declining prestige of the soldier, see Everard, *The Arriereban,* pp. 25ff.

58 Adams, *Soldier's Honor,* sig. B$_2$. Preacher after preacher came forward to tell the young men who drilled ("not by constraint but of a ready mind"—Davenport, *Royal Edict,* p. 15) in the artillery yards that soldiering was a profession which would do them honor. It is by no means far-fetched to suggest that these young men marched to prove themselves gentlemen. Samuel Buggs, whose audience was "for the most part tradesmen," told them that "you have entered now one of the two professions which are the only life and luster of true gentry." *Midland Soldier,* sig. A$_3$ and p. 35. Adams refers to his audience as made up of "truly generous gentlemen, citizens of London, of the society of arms." *Soldier's Honor,* dedication. Significantly, the artillery companies were also centers of Puritan activity: for the Honorable Artillery Company of London, see Valerie Pearl, *London and the Outbreak of the Puritan Revolution* (Oxford, 1961), pp. 170-173.

effort to distinguish one side from the other; he displayed little sense of Protestant militancy. "They have found them . . . dog-days . . . Such is the fury and rage of one against the other, that the fume and smoke thereof prognosticates the fire of conflagration, ready . . . to consume them all." "Oh Christian religion . . . thy reverend name [is made] the mask of war . . ."[59] In 1625 Bishop Bedell's translation of Paoli Sarpi's *The Free School of War*, published under the king's seal, provided Englishmen with an equally detached but far more playful view of warfare. Sarpi defended a group of Italian noblemen who had fought in Holland against the Spanish army and had in consequence been denied the sacraments by a Catholic priest. The denial obviously implied that warfare had some religious meaning. Sarpi disagreed with the priest but hardly took what could be called a Protestant position. "The only and true cause," he insisted, "why these gentlemen served under the States of Holland was a mere intent to learn the art of war . . . without having . . . regard unto the doctrine and religions professed in these countries . . ."[60] This view of aristocratic prerogative, turning Europe's religious upheaval into a "free school of war," was presumably approved by the king, but it was utterly foreign to the pious seriousness of the Puritans. Sarpi's defense of the "free school" contrasts sharply with the prayer of Alexander Leighton published a year earlier: "that our camps may be holy camps and our wars sanctified to the Lord."[61]

The new warfare had been launched under the aegis of ancient Rome: Roman drill, Roman discipline, Roman tactics—all were enthusiastically praised by Renaissance writers. But the martial valor of Christians was disparaged; even the Turks, it was said, made better soldiers though their camps were never holy nor their wars sanctified. To Machiavelli, it was the Christian religion itself which was at fault, teaching men the pacifist virtues.[62] Puritan writers vigorously denied this—knowing little of such virtues —and they were probably right. "Who can doubt that these will

---

[59] Robert Willan, *Conspiracy Against Kings, Heaven's Scorn* (London, 1622), pp. 2, 11-12. Willan asks why there is so much strife in the world, but steers away from any radical response. "The question is hard, and pressed too far, may prove curious." It will lead men to become Manicheans—that is, to emphasize (as many Puritans did) the power of Satan; p. 14.
[60] Paoli Sarpi, *The Free School of War*, trans. W. B. (London, 1625), sig. F₃ verso.
[61] Leighton, *Looking Glass*, p. 31.
[62] Machiavelli, *The Discourses*, book II, ch. ii.

adventure life in the field for religion and a just cause," one of the ministers asked, "that dare willingly yield their bodies to be burnt for their faith and profession?"[63] Christianity might produce a discipline and courage of its own. Braced by the sermons of his chaplain, excited by the mass prayer meetings, shouting hymns as he rode into battle, the pious Protestant warrior was not very far from a crusading fanatic. Such a Christian hero Machiavelli had never imagined.

VI

In the preceding pages, the Puritans have undoubtedly been made to appear far more warlike, even more militant than they actually were. There is no other way to explain the revolution except by emphasizing these elements in its historical background that came to the fore once the conflict had actually opened. Had it never opened, the saints might have continued to pursue their spiritual warfare and this would have appeared to the historian as nothing more than a particularly intense version of the ancient Christian struggle against the old Adam. But the military rhetoric that set saints against worldlings, the interest of the preachers in army order and drill, the erosion of traditional notions about the just (limited) war—all these made actual warfare more likely than it would otherwise have been. And they helped too in pushing the war, when it came, beyond resistance to revolution.

This was the effect of Puritanism: it made revolution available to the minds of seventeenth-century Englishmen as it had never been before. It trained them to think of the struggle with Satan and his allies as an extension and duplicate of their internal spiritual conflicts, and also as a difficult and continuous war, requiring methodical, organized activity, military exercise, and discipline. These ideas were the underlying themes of the new politics; permanent warfare was the central myth of Puritan radicalism. The preachers made warfare appear a particularly vivid and significant expression of the disorder of the age. Here moral confusion and social strain were turned into systematic enmity and this, in a sense, was the "secret history" of the English Revolution. After the king's execution, a Puritan minister described with awe the unexpectedness of the event: "The actions

---

63 Bernard, *Bible-Battles*, pp. 79-80. Leighton answers Machiavelli in a similar vein, *Looking Glass*, p. 25-28.

of God in such a day as this," wrote John Owen, "are . . . un-
suited to the expectations of men."[64] He was right and the point
can hardly be overstated. The prerevolutionary preachers who
urged the amateur soldiers of London's artillery yard to fight
against Satan for the glory of Christ had no prevision of Cromwell's army. Nevertheless, England was not unprepared for the
New Model; in some obscure way, men may even have been
waiting—for so many years the ministers had been calling them
to their tents. One of those ministers suggested that this long
preparation was an example of the cunning of God: "God can
work upon the hearts of men . . . the work shall be done though
they think not so."[65]

What finally made men revolutionaries, however, was not only
this secret preparation, but an increasingly secure feeling that
the saints did know the purposes of God, a more open and direct
reinforcement of their pride and contentiousness. This new, aggressive, and self-confident mood took hold of Puritan ministers
and gentlemen only when the idea of warfare was brought into
a fairly specific system of historical reference and prophecy. Beginning at some point before 1640, a group of writers, including
Joseph Mead of Cambridge University, began the work of inte-
grating the spiritual warfare of the preachers with the apocalyptic history of Daniel and Revelations.[66] The religious wars on the
continent and then the struggle against the English king were seen
by these men as parts of the ancient warfare of Satan and the
elect, which had begun with Jews and Philistines and would continue until Armageddon. This view, which preceded the revolution, marked a significant break with the military rhetoric of
Calvin and the Marian exiles, who had described conflict in ahistorical terms as a necessary feature of the Christian life, more
violent, perhaps, in periods of reform, but essentially continuous
and unrelenting. The victories that could be won were minimum
victories, grasped with the fiercest of wills, maintained with the

---

[64] John Owen, *The Advantage of the Kingdom of Christ in the Sinking of the
Kingdoms of the World* (London, 1651), p. 22.
[65] William Hussey, *The Magistrate's Charge for the People's Safety* (London,
1647), p. 23.
[66] For an excellent treatment of Christian millenarian thought, see E. L. Tuveson,
Millenium and Utopia: A Study in the Background of the Idea of Progress (Berkeley,
1949), on Mead, see pp. 76ff.

most severe of disciplines and yet only temporary. The shift to a more optimistic and historical theory of Christian warfare can probably be dated from the appearance of Mead's *Clavis Apocalyptica* in 1627.

This long and scholarly book was translated in 1643 by order of Parliament, with a "compendium" of world history added at the end for the use of less educated enthusiasts. It thus became the chief authority for the apocalyptic writers of the revolutionary period, though Mead would hardly have approved the extravagant conclusions that some of them, caught up in the excitement of the revolution, drew from his work. By and large, they accepted his interpretation of the millenium as an actual earthly kingdom (Mead did not say, however, that Christ would personally rule in this kingdom) coming into existence after the pouring of the last vial and the final overthrow of the beast. Previous Protestant writers had usually identified it with the first thousand years of the church and hence as a time long past. Mead's reversal of this position may be thought of as fulfilling one of the intellectual prerequisites of the revolution: it set Puritan activity within a world-historical context.[67] The effect upon the expression of patriotic and religious feeling may be suggested by the following quotation. Mead is interpreting an obscure passage from Revelations 16: "the third vial upon the rivers and fountains of the world of the beast."[68]

> The rivers and fountains ... are the ministers and defenders of the Anti-Christian jurisdiction, whether ecclesiastical, as Jesuits and other emissary priests, or even secular and lay as the Spanish champions ... Which thing concerning the ecclesiastical emissaries ... I think was fulfilled, when in our England, in the reign of Elizabeth of famous memory ... those bloody proctors for the authority of the beast were ... punished with death ... And not they alone, but the Spanish

---

[67] But compare the earlier treatise by Thomas Brightman, *A Revelation of the Apocalypse* (Amsterdam, 1611) in which the older, pessimistic view has been left behind and Mead's fully developed historical position anticipated. Brightman's apocalyptic vision suggested a kind of Protestant imperialism: "The victory [over the Pope] being obtained, the souls gather to the prey and do fill themselves with the spoils ... That whole late popish nation shall be subject afterward to the Reformed Church. Every country being a nourrison of the purer truth, shall have some part of the regions, before time given up to superstition, made subject to them." (p. 643).

[68] Joseph Mead, *The Key of the Revelation*, trans. by Richard More (London, 1643), p. 115 (second numbering).

champions for the cause of the beast, who were much more to be feared than they . . . thirsting for blood, drank blood in full draughts, especially in that memorable overthrow of the year 1588.

Thomas Twisse, prolocutor of the Assembly of Divines, who wrote the preface to the translation of Mead's book, credited him with having made possible a full historical description of "the martyrdom of God's saints . . . by the sword of war, first in the Low Countries, then in France, after that in Bohemia, then in Germany . . . and now amongst us . . . and that by the Anti-Christian generation."

Ideas of this sort apparently circulated among Puritans in the years directly before the revolution. When the fighting actually broke out, however, the first public defenses of the parliamentary position were written in terms of just-war theory. Ministers like Herbert Palmer (who later invoked the apocalyptic histories) argued that the soldiers of Essex fought only against the "malignants" who surrounded the throne and not against the king, "taking up arms for the defense of the kingdom" and not "against the king's person."[69] They refused to identify the royalists—let alone Charles himself—with Anti-Christ and the beast. They developed anew the old Huguenot theory of magistracy, but for the moment were as careful as the Huguenots had been to limit the use of the idea. "The power of the sword, by God's law, is not proper and peculiar to the king only," wrote Samuel Rutherford, "but given by God to the inferior judges." He went further and called into question that obedience to kings which Richard Bernard had still defended in 1629: the people ought to look less "to the authority of a king" and rather investigate on their own "the causes of war"—for obedience against God would be idolatry.[70] Still, the struggle was defensive only and could not, insisted Palmer, "be drawn to a necessary change of government."[71] These were the stock notions of the parliamentary lawyers; even in the first year of the fighting, however, they were supplemented and transformed by the bolder speculations of enthusiastic divines.

[69] [Herbert Palmer], *Scripture and Reason Pleaded for Defensive Arms* (London, 1643), pp. 25ff. See also Samuel Rutherford, *Lex Rex, or the Law and the Prince* (London, 1644; repr. Edinburgh, 1843), p. 139, and discussion in Bainton, "Congregationalism," pp. 5-8.

[70] Rutherford, *Lex Rex*, pp. 184, 187.

[71] [Palmer], *Scripture and Reason*, p. 58 (pagination irregular).

Thus the Presbyterian minister Francis Cheynell, speaking before the House of Commons in 1643: ". . . when the kings of the earth have given their power to the beast, these choice-soldiers [that is, the elect] will be so faithful to the King of kings, as to oppose the beast, though armed with kinglike power." Cheynell went on to stress the importance of rescuing the king from the beast and settling power once more upon his "royal person," but the emphasis of his oratory was clearly on the war rather than the rescue.[72]

The hastily offered arguments based on the theory of defensive war did not describe the struggle with the king as it appeared to the more radical of the Puritans. So the old descriptions of the warfare of saints and worldlings, of the onslaught of Satan and the methodical activity of the godly battalions shortly reappeared—in part, undoubtedly, as war propaganda, in part produced by the sheer momentum and excitement of the struggle itself. But wars, it should be said, had been fought among Christians for many centuries without similar rhetorical support. Throughout the Middle Ages, writes one historian, "even those who commented in the heat of political passion had never identified their enemies with Anti-Christ."[73] Such an identification is not necessary to civil war, but only to revolution. It was for this that the saints had been prepared and from the early forties, once the first shock of battle had been overcome, it was a revolution that they made. The very suddenness of the overturn suggested an opportunity provided by God. And the tense readiness of the Puritan spirit was fashioned for such an occasion: "When he gives us an opportunity, then is the time; when the iron is hot, then strike."[74] At such a moment, all men were called to act; there were great tasks to be done, enemies to be overcome. The world was rapidly divided into those who came forward and those who did not. "All people are cursed or blessed according as they do or do not join their strength and give their best assistance to the Lord's people against their enemies."[75] It was, Thomas

72 Francis Cheynell, *Sion's Momento and God's Alarum* (London, 1643), p. 10.

73 Beryl Smalley, *The Study of the Bible in the Middle Ages* (Oxford, 1941), p. 225; quoted in Tuveson, *Millenium*, p. 18. Joachim of Flora and Savonarola are exceptions to this general rule.

74 John Cotton, quoted in Mosse, *Holy Pretense*, p. 125.

75 Stephen Marshall, *Meroz Cursed* (London, 1641), p. 9.

Goodwin told the Commons in 1642, "an opportunity such as the last hundred years . . . have not afforded the like . . ." It was a divinely given chance to rebuild the Temple, "and if you will not do it," the preacher ominously told the parliamentarians, "God will do it without you." Images of violence and struggle recurred in Goodwin's sermon; these were the inevitable concomitants •of reformation. "Purge and reform the Temple," he insisted, "though you die for it." "I am confident," repeated John Arrowsmith, "that you never dreamt of reforming a church and state with ease."[76]

Stephen Marshall, the greatest of the parliamentary preachers, described the transition from just war to revolution in a sermon delivered before both houses in 1644. Abruptly turning to the soldiers present, he said, "Go now and fight the battles of the Lord . . . for so I will not now fear to call them . . . although indeed at the first nothing clearly appeared but only that you were compelled to take up arms for the defense of your liberties . . . all Christendom . . . do now see that the question in England is whether Christ or Anti-Christ shall be lord or king."[77] A year later, Thomas Coleman was even more forthright: "the weapons of the saint's warfare," he proclaimed before the Commons, "are as well offensive as defensive . . ." The members must expect "the militia of hell and the trained bands of Satan" to be armed against them.[78] Indeed, it was Satan, and not the saints, suggested the preacher Henry Wilkinson, who was on the defensive: the devil's cohorts must "be put into a posture of war," he wrote, "since [Parliament's] business lies professedly against the apocalyptical beast and all his complices . . ."[79]

Such a view made the struggle against the king purposive and total; it implied a whole set of meanings that the term civil war did not usually include. It required that the soldiers who fought against the apocalyptical beast be themselves saints; at the very

[76] Thomas Goodwin, *Zerubbabel's Encouragement to Finish the Temple* (London, 1642), pp. 51, 58; John Arrowsmith, *The Covenant-Avenging Sword Brandished* (London, 1643), p. 14.

[77] Marshall, *A Sacred Panegyric* (London, 1644), p. 21.

[78] Thomas Coleman, *Hopes Deferred and Dashed* (London, 1645), p. 12; this sermon created a considerable stir in the House—"it had so much of novelty in it . . . and so wholly took up the minds of many." See Francis Woodcock, *Lex Talionis: or, God Paying Every Man in his Coin* (London, 1646), sig. A$_4$ (preface).

[79] Wilkinson, *Babylon's Ruin, Jerusalem's Rising* (London, 1643), sig. A$_3$ (epistle).

least, it permitted them to pretend that saints they were. Warfare
and reformation were locked together and their range extended
into every area of church and state where the beast might lurk.
At times, the Puritan struggle would be waged, like ordinary
war, in the field; but at times it would be waged politically and
enemies sought out at home. "Search, search narrowly for that
[evil] which may remain, search every corner of the law . . .
search with candles, make a curious search . . ."[80] Evil men like
evil laws would have to be searched out; here the war against
Satan took the form of a purge. It was justified by pious references
to Moses' slaughter of the golden calf worshippers (Exodus 32:27)
—as in an important sermon by Samuel Faircloth in 1641. "The
divine policy and heavenly remedy, to recover a commonwealth
and church . . . endangered," said Faircloth, "is that those that
have authority under God totally abolish and extirpate all the
cursed things whereby it may be disturbed . . ." Even Moses had
been a "man of blood," declared William Bridge; his was an
example to be followed.[81] Who were the "disturbers" of the commonwealth and church? The list suggested by Gouge in 1627 may
be recalled: infidels, idolators, heretics, worldlings, persecutors—
"*yea, and false brethren.*" When the tension of the battlefield was
carried into domestic politics, the number of "false brethren"
was almost automatically increased. It was no longer possible for
men to be neutral or merely sympathetic or to bargain and make
their peace. The military world-view continually compelled a
reorganization of ranks and the exclusion of soldiers thought to be
disloyal or ungodly or not totally committed. This was only an
extension of the eternal "watchfulness" of the saints, but it turned
politics into a deadly business. Anything less, the saints might have
argued, would not be serious; anything less would not have suited
their exalted sense of purpose and their apocalyptic sense of
possibility. As satanic lust was overcome in their inner wars, so
in the revolution, as one of them said, "the Whore of Babylon shall
be destroyed with fire and sword."[82]

---

80 Thomas Case, *Two Sermons Lately Preached* (London, 1642), I, 16.

81 Faircloth, *The Troublers Troubled* (London, 1641), p. 24; Bridge, *A Sermon
Preached Before the House of Commons* (London, 1643), p. 18.

82 Quoted in William Lamont, *Marginal Prynne: 1600-1669* (London, 1963), p. 61.
Even Prynne, narrow-minded lawyer that he was, was carried away by the

VII

But Puritan conceptions of the apocalypse were not quite apocalyptical. Mead's work had made it possible for the saints to connect their holy commonwealth with the promised millenium, but
most of them still saw that achievement of that millenium as hard
work, painful and inescapable. Chiliastic prophets might proclaim the imminence of glory and await with enthusiasm the
great changes in nature that would herald the kingdom of God.
But a man like Stephen Marshall, sharing the enthusiasm and
adhering closely to Mead's system, nevertheless exhorted the
saints to consider Christ's work their own: *"thou* hast a part
in every deliverance."* Nor was it the task of the Puritan saints, as
some of the chiliasts urged, simply to conquer and destroy all
existing political and religious institutions. The new Jerusalem
had to be built; it could only be the product of reformation and
reconstruction. And even in the new Jerusalem discipline would
be necessary, pious magistrates as vigilant as ever.[83]

This view of the revolution was expressed most clearly by the
Independent divine John Owen. In a series of remarkable sermons
preached in the years after the king's execution, Owen developed
an interpretation of Daniel and Revelations that translated the
mystical apocalypse into practical political terms, much as Mead
had translated it into mundane historical terms. "All nations
whatever," Owen wrote in 1652, "which in the present state and
government have given their power to the dragon . . . shall be
shaken, broken . . . and turned off their old foundations . . .
All those wars . . . wherein the saints of God shall be eminently
engaged, are upon this account." The outcome of the wars would
be "that the civil powers of the world, after fearful shakings and
desolations, should be disposed of, into a useful subserviency to
the interest, power and kingdom of Jesus Christ." What form of
government this "subserviency" would take, Owen was unwilling
to say; he contented himself with describing the fullness of peace,
the purity and beauty of the ordinances, the multitudes of converts that were promised in the new society. "There are great and

---

millenarian enthusiasm of the early 1640's—and that enthusiasm, according to
Lamont, made him briefly a "radical" (pp. 59-64).

[83] Marshall, *The Song of Moses . . . and the Song of the Lamb* (London, 1643),
p. 21; see discussion in Tuveson, *Millenium,* pp. 87-90.

mighty works in hand in this nation," he told the Rump; "tyrants are punished, the jaws of oppressors are broken, bloody, revengeful persecutors disappointed, and we hope governors set up that may be just, ruling in the fear of the Lord . . ."[84]

Intently concerned with the actual, unending, mundane struggle—"*Satan never turns Christian*"—Puritan writers like Owen and Marshall tended to reject the more radical and mystical visions of the apocalypse. Political warfare and reconstruction were different in kind both from the mystic's waiting for Christ and from the efforts of the Fifth-Monarchy men to prepare the way for his return by an orgy of destructiveness.[85] Despite their new enthusiasm, latter-day Calvinists still described what may be called, in contrast to the chiliasts' dream, a minimum program: they had not been untouched by the worldly pessimism of their teacher. "To dream of setting up an outward, glorious, visible kingdom of Christ, which he might bear rule in . . . be it in Germany or in England, is but an ungrounded presumption."[86] Owen rejected the idea of Christ's personal arrival on English soil. It was men who must achieve, by effort and struggle, whatever could be achieved on "this molehill earth." And that meant organization, calculation, systematic endeavor; the discipline of warfare would be carried into the work of rebuilding society. It was this above all that distinguished the Puritan revolutionary from the chiliast.

From the initial act of political disobedience until the founding of the holy commonwealth, the Puritan emphasis was on vigilance and self-control. Before the saints went to war, wrote one of the ministers, it was necessary "to weigh the strength of a kingdom . . . in a balance, to make an estimate of, and compare together the power of [the] several parties or divisions of people in it with so much exactness as to determine which is the stronger and which the weaker . . ."[87] So the saint was a military strategist, holding tight rein on his forces, keeping them battle-ready and

84 John Owen, *A Sermon . . . Concerning the Kingdom of Christ and the Power of the Civil Magistrate* (Oxford, 1652), p. 15; *Advantage of the Kingdom of Christ*, pp. 5, 27ff.

85 See the work of the Fifth-Monarchy man, John Canne, *The Time of the End* (London, 1657), esp. pp. 194-200, for an example of the destructive zeal of the godly.

86 Owen, *Concerning the Kingdom of Christ*, p. 18.

87 John Goodwin, *Anti-Cavalierism or, Truth Pleading as well the Necessity as the Lawfulness of this Present War* (London, 1642), p. 23.

well-drilled, waiting for the opportune moment. "When the iron is hot, then strike." Like a general in the army, he measured his chances, he knew his enemy, he was impatient with negotiation and maneuver, he sought nothing but victory. All this, as has been said, was a state of mind as well as a new kind of warfare—and it was that state of mind which Puritanism created and introduced into the political arena.

CHAPTER NINE · CONCLUSION

Virtually all the modern world has been read into Calvinism: liberal politics and voluntary association; capitalism and the social discipline upon which it rests; bureaucracy with its systematic procedures and its putatively diligent and devoted officials; and finally all the routine forms of repression, joylessness, and unrelaxed aspiration. By one or another writer, the faith of the brethren, and especially of the Puritan brethren, has been made the source or cause or first embodiment of the most crucial elements of modernity.[1] Undoubtedly there is some truth in all these interpretations and in the preceding pages many examples have been given of "modern" elements in Calvinist theory and practice, or rather, of elements later incorporated into the modern world. It is now necessary to add, however, that this incorporation was a long and complex process, involving selection, corruption, and transformation; it was the result of men *working upon* their Calvinist heritage. Calvinism in its sixteenth- and seventeenth-century forms was not so much the cause of this or that modern economic, political, or administrative system as it was an agent of modernization, an ideology of the transition period. And as the conditions of crisis and upheaval in which Calvinism was conceived and developed did not persist, so Calvinism as an integral and creative force did not endure. It gave way to other social and intellectual forces which sustained something of its achievement but not everything—indeed, very far from everything.

1 See, for example, Charles Borgeaud, *The Rise of Modern Democracy in Old and New England*, trans. B. Hill (London, 1894); G. P. Gooch, *English Democratic Ideas in the Seventeenth Century* (New York, 1959); A. D. Lindsay, *The Modern Democratic State* (Oxford, 1943); Max Weber, *The Protestant Ethic and the Spirit of Capitalism*, trans. Talcott Parsons (New York, 1958)—and the enormous literature provoked by this book (a partial list and a critical discussion can be found in Charles H. and Katherine George, *The Protestant Mind of the English Reformation 1570-1640*, Princeton, 1961); C. J. Friedrich, "Introduction" to Althusius, *Politica Methodice Digesta* (Cambridge, Mass., 1932).

Calvinism was not a liberal ideology, even though congregational life was surely a training for self-government and democratic participation. The radically democratic Levellers probably had their beginning in the Puritan congregations, in the debates, for example, that preceded the elections of ministers and in the recriminations that so frequently followed.[2] Even when the choice of ministers was not open to the church membership, as it often was not, politics in the congregation was very different from the influence, intrigue, and patronage that prevailed at the bishop's or the king's court. Personal loyalty and deference, so highly developed among the courtiers, declined among the brethren. Calvinist voluntarism established instead the freely negotiated contract as the highest human bond; in its terms, Puritan writers described the connection of man and God, of the saint and his associates, of minister and church, of husband and wife. All these relations were entered into willingly and knowingly, and if men were thus to negotiate contracts they obviously required some knowledge of the contract's content and purposes. The preaching and writing of the ministers was designed to provide such knowledge; so was the discussion among lay Puritans of the sermons and the texts; so also the congregational debates, the reading, note-taking and diary-keeping of the newly political, newly educated saints. And all this was preparation also for the debates and elections, the pamphlets and parties of liberal politics.

But Puritanism was much more than this, as the previous description of the "attack upon the traditional world" and the "new world of discipline and work" ought to have made clear. The associations of the brethren were voluntary indeed, but they gave rise to a collectivist discipline marked above all by a tense mutual "watchfulness." Puritan individualism never led to a respect for privacy. Tender conscience had its rights, but it was protected only against the interference of worldlings and not against "brotherly admonition." And the admonitions of the brethren were anxious, insistent, continuous. They felt themselves to be living in an age of chaos and crime and sought to train conscience to be permanently on guard, permanently at war, against sin. Debate in a Puritan congregation was never a

---

[2] See Christopher Hill, *Economic Problems of the Church* (Oxford, 1956), pp. 298ff.

free and easy exchange of ideas; the need for vigilance, the pressures of war were too great to allow for friendly disagreement.
What lay behind the warfare of the saints? Two things above all:
a fierce antagonism to the traditional world and the prevailing
pattern of human relation and a keen and perhaps not unrealistic
anxiety about human wickedness and the dangers of social disorder. The saints attempted to fasten upon the necks of all mankind the yoke of a new political discipline—impersonal and
ideological, not founded upon loyalty or affection, no more open
to spontaneity than to chaos and crime. This discipline was not to
depend upon the authority of paternal kings and lords or upon
the obedience of childlike and trustful subjects. Puritans sought
to make it voluntary, like the contract itself, the object of individual and collective willfulness. But voluntary or not, its key-
note was repression.

Liberalism also required such voluntary subjection and self-
control, but in sharp contrast to Puritanism, its politics was
shaped by an extraordinary confidence in the possibility of both,
a firm sense of human reasonableness and of the relative ease
with which order might be attained. Liberal confidence made
repression and the endless struggle against sin unnecessary; it also
tended to make self-control invisible, that is, to forget its painful
history and naïvely assume its existence.[3] The result was that
liberalism did not create the self-control it required. The Lockeian
state was not a disciplinary institution as was the Calvinist holy
commonwealth, but rather rested on the assumed political virtue
of its citizens.[4] It is one of the central arguments of this conclusion that Puritan repression has its place in the practical history
of that strange assumption.

It is not possible to judge in any absolute terms the effectiveness
of this repression or the extent of the social need for it. It can
only be said that the Puritans *knew about* human sinfulness and
that Locke did not need to know. This undoubtedly reflects not
only different temperaments but also different experiences. The
very existence and spread of Puritanism in the years before the

---

[3] For some suggestion of that painful history, see Friedrich Nietzsche, *The
Genealogy of Morals*, trans. Francis Golffing (New York, 1956), esp. pp. 192ff. on
the genesis of conscience.

[4] For a discussion of Locke's theory of political virtue, see Peter Laslett's edition
of the *Two Treatises of Government* (Cambridge, 1960), 108ff.

revolution surely suggest the presence in English society of an acute fear of disorder and "wickedness"—a fear, it has been argued above, attendant upon the transformation of the old political and social order. The triumph of Lockeian ideas, on the other hand, suggests the overcoming of anxiety, the appearance of saints and citizens for whom sin is no longer a problem. The struggle against the old order seems largely to have been won by Locke's time, and the excitement, confusion, and fearfulness of that struggle almost forgotten. Lockeian liberals found it possible to dispense with religious, even with ideological, controls in human society and thought enthusiasm and battle-readiness unattractive. But this was only because the controls had already been implanted *in men.* In a sense, then, liberalism was dependent upon the existence of "saints," that is, of persons whose good behavior could be relied upon. At the same time, the secular and genteel character of liberalism was determined by the fact that these were "saints" whose goodness (sociability, moral decency, or mere respectability) was self-assured and relaxed, free from the nervousness and fanaticism of Calvinist godliness.

This, then, is the relation of Puritanism to the liberal world: it is perhaps one of historical preparation, but not at all of theoretical contribution. Indeed, there was much to be forgotten and much to be surrendered before the saint could become a liberal bourgeois. During the great creative period of English Puritanism, the faith of the saints and the tolerant reasonableness of the liberals had very little in common.

Roughly the same things can be said about the putative connection of Calvinism and capitalism. The moral discipline of the saints can be interpreted as the historical conditioning of the capitalist man; but the discipline was not itself capitalist. It can be argued that the faith of the brethren, with its emphasis upon methodical endeavor and self-control, was an admirable preparation for systematic work in shops, offices, and factories. It trained men for the minute-to-minute attentiveness required in a modern economic system; it taught them to forego their afternoon naps—as they had but recently foregone their saint's day holidays —and to devote spare hours to bookkeeping and moral introspection. It somehow made the deprivation and repression inevitable in sustained labor bearable and even desirable for the saints.

And by teaching self-control, it provided the basis for impersonal, contractual relations among men, allowing workmanlike cooperation but not involving any exchange of affection or any of the risks of intimacy. All this, Calvinism did or helped to do. Whether it did so in a creative fashion or as the ideological reflection of new economic processes is not immediately relevant. The saints learned, as Weber has suggested, a kind of rational and worldly asceticism, and this was probably something more than the economic routine required. They sought in work itself what mere work can never give: a sense of vocation and discipline that would free them from sinfulness and the fear of disorder.[5]

But Weber has said more than this; he has argued that systematic acquisition as well as asceticism has a Calvinist origin.[6] The psychological tension induced by the theory of predestination, working itself out in worldly activity, presumably drove men to seek success as a sign of salvation. The sheer willfulness of an inscrutable God produced in its turn, if Weber is correct, the willfulness of an anxious man and set off the entrepreneurial pursuit of better business techniques and more and more profit. At this point his argument breaks down. If there is in fact a peculiar and irrational quality to the capitalists' lust for gain, its sources must be sought elsewhere than among the saints. For Puritanism was hardly an ideology that encouraged continuous or unrestrained accumulation. Instead, the saints tended to be narrow and conservative in their economic views, urging men to seek no more wealth than they needed for a modest life, or, alternatively, to use up their surplus in charitable giving. The anxiety of the Puritans led to a fearful demand for economic restriction (and political control) rather than to entrepreneurial activity as Weber has described it. Unremitting and relatively unremunerative work was the greatest help toward saintliness and virtue.[7]

The ideas of Puritan writers are here very close to those of

5 This much of Weber's theory has no necessary connection with capitalism: it suggests that Puritanism fostered a rationalist "spirit," but not an acquisitive one. A similar view seems to be implied in Herbert Marcuse's discovery of a "protestant ethic" in Soviet Marxism; see *Soviet Marxism: A Critical Analysis* (New York, 1961), pp. 217, 222-223.

6 Weber, *Protestant Ethic*, pp. 171ff.

7 See discussion in George, *Protestant Mind*, Chapters Three and Four; also Kurt Samuelsson, *Religion and Economic Action*, trans. E. G. French (Stockholm, 1961).

such proto-Jacobins as Mably and Morelly in eighteenth-century France, who also watched the development of capitalist enterprise with unfriendly eyes, dreaming of a spartan republic where bankers and great merchants would be unwelcome.[8] The collective discipline of the Puritans—their Christian Sparta—was equally incompatible with purely acquisitive activity. Virtue would almost certainly require economic regulation. This would be very different from the regulation of medieval corporatism and perhaps it was the first sense of that difference that received the name *freedom*. It was accompanied by a keen economic realism: thus the Calvinist acknowledgment of the lawfulness of usury. But Calvinist realism was in the service of effective control and not of free activity or self-expression. Who can doubt that, had the holy commonwealth ever been firmly established, godly self-discipline and mutual surveillance would have been far more repressive than the corporate system? Once again, in the absence of a Puritan state the discipline was enforced through the congregation. The minutes of a seventeenth-century consistory provide a routine example: "The church was satisfied with Mrs. Carlton," they read, "as to the weight of her butter."[9] Did Mrs. Carlton tremble, awaiting that verdict? Surely if the brethren were unwilling to grant liberty to the local butter-seller, they would hardly have granted it to the new capitalist. The ministerial literature, at least, is full of denunciations of enclosures, usurers, monopolists, and projectors—and occasionally even of wily merchants.[10] Puritan casuistry, perhaps, left such men sufficient room in which to range, but it hardly offered them what Weber considers so essential—a good conscience. Only a sustained endeavor in hypocrisy could have earned them that. The final judgment of the saints with regard to the pursuit of money is that of Bunyan's pilgrim, angry and ill-at-ease in the town of Vanity, disdainful of such companions as Mr. Money-love and Mr. Save-all.[11]

Liberalism and capitalism appear fully developed only in a

[8] See, for example, Mably's *Entretiens de Phocion* (Paris, 1804); the restrictionist attitudes of Mably and Morelly are discussed in J. L. Talmon, *The Origins of Totalitarian Democracy* (New York, 1960), pp. 58ff.

[9] Quoted in Horton Davies, *The Worship of the English Puritans* (Westminster, 1948), p. 236.

[10] This literature is discussed in George, *Protestant Mind*, pp. 149ff.

[11] John Bunyan, *Pilgrim's Progress*, ed. J. B. Wharey (Oxford, 1928), pp. 95ff., 107ff.

secular form, that is, only after Puritanism is spent as a creative force. It seems likely that a certain freedom from religious controls and religious scruples is essential for their general triumph in modern Western society. This freedom may well have its origins in the Reformation, in the attack upon the established church and the traditional priesthood, but it was not the responsibility of the reformers; it lay beyond their intentions. The holy commonwealth would have been neither liberal nor capitalist—no more, indeed, than would the Jacobin Republic of Virtue. The spread of the capitalist and liberal spirits parallels the decline of radical enthusiasm. At the same time, however, radical enthusiasm in the years before its decline helped to shape the disciplinary basis of the new economy and politics. In a sense, worldly asceticism preceded entrepreneurial freedom, just as political zeal preceded liberalism. There is an historical interdependence, not easy to understand though vulgar moralists have made it a cliché, between discipline and liberty—or rather, between discipline and a certain sort of liberty.

II

Neither Max Weber nor any of his followers have ever demonstrated that the Englishmen who actually became Puritans, who really believed in predestination and lived through the salvation panic, went on to become capitalist businessmen. The burden of the evidence would seem to be against such a conclusion, though this is not certain; it is possible that businessmen are simply less likely to keep records of their spiritual struggles than of their economic affairs. The weight of such diaries, letters, and memoirs as we possess, however, suggests that the most significant expression of the new faith was cultural and political rather than economic. The saints were indeed activists, and activists in a far more intense and "driven" fashion than the men who came later: English gentlemen after their conversions attended to parliamentary affairs with a new assiduousness; pious mothers trained their sons to a constant concern with political life; enthusiastic apprentices took notes at sermons and studied the latest religious and political pamphlets. The outcome of Puritan activity was godly watchfulness, magistracy, and revolution.

Had the revolution succeeded, the discipline of the holy commonwealth, as of the Jacobin Republic of Virtue, would have required an institutionalized political activism. Each utopia would have proliferated a petty officialdom, a host of minor administrators busily enforcing the new rules and regulations. The ideas of John Eliot of Massachusetts suggest an image of the holy commonwealth as an over-governed society, with every tenth man an official. These zealous and conscientious magistrates—equipped with a realistic and intolerant sense of the sinfulness of their fellow men—would hardly constitute a modern bureaucracy, though once again their religious contentiousness may suggest the difficult, half-forgotten origins of modern bureaucratic discipline. The zeal of the saints seems to have little in common with the secular competence, functional rationality, and moderate devotion required of modern officials. Yet magistracy is a far better description of the saints' true vocation than is either capitalist acquisition or bourgeois freedom. It suggests most clearly the activist role that Puritanism called upon the saints to play in the creation and maintenance of a new moral order. This activity was political in the sense that it was always concerned with government—though not only or most importantly at the level of the state. For Puritans imagined the congregation as a "little commonwealth," debated worriedly over its constitution and sought means to discipline recalcitrant members; they saw the family as a voluntary community dominated by a godly father whom they described as a governor. And finally, they saw the self as a divided being, spirit at war with flesh, and there also they sought control and government.

Once Calvinism and Puritanism have been described in the political language of repression and war it becomes easier to answer the question posed in the first chapter of this book: why did particular groups of Englishmen and Frenchmen, Scots and Dutchman become Calvinists and Puritans? They did so, it may be suggested, because they felt some need for the self-control and godly government that sainthood offered. This is to push Weber's explanation of capitalism a step further back: he has argued that Calvinism was an anxiety-inducing ideology that drove its adherents to seek a sense of control and confidence in methodical work and worldly success. But he has not even raised the question of why men should adopt an anxiety-inducing ideology in the first place, a question to which his own concept of "elective affinity" offers a possible answer.[12] Now it is probably not true that Calvinism *induced* anxiety; more likely its effect was to confirm and explain in theological terms perceptions men already had of the dangers of the world and the self. But what made Calvinism an "appropriate" option for anxiety-ridden individuals was not only this confirmation, but also the fact that sainthood offered a way out of anxiety. Puritan "method" led to tranquillity and assurance through the "exercises" of self-control and spiritual warfare, and it then led to the political order of the holy commonwealth through the corresponding "exercises" of magistracy and revolution.

Men were likely to become saints, or rather, it is understandable that certain men should have become saints, if their social and personal experiences had been of a certain sort.[13] Three different sets of experiences have been discussed in the preceding pages: that of discontented and fearful noblemen like the French Huguenots who sought some way to adjust to a modern political order; that of clerical intellectuals, newly freed from corporate ties (and from the privileges that went along with those ties) and especially sensitive to the ambiguities of their own position and the disorder of their society; and finally that of new or newly educated gentlemen, lawyers and merchants, nervously making their way in university, parliament, and city, with a claim to stake in the political and social worlds. None of these group experiences make individual conversion predictable; each of them makes it comprehensible. Thus the moderate Calvinism of a man like Philip de Mornay can be viewed as the willful effort of an educated and ambitious French gentleman to demonstrate to himself as well as to others his worthiness for political office—a demonstration that required a rigid rejection of Renaissance pleasure and extravagance. The fanatical self-righteousness of that first Puritan John Knox, a Scottish peasant's son set loose in Europe by war and revolution, can best be understood as in some sense a function

12 *From Max Weber: Essays in Sociology,* trans. and ed. H. H. Gerth and C. Wright Mills (London, 1948), pp. 284-285.
13 The notion of "appropriate" or understandable behavior is used here in the sense suggested by William Dray, *Laws and Explanation in History* (Oxford, 1957), especially Part V. But for any full scale explanation of Puritanism in these terms it would probably be necessary to extend considerably Dray's conception of "rational action." See Samuel H. Beer, "Causal Explanation and Imaginative Re-enactment," *History and Theory* 3:23-24 (1963).

of his exile. Righteousness was a consolation and a way of organizing the self for survival. When John Whitgift, the future archbishop, cruelly taunted Thomas Cartwright for "eating at other men's tables," he was perhaps suggesting an important source of Cartwright's ideas of congregational unity and ministerial status. And finally, it can be argued, country gentlemen like John Winthrop and Oliver Cromwell, educated at Cambridge, knowledgeable but uneasy in London, full of new and vague aspirations, sought in Puritanism a self-confidence equal to their hopes and became saints on their way, as it were, to becoming governors of new worlds and new societies.

It should be noted that the elective affinity of aristocrats, ministers, gentlemen, merchants, and lawyers with the Calvinist and Puritan ideologies did not lie only in the anxiety they all shared, but also in the *capacity* they all shared to participate in those "exercises" that sainthood required. They were the "sociologically competent"—as has already been argued—they were ready for magistracy and war. The Calvinist faith did not appeal to men, however anxious, below the level of such competence. Laborers and peasants were more likely, if they were free at all from traditional ways, to adopt some more pacific or chiliastic faith whose promise did not depend upon their own hard work, that is, upon the control of themselves and the cruel, unwearying repression of others.

Puritanism cannot, then, be described simply as the ideological reflex of social disorder and personal anxiety; it is one possible response to the experiences of disorder and anxiety, or rather, it is one possible way of perceiving and responding to a set of experiences that other men than the saints might have viewed in other terms. There were both merchants and gentlemen, for example, who obviously enjoyed the very freedoms that frightened the saints so much—mobility, extravagance, individuality, and wit—and who eagerly sought out the Renaissance cities and courts where such freedoms were cultivated. And from among these new urbanites undoubtedly came many capitalists and liberals. It would not be easy to explain in particular cases why the court of James I held such attractions for some members of the English gentry while it was vicious and iniquitous in the eyes of others. No more is it readily comprehensible why some of the newcomers to

the burgeoning city of London merged into the mob or explored
the exciting underworld, while others hated the "wickedness" of
the city and sought out virtuous brethren and a sense of security
and confidence in the Puritan congregations. All that can be
said is that some of the men living in this age of social transformation found what was for them a suitable response in Calvinist
ideology. In England, Puritanism was their effort to capture control of the changing world and their own lives—hence the insistent concern of the saints with order, method, and discipline.

III

The Puritan concern with discipline and order, however, is not
unique in history. Over and over again since the days of the
saints, bands of political radicals have sought anxiously, energeti-
cally, systematically, to transform themselves and their world. The
choice of sainthood, then, need not be described simply as a
reasonable choice for sixteenth and seventeenth-century Englishmen to have made; it can be related systematically to other choices
of other men in similar historical circumstances.

The very appearance of the Puritan saints in English history
suggests the breakdown of an older order in which neither Protestant autodidacts, political exiles, nor voluntary associations of lay
brethren were conceivable. At the same time that breakdown provides the context within which the choice of sainthood seems
reasonable and appropriate, though not in any individual case
predictable. It is possible to go further than this, however, and
argue that given the breakdown of the old order, it *is* predictable
that some Englishmen would make that reasonable choice. And
further than this: given similar historical circumstances, Frenchmen and Russians would predictably make similar choices. Englishmen became Puritans and then godly magistrates, elders and
fathers in much the same way and for many of the same reasons
as eighteenth-century Frenchmen became Jacobins and active citizens, and twentieth-century Russians Bolsheviks and professional
revolutionaries—and then in Lenin's words "leaders," "managers,"
and "controllers."[14] The Calvinist saints were the first of these

14 Lenin, *The Immediate Tasks of the Soviet Government* (1918) in *Selected
Works* (New York, 1935-37), VII, 332-333. It was necessary, Lenin wrote, "to discover
real organizers, people with sober minds and a practical outlook, people who

bands of revolutionary magistrates who sought above all control and self-control. In different cultural contexts, at different moments in time, sainthood will take on different forms and the saints will act out different revolutions. But the radical's way of seeing and responding to the world will almost certainly be widely shared whenever the experiences which first generated that perception and response are widely shared, whenever groups of men are suddenly set loose from old certainties.

That older order in which Puritanism was unimaginable has been described in the preceding pages as a traditional society, that is, a society in which hierarchy is the fundamental ordering principle; patriarchy, personal loyalty, patronage and corporatism are the key forms of human relations; and passivity is the normal political posture of common men. At some point in the later Middle Ages, the complex institutional structure of European traditionalism began to weaken and erode; its philosophical rationalizations were called into question by bold speculators free, more or less, from traditional controls. Then there began a long˙ period of transition, in which moments of rapid and explosive change alternated with moments of stalemate and frustration. Individual men experienced at once a new and exhilarating sense of freedom and mobility and an acute anxiety and fearfulness, both of which may be summed up in the Puritan notion of "unsettledness." Only gradually, at different times in different countries, did there emerge a new society, whose members were at least formally equal, their political relations impersonal, based either upon negotiation and contract or upon a uniform coercion. In this society the activity of the organized "people" was as necessary to social discipline as was popular passivity in the traditional world.[15] The old order was imagined to be natural and eternal, but it is in the nature of the new that it be regularly renewed. It is the product of art and will, of human doing. If traditionalism was stable, modernity is founded upon change. Even so, however, it represents a routinization of the frenetic mobility that marked

---

combine loyalty to socialism, with ability without fuss (and in spite of fuss and noise) . . ." Compare this with Cromwell's plea for men "conscientious in employment."

15 The importance of "participation" in modern politics is urged by Daniel Lerner, *The Passing of Traditional Society* (Glencoe, Ill., 1958), esp. pp. 57ff.

the period of transition and of the zeal and anxiety that drove men forward during that exciting and painful time.

The significance of Puritanism lies in the part it played between 1530 and 1660. Those were crucial years of struggle and change in England and those were the years when Calvinism was a forceful, dynamic faith. After the Restoration, its energy was drawn inward, its political aspirations forgotten; the saint gave way to the nonconformist. Or, Lockeian liberalism provided an alternative political outlook. But Puritanism cannot be explained by reference either to its survivals or its transformations; it is necessary to confront the historical reality of those years when it was still an integral creed. In those years, Puritanism provided what may best be called an *ideology of transition*. It was functional to the process of modernization not because it served the purposes of some universal progress, but because it met the human needs that arise whenever traditional controls give way and hierarchical status and corporate privilege are called into question.[16] These needs can be met in other ways: by ideologists of nostalgia, for example, who glorify the old security and the old bondage. But they are met most effectively by doctrines like Puritanism that encourage a vigorous self-control and a narrowing of energies, a bold effort to shape a new personality against the background of social "unsettledness." Once such a personality has been achieved, the saints proceed to shape society in the image of their own salvation; they become what the ideologists of nostalgia can never become: active enemies of the old order. Thus when country gentlemen have experienced a conversion like Cromwell's, they are transformed not only into saints but also into parliamentary intransigents, attacking the traditional hierarchy root and branch and experimenting with new forms of political association.

But though they appear in history as revolutionaries, who destroy the old order and kill the king, the primary source of the saints' radical character lies in their response to the *dis*order of the transition period. The old order is only a part, and not the most important part of their experience. They live much of their lives amidst the breakdown of that order or (as with the clerical intellectuals) in hiding or exile from it. Much as they hated

16 This view of radical ideology was first suggested by Adam Ulam in his study of Marxist thought, *The Unfinished Revolution* (New York, 1960).

bishops and courtiers, then, the Puritan saints hated and feared vagabonds more and dreaded the consequences of the vagabonds in themselves, their own "unsettledness." "Masterless men" are always the first products of the breakdown of tradition and the saints hardly thought such men less dangerous than did their former masters. Without the experience of masterlessness, the Puritans are unimaginable. Sainthood is one of the likely results of that experience, or rather one of the ways in which men seek to cope with that experience. Hobbist authoritarianism is another way—and the contrast between Hobbes' appeal to sovereign power and the Puritan's struggle for self-control suggests the difficulty of describing sainthood, in Erich Fromm's terms, as an "escape from freedom."[17]

Fromm is certainly right, however, in viewing the saint in the context of "freedom." The Puritans were in no sense the products of a new order slowly growing up within traditional feudal society, as Marxist theory would have it. They were the products —though that word hardly suggests their extraordinary activism— of disorder. They inherited the critical and destructive work of writers like Machiavelli and Luther and they continued that work only after they had organized themselves to survive in the midst of criticism and destruction. They were second-generation men: they arrived in a world where courageous heretics and philosophers had already challenged the traditional masters; they encountered the difficulties of this world by being born again, by rejecting masterlessness and finding a new master in themselves and a new system of control in their godly brethren.

Coping with disorder meant being reborn as a new man, self-confident and free of worry, capable of vigorous, willful activity. The saints sometimes took new names, or gave new names to their children, to signify this rebirth. If the experience of "unsettledness" had made them anxious, depressed, unable to work, given to fantasies of demons, morbid introspection, or fearful daydreams such as Calvin had suggested were common among fallen men, then sainthood was indeed a triumph of character formation. Here the analogy with the Bolsheviks is worth pursuing. Lenin's diatribes against "slovenliness . . . carelessness, un-

17 Erich Fromm, *Escape from Freedom* (New York, 1941), pp. 84-98.

tidiness, unpunctuality, nervous haste, the inclination to substitute discussion for action, talk for work, the inclination to undertake everything under the sun without finishing anything" were intended first of all as attacks upon his fellow radicals and exiles— whatever their value as descriptions of the "primitive" Russia he hated so much.[18] The first triumph of Bolshevism, as of Puritanism, was over the impulse toward "disorganization" in its own midst: here, so to speak, was Satan at work where he is ever most active—in the ranks of the godly. It should not be forgotten, however, that this was a triumph also over the impulse toward free thought and spontaneous expression that manifests itself with especial vigor in the period of masterlessness and with which modernity has, up to a point, made its peace. This was the sacrifice which the saints found necessary in their terrible struggle for self-control. The Puritans vigorously attacked Renaissance experimentation in dress and in all the arts of self-decoration and hated the free-wheeling vagabonds who roamed the countryside and crowded into cities, never organizing themselves into families and congregations. They dreaded the dance and the drama, tore down maypoles and closed playhouses; they waged a long, bitter and unending war against fornication. In a similar fashion, the Jacobin leader Robespierre attacked the hedonism and censured the morals of the new bourgeoisie and spitefully connected the radical free thought of the Enlightenment with anti-revolutionary conspiracy. Atheism, he declared, is aristocratic.[19] And again Lenin, preaching with all the energy of a secular Calvinist against free love: "Dissoluteness in sexual life is bourgeois, [it] is a phenomenon of decay. The proletariat is a rising class . . . It needs clarity, clarity and again clarity. And so, I repeat, no weakening, no waste, no destruction of forces."[20]

In fact, Lenin's morality had little to do with the proletariat and the "dissoluteness" he attacked had little to do with the bourgeoisie. He might as well have talked of saints and worldlings as the Puritans did. The contrast he was getting at was between

18 *How to Organize Competition* (1917, repr. Moscow, 1951), p. 63; also *Letters*, trans. and ed. Elizabeth Hill and Doris Mudie (New York, 1937), p. 113.

19 Quoted in A. Aulard, *Christianity and the French Revolution* (Boston, 1927), p. 113.

20 Quoted in Klara Zetkin, "Reminiscences of Lenin," in *The Family in the U.S.S.R.*, ed. Rudolf Schlesinger (London, 1949), p. 18.

those men who had succumbed to (or taken advantage of!) the disorder of their time—speculators in philosophy, vagabonds in their sexual lives, economic Don Juans—and those who had somehow pulled themselves out of "unsettledness," organized their lives and regained control. The first group were the damned and the second the saved. The primary difference between them was not social, but ideological.

All forms of radical politics make their appearance at moments of rapid and decisive change, moments when customary status is in doubt and character (or "identity") is itself a problem. Before Puritans, Jacobins, or Bolsheviks attempt the creation of a new order, they must create new men. Repression and collective discipline are the typical methods of this creativity: the disordered world is interpreted as a world at war; enemies are discovered and attacked. The saint is a soldier whose battles are fought out in the self before they are fought out in society. Revolution follows from Puritan sainthood—that is, from the triumph over Satanic lusts—and also from Jacobin virtue and from the Bolshevik "steeling" of character; it is the acting out of a new identity, painfully won. This connection between sainthood and revolution is nicely illustrated in John Milton's eulogy of Cromwell: "A commander first over himself; the conqueror of himself, it was over himself he had learnt most to triumph. Hence he went to encounter with an external enemy as a veteran accomplished in all military duties . . ."[21] In traditional societies, this self-conquest is not necessary—except for relatively small numbers of men who for personal reasons choose monasticism as a way of life. In modern societies, it is routine. But there is a point in the modernization process when large numbers of men, suddenly masterless, seek a rigid self-control; when they discover new purposes, dream of a new order, organize their lives for disciplined and methodical activity. These men are prospective saints and citizens; for them Puritanism, Jacobinism, and Bolshevism are appropriate options. At this point in time, they are likely options.

This is not to reduce political radicalism to the psychological therapy of "unsettled" men. The "unsettledness" which Knox, Cartwright, and Cromwell experienced, with all its attendant fearfulness and enthusiasm, sometimes disfiguring and sometimes ennobling, was only a heightened form of the feelings of many of their fellow Englishmen—for ultimately the sociological range of the Puritan response was very wide. Of course, "unsettledness" was not a permanent condition and so sainthood was only a temporary role. The Puritans failed in their effort to transform England into a holy commonwealth and, in one way or another, their more recent counterparts have also failed. Sainthood mediated the dangerous shift from one social routine to another; then it survived only as a remembered enthusiasm and a habitual self-control devoid, as Weber's capitalism is, of theological reason. What this suggests, however, is not that holiness was an impractical dream, the program of neurotic, muddled, or unrealistic men. In fact, Puritan ministers and elders (and fathers) had considerable political experience and the holy commonwealth was in part achieved—among those men who most needed holiness. Nor is it correct to argue from the inability of the saints to retain political power that Puritanism represented only a temporary triumph of "ideas" over "interests," of the holiness doctrine over the ultimately more significant secular purposes of gentlemen, merchants, and lawyers.[22] For what needs to be explained is precisely why the saints over a long period of time acquired such an intense interest in ideas like predestination and holiness. Puritan ideology was a response to real experience, therefore a practical effort to cope with personal and social problems. The disappearance of the militant saints from English politics in the years after the Restoration suggests only that these problems were limited in time to the period of breakdown and psychic and political reconstruction. When men stopped being afraid or became less afraid, then Puritanism was suddenly irrelevant. Particular elements of the Puritan system were transformed to fit the new routine—and other elements were forgotten. And only then did the saint become a man of "good behavior," cautious, respectable, moved only by a routine anxiety and ready to participate in a Lockeian society.

22 This is the view of revolutionary enthusiasm suggested in Crane Brinton's book on the French Revolution, *Decade of Revolution* (New York, 1934), and again in his *Anatomy of Revolution* (New York, 1938).

IV

It is now possible to suggest a model of radical politics based on the history of the English Puritans and developed, at least in part, in their own terms. Such a model may serve to reveal the crucial features of radicalism as a general historical phenomena and to make possible a more systematic comparison of Puritans, Jacobins, and Bolsheviks (and perhaps other groups as well) than has been attempted here.

(1) At a certain point in the transition from one or another form of traditional society (feudal, hierarchical, patriarchal, corporate) to one or another form of modern society, there appears a band of "strangers" who view themselves as chosen men, saints, and who seek a new order and an impersonal, ideological discipline.

(2) These men are marked off from their fellows by an extraordinary self-assurance and daring. The saints not only repudiate the routine procedures and customary beliefs of the old order, but they also cut themselves off from the various kinds of "freedom" (individual mobility, personal extravagance, self-realization, despair, nervousness, vacillation) experienced amidst the decay of tradition. The band of the chosen seeks and wins certainty and self-confidence by rigidly disciplining its members and teaching them to discipline themselves. The saints interpret their ability to endure this discipline as a sign of their virtue and their virtue as a sign of God's grace. Amidst the confusion of the transitional period, they discover in themselves a predestination, a firm and undeviating sense of purpose, an assurance of eventual triumph.

(3) The band of the chosen confronts the existing world as if in war. Its members interpret the strains and tensions of social change in terms of conflict and contention. The saints sense enmity all about them and they train and prepare themselves accordingly. They keep watch and continually calculate their chances.

(4) The organization of the chosen suggests the nature of the new order they seek, but also reflects the necessities of the present struggle.

(a) Men join the band by subscribing to a covenant which testifies to their faith. Their new commitment is formal, impersonal, and ideological; it requires that they abandon older loyalties not founded upon opinion and will—loyalties to family, guild, locality, and also to lord and king.

(b) This commitment is voluntary, based upon an act of the will for which men can be trained, but not born. It is not possible to take one's place in the chosen band through any sort of patronage. To be chosen, one must choose.

(c) The commitment and zeal of prospective saints must be tested and proven. Hence it is not easy to choose sainthood and the band of the chosen remains exclusive and small, each of its members highly "talented" in virtue and self-discipline. Even after men have been accepted as saints, they must still demonstrate their godliness on every possible occasion. They are subject to examination and as they could once have been rejected so they can always be purged. The godly tension which the saints maintain is thus in vivid contrast to the apathy of worldlings, secure and at their ease with their customs and traditions.

(d) Within the band of the chosen, all men are equal. Status counts for little. Members are measured by their godliness and by the contributions they can make to the work at hand.

(5) The acting out of sainthood produces a new kind of politics.

(a) The activity of the chosen band is purposive, programmatic, and progressive in the sense that it continually approaches or seeks to approach its goals. This activity may be defined as an organized effort to universalize sainthood, to reconstruct or reform the political or religious worlds according to objective criteria (revealed, predetermined, written), without any regard for the established forms.

(b) The activity of the saints is methodical and systematic. Politics is made into a kind of work, to which the chosen are required to commit themselves for long periods of time. At work they must suppress all purely personal feelings and behave in a disciplined fashion. They must learn to be patient and to concern themselves with detail. Above all, they must work regularly and hard.

(c) The violent attack upon customary procedures sets the saints free to experiment politically. Such experimentation is controlled by its overriding purposes and the right to engage in it is limited to the chosen few who have previously accepted the discipline of the band. It is not a grant of political free-play, but it does open the way to new kinds of activity, both public and secret. The saints are entrepreneurs in politics.

(6) The historical role of the chosen band is twofold. Externally, as it were, the band of the saints is a political movement aiming at social reconstruction. It is the saints who lead the final attack upon the old order and their destructiveness is all the more total because they have a total view of the new world. Internally, godliness and predestination are creative responses to the pains of social change. Discipline is the cure for freedom and "unsettledness." As romantic love strengthens the bonds of the conjugal family, so ideological zeal establishes the unity of the nonfamilial brethren and makes it possible for men to feel secure outside the traditional system of connections.

One day, however, that security becomes a habit and zeal is no longer a worldly necessity. Then the time of God's people is over. In this world, the last word always belongs to the worldlings and not to the saints. It is a complacent word and it comes when salvation, in all its meanings, is no longer a problem. But the saints have what is more interesting: the first word. They set the stage of history for the new order.

Once that order is established, ordinary men are eager enough to desert the warfare of the Lord for some more moderate pursuit of virtue. Once they feel sufficiently secure as gentlemen and merchants, as country justices and members of Parliament, they happily forego the further privilege of being "instruments." Hardly a moment after their triumph, the saints find themselves alone; they can no longer exploit the common forms of ambition, egotism, and nervousness; they can no longer convince their fellow men that ascetic work and intense repression are necessary. The experience of other revolutionaries has been similar: the history of their success is brief. An enthusiastic poet of the Bolshevik Revolution, for example, wrote as early as 1924 that his verse was no longer needed.[23] The vanguard, he suggested (not quite accurately) had settled down to a new routine:

[23] Sergei Esenin, "Soviet Russia," trans. George Reavey, *Partisan Review* 28:379-382 (1961).

> I see before me
> Villagers in Sunday best
> Transact a meeting as if attending church.

The good old cause had quickly become only a memory:

> Wrinkling his reminiscent forehead,
> A lame Red Army man with drowsy face
> Grandly expatiates upon Budyonny
> And the Reds who captured Perekop by storm.

And the "rebel soul" felt like an alien again:

> What a misfit I've become
> . . . I feel a foreigner in my land.

So too the Puritan saint was a stranger before his revolution, and
after. There was a difference, of course, for the new routine em-
bodied many aspects of his radical faith. But the enthusiasm, the
battle-readiness, the confident enmity, the polemical eagerness, the
sense of unity among the brethren, the first pride of self-control—
all these were gone. Something of the tension, vigilance, and
excitement they suggest might have been maintained in the
holy commonwealth, but not in the world of the Restoration or
the Whigs. They had helped carry men through a time of change;
they had no place in a time of stability. They had been elements of
strength in an age of moral confusion and of cruel vigor in an age
of vacillation. Now it was suggested that saintly vigor had its own
pathology and conventionalism its own health; peace had its virtues as well as godly warfare.

BIBLIOGRAPHICAL NOTE

INDEX

BIBLIOGRAPHICAL NOTE

The purpose of this note is to discuss briefly certain aspects of the source material which may be of interest to the general reader and to describe the principles of selection which I adopted in the course of my research. At the same time I should like to acknowledge some intellectual debts and to note some crucial disagreements.

There exist two series of English translations of Calvin's sermons and commentaries. Both are incomplete; indeed, many of the sermons have never been published in any language and are only now being edited; others have apparently been lost (see T. H. L. Parker, *The Oracles of God: An Introduction to the Preaching of John Calvin*, London, 1947, and *Supplementa Calviniana*, London, 1962). The first series of translations is Elizabethan, the work of a group of talented and amazingly industrious writers, including the well-known Arthur Golding, friend of Sir Philip Sidney and translator also of Ovid. These men worked sometimes from the Latin, sometimes from the French, with great accuracy and linguistic skill. (Calvin delivered his sermons in French, without notes; they were taken down in shorthand by his secretaries and, some of them, published in French. The commentaries were often delivered in the form of lectures, presumably in French, but these were first published in Latin and only later in French translations. The bulk of the work is enormous and it is not entirely clear just how much of the writing, editing, and translating is Calvin's own and how much is his secretaries'. A complete list of the published work can be found in the *Corpus Reformatorum*, vol. LIX.) In 1844, the newly formed Calvin Translation Society of Edinburgh proposed to republish the Elizabethan translations and brought out a short prospectus (available in the British Museum) cataloguing and defending them. "Everyone acquainted with the English books of that period," the prospectus announced, "is fully aware of the admirable fidelity of the old translations. There is a force and pith in the old structure of our language . . . which is greatly weakened or entirely lost in the idiom in which translators of the present day must write." This may well be true; in any case, it was these old translations that the Puritans read and I have quoted from them wherever possible. Unfortunately, the C.T.S. then proceeded to publish a whole series of new translations, not precisely duplicating the earlier series; certain commentaries not previously translated were now brought out, but most of the sermons were ignored. The Victorian editions are sometimes more accurate and sometimes less so, but they are consistently less interesting and forceful in their language and do not come so near as do the Elizabethan versions to Calvin's own directness. For no obvious reason, a new translation of the commentaries was begun in 1959 under the editorship of David and Thomas Torrance.

The *Institutes* also had its Elizabethan translator: he was Thomas Norton, coauthor of *Gorboduc,* Elizabethan M.P., savage persecutor of the Catholics. His work too is lively, accurate, intelligent. But the *Institutes,* unlike the sermons and commentaries, was not verbally delivered and transcribed by secretaries, but worked out with enormous care by Calvin himself; the book requires and deserves frequent retranslation. A precise rendering of each word is necessary and, as the years go on, the reader requires a more and more elaborate critical apparatus. I have quoted from the early nineteenth-century translation of J. E. Allen, which has been for many years the standard American text. A new translation by F. L. Battles, edited by John T. McNeill, which ought to replace Allen, appeared in 1961, after my own work on Calvin was largely completed.

André Biéler's recent book *La Pensée économique et social de Calvin* (Geneva, 1959), provides the best available interpretation of the Calvinist corpus. Biéler quotes extensively from the commentaries and sermons and avoids the common error of overemphasizing the importance of the *Institutes.* I have cited his study only occasionally because it is a work that requires more extensive analysis and criticism than I could possibly afford it in this book. It is enough to say that I believe Biéler seriously underestimates the repressive features of Calvin's doctrine and of his Genevan commonwealth. But his view of Calvinism as a modernizing ideology, an ideology of social reconstruction, is substantially the one that I also have adopted. A useful corrective to Biéler is George Lagarde, *Recherches sur l'esprit politique de la Réforme* (Paris, 1926), a brilliant book, which I take to be the best general introduction to Protestant political thought. There is, in my opinion, no adequate study of Huguenot ideology either in English or French. J. W. Allen's *History of Political Thought in the Sixteenth Century* (London, 1951), and Pierre Mesnard's *L'Essor de la philosophie politique au XVIe siècle* (Paris, 1951), provide useful introductions.

The literature of the English Puritans is so enormous, so varied in style and genre, that the only plausible guide is Pollard and Redgrave's *A Short Title Catalogue of Books Printed in England, Scotland and Ireland and of English Books Printed Abroad, 1475-1640* (London, 1948). This has the advantage of including it all and the disadvantage of including everything else. A bibliography remarkable in its range and extremely useful for students of Puritan politics is provided by W. K. Jordan in his *The Development of Religious Toleration in England* (Cambridge, Mass., 1932-1940), vol. IV. There is a select bibliography (with some surprising omissions) of Tudor Puritan writings in M. M. Knappen, *Tudor Puritanism: A Chapter in the History of Idealism* (Chicago, 1939). And useful lists of texts from the Jacobean and Caroline periods are available in William Haller, *The Rise of Puritanism* (New York, 1939), emphasizing the hagiographical literature, and in C. and K. George, *The Protestant Mind the English Reformation, 1570-1640* (Princeton, 1961). A complete list of the sermons and treatises upon which my book is based can be found in the copy of my doctoral dissertation on deposit in the Harvard University Archives.

It would not be impossible to read all the Puritan sermons published between 1550 and 1660. Godfrey Davies has estimated in his article "English Political Sermons, 1603-1640," *Huntington Library Quarterly* 3:1-2 (1939), that at least 340,000 sermons were preached in English and Welsh parishes from the turn of the century to the Revolution. But of these, he suggests, only about forty a year, or 1,600 for the whole period, were printed—though this is exclusive presumably of sermon collections and also of biblical commentaries and theological treatises (often delivered from the pulpit before being written up for publication), so the figure may be too low. During the revolution, the number of sermons printed each year probably increased. More than 200 sermons were preached before the Houses of Parliament and subsequently published in the 1640's alone. Of this literature, I have in fact read only a small part: several hundred sermons. But I have tried to read extensively among published sermons of six types, in all of which political issues came to the fore: (1) Court sermons: especially those preached in the presence of James I when a wide range of opinion was still represented at court. (2) The St. Paul's Cross sermons: these were generally proclamations of government policy, but the government was not of a single mind, nor did it always exercise effective control over the pulpit, and so several important Puritan ministers preached at the Cross in the teens and twenties of the seventeenth century. A register of all the sermons, published and unpublished, preached at the Cross is provided by M. Maclure, *The Saint Paul's Cross Sermons, 1534-1642* (Toronto, 1958). (3) Sermons preached at city elections. (4) Assize sermons: there are a large number of these, preached at the Quarter Sessions. The printed texts are so often by Puritan ministers that they would be worth investigating as a source of information on the religious predilections of the rural justices: who chose the preachers? how was it decided which sermons were to be published? (5) Sermons preached to the city military companies, and especially to the Honorable Artillery Company of London: the London company gathered once a year for a sermon and these were sometimes published. All the published sermons are by well-known Puritan ministers and they are extraordinarily similar in theme, imagery, and doctrine. (6) Parliamentary sermons: these are relatively rare before 1640; after that they are published at the rate of two or more a month. The most eloquent preachers in all England were called to London; their work is a running commentary on the revolution. A selection of these sermons, and especially of those of Stephen Marshall and John Owen, edited for modern readers, would provide one of the best possible introductions to the politics and religion of the Puritan revolutionaries. (A collection of Owen's works was published in 1862, edited by W. H. Goold.) A great many parliamentary sermons are included in the extensive bibliography provided by W. Fraser Mitchell in his valuable book *English Pulpit Oratory from Andrewes to Tillotson* (London, 1932).

In analyzing this literature (and also the tracts and treatises of the Puritan ministers) I have by and large avoided the conventional topics of political thought—the origin and forms of the state, obligation, resistance, and so forth—on which the Puritans had little to say that was new or striking or particularly revealing of their own hopes and intentions. I have tried instead to gain some entrance into Puritan political thinking by concentrating on language and especially on the imagery used to describe the various forms of "order" in which the English saints were so persistently interested. I have been helped a great deal in this effort by the work of other scholars, and most often by that of literary historians and critics. E. M. W. Tillyard's *The Elizabethan World Picture* (London, 1943), is the best starting point for the study of the imagery of cosmic order, though Tillyard does not make many distinctions and does not differentiate the Puritans from other more traditional Elizabethan writers, as I have sought to do. Robert West's fine monograph *Milton and the Angels* (Athens, Ga., 1955), contains the best discussion of the Puritan view of angelic ranks and orders. Sir Herbert Grierson's *Cross-Currents in Seventeenth Cen-*

tury English Literature (London, 1948), and Ian Watt's *The Rise of the Novel* (Berkeley, 1959), are very suggestive as to the Puritans' conception of conjugal love and familial order. Perry Miller's examination of covenant theology in his *The New England Mind: The Seventeenth Century* (Cambridge, Mass., 1952), is crucial for an understanding not only of the relations between man and God in Puritan thought, but also for those between man and man. Miller's work has provoked considerable discussion and controversy, most of it, however, concerned with narrowly theological problems. Most important of all, William Haller's *The Rise of Puritanism* (New York, 1939), a classic of modern scholarship, describes in an eloquent and utterly convincing fashion the new imagery of "wayfaring and warfaring," pilgrimage and struggle, which is, I believe, the key to Puritan politics.

Two other studies have also been helpful in getting at revealing and distinctive features of Puritan thought: George L. Mosse's *The Holy Pretense* (Oxford, 1957), on the casuistry of political behavior; and E. L. Tuveson's *Millennium and Utopia: A Study in the Background of the Idea of Progress* (Berkeley, 1949), on the connections between religious and political conceptions of purpose and possibility. My own reading in Puritan literature has frequently been guided by the notes and bibliographies of these books and of those listed above.

Scholarly work on Puritanism is almost as vast as is the work of the Puritans themselves. Like the literature dealing with the French Revolution, its history is also the history of European culture. Puritan repression and Jacobin terror are themes to which writer after writer has returned and each return is an adventure in self-discovery as well as in historical analysis. My own indebtedness to Max Weber's *The Protestant Ethic and the Spirit of Capitalism* (trans. Talcott Parsons, New York, 1958), the most adventurous of all the books on Puritanism, is obvious throughout; I have tried to make it explicit in the first chapter. Weber's book, along with the work of Marx's earliest disciples, marks the most significant turning-point in the history of Puritan histories: the shift from denominational biographies and genealogies to sociological analyses. An extraordinary literature of academic monographs and articles derives from *The Protestant Ethic*, but I have not attempted any summary of it since my chief intention was to pursue an analogous but not identical line of thought, studying the relation of Puritanism not to economic but to political activity.

Since the publication of R. H. Tawney's *Religion and the Rise of Capitalism* (New York, 1926), an interesting but theoretically imprecise combination of Weber's ideas with those of the Marxists has been

pervasive in the academic literature. Curiously, the Marxists themselves have not (until very recently with the triumph of various sorts
of revisionism) been at all successful in dealing with the Puritans.
Eduard Bernstein's *Cromwell and Communism: Socialism and Democracy in the Great English Revolution*, trans. H. J. Stenning (London, 1930), is typically unsympathetic to and uninterested in religious
thought. But the work of Christopher Hill—*Economic Problems of
the Church* (Oxford, 1956); *Puritanism and Revolution* (London,
1959); *A Century of Revolution* (London, 1961); *Society and Puritanism in Pre-Revolutionary England* (London, 1964)—has at last definitely established the value of a Marxist approach to Puritan history.
The most recent and probably the most important of Hill's books,
Society and Puritanism, appeared too late for citation in my notes. His
earlier works are cited frequently and are of enormous importance for
all students of Puritanism, both as a source of information and as a
basis for theoretical discussion—and argument. My own argument
with Hill is quite simple: whereas he treats Puritanism as the social
religion of the "industrious sort" (merchants and artisans), I have
tended to treat it as the political religion of intellectuals (ministers)
and gentlemen.

One last note: in studying Puritan political activity, the career of
Oliver Cromwell is crucial. He is, in Emerson's phrase, the "representative man" among the English saints. I have always found Thomas
Carlyle's view of Cromwell as a revolutionary hero and an Anti-Whig
attractive and (up to a point) convincing, and have chosen to quote
Oliver in Carlyle's *Letters and Speeches* (London, 1893; first published
1845) rather than in the more scholarly version of W. C. Abbott, *Writings and Speeches* (Cambridge, Mass., 1937-1947). C. H. Firth's *Oliver
Cromwell and the Rule of the Puritans in England* (London, 1929),
is probably the best conventional biography. Robert Paul's *The Lord
Protector: Religion and Politics in the Life of Oliver Cromwell* (London, 1955), is a sensitive and valuable attempt to probe the relation
between Puritan faith and political radicalism, an attempt I hope I
have carried forward.

INDEX